Graphic Details

Graphic Details

Jewish Women's Confessional Comics in Essays and Interviews

Edited by SARAH LIGHTMAN

McFarland & Company, Inc., Publishers

Jefferson, North Carolina

FORWARD The media sponsor of the exhibit "Graphic Details" is *The Jewish Daily Forward*/forward.com, America's national Jewish news outlet. *The Jewish Daily Forward* takes great pride in the project, which began with the article by Michael Kaminer that appears in this volume. The exhibition has subsequently been seen by audiences across North America and in Great Britain, informed by a catalogue that was also produced by *The Jewish Daily Forward*.

"Graphic Confessions of Jewish Women: Exposing Themselves Through Pictures and Raw Personal Stories" by Michael Kaminer originally appeared in *The Jewish Daily Forward* on December 12, 2008.

"Sticking Their Tongues Out at the World" by Dan Friedman is adapted from "Up Close, Personal & Brutally Specific: A Very Particular Sub-Genre with Broad Ramifications" in *The Graphic Details Catalogue.*

"The Latest Revolutionary Chapter?" by Zachary Paul Levine is adapted from "The Latest, Revolutionary, Chapter" in *The Graphic Details Catalogue.*

LIBRARY OF CONGRESS CATALOGUING-IN-PUBLICATION DATA

Graphic details : Jewish women's confessional comics in essays and interviews / edited by Sarah Lightman.
p.   cm.
Includes index.

ISBN 978-0-7864-6553-8 (softcover : acid free paper) ∞
ISBN 978-1-4766-1590-5 (ebook)

1. Autobiographical comic books, strips, etc.—History and criticism.
2. Jewish women in literature.   3. Jewish women in art.
4. Jewish women cartoonists.   I. Lightman, Sarah, 1975– editor.
PN6714.G738 2014   741.5'3522—dc23   2014018810

BRITISH LIBRARY CATALOGUING DATA ARE AVAILABLE

Cover graphics: self-portraits of the artists from top to bottom: Aline Kominsky-Crumb, Corinne Pearlman, Racheli Rottner, Vanessa Davis, Bernice Eisenstein, Miriam Libicki, Sharon Rudahl, Ilana Zeffran, Sarah Lightman, Laurie Sandell, Sarah Glidden, Sarah Lazarovic, Ariel Schrag, Miriam Katin, Diane Noomin, Lauren Weinstein, Miss Lasko-Gross, Trina Robbins

Printed in the United States of America

McFarland & Company, Inc., Publishers
Box 611, Jefferson, North Carolina 28640
www.mcfarlandpub.com

To the 18 artists in this book and to all the women around the world who are bravely making comics about their own lives.

Table of Contents

Preface and Acknowledgments: Imagetextlines—Confessions of a
    Co-Curator, Editor and Artist (Sarah Lightman)   1

Part I: Introductions

Graphic Confessions of Jewish Women: Exposing Themselves Through
    Pictures and Raw Personal Stories (Michael Kaminer)   18

Sticking Their Tongues Out at the World (Dan Friedman)   21

The Latest Revolutionary Chapter? (Zachary Paul Levine)   25

Telling Their Own Stories (Sarah Jaffe)   29

Part II: Essays

Herstory of Jewish Comic Art

Charlotte Salomon, Graphic Artist (Ariela Freedman)   38

The Book of Sarah—Life or Reconstruction? Situating Sarah
    Lightman's Illustrated Diary (Pnina Rosenberg)   51

Mi Yimtza? Finding Jewish Identity Through Women's
    Autobiographical Art (Evelyn Tauben)   61

Our Drawn Bodies, Our Drawn Selves

Fetal Attractions: Diane Noomin's "Baby Talk: A Tale of 3 4
    Miscarriages" (1995) and My *Journal of a Miscarriage, 1973*
    (Joanne Leonard)   79

Graphic Lesbian Continuum: Ilana Zeffren (Heike Bauer)   98

Traces of Subjectivity: The Embodied Author in the Work
    of Ariel Schrag (Natalie Pendergast)   110

Comic Comedy

The Turd That Won't Flush: The Comedy of Jewish Self-Hatred in
    the Work of Corinne Pearlman, Aline Kominsky-Crumb,
    Miss Lasko-Gross and Ariel Schrag (David Brauner)   131

The Comedy of Confession (Judy Batalion)   149

Part III: Interviews

BERNICE EISENSTEIN and the Persistence of Memory
(Michael Kaminer) 162

How to Understand SARAH GLIDDEN in 2,000 Words or Less
(Michael Kaminer) 167

SARAH LAZAROVIC: On Politics, Big Glasses and Not Shopping
(Michael Kaminer) 173

"A portrait of the world through my eyes": An Interview with
MISS LASKO-GROSS (Tahneer Oksman) 176

Thinking Panoramically: An Interview with LAUREN WEINSTEIN
(Tahneer Oksman) 185

"I thought hand wringing about my peculiar form of British-Jewish
assimilation was a little niche I had": CORINNE PEARLMAN Lays
Down Her Jewish Cards (Paul Gravett and Sarah Lightman) 195

From the Other Side of the World to North America: An Interview
with RACHELI ROTTNER (Noa Lea Cohn) 205

Part IV: "Graphic Details"
Artists, Artworks and Confessions

Vanessa Davis (Tahneer Oksman) 214

Bernice Eisenstein (Malcolm Lester) 219

Sarah Glidden (Julia Wertz) 222

Miriam Katin (Ranen Omer-Sherman) 228

Aline Kominsky-Crumb (F. K. Clementi) 234

Miss Lasko-Gross (Rob Clough) 240

Sarah Lazarovic (Alison Broverman) 245

Miriam Libicki (Ranen Omer-Sherman) 249

Sarah Lightman (Roger Sabin) 253

Diane Noomin (Sarah Lightman) 256

Corinne Pearlman (Arthur Oppenheimer) 262

Trina Robbins (Rachel Pollack) 266

Racheli Rottner (Ariel Kahn) 269

Sharon Rudahl (Paul Buhle) 271

Laurie Sandell (Michael Kaminer) 277

Ariel Schrag (Noah Berlatsky) 283

Lauren Weinstein (Nicole Rudick)   288

Ilana Zeffren (Gil Hovav)   292

About the Contributors   297

Index   301

Preface and Acknowledgments

Imagetextlines—Confessions of a Co-Curator, Editor and Artist

Sarah Lightman

"The show is a kind of *yichus*[1] of autobiographical comics by Jewish women."[2]

"Graphic Details: Confessional Comics by Jewish Women" is an internationally touring exhibition that has opened at the Cartoon Art Museum, San Francisco (2010); Koffler Center of the Arts, Toronto (2011); Yeshiva University Museum, New York (2011–2012); Washington DC Jewish Community Center (2012); and Oregon Jewish Museum, Portland (2012–2013). It has evolved into an eight-page catalogue, numerous panel discussions, guided tours, workshops, a one-day symposium and now this book. As a result of the success of "Graphic Details," the comics displayed in the show have since been in museums and galleries, in newspapers and magazines, and discussed on the radio and on TV programs. The artwork has been displayed as framed pages of original artwork, on walls and in vitrines, in filmed interviews, performances and presentations. These comics have been seen by thousands of visitors and read about in hundreds of press articles and interviews, from Canada's *National Post*[3] to San Francisco's *The Bay Area Reporter*,[4] from Israel's *Haaretz*[5] to *The Washington Post*.[6] That is huge exposure for artworks that are in reality very small scale and often began as self-published 'zines. Many of the images in "Graphic Details" are black and white, in ink, wash or pencil. And, in a satisfying twist, my contribution to the show has also included my triptych "Dumped Before Valentine's."

In "Dumped Before Valentine's [Day]" (2007), I sat facing the River Thames, on a bench outside the Tate Modern Gallery, London [Figs. 80–82]. My phone rings, my soon-to-be-ex-boyfriend lets me know that he will not, after all, be turning up. These three drawings concisely present my changing social status as I become unwillingly newly single, just before the international day of romantic love. But I was not just socially alone. While a student at the Slade School of Art—creating a visual autobiography—I felt another distinct sense of isolation. No other art students had embarked on similar projects, jointly exploring their religious backgrounds and personal histories in a visual narrative form. I found myself, a Jewish woman comic artist, without peers. I was situated professionally parallel to this bench outside the Tate, my artwork and practice positioning me, unwillingly and uncomfortably, outside the academy.

My email to Michael Kaminer in 2009 changed all that. I was responding to his article "Graphic Confessions of Jewish Women: Exposing Themselves Through Pictures and Raw Personal Stories" for *The Jewish Daily Forward* and between us we would bring comics by Jewish women into established art spaces, and in the process find me the creative family I had always hoped for. I had already curated "Diary Drawing" (2008), a touring show that included the work of two Jewish women who made autobiographical comics, Ariel Schrag and Miriam Katin. I suggested to Michael in an email we curate a show together based on his article and between us we drew up a list of 15 other artists from Israel, America, Canada and England who fitted our remit.

The artworks in "Graphic Details" cover much of life experience—the unhappy childhoods of Aline Kominsky-Crumb in *Wise Guys* (1995) [Figs. 71–72], and of Laurie Sandell in *The Impostor's Daughter* (2009) [Figs. 95–99]; the awkward school days in Lauren Weinstein's "Last Dance" (2006) [Fig. 41]; the burgeoning love affairs and broken hearts in Miriam Katin's "Eucalyptus Nights" (2006) [Figs. 65–68] and Sharon Rudahl's "The Star Sapphire" (1975) [Figs. 91–94]. Bodily functions and friendship feature in Miss Lasko-Gross's "The Turd" (2009) [Figs. 37–38], Ariel Schrag's "Shit" (2003) [Figs. 100–101] and the personal tragedy of "Baby Talk: A Tale of 3 4 Miscarriages" by Diane Noomin (1993) [Figs. 21–22, 83–86]. The success of the show is a reflection of the relevance, immediacy and insight of these artworks, with their honest coverage of the Jewish women, but also importantly more general, life experience.

There have been multiple comics exhibitions before, but "Graphic Details" is unique in its highlighting of the work of female Jewish comics artists. As a curator I had a feminist agenda. The "Graphic Details" exhibition, with over 80 artworks, redresses the uphill struggles previous generations of women comics artists would have experienced. The exhibition was a chance to expose their stories in mainstream environments; the galleries were beautiful spaces where intimate stories were relayed and where their, and my, art became valued and appreciated. From sex shops to synagogues, featuring both heart-breaking and heartbroken Israeli soldiers, some stories may seem shocking; but perhaps the real scandal is the realization that a show like "Graphic Details" hadn't happened before.

"'Old school sexism' necessitates 'old school feminism'"[7]

Jews have contributed significantly to the world of comics. Jewish comic creators include Jerry Siegel's and Joe Shuster's *Superman* (1938), Art Spiegelman's PulitzerPrize–winning *Maus* (1991), and Will Eisner's *Contract with God, and Other Tenement Stories* (1978). But where were the women comic artists? Were there any?

As I began my talk about "Graphic Details" at the *Limmud* Conference at Warwick University in December 2012, an audience member asked me: "Are there *really* any Jewish women comics artists?" And, if there are, the next question would be: "Why don't we know about them?" A short answer, in traditional Jewish fashion, would be more questions: "How *could* we know about them?" "How do we hear about the artists we do know about?"

We know about artists through many arenas: artists' books, group shows and retrospectives in museums, in catalogues, postcards and press that accompany the shows. But if an artist does not have access to these means of production, cannot get exposure, for example through galleries and art collections, and does not have allies in the press, how will the artist reach greater audiences? This was the predicament of many female comics artists, until very recently.

Alisia Grace Chase argues in her eloquent and forceful essay "'Draws Like a Girl': The Necessity of Old School Feminist Interventions in the World of Comics and Graphic Novels" that comics exhibitions remain one of the last unreconstructed bastions of fine art.[8] Previous art shows about comics, even recent ones about Jews and comics, have not facilitated the restoration of a balanced history. From November 2005 through March 2006, the Hammer Museum and the Museum of Contemporary Art in Los Angeles presented the touring exhibition "American Masters of Comic Art." Trina Robbins, "Graphic Details" artist and *herstorian*, subsequently observed:

> Of the 15 cartoonists represented ... there was not one woman in the show. Why? Why Chester Gould's Dick Tracy, with its grotesque villains, and not Dale Messick's Brenda Starr, with her grotesque villains? [...] Why Lyonel Feininger, who drew the Kinder-Kids for less than a year, and not Nell Brinkley, who drew her strips for 30 years [...] I couldn't possibly explain [why this had happened] better than Ursula Le Guin [does]. In her foreword to *She's Fantastical, The First Anthology of Australian Women's Speculative Fiction* [2003], she writes: "Men ran the publishing houses and all the machinery of evaluation and criticism. Editors seldom print and critics seldom praise a work outside the conventions they uphold."
> All you have to do is change "writing" to "drawing."[9]

"Masters of American Comics," as it was later called, also toured the Newark Museum and the Jewish Museum New York in 2006–2007. The inaccuracies of representation are articulated by Chase, who writes that through the

> selection of predominantly white, middle class, male artists who were chosen for the "Masters" show, some industry bloggers pointed out that there have never been as many women working in comics and graphic novels as there are now.[10]

More recently, a touring show about Jews and Comics entitled "From Superman to the Rabbi's Cat" traveled across Europe and Australia. This show's title, again, draws emphasis to the male, not female, contribution to comics. The Rabbi's Cat was male, and the artist Joann Sfar is a French male; thus both creators and creations that bracket the title are male. And even though the show also included the work of women comic artists including Miriam Katin, Aline Kominsky-Crumb and Diane Noomin, these artists were never the focal point.

This was clearly illustrated when I attended the conference for this show in Paris in 2007. Following fervent question and answer sessions with Joe Kubert and other male artists there was a panel on women and comics, with Katin, Kominsky-Crumb and Noomin, but by then the organizers had run out of time for questions. The exuberance of fan-boys had managed to push out the women, once again. At that moment I knew there was more to be explored on the topic of Jewish women and comics. I promised myself I would chair a conference with Jewish women comic artists, placing them, their work, and discussion around their work at the center, not the sidelines. A little over five years later I co-chaired "Talking about Jewish Women and Comics" with Tahneer Oksman and Amy Feinstein—a one-day symposium inspired by the artwork of "Graphic Details" at Yeshiva University Museum, New York, where many artists from the show spoke, including Diane Noomin and Miriam Katin.

What was the best way to change this imbalance of representation in galleries? By returning to the gallery, but this time ensuring that this show would highlight female artists. But it would not suffice to just challenge the selection of artwork, as Chase notes:

> [The] choices made by the "Masters" curators not only erase female artists' contribution to the field of comics and graphic novels, but also ignore feminist methodologies, and thus, not surprisingly, recycle totally antediluvian notions about art and artists.[11]

Thus "Graphic Details" also looks to continue the work of Rozsika Parker and Griselda Pollock's *Old Mistresses: Women, Art and Ideology* (1981), a book that explores why women have been excluded and erased from the history of art and what this reveals about the teaching and writing of art history.

It still is women who continue to do the job of disinterring a hidden history, and claiming and naming women artists for posterity. As Curator Ute Meta Bauer articulated to Katy Deepwell in relation to her exhibition "?," there is both immediate and long-term importance in museum representation: "Museums have great potential and they are the spaces in which art history is written. So if we want to be inscribed, we have to use them."[12]

Fortunately there have been significant developments since 2006, and the success and longevity of "Graphic Details" has, I believe, been a testament to a redressing of the balance of power in art galleries and art institutions, Jewish and elsewhere, that may have previously blighted previous generations. In fact, the majority of sites to which "Graphic Details" has toured, so far, have all been institutions where the CEOs and directors are women—Lori Starr at Toronto's Koffler Centre of the Arts, Carole Zawatsky at Washington DC's Jewish Community Center, Judy Margles at Oregon Jewish Museum, Portland, and Jo Ann Arnowitz at the Jewish Museum of Florida. So, this changing power base is not a development unique to comics, but is shared by the wider art world in general, as feminist art critic Katy Deepwell recognized in her interview with Catherine de Zegher about her exhibition "Inside the Visible: An Elliptical Traverse of Twentieth Century Art, in, of, and from the Feminine" when she states: "It seems that all the places 'Inside the Visible' is being shown have women directors."[13]

"Graphic Details" also addresses other concerns in feminist curation. Margaret D. Stetz in "Feminist Exhibitionism: When the Women's Studies Professor is a Curator," writes: "If the public cannot come to the feminist classroom, the valuable ideas generated within the feminist classroom can go out to the public by other means."[14] Stetz notes that those who might not attend a lecture, or read an article, would go to a gallery and this is a way to bring feminist arguments to the wider community. The title "Graphic Details: By Jewish Women Confessional Comics" foregrounds the word "women" in the title—perhaps suggesting that the works may only speak to that one group in society. But does "Graphic Details" continue what Malin Hedlin Hayden and Jessica Sjöholm Skrubbe describe as "the prevalent trajectory in art historical practice: namely a sex-biased structure?"[15] Perhaps it does, but then as Chase herself argues the exclusion of women in previous comics shows suggests, "'old school' sexism necessitates 'old school feminism.'"[16] Something far subtler is also happening, something specifically revolutionary with regard to the combination of artists and their inherited history and culture in "Graphic Details." The show's content begins from the female standpoint and addresses universal experiences. This is a major reconfiguration of the traditional flow of information about Jewish life and ritual. For example, for generations, in prayer the descriptions of God have been masculine: "The presence of the masculine is so strong within Jewish prayer, and the omission of the feminine so glaring," writes Tova Hartman in her essay "The Paternal Voice in Liturgy."[17] Hartman, however, is not inclined to change the wording of the prayers; instead she is satisfied with reimagining the meanings for each of these masculine terms. Hartman explains: "'Our Father' could potentially come to signify not exclusively a ruling and judging God but a nurturing God: He may come to hold maternal qualities as well."[18] This logic could be applied in relation to Jewish narrative, where the male experience and history is the source of "universal" knowledge and understanding—and thus again "he" covers both "he and she." "Graphic Details" reverses this direction in the innate structure of the show.

"Graphic Details" as a touring entity divides 80 works into four sections. These are

"The Whole *Mishpocha*" (Hebrew for families), about families, romantic bonds and sibling rivalries; "Who Fashioned Humanity," which stems from the religious blessing said after going to the bathroom, about toilet mishaps and bathroom blunders; "If I Am Not for Myself," about everyday conflicts involved in being Jewish, such as those of engaging with the wider Jewish community and Israel; and "Facing Trauma," about personal, as well as collective, tragedy. These themes draw out from *these women's stories*—the specific to the universal—and enable the wider resonance of the stories to become apparent—"she" covers both "she" and "he."

Art *in* Comics

Curating a show of original comic artwork is not a new practice, but it still manages to make the ordinary feel extraordinary, and even more so in a show of artwork of the everyday. For many viewers, their first introduction to comics was through newspapers, but often the quality of the reproduction meant the artist's skill was not shown clearly. "Graphic Details" is a show of original comics in museum and gallery settings. There have been numerous exhibitions of comics in an art gallery but I knew that recognizing the art *in* comics would be a surprise to many viewers. Kim Munson discusses this happening 30 years ago in "The Comics Art Show" (1983)[19] co-curated by John Carlin and Sheena Wagstaff. She described it as the "breakthrough exhibition that presented comic art as equal to fine art." Years later, audience responses are still the same. The phrase "Oh my god I didn't think of this comic art being as the same quality as fine art,"[20] Brian Walker's recollection of the public response to "The Comics Art Show," could well have come from the mouths of spectators in any of the cities in which "Graphic Details" has been shown.

In an exhibition that focuses on life stories, displaying the original artworks gives additional resonance. Many of the comics pages in "Graphic Details" have already been published in collections and graphic novels, or featured online. When the works are exhibited as pages, not in books, they are exposed and unbound, unprotected—and as such, are revelatory. Books require examination in a way different to pages—they ask to be both read and viewed. These works, like our own lives, reflect human frailty and folly; we see the marks and mistakes, the histories and the physicality of the page, worn or pristine, aging or polished. The works on display in "Graphic Details" are small enough that they require face-to-face encounters; they ask us to spend time on them, with them, to read them, follow the rhythms of their texts, hear our minds speak their speech bubbles. As Andrei Molotui says, they reveal "the palimpsest of marks that do not show up on the printed page."[21] There is a secret history you can only see, that the work will only let you see, in the original. Though some works are printed, in a number, the hand-painted watercolors lead us through the thought process in the touches that litter the edges of the paper, as the artist chooses her palette. We are invited to see her process, creativity, and life in action: the visualizing of experiences, of memories and her stories. The papers share the narrative movement by telling the story of the artist.

Coverage, Not Cover Up

"Men ran the publishing houses and all the machinery of evaluation and criticism,"[22] stated Trina Robbins. The eight-page catalogue for "Graphic Details" was designed like the newspaper *The Jewish Daily Forward*, our sponsor. Where in the past it might have been difficult for a woman comic artist to get reviewed and featured, here, we were giving the comics artists their own newspaper. Additionally, this format paid homage to the earlier history of comics being published in newspapers.

The reference to newspapers also reveals how "Graphic Details" has used museums and gallery spaces as springboards for wider coverage of the art. My co-curator Michael Kaminer's skillful and dynamic press releases, and the sheer power of the artworks, meant we have been featured in Jewish and non–Jewish press, online and on TV. "Graphic Details" used the gallery, and also all other means available, to imprint onto the public imagination. "Graphic Details" attracted a mixed audience, and to reflect this we invited a variety of academics, journalists and enthusiasts to respond to themes they saw in the artwork. We also included information about each of the artists, who were identified by a self-portrait drawing. Our catalogue had comics you could hold in your hand, fold up, and you could even take reproductions in the catalogue home with you after seeing the show.

A Book of Their Own

My ambition was to create a book of a show, though, ironically, this decision may seem to oppose my initial focus of bringing comics out of books and into art galleries. But I wanted to do more than turn original works into reproductions again. I returned to that initial premise of re-engaging with "old school feminism," and also to look back on the actions of earlier comic artists. As F.K. Clementi writes:

> Will Eisner is credited with having published the first Jewish graphic autobiography at a time when women artists would rarely be published. But it was a woman who was the first Jewish graphic autobiographical artist. Charlotte Salomon gouached her life in images with texts, until the Nazis ended her story in Auschwitz.[23]

Clementi makes a point that is central to the premise of "Graphic Details." Women in previous generations were not gaining the same exposure or, crucially, access to the publishing world as their male counterparts. As a consequence the history of comics is incomplete and inaccurate, with only the male comics artists being credited for their innovations. This, in turn, led to fewer women being featured in shows, catalogues and collections—creating a cyclical process of exclusion.

While "Graphic Details" does not claim to be a comprehensive survey of Jewish women's autobiographical comics, it has created a platform to show the range, breadth and depth of work, which was being made from the 1970s and beyond. And though many of the new generation of artists are already well known, there will always be a few surprise contenders. Among the many essays in the book, we first look at an artist who is not included in "Graphic Details" but who inspired many artists in the show—the remarkable Charlotte Salomon and her *Life? or Theatre?* created between 1941 and 1943. Her work continues to inspire us— and I am grateful to the Jewish Museum of Amsterdam for granting us permission to reproduce one of Salomon's images to sit among the other artists' work in this book.

Since it was harder for women to get publishing deals, they often set up on their own. And notably a number of artists in "Graphic Details" have been involved in enabling women's comics to be published: Trina Robbins and Diane Noomin both edited at various points all-women comics anthologies including *Wimmin's Commix* (1972–1992) and *Twisted Sisters*

(1976–1995) in the United States. Corinne Pearlman is creative manager and graphics editor of Myriad Editions, operating now in the UK, and has a reputation for publishing works by women and featuring female experience.

Though "Graphic Details" has been welcomed in the U.S. and Canada my expectation is this book will travel farther than the original exhibition. In addition to creating a perpetual record of the show, another reason for creating this book was to celebrate the wonderful array of responses to "Graphic Details," reflected in the range of contributions. We have journalists and academics, as well as an artist, an editor, a performer, a curator, and even a chef. What, I hope, is evident in this book is the work's impact, importance and capacity to fascinate and inspire, and not just a female, Jewish audience. I hope this book will join the growing library of books on autobiographical comics, women and comics, and Jews and comics including Elizabeth El Refaie's *Autobiographical Comics: Life Writing in Pictures* (2012), *Graphic Subjects: Critical Essays on Autobiography and Graphic Novels* edited by Michael Chaney (2011), and Hillary L. Chute's *Graphic Women: Life Narrative and Contemporary Comics* (2010), as well as *Jewish Images in the Comics* (2012) by Fredrik Strömberg, Samantha Baskind and Ranen Omer-Sherman's *The Jewish Graphic Novel: Critical Approaches* (2008), and *Jews and American Comics: An Illustrated History of an American Art Form* (2008) by Paul Buhle.

Introductions

The book opens with four introductory essays that reflect the journey and development of "Graphic Details" from an article in a newspaper to a sponsored touring show that has since been written about in numerous newspapers. Michael Kaminer's article in *The Jewish Daily Forward* inspired the exhibition "Graphic Confessions of Jewish Women: Exposing Themselves Through Pictures and Raw Personal Stories." Another introduction is *The Jewish Daily Forward* (sponsor of "Graphic Details") managing editor Dan Friedman's "Sticking Their Tongues Out at the World," which celebrates the power and honesty of the artworks and explains why he has named Miss Lasko-Gross's image (which was produced especially for the show) "The Tongue Mothers." The next introduction is by Zachary Paul Levine, curator at Yeshiva University Museum, New York—the third institution that hosted "Graphic Details." Levine was instrumental in transforming "Graphic Details" into a touring show, and in "The Latest Revolutionary Chapter?" Levine places the exhibition squarely within Jewish literary tradition, notably contextualizing the women creating work about their lives as a continuation of the writings of Glückel of Hameln. Finally, journalist Sarah Jaffe travels through the show highlighting examples of exposure—where sex is messy, and women acknowledge their own desires—but where there is still much unsaid. Jaffe writes: "Comics require the reader to fill in the gaps between panels, but autobiographical comics require the reader to fill in the spaces of a life."[24]

Essays

These essays situate the artwork of "Graphic Details" in relation to other artists and contemporary critical theories. The authors make wide-ranging connections and associations between fine art, cinema, Jewish studies, queer theory, performance and comedy. Many of the essays in this book were first read as papers at the "Talking about Jewish Women and Comics" symposium on February 28, 2012, at Yeshiva University Museum. This part opens with a comic by Corinne Pearlman, "Confessions about Jewish Women and Comics Symposium: Academia or Comics?" (2012). Pearlman draws herself talking about her own artwork: "I will now refer to the character in the strip as CP and the author as Corinne Pearlman" [Fig. 9]. Pearlman's comic visualizes an act of differentiation that is applied in many of the essays that follow, separating the drawn artist "CP" from the creating artist "Corinne Pearlman."

The essays that follow are organized to reflect three themes central to "Graphic Details": rewriting history in "Herstory of Jewish Comic Art," bodies and sexuality in "Our Drawn Bodies, Our Drawn Selves," and Jewish humor in "Comic Comedy."

"Herstory of Jewish Comic Art" begins with Ariela Freedman's "Charlotte Salomon, Graphic Artist" which introduces a detail of Bernice Eisenstein's epigram to *I Was a Child of Holocaust Survivors* (2006)—an image of Charlotte Salomon advising Eisenstein on her art. Freedman writes that the work of Charlotte Salomon has been consistently ignored by many comics historians and academics. Referencing Walter Benjamin and Griselda Pollock, Freedman's visual analysis places Salomon rightfully as a founder of the graphics form. Pnina Rosenberg continues to address the long shadow of Charlotte Salomon by exploring her impact on my own ongoing visual autobiography *The Book of Sarah*. Rosenberg explores how Marianne Hirsch's theory of postmemory also links my work to that of Christian Boltanski, Ruth Kestenbaum Ben-Dov and Daniela Rosenhouse-Ben Zion. Evelyn Tauben's "*Mi Yimtza*? [Who Can Find?] Finding Jewish Identity Through Women's Autobiographical Art" addresses questions central to "Graphic Details"—the tensions of belonging in the work of Jewish women artists. Tauben looks first at the comics of Miriam Libicki, Liana Finck, Sarah Glidden, and Miriam Katin and then turns to fine artists including Melissa Shiff and Helène Aylon—who also address tradition and Jewish experience in their artwork.

In "Our Drawn Bodies, Our Drawn Selves," we pay homage to the great feminist publication *Our Bodies, Ourselves*,[25] with essays that explore female bodies and sexuality. The opening essay introduces photographer Joanne Leonard who writes movingly of her own artwork *Journal of a Miscarriage, 1973* in relation to Diane Noomin's "Baby Talk: A Tale of 3̶ 4 Miscarriages" (1995). The fascinating differences and parallels between their works reveal how two artists can address similar topics and experiences without knowing of each other's work at the time. In "Graphic Lesbian Continuum: Ilana Zeffren," Heike Bauer presents Zeffren's comics as work that ensures female-identified sexuality is not overlooked. The constant presence of Zeffren's cats breaks up the preconceived notions of family and the artist also retains Hebrew in the comic even when the texts are translated, to suggest a transnational element to her weekly autobiographically inspired column. Natalie Pendergast's "Traces of Subjectivity: The Embodied Author in the Work of Ariel Schrag" discusses the dramatizing techniques Schrag uses in her comics. These include her drawing styles, her use of caricature and also her use of font as a performer in her story. Schrag's portrayal of her explorations of sexuality invites the reader to share her journey.

In "Comic Comedy" two essays explore the Jewish humor in "Graphic Details." In "The Turd That Won't Flush: The Comedy of Jewish Self-Hatred in the Work of Corinne Pearlman, Aline Kominsky-Crumb, Miss Lasko-Gross and Ariel Schrag," David Brauner explores definitions of and the application of self-hatred in these satirical comics. Judy Batalion gives a tour of "Graphic Details" that is signposted with comedic terms. Breaking down different techniques used by Jewish comedians, Batalion explains how artists in the exhibition use self-deprecation, anti–Semitic jokes and wordplay.

Interviews

The next part of the book includes seven interviews with artists exhibiting in "Graphic Details." My hope is it will prove a valuable resource for enthusiasts and academics—as these interviews capture directly the voices of many of the artists in the exhibition and give them a space to talk about their artistic processes and inspirations. Michael Kaminer interviews three of the artists in the exhibition. His first interview is with Bernice Eisenstein, who describes how it felt to draw those no longer alive, how Charlotte Salomon and Alfred Kantor inspired her, and how ink and pen drawings suited her subject matter. In "How to Understand Sarah Glidden in 2,000 Words or Less," Glidden explains how memory is not "unfiltered"; she discusses the contribution of daydreaming to her comics production, and shares her surprise at the Jewish community's response to her book *How to Understand Israel in 60 Days or Less* (2011). "Sarah Lazarovic: On Politics, Big Glasses and Not Shopping" exposes the artist's editorial process in her cartoons and references her upcoming book *A Bunch of Pretty Things I Did Not Buy* (Penguin Viking 2014).

Tahneer Oksman contributes two insightful interviews. In "'A Portrait of the World through My Eyes': An Interview with Miss Lasko-Gross" Lasko-Gross addresses themes of authority, Jewishness and identity as well as the risks involved in old school classmates reading her comics. In "Thinking Panoramically: An Interview with Lauren Weinstein," the artist describes how she chose comics after art school as her medium and how creating *Girl Stories* was far more masochistic than cathartic. In the next interview Paul Gravett and I ask Corinne Pearlman about her dual role as comic artist and graphics director of Myriad Editions, as well as her comics column in the *Jewish Quarterly*. I was delighted that Noa Lea Cohn interviewed Racheli Rottner. This is the first time Rottner has been featured in an English language interview. It is fascinating to learn how this Israeli Orthodox artist discovered comics through Dudu Geva and formed her own visual language, using cockroaches as a metaphor.

"Graphic Details" Artists, Artworks and Confessions

The final part of the book includes short biographies of all the artists in "Graphic Details" and examples of their artwork from the show. Since the work in the show is personal and intimate, I wanted the artists themselves to invite commentary from chosen peers in the "Confessions" section. The following contributors add personal reflections and insights on the featured artists and their works: Noah Berlatsky, Alison Broverman, Paul Buhle, F.K. Clementi, Rob Clough, Gil Hovav, Ariel Kahn, Michael Kaminer, Malcolm Lester, Tahneer Oksman, Ranen Omer-Sherman, Arthur Oppenheimer, Rachel Pollack, Nicole Rudick, Roger Sabin and Julia Wertz.

Imagetextlines

"Graphic Details" celebrates visual herstory. I was inspired by Amoz Oz and Fania Oz-Salzberger in *Jews and Words* (2012) and their use of the term "textlines" to describe the

Fig. 1. Corinne Pearlman, "Playing the Jewish Card: Show & Tell," 2009, ink and pen on paper.

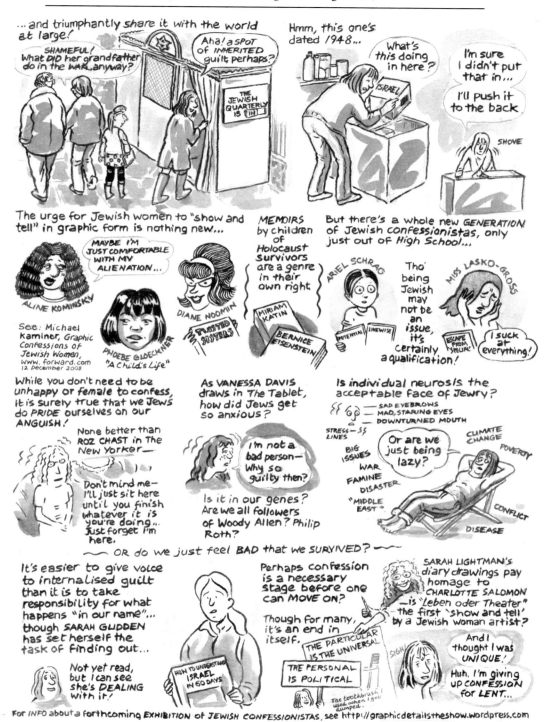

Fig. 2. Corinne Pearlman, "Playing the Jewish Card: Show & Tell," 2009, ink and pen on paper.

literary heritage of the Jewish people. While the term *yichus* is Yiddish for family status and lineage, the artists of "Graphic Details" are not related by blood but rather are linked through their text and image heritage and creativity, their "Imagetextlines." Jewish tradition states that the Jewish line is matrilineal, yet it should be noted that much Biblical literature concerns itself with the male line, and the *Talmud* (a central text of Judaism) on the whole has traced male intellectual endeavor through (male) rabbis and their discussions. "Graphic Details" emphasizes the construction of a female creative visual lineage, and includes, among others, Aline Kominsky-Crumb, the self-appointed "Grandmother of whiny tell-all comics."[26]

"And I thought I was UNIQUE!"[27]

Corinne Pearlman's "Show and Tell" (2009) [Figs. 1–2] humorously suggests her unhappiness at discovering other Jewish women comics artists who made autobiographical art: "And I thought I was UNIQUE!" For myself, after feeling isolated at art school and having few peers working in a similar way, nothing could have been more welcome. I used to work alone in my studio, desperately wanting to find a creative community, so as to place my work and myself in a context and a tradition. The impact of "Graphic Details" will, I believe, continue to grow wherever the show and its coverage spreads. I want this book to be a source of inspiration for artists and researchers and a reference for those in their studios.

In her essay "Celebrating 35 Years of Jewish Women's Stories" Susan Schnur explores the success of *Lilith Magazine*, which records "Jewish women's lives with exuberance, rigor, affection, subversion and style."[28] Shnur argues: "We don't believe the memory is private. We hold the common place is sacred [...] Because the unheard voices of Jewish women signifies a crime."[29] I would argue that it is not just the failure to hear women's voices that needs rectifying but the fact that artwork by Jewish women comics artists has gone unseen and unappreciated. Through this book the artwork of "Graphic Details" is made accessible and can offer inspiration to other comics artists. Every time the show opens in a new site, comics artists approach me about their work. May this book build many more connections and continue to inspire women to make comics about their lives.

To return to Salomon: we are audiences to others' stories. And more than that—their stories change us. The ripples of *Life? or Theatre?* were felt earlier. This is emphasized by Mary Lowenthal Felstiner in her book *To Paint Her Life: Charlotte Salomon in the Nazi Era* (1997) recalling a meeting between two fathers who had both tragically lost their creative and talented daughters in the Holocaust. In 1946 Albert and Paula Salomon, Charlotte's father and stepmother, visited Villefranche where Charlotte had lived before she was deported. There they received the package that contained hundreds of drawings that formed *Life? or Theatre?* The Salomons opened the package when they returned to their home in Amsterdam:

> One day Paula and Albert Salomon were visited in Amsterdam by close friend Otto Frank, with his daughter Anne's manuscript in his hand. He told them he couldn't bear to read it through. Would they? Was it worth anything, did they think? It had to be, Paula said, surely with [Char]Lotte's thousand scenes in mind.[30]

Salomon's book helped another book come to light. May this book achieve the same.

Acknowledgments

I would firstly like to thank my exhibit co-curator Michael Kaminer—his vivid and dynamic article "Graphic Confessions of Jewish Women: Exposing Themselves Through Pictures and Raw Personal Stories" in *The Jewish Daily Forward* inspired the show. I want to thank all the artists in "Graphic Details" for lending their wonderful artwork and being a delight to work with: Vanessa Davis, Bernice Eisenstein, Sarah Glidden, Miriam Katin, Aline Kominsky-Crumb, Miss Lasko-Gross, Sarah Lazarovic, Miriam Libicki, Diane Noomin, Corinne Pearlman, Trina Robbins, Racheli Rottner, Sharon Rudahl, Laurie Sandell, Ariel Schrag, Lauren Weinstein and Ilana Zeffren. I am grateful for their generosity in giving permission to reproduce their works in this book.

It was a pleasure to work with my co-chairs, Tahneer Oksman and Amy Feinstein, on the one-day symposium "Talking About Jewish Women and Comics" on February 26, 2012, at Yeshiva University Museum, where many of these essays were first given as papers. I would also like to thank all the other contributors to this book, for their essays, interviews and texts on the artists.

I would like to extend a very special thank you to Ann Miller and Deborah Harris; their support and guidance have been invaluable. I am grateful to all my readers for their advice: Janaya Lasker-Ferretti, Maggie Gray, Esther Solomon, Lise Tannahill, Christine Ferguson, Nancy K. Miller, Steve Hart, Roger Sabin, Alex Fitch, Maeve Thompson-Starkey, Althea Greenan and Elicia Spencer-Mills. I'd also like to thank all those who helped me source permissions for images: Lora Fountain, Tony Bennett, Adam Baumgold, Eric Reynolds and Paul Baresh.

The show "Graphic Details" has developed with the ongoing support of *The Jewish Daily Forward* and in particular Dan Friedman, Bob Goldfarb, Barry Surman and Jane Eisner. The exhibition has toured many sites in the U.S. and Canada. There have been many individuals who have helped us, and I would like to take this opportunity to thank Jo Ann Arnowitz at Jewish Museum of Florida, Judy Margles at the Oregon Jewish Museum, Carole Zawatsky and Josh Ford at Washington DC's Jewish Community Center, Jacob Wisse, Zachary Levine and Rachel Lazin at Yeshiva University Museum, Lori Starr, Mona Filip, Evelyn Tauben and Tony Hewer at Koffler Centre of the Arts, Toronto, and Andrew Farago and Summerlea Kashar at the Cartoon Art Museum, San Francisco.

I would also like to acknowledge the support of the University of Glasgow. My final thank you is to my wonderful husband, Charlie, for his care and attention toward both this book and its editor.

Group from *Likewise* by Ariel Schrag. Copyright © 2009 Ariel Schrag. I would also like to thank Anton Kras for enabling this image to be reproduced: Charlotte Salomon 4181—"Franziska's Suicide." *Life? or Theatre?* Collection Jewish Historical Museum, Amsterdam. © Charlotte Salomon Foundation, Charlotte Salomon.®

NOTES

1. *Yichus* in Hebrew is defined as pedigree and family status. The artists of "Graphic Details" are not linked by a family line, but are linked by a creative lineage of artwork and talent. Leo Rosten expands in *The Joys of Yiddish:* "*Yiches* refers to more than pedigree or family 'name' for *yiches* must be deserved, earned as well as inherited" (433).
2. Sarah Lightman and Michael Kaminer, "Trauma and Triumph for Artists of Graphic Details Vulnerability Means Power," *Graphic Details Catalogue,* New York: *The Jewish Daily Forward,* 2010.
3. Melissa Leong, "The Oy of Comics," *National Post,* February 24, 2011.
4. Sura Wood, "Color & Line with XX Chromosomes," *Bay Area Reporter,* September 30, 2010.
5. Nirit Anderman, *Haaretz,* October 11, 2010.
6. Mark Jenkins, "DCJCC Showcases some wonder women of underground comics," *The Washington Post,* August 23, 2012.
7. Alisia Grace Chase, "'Draws Like a Girl': The Necessity of Old School Feminist Interventions in the World of Comics and Graphic Novels," *Feminism Reframed: Reflections on Art and Difference* (Newcastle: Cambridge Scholars, 2008) 61–83.
8. Chase, 82.
9. Trina Robbins email, November 4, 2010.
10. Chase, 62.
11. Chase, 64.
12. Katy Deepwell, "Curating New Narratives interviews Ute Meta Bauer," *n. paradoxa* 10 (2002): 65–74.
13. Katy Deepwell, Interview with Catherine de Zegher, curator of "Inside the Visible: An Elliptical Traverse of Twentieth Century Art, in, of, and from the Feminine," *n.paradoxa* 1 (1996): 60.
14. Margaret D. Stetz, "Feminist Exhibitionism: When the Women's Studies Professor is a Curator," *NWSA Journal* 1, no. 2 (Summer 2005): 208–216.
15. Malin Hedlin Hayden and Jessica Sjöholm Skrubbe, Preface, *Feminism Is Still Our Name: Seven Essays on Historiography and Curatorial Practices* (Newcastle: Cambridge Scholars, 2010) xiii–xviii.
16. Chase, 82.
17. Tova Hartman, "The Paternal Voice in Liturgy," *Feminism Encounters Traditional Judaism* (Waltham, MA: Brandeis University, 2007) 63.
18. Hartman, 78.
19. Kim Munson, "Revisiting The Comics Art Show," *IJOCA* (Fall 2012): 264.
20. Brian Walker, phone interview, 2009, quoted in Munson, *IJOCA* (Fall 2012): 276.
21. Andrei Molotui, quoted in Mark Staff Brandl, "Two New Art Terms: A New Artistic Development: *Gallery Comics* and A New Compositional Form: *Iconosequentiality,*"May 8, 2006. Accessed February 19, 2013.
22. Trina Robbins email, November 4, 2010.
23. F.K. Clementi, "Rottweilers, Please Take Note," *Graphic Details Catalogue,* 7.
24. Sarah Jaffe, "Telling Their Own Stories," Graphic Details: Confessional Comics by Jewish Women, 34.
25. *Our Bodies, Ourselves* (Boston: New England Free Press, 1971).
26. Roland Chambers, "Hillary Chute on Graphic Narratives," *Five Books.* http://fivebooks.com/interviews/hillary-chute-on-graphic-narratives?page=2. Accessed February 19, 2013.
27. Corinne Pearlman, "Playing The Jewish Card: Show and Tell," 2009, 2.
28. http://lilith.org/about/mission/. Accessed June 20, 2013.
29. Susan Schnur, "Celebrating 35 Years of Jewish Women's Stories," *Lilith* (Fall 2011): 17–22, 22.
30. Mary Lowenthal Felstiner, *To Paint Her Life: Charlotte Salomon in the Nazi Era* (Berkeley: University of California Press, 1997) 218.

BIBLIOGRAPHY

Baskind, Samantha, and Ranen Omer-Sherman. *The Jewish Graphic Novel: Critical Approaches.* New Brunswick: Rutgers University Press, 2008.
Brandl, Mark Staff. "Two New Art Terms: A New Artistic Development: *Gallery Comics* and A New Compositional Form: *Iconosequentiality.*" Sharkforum.org. May 8, 2006. Accessed March 1, 2013.

Buhle, Paul. *Jews and American Comics: An Illustrated History of an American Art Form.* New York: The New Press, 2008.

Chainey, Michael A., ed. *Graphic Subjects: Critical Essays on Autobiography and Graphic Novels.* Madison: University of Wisconsin Press, 2011.

Chase, Alisia Grace. "'Draws Like a Girl': The Necessity of Old-School Feminist Interventions in the World of Comics and Graphic Novels." *Feminism Reframed: Reflections on Art and Difference.* Newcastle: Cambridge Scholars, 2008. 61–83.

Chicago, Judy, and Frances Borzello. *Frida Kahlo: Face to Face.* New York: Prestel, 2010.

Chute, Hillary L. *Graphic Women: Life Narrative and Contemporary Comics.* New York: Columbia University Press, 2010.

Clementi, F.K. "Rottweilers, Please Take Note." *Graphic Details: Confessional Comics by Jewish Women Catalogue.* New York: *The Jewish Daily Forward*, 2010.

Deepwell, Katy. "Curating New Narratives interviews Ute Meta Bauer." *n.paradoxa* 10 (2002): 65–74.

_____. Interview with Catherine de Zegher, curator of "Inside the Visible: An Elliptical Traverse of Twentieth Century Art, in, of, and from the Feminine." *n.paradoxa* (1996): 57–67.

Eisner, Will. *A Contract with God, and Other Tenement Stories.* New York: Baronet Books, 1978.

Felstiner, Mary Lowenthal. *To Paint Her Life: Charlotte Salomon in the Nazi Era.* Berkeley: University of California Press, 1997.

Hartman, Tova. *Feminism Encounters Traditional Judaism.* Waltham, MA: Brandeis University, 2007.

Hayden, Malin Hedlin, and Jessica Sjöholm Skrubbe. *Feminisms Is Still Our Name: Seven Essays on Historiography and Curatorial Practices.* Newcastle: Cambridge Scholars, 2010.

Munson, Kim. "Revisiting The Comics Art Show." *IJOCA* (Fall 2012): 264–288.

Le Guin, Ursula. *She's Fantastical: The First Anthology of Australian Women's Speculative Fiction, Magic Realism and Fantasy.* Melbourne: Sybylla Co-operative Press, 2003.

Lightman, Sarah, and Michael Kaminer. "Trauma and Triumph for Artists of Graphic Details Vulnerability Means Power." *Graphic Details: Confessional Comics by Jewish Women Catalogue.* New York: *The Jewish Daily Forward*, 2010.

Oz, Amos, and Fania Oz-Salzberger. *Jews and Words.* New Haven: Yale University Press, 2012.

Parker, Roziska, and Griselda Pollock. *Old Mistresses: Women, Art and Ideology.* Edinburgh: Pandora, 1981.

Refaie, Elisabeth El. *Autobiographical Comics: Life Writing in Pictures.* Jackson: University of Mississippi Press, 2012.

Rosten, Leo. *The Joys of Yiddish.* London: Penguin, 1971.

Schnur, Susan. "Celebrating 35 Years of Jewish Women's Stories." *Lilith* (Fall 2011): 17–22.

Stetz, Margaret D. "Feminist Exhibitionism: When the Women's Studies Professor is a Curator." *NWSA Journal* 1, no. 2 (Summer 2005): 208–216.

Part I:
Introductions

Graphic Confessions
of Jewish Women

Exposing Themselves Through Pictures
and Raw Personal Stories

MICHAEL KAMINER

Before you even see her face, Vanessa Davis's naked breast makes an appearance in the first panel of *Spaniel Rage*, her acclaimed book of diaristic comics. She's vomiting into a garbage can on page two. By the third page, she's servicing two clowns in an X-rated thought bubble. Rude? Shocking? Indecent? Try "charming, funny, and honest." That's how *Ghost World* auteur Daniel Clowes, the closest thing to an indie laureate, described Davis's work. And a growing number of fans are embracing the kind of raw, revealing autobiographical comics produced by a new generation of young, female, Jewish graphic novelists, such as herself.

While women have been writing frank confessional cartoons since the early 1970s, the context has changed. Brutal sexism defined underground comics back then, with females mostly depicted as fawning objects for a largely male readership. Blunt confessional comics were a throat-grab from women who dared male readers to confront real, unvarnished female characters.

Today's autobiographical comics come as less of a cultural jolt. For one thing, women have become a formidable presence in comics. Personal problems have also supplanted gender politics as a dominant theme. But these young artists are just as ruthlessly honest, presenting their bodies as nakedly as their emotions. They're also finding a new crop of audiences, weaned on blogs and tell-all Facebook pages, even hungrier for first-person intimacy. Even if the content of their work isn't especially Jewish, it reflects the kind of unfiltered sharing that Jews do especially well. "Jews are more likely to be in therapy," says Miss Lasko-Gross, whose pungent, thickly atmospheric *Escape from "Special"* chronicles the turbulent inner life of hyper-perceptive high-school student Melissa, a thinly veiled stand-in for her creator. "We're willing to be open about things that aren't necessarily flattering," Gross says. "It's probably the same reason there are a lot of Jewish comedians. We've got lots of problems, and we like to talk about them."

In *A Mess of Everything* (2009), Gross's long-awaited sequel to *Special*, Melissa returns as a highschooler coping with addiction, anorexia, and teenage malaise. Among its "no-she-didn't" moments: an epic battle with a recalcitrant, floating turd. "There's nothing I'm ashamed of," says Gross, 29, who lives on New York's Lower East Side. Exposing oneself through art is "a very Hebe-y thing to do," agrees Ariel Schrag, whose humane, poignant *Potential* won an Eisner, the comics equivalent of an Oscar. Like its predecessors, *Awkward* and *Definition*, the book was written while Schrag was still in high school; with almost naive openness, all of them pitilessly chronicle her adolescence and coming out. A film version of *Potential* is in development, and *Likewise*—a much-anticipated sequel—will appear in April. In terms of sharing her neuroses, "Woody Allen was a big influence on me. My comics are very Jewish in that sense," Schrag says.

Jewish identity itself isn't a dominant theme among these younger female comics artists; instead, it hovers at the margins of books such as *Spaniel Rage* and *Potential*. One exception is Lauren Weinstein, whose hilariously awkward autobiographical strips appear on the teen site Gurl.com and in her *Girl Stories* collection. In the online strip "Chanukah Blues," a tween girl argues the relative merits of winter religious holidays with a goyish-looking classmate. Weinstein also contributed "Horse Camp," about a lone Jewish girl at a Christian sports camp, to the Schrag-edited cartoon compilation *Stuck in the Middle*. "I don't do a lot of stuff explicitly confronting my Jewishness, but it's important for me never to shrug it off. I let it enter where it's appropriate," Weinstein says.

There is, in fact, a rich history of Jewish artists who lay out their own hang-ups in their work, says Samantha Baskind, Associate Professor of Art History at Cleveland State University and co-editor of *The Jewish Graphic Novel*. "But I think what links these younger graphic novelists is their approach as women rather than as Jews. A lot of their material is teenage anxiety."

Although their trials are more personal than political, today's young women artists "are definitely following in the footsteps of women in the 1970s underground," says Trina Robbins, the San Francisco-based writer and "herstorian" who created the first all-women comic, "Girl Fight," in 1970. Robbins considers Aline Kominsky-Crumb's infamous 1972 strip "Goldie: A Neurotic Woman" as the birth of female-authored autobiographical comics; it depicted the artist pleasuring herself with vegetables. The tendency toward self-revelation in comics is, Robbins says, "a Jewish cultural thing. We're not those quiet white Protestants who speak few words and act polite. We're noisy, we're always talking, and we're not embarrassed about it." More precisely, says Paul Buhle, author of "Jews and American Comics," "there's a Jewish self-identification in these artists' sense of humor, their unashamed discussion of personal lives, their dealings with angst and unhappiness through a pop-culture art form." Like Robbins, Buhle connects artists like Davis, Schrag, and Gross to the 1970s underground, "when extremely talented young women did comics about themselves and their lives in ways more frank, shocking, and vulgar than any artist could have been outside of *Tijuana* bibles." A few young Jewish female cartoonists have tackled political situations with the same fierce honesty others bring to personal histories. In *jobnik!* [Figs. 7, 78–79] her delicately drawn account of a tumultuous year-long stint in the Israel Defense Forces, Miriam Libicki's takes on Israeli society, culture, and men cut as deep as her self-analysis (she tends "to fall in love with anything that moves"). "It was just ripped from a diary. But it was fascinating to people because of Israel and the military setting," says Vancouver-based Libicki, 27, who's releasing a complete, self-published *jobnik!* collection this month.

Likewise, Sarah Glidden's elegant *How to Understand Israel in 60 Days or Less* (Part 1) [Figs. 45–47, 61–64] turns her own misconceptions into a whimsical but cutting memoir of a Birthright Israel trip, replete with sharp-eyed observations about Holy-Land quirks. Glidden's expanding the series after winning a book deal with Vertigo, the edgy "mature" division of publishing giant DC Comics.

As for Vanessa Davis, the minutiae of daily life will continue providing an endless source of material, no matter how awkward. "My mom asked about the boob, and I told her it was from a movie," says Davis, 29, currently finishing a *Spaniel Rage* sequel at her Santa Rosa, California, home studio. "But I'm doing these stories because they come naturally to me. I find a lot of personal comfort in the notion of recording things. Your memory fades. You lose things. Life is so ephemeral."

Sticking Their Tongues Out
at the World

DAN FRIEDMAN

When Michael Kaminer first approached *The Jewish Daily Forward* about publishing an article that eventually transformed into the "Graphic Details" exhibition, I'd just finished teaching Scott McCloud's astounding *Understanding Comics: The Invisible Art* (1994).[1] After Art Spiegelman's *Maus* (2003) few people could doubt the practical possibilities of graphic novels, and after McCloud I was a believer in the theoretical seriousness of this flourishing and popular art form.[2] The pitch, though, seemed a little too particular—confessional, Jewish and women, all at once? I'd heard of Aline Kominsky-Crumb and, more recently, had seen some of Ariel Schrag's work so I was willing to believe that there were maybe three contemporary artists who, though demonstrably women, might only vaguely be Jewish or confessional. It seemed interesting enough to give a green light but when the draft article came in I was blown away by the volume of excellent art and women artists for whom being Jewish was a central preoccupation.

By the time it was published in December 2008, "Graphic Confessions of Jewish Women: Exposing Themselves Through Pictures and Raw Personal Stories" had been pared down.[3] The story of the trend—its sheer scale and vigor—was getting lost in the critical and academic affirmations of art produced by women prepared to display the sometimes unpretty results of self-scrutiny. The examples of startlingly talented Jewish women producing starkly confessional graphic work were simply too numerous. And, in that scaling back, came Kaminer and Sarah Lightman's idea for a show that would present a more complete picture.

And, for the show that is in front of you, that comprehensiveness is all the more fitting. Because the proof is overwhelming—from Vanessa Davis's breast at the start of *Spaniel Rage* (2005) (and also in the article "Graphic Confessions") through to Sarah Glidden's journey of self-discovery at the end—that these works represent a community of artists that is brutally and uncompromisingly dedicated to providing complete, unexpurgated, and often difficult pictures. The pictures it produces are of life as it is lived with its messy physicality and its intrusive ideologies, its daily difficulties and occasional hells, its brief successes and its awkward moments.

From the first brief pitch in late 2008, to a fully-fledged exhibition opening in late 2010, it has been a long but rapid journey. That is testament to the work of Kaminer and Lightman and the belief of the hosting institutions. Shortly after the first reprinting, a number of the "Graphic Details: Confessional Comics by Jewish Women" catalogues were sitting in *The Jewish Daily Forward* offices awaiting distribution. Sandra McIntyre, then our Executive's Assistant, saw Miss Lasko-Gross's large and striking painting on the cover and came to ask me about this specially commissioned image [Fig. 3].

"What is that picture all about?"

As I explained to her what I had thought was a simple, graphically appealing and provocative image I realized that Lasko-Gross had put her finger on some of the key issues of the show and produced a symbolically apt cover for our exhibition. The tongue at the center of the image has a number of different meanings dependent upon its context. As an organ of sense and consumption it connotes taste; as the primary organ of articulation it has provided a number of languages with the words for language or speech; as an internal muscle that can extend to the external world it can display rudeness or intimacy and, sometimes, both—even in a scandalous way.

Though I don't know whether Lasko-Gross's picture has a name, I call it "The Tongue Mothers." It suggested itself to me because she made the picture around the time when she gave birth to her first child, but the name refers both to the women at either side of the tongue (the women, or "mothers" of the tongue) and also to the generative properties of expression (the tongue begets expression, it "mothers"). I think it's a good name, because the picture calls on all of these aspects to send a strong message about the type and tone of

Fig. 3. Miss Lasko-Gross, *Self-Portrait*, 2008-09, paint on canvas.

the work both within the exhibition and represented by it. In almost all cases and entirely as a whole the artists are deeply eloquent. These are artists of the pen as much as artists of the brush.

Long overlooked, women's autobiographical comics are as varied in style, topic and approach as the artists who make them. Though Jewish women were of crucial importance in this genre (as other essays in this collection detail), the Jewish artists in the show are necessarily a smaller sample. Yet, the "Graphic Details" artists have a variety of different approaches influenced by—but not limited to—their multiple nationalities: Canadian, English, American and Israeli. While Vanessa Davis's comic recounting of her trip to the sex shop [Fig. 7] and Miriam Katin's account of her sexual assault in the Israeli army [Figs. 65–68] might seem to be radically different, they're both up-close and personal stories about how women are co-opted and used by a patriarchal society. They are both sharply personal insights into the ways that gendered superstructures are experienced in the world by young women.

Just like the homunculus (womunculus?) on the tongue, their linguistic expression starts as a self-address and, in genre, takes the form of a self-examination. This is not glancing, contingent scrutiny but observation and evaluation that looks the artist right in the face— and in an intimate way. The effect of this type of expression is provocative, often deliberately so. Diane Noomin's section on DiDi Glitz's miscarriages [Figs. 21–22, 83–86] and Lasko-Gross's own contribution, "The Turd"—from *A Mess of Everything* (2009) [Figs. 37–38], both challenge us with their problems, as either generalizable or as *sui generis*. [4] These women are confident enough to stick their tongue out at society when they think it's warranted.

The self-representation that happens in the exhibition and the work that it stands for would be worthy of a monograph or two. The fact that Lasko-Gross has two versions of herself regarding one another across the divide of a tongue shows not just a degree of self-consciousness that one might expect from this kind of art, but a highlighting of the primacy of representing self-regard. For women, and especially Jewish women, knowing how to look at yourself is a crucial factor in combating the pervasive stereotypes provided for the male gaze.

As John Berger's *Ways of Seeing* (2008)[5] and Laura Mulvey's "Visual Pleasure and Narrative Cinema" (1975)[6] point out, women have been portrayed over and over again in art and cinema for the enjoyment of the male gaze. In importantly distinct ways, Jews have also struggled against pervasively anti–Semitic portrayals of themselves in various media. In "The Tongue Mothers" Lasko-Gross takes up her brush against those historical trends and, in a striking image, opposes them. Some of what I've said above is an expanded version of what I told Sandra. But, in short, the picture introduces a show of a variety of artists who, though talented, can show themselves behaving badly: they're bright, they're autobiographical Jewish women artists, and they're rude when they want to be.

NOTES

1. Scott McCloud, *Understanding Comics: The Invisible Art* (New York: HarperCollins, 1994).
2. Art Spiegelman, *Maus* (London: Penguin, 2003).
3. Michael Kaminer, "Graphic Confessions of Jewish Women: Exposing Themselves Through Pictures and Raw Personal Stories," December 4, 2008, *The Jewish Daily Forward.* http://forward.com/articles/14657/graphic-confessions-of-jewish-women/.
4. Miss Lasko-Gross, *A Mess of Everything* (Seattle: Fantagraphics, 2009).
5. John Berger, *Ways of Seeing* (London: Penguin Classics, 2008).
6. Laura Mulvey, "Visual Pleasure and Narrative Cinema," *Screen* 16.3 (Autumn 1975): 6–18.

BIBLIOGRAPHY

Berger, John. *Ways of Seeing*. London: Penguin Classics, 2008.

Davis, Vanessa. *Spaniel Rage*. Oaklnad: Buenaventura Press, 2005.

Kaminer, Michael. "Graphic Confessions of Jewish Women: Exposing Themselves Through Pictures and Raw Personal Stories." December 4, 2008, *The Jewish Daily Forward*. Retrieved from http://forward.com/articles/14657/graphic-confessions-of-jewish-women/

Lasko-Gross, Miss. *A Mess of Everything*. Seattle: Fantagraphics, 2009.

McCloud, Scott. *Understanding Comics: The Invisible Art*. New York: HarperCollins, 1994.

Mulvey, Laura. "Visual Pleasure and Narrative Cinema." *Screen* 16.3 (Autumn 1975): 6–18.

Spiegelman, Art. *Maus*. London: Penguin, 2003.

The Latest Revolutionary Chapter?

ZACHARY PAUL LEVINE

Hilarious. Painful. Embarrassing. Revolutionary ... and perhaps part of a long literary tradition? Although the majority of works in "Graphic Details: Confessional Comics by Jewish Women" forgo deep interrogation of its meaning, their authors unpack the profound relevance of Jewishness for themselves by positioning their works within the broader context of contemporary Jewish literature.

Iconic Jewish authors have confessed beautiful, ugly and comical images of their Jewish experiences. From Theodor Herzl's comic yet pointed rendering of European Jews' emaciated national spirit in *Altneuland* (1902) to Woody Allen's images of an imagined *nebbishy* upbringing beneath "The Cyclone Rollercoaster" in Coney Island in *Annie Hall* (1977), from the hundreds of frank and insightful autobiographies created for The Jewish Institute for Jewish Research (YIVO),[1] memoir competitions of the 1920s and 1930s, to Philip Roth's jarring and rebellious discussion of his manifold youthful frustrations,[2] and from the bellicose images of Queens Jews on *Seinfeld* (1990–1998), to established and emerging Jewish authors and artists grappling with being American (or British or Israeli or German, etc.) and Jewish today. These types of stories have offered generations an invitation and a blueprint for describing the individual's experience of being Jewish, as well as a way for successive generations of Jewish writers and artists to grapple with, if not react against, ideas of Jewish culture, Jewishness, and the relevance of Jewish historical experience in contemporary life.

Arguably, the first Jewish confessional autobiographer was Moses, writing in the *Torah* about himself and his own shortcomings as a leader. And certainly among the best-known medieval Jewish autobiographies is Rabbi Leon Modena's 17th century confessional memoir.[3] Hardly point-by-point recollections of the piety and glory, the authors revealed themselves as emotionally complex figures who continually wrestle with—and frequently lose out to— anger, gluttony, and egoism. Such confessional writing has probably existed for as long as there has been Judaism. We see it across the centuries, in Maimonides' letters about his daily routines,[4] and in numerous introductions to Jewish liturgical and legal texts. These texts humanize their authors, giving life and personality to some of the most recognizable names associated with Judaism and Jewish history.

Writing about one's experiences in a private journal or for a select audience was common in Jewish history, though the practice has expanded widely only in the last few centuries. As literacy expanded and Enlightenment ideas took greater hold in European societies, memoirs emerged as a witness to the lives of people beyond the elites, and to groups on the margins of society. In part, because memoirs and biographies captured so much of the daily life of non-elites, and especially for women, they have become recognized as a distinct and important part of Jewish literature. Think of the 17th century autobiography by the Jewish businesswoman Glückel of Hameln.[5] Though she wrote the book specifically for her family, Glückel tells us so much about the daily lives and worldviews of Jews, and in particular Jewish women on the cusp of the Enlightenment. Her memoirs have become required reading for any student of Jewish history.

The works appearing in "Graphic Details" emerged from the desire of a marginalized people to tell their stories in their own words and through images. They may have seen their provenance in the alternative comics scene of the 1970s, but these works are part of Judaism's long literary tradition. Yet, only a handful are explicitly about Judaism and Jewish history. So what then makes them Jewish? The answer, as Michael Kaminer and Sarah Lightman note, is that because these artists identify themselves as Jews, and because their work is autobiographical, then their works are, at least in some respect, *de facto* commentaries on their own experience as Jews. Indeed, Jewish autobiographers frequently, if not characteristically, position Judaism as one of many identities and heritages that shape their personalities, provoke and constrain their choices, and give their lives direction and meaning. More to the point, an autobiography is necessarily about how an individual wrestles with ever-changing ideas, events, people and identities, of which Judaism is only ever one part. It is unsurprising that only a handful of the artists explicitly concern themselves with Judaism and Jewish history.

The confessional memoir genre's lineage in Jewish literature is clear, but it has rarely been combined with images. Jews everywhere have always had a visual culture that is inextricably connected to the world around them. Jewish narrative storytelling through pictures goes back at least to the famous third century synagogue at Dura-Europus (today in Syria), which employed artistic styles common in Rome.[6] The tradition continued through illuminated Hebrew manuscripts including *Haggadot* that prescribe the order of the Passover *Seder* Meal, as well as prayer books, medical and legal texts, stretching as far back as the 13th century. However, these works were about the Jewish people, and tell the story of "us"—that is, of the Jewish nation and community, and its heroes. Rarely, if ever, did they focus on the author, let alone his/her (mostly his) deepest, darkest confessions.

Jewish women's confessional comics are, by contrast, revolutionary: each is a story of "me" rendered in graphic detail, meant for a wide audience. Then again, their deeply personal confessions invite us to take a look at ourselves and see something of our own biographies. Each comic's unique and personal observations provide a kernel of insights into the universal Jewish experience. Each is about an individual Jew's negotiation through a multifaceted culture, and each story relates something about the discrete ways that many Jews have perceived and conceived of Jewishness with respect to the social and cultural world around them. This connection between the personal and the communal places the pieces in "Graphic Details" squarely within the Jewish literary tradition. Though the comic art medium might suggest that they constitute a revolution in Jewish literature, their striking continuity with Jewish memoirs suggests that they might be, rather, an evolution.

Communicating this argument that these and similar comic works have a place within Jewish literature was the primary goal for the "Graphic Details" exhibition at Yeshiva University Museum and in subsequent venues [Fig. 4]. The project required the depiction and exploration of familiar and often clichéd tropes about contemporary Jews: spoken English peppered with Yiddish; persistent references to the vanquished "old world" and lore of family suffering; images of middle-class consumption; a guilty ambivalence if not contempt for

Fig. 4. Installation shot, "Graphic Details: Confessional Comics by Jewish Women," Yeshiva University Museum. Photograph by Zachary Paul Levine, courtesy Yeshiva University Museum.

Jewish religion as a mainstay of an author's Jewishness. Our task was to treat these ideas as cultural and historical artifacts for the visitor to investigate. The framed comics on the gallery walls and in the cases emphasized the gravitas and the artistry of the comic book narrative and its use of familiar and stereotypical images and tropes. A video portion featuring artists reading and commenting on their featured pieces further emphasized the seriousness of their storytelling in the otherwise characteristically playful and accessible comic book form.

Visitors and our colleagues appear to have embraced this argument. Many of the people who walked through the gallery doors came away with an understanding that the stories and medium appearing in "Graphic Details" are not just part of Jewish literature, and not just part of Jewish history and heritage, but refract their own experiences as Jews and their own ideas of the meaning and value of Judaism and Jewishness.

NOTES

1. Jeffery Shandler, ed., *Awakening Lives: Autobiographies of Jewish Youth in Poland Before the Holocaust* (New Haven: Yale University Press, 2001).

2. Philip Roth, *Portnoy's Complaint* (New York: Random House, 1969).

3. Leone Modena, *The Autobiography of a Seventeenth-Century Venetian Rabbi: Leon Modena's Life of Judah*, trans. Mark R. Cohen (Princeton: Princeton University Press, 1988).

4. Moses Maimonides, and David Yosef, *She'elot u-teshuvot Rabenu Mosheh ben Maimon "Pe'er ha-dor"* (Yerushalayim: Mekhon Or ha–Mizrah, Mekhon Yerushalayim, 1983) 143.

5. Glückel, *The Memoirs of Glückel of Hameln*, trans. Marvin Lowenthal (New York: Schocken Books, 1987).

6. See *Edge of Empires: Pagans, Jews, and Christians at Roman Dura-Europos*, eds. Jennifer Y. Chi and Sebastian Heath (New York: Institute for the Study of the Ancient World, New York University, 2011). Also see Steven Fine, *Art & Judaism in the Greco-Roman World: Toward a New Jewish Archaeology* (Cambridge: Cambridge University Press, 2005).

BIBLIOGRAPHY

Annie Hall. Dir. Woody Allen. United Artists, 1977.

Chi, Jennifer Y., and Sebastian Heath, eds. *Edge of Empires: Pagans, Jews, and Christians at Roman Dura-Europos*. New York: Institute for the Study of the Ancient World, New York University, 2011.

Fine, Steven. *Art & Judaism in the Greco-Roman World: Toward a New Jewish Archaeology*. Cambridge: Cambridge University Press, 2005.

Glückel. Th*e Memoirs of Glückel of Hameln*. Trans. Marvin Lowenthal. New York: Schocken Books, 1987.

Maimonides, Moses, and David Yosef. *She'elot u-teshuvot Rabenu Mosheh ben Maimon "Pe'er ha-dor."* Yerushalayim: Mekhon Or ha–Mizrah, Mekhon Yerushalayim, 1983.

Modena, Leone. *The Autobiography of a Seventeenth-Century Venetian Rabbi: Leon Modena's Life of Judah*. Trans. Mark R. Cohen. Princeton: Princeton University Press, 1988.

Roth, Philip. *Portnoy's Complaint*. Princeton: Random House, 1969.

Seinfeld, Jerry, and Larry David. *Seinfeld*. Sony Pictures Television, 1990–1998.

Shandler Jeffrey, ed. *Awakening Lives: Autobiographies of Jewish Youth in Poland before the Holocaust*. New Haven: Yale University Press, 2001.

Telling Their Own Stories

SARAH JAFFE

It's almost a cliché: the Jewish writer or artist examining and obsessively re-examining their life. Over and over, loudly, and in public. But it's less of a cliché for it to be a woman. For women to claim the space to self-examine in public is still transgressive. For women to be accepted as individuals with individual problems instead of making a statement about All Women Everywhere is still too often difficult. For women even to talk about things considered "unpretty" is transgressive.

Even non-comic folk have heard of R. Crumb and Harvey Pekar; many people have some idea of autobiographical comics as a sort of inverse of superhero books. Superheroes are impossibly pretty, perfect, every bit of their lives is heightened drama, and for Superman to be ugly he puts on glasses. Indie confessional comics are often purposefully ugly, showing life not only warts and all but with a few extra warts for good measure. Not only am I not a superhero, they say, I am going to lay out all the worst parts of me and dare you to like me anyway.

"Confessional" is a tough word to get past. When applied to Jewish authors, it doesn't take on the same religious connotation—there's no tradition of spilling your personal sins to another to get absolved of them. Instead, we fast once a year and wipe our slate clean for the next, we confess that we are sinners collectively, but frown on confessing our personal sins to anyone but God. So it makes sense that the women here aren't looking for absolution. They're staking their claim to space; to the same space the men get to tell their stories. Sometimes they're ugly stories, sometimes they're shockingly beautiful.

One can imagine Harvey Pekar, certainly a forefather of many of these creators, grumbling: "Confessional? I haven't committed a crime!" And indeed the idea of a confession, in addition to its religious overtones, echoes the idea of a crime. Is it a crime, then, to be Jewish, to be female, to write yourself and draw yourself as you appear, or as you would like to, or would like others to see you? Drawings, after all, are necessarily subjective, dependent on skill and style and a thousand choices.

Ariel Schrag and Miss Lasko-Gross tell embarrassing stories about shit in "Shit" (2003) [Figs. 100–101] and "The Turd" (2009) [Figs. 37–38] respectively. Lauren Weinstein opens up her thoughts and fears about pregnancy. Bodies are front and center in these comics, not only their shapes and sizes but also their inevitable functions, usually glossed over, hidden away. And since in comics the autobiographer not only "confesses" to the page but also presents herself physically on it, these artists present us with pictures of themselves that are deliberately unpretty, that challenge the traditionally male comics gaze that's filled the world with

Fig. 5. Miriam Libicki, *jobnik!* (Coquitlam, BC: Real Gone Girl Studios, 2008) 32, pencil on paper.

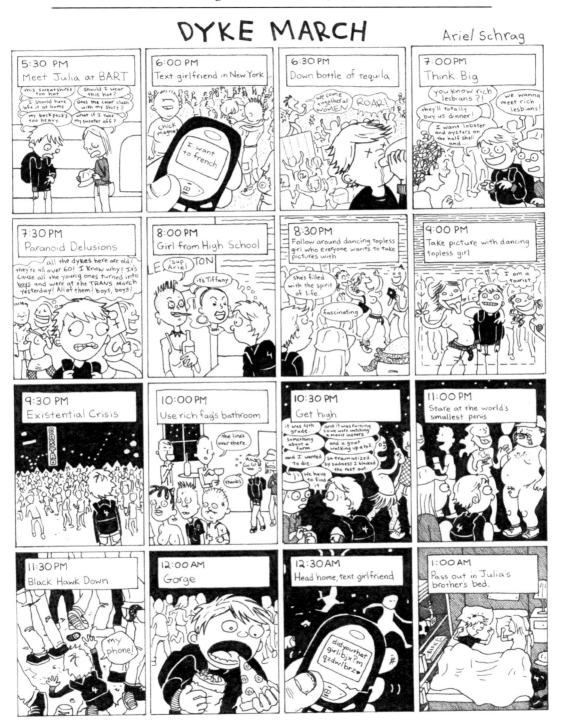

Fig. 6. Ariel Schrag, "Dyke March," 2005, ink on paper.

scantily-clad superheroines. (Wonder Woman, 1941, might be wearing pants now, but she sure is still the prettiest thing you've ever seen.)

The idea of "confession" can supplant the idea of craft though—as if one simply vomits up feelings and has been lucky enough to have feelings people may be interested in. Liz Phair, a musician known for her "confessional" songwriting, has pointed out that she was pigeonholed as someone who would just blurt out her feelings, her life story, rather than as someone who could create a character.

The idea that women just feel and men create and innovate can be a dangerous consequence of grouping women together under the moniker "confessional." But comics themselves require a degree of craft that belies that idea—one must take the time to draw, to stage, to frame an action—one has to show, not tell, by virtue of the medium itself. And because comics are sequential, a narrative is necessary. These artists can no more simply draw feelings than they can just write: "I feel." These women have situated themselves in a story— a story that serves more purposes than just navel-gazing. Their stories take you from one place to another and many in between, and illustrate inner lives as beautifully as outer lives.

There is politics here as well; again, not at all rare to comics, but certainly rare to comics where women are telling their own stories. Sarah Glidden and Miriam Libicki tackle Israeli politics, Libicki from inside the only army in the world to draft women along with men in *jobnik!* (2008) [Figs. 5, 78–79] while Sarah Glidden draws not only on her trip to Israel and her very visceral interactions with the people there, but also her inner conflicts along the way in *How to Understand Israel in 60 Days or Less* (2010) [Figs. 45–47, 61–64]. Glidden dramatizes the clash between her political beliefs and the Israel she is confronted with in a court case—"Birthright is trying to brainwash me vs. Birthright is actually pretty reasonable"[1]—that recurs again and again throughout her narrative. Her "confession" here is a confession about her confusion about politics, a sudden lack of certainty.

So often that's the subject of "confessional" personal comics, anyway. The space where nothing is certain, where the creator can't tell you exactly what's going on. The text, narration, thought balloons or words say one thing, while the images tell you something else. It's that tension that makes them poignant.

In Libicki's work the tension is between the political, going on all around her, and her own small tragedies. The year is 2000; Sharon's visit to the Temple Mount the background. Yet Libicki gives us the politics in the form of radio broadcasts in the background, the soundtrack to her day-to-day existence as a "jobnik," a soldier in a non-combat role. She is willing to put her sexuality front and center, confessing perhaps to the sin of ignoring history happening all around her while she worries about love. And who hasn't occasionally made her own heartbreak the center of the universe? It's beautifully displayed in one panel, with the daily news printed behind her, as if from a newspaper, on one half, and in front of her just the name "Asher."[2]

In most of these women's work, in their stories about love, the expected female territory is shifted, opened up differently. Sex isn't prettified; it's depicted in all its messiness. Love isn't the end of the story; it's the beginning, or a speed bump along the way. Ariel Schrag looks at (and laughs at) the "Dyke March" (2005) [Fig. 6] and Libicki dishes up her inevitable heartbreak from her soldier fetish. So many of them confess to wanting. Desire, still so hard for women to cop to. Miriam Katin's desire for a Sephardic man in "Eucalyptus Nights" (2006) (she too is in the Israeli army, and she too foregrounds emotion over war) against the wishes of her family [Figs. 65–68]. Vanessa Davis's trip to a sex-toy shop in "Toys in Babeland" (2005) [Fig. 7]. The subtext in Sarah Lightman's "Dumped Before Valentine's"

(2007) [Figs. 80–82] of course, is wanting someone who doesn't want you. Libicki's book is an examination over and over of her desires, of the trouble that comes from giving sex when you want love, or from not knowing which is which. Laurie Sandell tells the story of depression—a familiar subject for a women's memoir, especially these days, but rendered poignant in a few spare lines, "confessing" her hurt and pain and destructive behaviors in *The Impostor's Daughter* (2009) [Figs. 95–99]. Checking herself in for help.

Fig. 7. Vanessa Davis, "Toys in Babeland," 2005, ink on paper.

But is telling your story itself a kind of asking for help? Or is it, instead, a way of demanding what you want—demanding attention, to whatever your subject is? Do you make yourself more important, or less so? How much of yourself are you offering? In an interview for *Bust* Libicki said:

> It's distasteful if your protagonist is a naked plea for love from the readers, though in actuality, having some big flaws that stand out usually makes a character more sympathetic. No one can tell the utter truth about themselves, cause it's both a lot simpler and more complicated than we can see from the inside. You either pump yourself up or put yourself down. Clearly, putting yourself down is more honest and brave when you had the choice to go in the other direction.[3]

But she also noted that "when you go too far in self-deprecation, it just folds right back into self-aggrandizement."[4] The desire for kudos for bravery in confessional literature, whether in comics or in prose, is just as dishonest as glossing oneself into a superhero.

And so, how true are any of these true confessions? How honest are these honest stories? Comics require the reader to fill in the gaps between panels, but autobiographical comics require the reader to fill in the spaces of a life, to understand that there are things left out of these stories as well as the things included. Sometimes by telling you the worst thing that's happened—or the best thing—artists run the risk of being boiled down to that one thing alone. It's the continuing nature of this work that makes it truly special, not the worst confessions. It's the simple, mundane moments that make you realize that there's more to this story—this woman's story, this Jewish woman's story, this Jewish woman artist's story—than what you see on the page.

None of these cartoonists is doing this to be brave or to get your acceptance; none of them is speaking for all women or all Jewish women. Instead, maybe the most transgressive, the most challenging thing about these memoirs is that, placed up against one another, they force us to see just how wrong we are to make sweeping statements about a female experience, a Jewish experience, a comic, a graphic memoir, a cartoon. They're just telling their own stories.

NOTES

1. Sarah Glidden, *How to Understand Israel in 60 Days or Less* (New York: Vertigo, 2010) 107.
2. Miriam Libicki, *jobnik!* (Vancouver: Real Gone Girl Studios, 2008) 64.
3. Sarah Jaffe, "Miriam Libicki Talks Comics, Art, and Judaism" *Bust*, July 20, 2009. http://www.bust.com/blog/miriam-libicki-talks-comics-art-and-judaismhtml.html. Accessed January 22, 2013.
4. Ibid.

BIBLIOGRAPHY

Marston, William Moulton. "Wonder Woman." *All Star Comics*. New York: All American Publications, 1945.

Glidden, Sarah. *How to Understand Israel in 60 Days or Less* 2010. New York: Vertigo, 2010.

Jaffe, Sarah. "Miriam Libicki Talks Comics, Art, and Judaism." *Bust*, July 20, 2009. http://www.bust.com/blog/miriam-libicki-talks-comics-art-and-judaismhtml.html. Accessed January 22, 2013.

Libicki, Miriam. *jobnik!* Vancouver: Real Gone Girl Studios, 2008.

Sandell, Laurie. *The Impostor's Daughter*. New York: Little, Brown, 2009.

Part II:
Essays

Fig. 8. Corinne Pearlman, "Confessions About Jewish Women & Comics Symposium: Academia? or Comics?," 2012, ink on paper.

Fig. 9. Corinne Pearlman, "Confessions About Jewish Women & Comics Symposium: Academia? or Comics?," 2012, ink on paper.

Charlotte Salomon, Graphic Artist

ARIELA FREEDMAN

Bernice Eisenstein's book *I Was a Child of Holocaust Survivors* (2006) begins with a bird's eye view drawing of five writers seated around an octagonal table [Fig. 10]. We might call them Holocaust writers, though we need to remain attuned to their differences: theorist and philosopher Hannah Arendt, novelists and memoirists Primo Levi and Elie Wiesel, the fantasy and fiction writer Bruno Schulz, who was murdered while reportedly writing a book titled *The Messiah*, and, in the tightest corner, the graphic artist Charlotte Salomon. They emerge from the table like petals on a flower, or like the dimensional figures of a pop-up book, their heads large and heavy on foreshortened torsos. Each has a few words of advice to Eisenstein as she embarks on her project, pictured in speech bubbles and hand-lettered. Levi, Wiesel and Arendt warn of the inadequacy of language, the difficulty of coming to terms with evil and with suffering, while Schulz speaks of the desire for external affirmation: "a friend."

But it is Salomon who points Eisenstein toward the autobiographical elements of her project and toward the work of witnessing as also a work of recollection. "You must first go into yourself," she says, "into your childhood—to be able to get out of yourself."[1] Of the guests at the table, she is by far the least well known, which is perhaps subtly indicated by the meagerness of her corner. Yet her work is the closest to Eisenstein's project: an autobi-fictionalography, beginning in childhood and employing both word and image.

Charlotte Salomon was a young Jewish artist from Berlin who fled Germany after *Kristallnacht*—also known as the Night of Broken Glass—and hid in the South of France. From 1940 to 1942, she created over 1,300 small gouached paintings and sketches that together comprised a fictionalized autobiography. She rejected about 500 of these, leaving a narrative sequence of nearly 800 paintings. She tells the loosely veiled story of her own life and family history, beginning with her aunt's suicide [Fig. 11] in 1913 and ending with her own exile to France in 1933 and her decision to begin this work of art. She balances autobiography and testimony, personal history and the history of German Jewish culture in Weimar Berlin, thus anticipating the dual focus on personal and historical narrative that has characterized so many significant works of contemporary comics.

Charlotte Salomon's *Leben? oder Theater? Ein Singespiel* might be the most powerful Jewish women's graphic narrative ever drawn and written. But it is almost entirely absent in critical discourse on comics and on graphic narrative. Salomon is frequently left out of genealogies of comics, and until recently, of holocaust writers. Mary Lowenthal Felstiner, who is the critic most responsible for bringing Salomon's work to a wider audience, describes giving a lecture about Salomon in 1979, and a woman in the back of the audience crying out: "Why haven't I ever heard of this?"[2] That was my reaction when I first learned about her work last Spring, from a short section in Robert Peterson's *Comics, Manga and Graphic Novels: A History of Graphic Narrative* (2010). I found Peterson's single brief mention after spending two years trying to figure out the field of comics, and reading a number of comics

Fig. 10. Excerpted from *I Was a Child of Holocaust Survivors* by Bernice Eisenstein, 7. © 2006 Bernice Eisenstein. Reprinted by permission of McClelland & Stewart.

Fig. 11. Charlotte Salomon 4181—"Franziska's Suicide." *Life? or Theatre?* Collection Jewish Historical Museum, Amsterdam. © Charlotte Salomon Foundation, Charlotte Salomon.®

histories and genealogies for a review article for the journal *Literature Compass* on the state of the field. Salomon is not mentioned in my article, because none of the comics historians and theorists I read seemed to know anything about her: not McCloud, not Groensteen, not Kunzle, not Witek, not even Hillary Chute, who had devoted an entire book to the work of female graphic memoirists without mentioning Salomon even once. Though in part Salomon's absence has to do with the liminal, intermedial quality of her work, her exclusion is also symptomatic of the general neglect of women comics artists among many comics historians and critics, an omission that has only begun to be corrected in the last few years. Salomon's work is a crucial part of the lineage of women comics artists that the "Graphic Details" exhibition traces, and of the history of the medium.[3] For me, as for so many, Salomon was a galvanizing find; the process of discovering her is ongoing.

Part of the reason for Salomon's absence from comics history is that *Leben? oder Theater?* is not a comic, strictly speaking; it was not drawn to be mass-produced, which is so often part of the definition of contemporary comics, and was created largely in isolation from a comics tradition. Early comics histories have often emphasized the centrality of print. According to David Kunzle, the rise of comics follows the rise of the printing press; comics are a medium designed for reproduction.[4] By contrast, Salomon's work is *sui generis*; it is hard to imagine how she imagined her work would be seen at all, let alone how it might be adequately duplicated. Salomon works in an artistic idiom informed by painting, film and music, but there seems to be little correspondence between her work and the German-language comics artists who were her predecessors, notably Rodolphe Töpffer and Wilhelm Busch, both considered fathers of the medium. She paints, rather than draws; usually uses full page spreads rather than panels, though occasionally she will split the page horizontally into long, thin segments of time, and instead of putting dialogue either along the margins or in speech balloons, she draws it on the overlays that accompany her paintings, or alongside the paintings themselves. Though her work occasionally is reminiscent of caricaturist George Grosz, it's often closer to expressionism. Michael P. Steinberg compares her color washes to Rothko, and her almond-eyed oval faces to Modigliani, and her series certainly belongs in the pantheon of painting, even as it exceeds familiar art historical narratives. As Griselda Pollock writes: *Life? or Theatre?* is one of the twentieth century's most challenging art works... Yet, I, for one, am not sure that I can know fully what I am looking at."[5]

But what if we say we are looking at a comic? Examining *Leben? oder Theater?* as graphic narrative rather than as an artist's book means seeing Salomon as a founder rather than as an exception. Salomon's work provides a valuable precedent for one of the most significant movements in contemporary comics, graphic memoir and testimonial, which otherwise does not emerge until the American alternative comics of the 1970s and the European ones of the 1990s. In her playful, leading, and questioning opening title: "Life? or Theatre?" she introduces the tension inherent in staging an autobiography. In her mutual claim to comics and high art, Salomon anticipates the move of contemporary comics back to the gallery wall. Her foregrounding of the personal and domestic against an implicated dark history prefigures the attempts of writers like Spiegelman, Satrapi or Eisenstein to map their own stories. Her bold, iconic use of color startles in the context of a story that we are accustomed to being told in black and white. Her radical use of the full frame and her surprising, expressive, talking heads point to structural and aesthetic choices that have rarely been repeated. Aside perhaps from Nakazawa's *Barefoot Gen*, Salomon's is the longest, most ambitious graphic testimony ever told, with 769 included gouaches and nearly another 500 discarded ones that bleed off the edge of the story. *Leben? oder Theater?* is something rich and strange: an ambitious graphic narrative on a scale that has not yet been replicated, that in many ways anticipates the conventions and preoccupations of contemporary graphic memoirs.

Trying to find a name for Salomon's "strange work," Griselda Pollock turns to Walter Benjamin who wrote in *Berlin Chronicle:* "For a long time, years really, I have toyed with the idea of structuring the space of my life—bios—graphically on a map ... I have devised a sign system, and on the ground of such a map there would be a real hustle and bustle."[6] Salomon's self-mapping—what Pollock calls the theatre of memory—follows this spatial logic. As McCloud and others have argued, in comics space is time: we read time by the way it is laid out on the page. Benjamin imagines this spatialization of memory as not only a map but a labyrinth: "So many primal relationships," he writes, "so many entrances to the maze."[7] That seems right both in relation to Salomon's work and in relation to the project of autobiographic comics as a whole; we follow not just a representation of the past but a series of clues, and we get lost.

Pollock's mention of Benjamin's essay is fleeting, but it's worth reading on. Benjamin continues:

> For autobiography has to do with time, with sequence and what makes up the continuous flow of life. Here, I am talking of a space, of moments and discontinuities. For even though months and years appear here, it is in the form they have at the moment of commemoration. This strange form—it may be called fleeting or eternal—is in neither case the stuff that life is made of... The atmosphere of the city that is here evoked allots them only a brief, shadowy existence.[8]

Benjamin's description could well be of comics that specialize in gaps and discontinuities out of formal necessity. We experience memory not as a coherent flow—and here perhaps Benjamin is quarreling with his predecessor, Bergson, and with Proust, whom he adored—but in the discontinuous instant of remembrance, a time out of time. Benjamin emphasizes the artificiality of this act of memory, its fictiveness, since it is not "the stuff that life is made of." The "brief, shadowy existence" allotted by the chronicle is the haunted space (not time) of the past.

It's useful to juxtapose Benjamin's strange figure with what Salomon calls her *"merk-würdigen Arbeit"*—her strange work. She writes in her preface:

> Since I myself needed a year to discover the significance of this strange work, many of the texts and tunes, particularly in the first paintings, elude my memory and must—like the creation as a whole so it seems to me—remain shrouded in darkness. CS.[9]

Memory is elusive and retrospective; the work is defined by its shadows and absences and retains a mystery, despite its intensity.

Salomon prefaces the work with an epigraph from Psalm 8: "What is man that thou art mindful of him; that earthly worm that thou should set thine heart on him?" On the top right hand corner of the page, the quotation helps inscribe the work in a Jewish tradition of inquiry and struggle with divine mystery. Like the opening question, *Leben? oder Theater?* the query remains unanswered, and the stylized, circular red question mark underneath the psalm echoes the blue question mark of the title, and emphasizes the very form of inquiry, the urgent and unanswerable question. Salomon's choice of the psalm as an epigraph is leading, since in general the work is thicker with references to secular culture, and particularly to German poetry and music. By beginning with the psalm, she writes the work into the lineage of Jewish text and tradition. And the quotation itself, whose translation emphasizes an earthly abjectness that is not as explicit in the original, asks the question posed by the title of another holocaust testimony, this one taken from Primo Levi's reaction to Dante's *Se questo è un uomo*—if this is a man? "Consider if this is a man," Levi writes, "Who works in the mud, Who does not know peace, Who fights for a scrap of bread, Who dies because of a yes or a no."[10] What is man? Salomon asks, or more accurately, what is woman? What is a Jewish woman in a time and place that strips her of her rights and identity?

I'd like to call attention to one last element of this page, Salomon's insignia, here incarnadine and enclosed in a circle, like a wax seal, elsewhere floating on the lower left hand side of the page. Salomon marks many of her pages with this signature, a fluid, often linked C and S, found somewhere in the corners of the painting. Salomon signs nearly every page of her work and appears in her *roman à clef* not only under the mask of Charlotte Kann, the heroine of *Leben? oder Theater?*, but in this ubiquitous signature. Her signature is not only striking and ever-present, it is, as Carolyn Austin argues, repeatedly echoed in the shape of her body and the maternal bodies of the pictorial narrative. Salomon's work is a writing of the body; her body and name combine in one linked, fluid sign. The signature mobilizes what Benjamin might call "an arsenal of masks,"[11] not a proper name but a multiplicity of inheritances and allegiances, which together stamp Salomon's life and work.

The signature also points us toward Salomon's incorporation of text and narration throughout the text. She begins with the thick painted words of her preface, and later writes the textual portions—dialogue, narration and musical cues—onto semi-translucent pieces of paper that she taped over the paintings. Sometimes she wrote in pencil, and sometimes she painted the words; she used the surface of the paper freely, varying the size of her handwriting to draw attention to different parts of the text, using looping arrows and numbers to point the reader to the order of the paragraphs, writing both horizontally and vertically and sometimes tracing the writing alongside the images below, so that it becomes another skin for the picture. The text maps the images, but also complicates them. To take one striking example, when Franziska throws herself from the window, the overlay traces her body with the words of the song that was introduced as a motif at her wedding: "Wir winden dir den Jungfernkranz"/"We twine for thee the maiden's wreath," from Carl Maria von Weber's 1821 opera *Der Freischütz*. The words themselves twine along her fallen body [Fig. 11 without overlay]. We read them, unconventionally, from bottom to top. Even as her body is depicted falling, the letters lead us up in an ascent reminiscent of the earlier gouache, where Franziska tells the young Charlotte about the angels ascending to heaven. The words of the lyric, thickly traced, emphasize the tragedy foreshadowed at the wedding, and rewrite the story of Weber's opera in which the young woman, Agathe, is protected by the bridal wreath that deflects the bullet meant to kill her. The bridal wreath—and marriage, more generally—writes Franziska into her suicide plot.[12]

This image is the first close-up of a human figure in the series, and only the second painting to focus on a single subject in the frame. The sudden switch to the single body makes her seem enormous on the page. We have moved from the dollhouse world of miniatures to the exaggerated, oversized world of tragedy. Even as her body becomes more abstract in this rendition, the letters become pictorial. Franziska's arm hides her face, her body is crumpled, her arms and legs fluid, and the realistic backdrops of the earlier pictures are shed for a thick collage of brush strokes. The letters emphasize the shape of her fallen body and serve as extensions of the pattern. By contrast, the narration, in pencil and in the corner, is so demure as to almost be invisible. "Franziska died immediately, the apartment being on the third floor. There is nothing more to be done about the tragedy." The resigned "nothing more to be done" is put in tension with the charged forcefulness of the image. The picture is followed by a series of close-ups of giant mourners: first Mrs. Knarre, monumental and static in grays and blues, then Albert, frenzied against a backdrop of red, and then the death notice which conspicuously omits any mention of suicide.[13]

In part, Salomon's emphasis on family history implies a restoration of identity. This is who I am, the work claims, and this is where I come from. Salomon's work begins with family history, like a novel by Thomas Mann, and moves slowly toward both the heroine's life and the birth of her art. But alongside her personal drama, Salomon charts the way the city is changing, as her Berlin streets move from melancholy blues and vibrant yellows to what Pollock calls "fecal fascist brown."[14] One could argue that her emphasis on the personal story of this Jewish family, even in the light of these historic sea changes, is a way of preserving the individual among the mass movements that swept the mid–20th century, and amid the genocide that sought to obliterate them. The emphasis on subjectivity is an act of defiance.

When Salomon describes the rise of the Third Reich, she writes of the progressive erasure of Jews from the public spheres of Germany and the stripping of their rights and place. Here is her bitter and brittle description.

> The swastika—a symbol bright of hope. The day for freedom and for bread now dawns—Just at this time, many Jews—who, with all their often-unmistakable efficiency, are perhaps a pushy and insistent race, happened to be occupying government and other senior positions. After the Nazi takeover of power they were all dismissed without notice. Here you see how this affected a number of different souls that were both human and Jewish.[15]

Salomon's irony ventriloquizes the Nazi point of view, as even her swastikas, as Mary Lowenthal Felstiner points out, are inverted. Through this mirroring effect, she subverts the Nazi victory, insisting on the humanity and identity of the "*menschlich-jüdischen*," both Jews and men.

Both the content of Salomon's work and the style of figure drawing emphasize the essential humanity of the "*menschlich-jüdischen*." The sloe-eyed, sometimes fair-haired women Salomon likes to draw are nothing like the racist cartoons published by Nazi papers like *Der Stürmer*. Salomon is interested in the liminality of not looking Jewish; she sits on benches and at cafes that are *Judenrein* (free of Jews), and is undetectable. The Nazis in the ministry of culture, on the other hand, imply a bitter joke: small, dark, grotesque, chinless and jug-eared like George Grosz's caricatural paintings, they are anything but the Aryan heroes of a Leni Riefenstahl film, anything but advertisements for the beautifying power of racial purity. In the meantime, Dr. Singsang leans against the wall behind them, slender and elegant, looking like young Werther.[16] Embedded in Salomon's comic is a reflection on caricature, that representational trap of cartoonish drawing. As images move closer to semaphore, they are more and more prone to racializing shorthand and distorted representation, and racist caricature haunts the early history of comics and cartoons. As Jeet Heer writes: "The affinity of comics for caricature meant that the early comic strips took the existing racism of society and gave it vicious and virulent visual life."[17] By contrast, Salomon draws her figures to emphasize the ironic failure of racial profiling and racist representation.

On the deportation list, Salomon names her profession as Graphic Artist. We need to put this act of self-naming alongside another audacious moment of auto-identification. When Kann, Salomon's alter ego, is asked if she is a Jew at the art school she replies, drawing herself up: "Of course I am."[18] The activity of making art and imagining a future and an audience for oneself as an artist was almost impossible for a Jewish woman in Berlin in the late 1930s. Her work charts the progressive narrowing of her world as a Jew in Berlin, and moves from the dense, delightful interiors and landscapes of the early pages—depictions of a time when German Jews could travel, live luxuriously, share the baggage of any citizen— to the later scenes, when characters are stripped of anchoring decor and are merely outlines, as all European Jews found themselves stripped of property and identity. Salomon shifts her representational strategies, from the dollhouse images of the early paintings, the bird's-eye-view interiors and elaborately realized exteriors, to the slashed brushstrokes, bleeding outlines and muddied colors and of paintings located late in the series. When war comes to France, the date is circled and centered on the page, and the planes that drop bombs on France are merely painted X's, their bombs dark and bloody.[19] Images have become bare semaphores, stripped signifiers of meaning. When the refugees flee the air raids and huddle together in a railway car, they have no faces.[20] There is an urgency and speed to the style here, which likely resulted from the increasingly strenuous and harried circumstances of Salomon's life. Colors become less representational, and more expressionistic, and the dominant tone is anxiety. Detail drops away and setting drops away, as if to mimic these vanished subjects, this vanishing world. When Charlotte says to her grandfather: "You know, grandfather, I have a feeling that the whole world needs to be put together again," there is a childlike sketch of the frame of a house behind them, a refuge—or an idea of refuge—which is more and more virtual, which is, in fact, nearly gone.[21] Time is running out and the images are running dry.

Salomon's work is a *kunstlerroman* as well as a *bildungsroman*, the narrative of her coming of age as an artist. Her disastrous journey into exile brings her closer to the revelation that will power her most significant work: the book ends with the epiphany that this is the work she was meant to create, looping back, as many critics have noted, to its own beginnings. Even so, there is something Salomon leaves out: Gurs, the camp where she was held in May–June of 1940, before being released to care for her sick grandfather. Griselda Pollock argues that Gurs is the structuring absence in the work. She writes:

> That she never imaged the brief moment of her incarceration in the concentration camp suggests that this experience was the degree zero around, or rather against, which this vast colorful musical life-map of past and present was generated, its brilliant Mediterranean blue piercing and cleansing the fecal fascist brown of recent traumatic imprisonment in a sea of mud, to become the ground upon which this theatre of memory could be enacted as answer to that question posed to the window in the hotel.[22]

The vast edifice of memory that Salomon erects rises up around a significant absence. By ending her book in 1933, Charlotte Kann, Salomon's alter ego, turns her back not only on the reader but on history and on the unspeakable future. Indeed, we might situate Salomon's work in a version of Kafka's three impossibilities: the impossibility of writing as a Jew, the impossibility of writing as a woman, the impossibility of writing as a German. We might look also to Kafka's uncanny bracket on:

> The fourth impossibility, the impossibility of writing (since the despair could not be assuaged by writing, was hostile to both life and writing; writing is only an expedient, as for someone who is writing his will shortly before he hangs himself—an expedient that may well last a whole life).[23]

Kafka's depiction of the act of making art as a life-long suicide note that is at the same time a deferral of dying resonates with Charlotte Salomon's choice: to commit suicide or to create something radically new. But Salomon's art is less desperate than that analogy might imply, and braver. For all that Salomon's art bears marks of trauma—elision, fragmentation, absence, compulsive repetition, haunting—her insistence on creativity and identity implies something more active than the passive status of the victim of history, and more specific than the vague platitudes of trauma narrative. Her story bears testimony not to the inchoateness of loss, but to a vital, complicated and difficult family history. To send a work like that into an uncertain future implies a staggering leap of faith in the possibility of future audience and the redemptive ability of art.

And there was a future for Salomon's legacy, which had seemed destined to disappear into obscurity. The visual fecundity and narrative power of Salomon's life work has only begun to be explored by critics. Luckily, artists have been quicker to find her. When Maira Kalman had a show at the Jewish Museum in New York, her works were housed in the same rooms that previously held Charlotte Salomon's paintings. Kalman was pleased with the symmetry—moving into a space that had housed Salomon's paintings, when her work chose to carry on that same spirit. In an interview in *The Jewish Daily Forward* Kalman said:

> Also, it's incredibly poignant because those rooms housed an exhibition about Charlotte Salomon, whose work I adore. She was a young woman who lived in Germany before the Holocaust and wrote and painted about her life and crazy family. She was killed in a concentration camp, but the paintings were saved—over a thousand gouaches. I encountered her some years into my career, and there was a kinship, an electric moment.[24]

Kalman frequently cites Salomon as "a major influence," calling the series "glorious works. To me they're perfect."[25] Salomon's stylistic signature is everywhere in Kalman's work, from the flattened representation of interiors and brush-painted words to the love of color and distillation of autobiography and history. Even the question of identity—what it means to make art as a Jewish woman—is parsed by Kalman in a way that illuminates Salomon's project: "Having an observer's view, a sense of humor, a sense of the absurd, and a sense of tragedy are, on some level, Jewish qualities."[26]

Salomon's influence on Kalman is evident not only in her color sense and combination of word and image, but in her irony and in her humor. Her affective, visceral response to Salomon's work—to the electric moment—implies a genealogy of influence that is embodied and affectionate.

Other artists have sought to inhabit the space opened up by Salomon, often through mimetic strategies that seek to inhabit her artwork. As Sarah Lightman writes in a forthcoming essay: "As Salomon merges into her art, she is constantly becoming animated and re-animated by her readers—Salomon's artistic life and story, at least, continues."[27] As part of her essay "Life Drawing," Lightman drew the cover of Felstiner's biography *To Paint Her Life,* as an act of homage: "Re-drawing Salomon, bringing her into my present, to show how her work, and Felstiner's book, have been absorbed into my own drawings and creative life"[28] [Fig. 12]. Lightman's reproduction of the cover of Felstiner's book is a doubled reclamation: by paying homage to both Felstiner and Salomon she implies that influence is less a shadow than an illumination, passed down through generations.

Finally, Salomon's legacy is also evident in the newest generation of Jewish female cartoonists. Vanessa Davis writes about her mother giving her a "huge, comprehensive book of Charlotte Salomon paintings, which made a big impact on me as a teenage girl: they were so free-flowing and diaristic and documentary."[29] In another interview, "A Womanly Chat," she elaborates on this early encounter:

Fig. 12. Sarah Lightman, "To Paint Her Life," 2011, pencil on paper.

Around that time, I got *Twisted Sisters 2* and a couple of *Dirty Plottes* [by Julie Doucet], and I also discovered the work of Charlotte Salomon. I was really into it, but I tried to incorporate their influence into my painting rather than draw comics. It wasn't until I was much older that it even occurred to me I could try drawing comics.[30]

It may be useful to think of Davis as a hybrid of the contemporary avant-garde brutalist Julie Doucet and the non-linear autobiographical paintings of Charlotte Salomon. Davis's work is distinguished by the use of the full page and by lush use of color. Her tracing of time through the comics page without the benefit of panels to imply its passage unfolds in a non-linear zigzag highly reminiscent of Salomon's incorporation of multiple moments in a single frame. In Davis's joyful, humorous comics we can glimpse a less haunted trace of Salomon and of Salomon's continuing presence in Jewish women's comics.

Clearly, Salomon is a guiding spirit, and not only at Eisenstein's table: you can see her stylistic fingerprint in the ghostly lovers at the edges of Eisenstein's narrative, and her large table scenes; you can also see her influence in Maira Kalman's painted words and intense colors, in Sarah Lightman's search for a form to encompass her engagement with family history and Jewish tradition, and in Vanessa Davis's non-linear page layouts and painterly comics. For all that *Leben? oder Theater?* is a memory book, it ends with an inaugural celebration of creativity, looping back to its own beginnings, and to a world of possibility; one in which her artistic descendants will name themselves in part through the gift of her work, her courage and her vision.

NOTES

1. Bernice Eisenstein, *I Was a Child of Holocaust Survivors* (New York: Riverhead Books, 2006) 7.
2. Mary Lowenthal Felstiner, *To Paint Her Life: Charlotte Salomon in the Nazi Era* (New York: HarperCollins, 1994) xi.
3. In "Life Drawing: The Visual Autobiography of Jewish Women Artists," Sarah Lightman writes that *LOT* is "arguably one of the first autobiographical comics." Lightman's work on Salomon is an exception in the comics field. Perhaps her recent entry on Salomon in Paul Gravett's *1001 Comics You Must Read Before You Die* (Universe, 2011) will help bring Salomon's challenging and prescient work to the attention of comics scholars.
4. David Kunzle, *The Early Comic Strip: Narrative Strips and Picture Stories in the European Broadsheet from c.1450 to 1825* (*History of the Comic Strip, Volume 1*) (Berkeley: University of California Press, 1973) 3.
5. Griselda Pollock, "Theatre of Memory: Trauma and Cure in Charlotte Salomon's Modernist Fairy-Tale," in *Reading Charlotte Salomon*, eds. Michael P. Steinberg and Monica Bohm-Duchen (Ithaca: Cornell University Press, 2006) 54–55.
6. Walter Benjamin, "Berlin Chronicle," in *Selected Writings: 1931–1934. Volume 2, Part 2*, eds. Howard Eiland and Michael W. Jennings (Boston: Belknap Press of Harvard University Press, 2005) 596.
7. Benjamin, 31.
8. Benjamin, 612.
9. Charlotte Salomon, *Leben? oder Theater? Ein Singespiel.* http://www.jhm.nl/collection. Jewish Historical Museum, Amsterdam. Accessed March 29, 2012. (C:LT) 4.
10. Primo Levi, *Survival in Auschwitz* (New York: Touchstone Books, 1995) 12.
11. Benjamin, 375.
12. Salomon, 19.
13. Salomon, 20–22.
14. Griselda Pollock, "Life-Mapping," *Conceptual Odysseys: Passages to Cultural Analysis*, ed. Griselda Pollock (London: I.B. Tauris, 2007) 63–90.
15. Salomon, 142.
16. Salomon, 151.
17. Jeet Heer, "Racism as a Stylistic Choice and Other Notes." http://www.tcj.com/racism-as-a-stylistic-choice-and-other-notes/. Accessed April 3, 2012.
18. Salomon, 164.
19. Salomon, 530.
20. Salomon, 538.

21. Salomon, 548.
22. Pollock, "Life-Mapping," 84–85.
23. Franz Kafka, "Franz Kafka to Max Brod, June 1921," *Letters to Friends, Family and Editors* (New York: Schocken Books, 1977) 289.
24. Maira Kalman, "Q&A: Maira Kalman on the Illustrating Life," interview with Jillian Steinhauer. http://blogs.forward.com/the-arty-semite/. Accessed April 3, 2012.
25. Maira Kalman, "In My Home Office: Maira Kalman," interview with Jackie Cooperman. http://online.wsj.com/article/. Accessed April 3, 2012.
26. Maira Kalman, "Q&A: Maira Kalman on the Illustrating Life."
27. Sarah Lightman, "Life Drawing: The Visual Autobiography of Jewish Women Artists," in *The Routledge Handbook to Modern Jewish Cultures*, eds. Nadia Valman and Laurence Roth (New York: Routledge, 2013), draft. 3.
28. Sarah Lightman, draft 3.
29. Vanessa Davis, "Vanessa Davis is a Self Made Woman," interview with Alex Dueben. http://www.comicbookresources.com/?page=article&id=29157. Accessed April 3, 2012.
30. Vanessa Davis, "A Womanly Chat with Vanessa Davis," interview with Chris Mautner. http://robot6.comicbookresources.com/2010/07/sdcc-10-an-interview-with-vanessa-davis/. Accessed April 3, 2012.

BIBLIOGRAPHY

Austin, Carolyn F. "The Endurance of Ash: Melancholia and the Persistence of the Material in Charlotte Salomon's *Leben? oder Theater?*" *Biography* 31.1 (2008): 103–132. *Project MUSE*. Accessed March 28, 2012. http://muse.jhu.edu/.
Benjamin, Walter. *Selected Writings: 1931–1934. Volume 2, Part 2*. Eds. Howard Eiland and Michael W. Jennings. Boston: Belknap Press of Harvard University Press, 2005.
Chute, Hillary. *Graphic Women: Life Narrative and Contemporary Comics*. New York: Columbia University Press, 2010.
Davis, Vanessa. *Make Me a Woman*. Montreal: Drawn and Quarterly, 2010.
_____. "Vanessa Davis Is a Self Made Woman." Interview with Alex Dueben. http://www.comicbookresources.com/?page=article&id=29157. Accessed April 3, 2012.
_____. "A Womanly Chat with Vanessa Davis." Interview with Chris Mautner. http://robot6.comicbookresources.com/2010/07/sdcc-10-an-interview-with-vanessa-davis/. Accessed April 3, 2012.
Eisenstein, Bernice. *I Was a Child of Holocaust Survivors*. New York: Riverhead Books, 2006.
Felstiner, Mary Lowenthal. *To Paint Her Life: Charlotte Salomon in the Nazi Era*. New York: HarperCollins, 1994.
Freedman, Ariela. "Comics, Graphic Novels, Graphic Narrative: A Review." *Literature Compass* 8 (2011): 28–46.
Gravett, Paul. *1001 Comics You Must Read Before You Die: The Ultimate Guide to Comic Books, Graphic Novels and Manga*. New York: Universe, 2011.
Groensteen, Thierry. *The System of Comics*. Jackson: University Press of Mississippi, 2007.
Heer, Jeet. "Racism as a Stylistic Choice and other Notes." http://www.tcj.com/racism-as-a-stylistic-choice-and-other-notes/. Accessed April 3, 2012.
Hirsch, Marianne. "Mourning and Postmemory." In *Graphic Subjects: Critical Essays on Autobiography and Graphic Novels*. Ed. Michael Chaney. Madison: University of Wisconsin Press, 2011.
Kalman, Maira. "In My Home Office: Maira Kalman." Interview with Jackie Cooperman. http://online.wsj.com/article/. Accessed April 3, 2012.
_____. "Q&A: Maira Kalman on the Illustrating Life." Interview with Jillian Steinhauer. http://blogs.forward.com/the-arty-semite/. Accessed April 3, 2012.
Kafka, Franz. "Franz Kafka to Max Brod, June 1921." *Letters to Friends, Family, and Editors*. New York: Schocken Books, 1977.
Kunzle, David. *The Early Comic Strip: Narrative Strips and Picture Stories in the European Broadsheet from c.1450 to 1825 (History of the Comic Strip, Volume 1)*. Berkeley: University of California Press, 1973.
Levi, Primo. *Survival in Auschwitz*. New York: Touchstone Books, 1995.
Lightman, Sarah. "Life Drawing: The Visual Autobiography of Jewish Women Artists." In *The Routledge Handbook to Modern Jewish Cultures*. Eds. Nadia Valman and Laurence Roth. New York: Routledge, 2013.
McCloud, Scott. *Reinventing Comics: How Imagination and Technology Are Revolutionizing an Art Form*. New York: Harper, 2000.
_____. *Understanding Comics: The Invisible Art*. New York: Harper, 1993.
Nakazawa, Keiji. *Barefoot Gen, Vol. 1: A Cartoon History of Hiroshima*. San Francisco: Last Gasp, 2004.

Peterson, Robert. *Comics, Manga, and Graphic Novels: A History of Graphic Narrative*. Santa Barbara: Praeger, 2010.

Pollock, Griselda. "Theater of Memory: Trauma and Cure in Charlotte Salomon's Modernist Fairy-Tale." In *Reading Charlotte Salomon*. Eds. Michael P. Steinberg and Monica Bohm-Duchen. Ithaca: Cornell University Press. 34–72.

_____, ed. "Life-Mapping." *Conceptual Odysseys: Passages to Cultural Analysis*. London: I.B. Tauris, 2007. 63–90.

Salomon, Charlotte. *Leben? oder Theater? Ein Singespiel*. http://www.jhm.nl/collection. Jewish Historical Museum, Amsterdam. March 29, 2012.

Satrapi, Marjane. *Persepolis: The Story of a Childhood*. New York: Pantheon, 2003.

Spiegelman, Art. *Maus I: A Survivor's Tale: My Father Bleeds History*. New York: Pantheon, 1986.

_____. *Maus II: A Survivor's Tale: And Here My Troubles Began*. New York: Pantheon, 1992.

Steinberg, Michael. "Reading Charlotte Salomon: History, Memory, Modernism." In *Reading Charlotte Salomon*. Eds. Michael P. Steinberg and Monica Bohm-Duchen. Ithaca: Cornell University Press, 2006. 1–20.

Ware, Chris. "Introduction." *McSweeneys Quarterly Concern 13*. San Francisco: McSweeneys, 2004.

Witek, Joseph. *Comic Books as History: The Narrative Art of Jack Jackson, Art Spiegelman, and Harvey Pekar*. Jackson: University Press of Mississippi, 1989.

Young, James E. "The Holocaust as Vicarious Past: Art Spiegelman's *Maus* and the Afterimages of History." *Critical Inquiry* 24, no. 3 (Spring 1998): 666–699.

The Book of Sarah—
Life or Reconstruction?

Situating Sarah Lightman's Illustrated Diary

PNINA ROSENBERG

The Book of Sarah as Postmemory

Sarah Lightman's *The Book of Sarah* (1995–ongoing) develops an innovative language as it tells and depicts a process that is as ancient as humanity, the telling of one's life. Taking on the forms of the scroll, diary, and comics concomitantly, Lightman's work delves into her past and reveals layers of memory, or more specifically, postmemory. Literary scholar Marianne Hirsch describes this particular kind of memory in *Family Frames: Photography, Narrative, and Postmemory* (1997):

> Postmemory is distinguished from memory by generational distance and from history by deep personal connection. Postmemory is a powerful and very particular form of memory precisely because its connection to its object or source is mediated not through recollection but through an imaginative investment and creation.[1]

The raw materials in *The Book of Sarah* are photographs taken from her familial album, a practice that has become quite prevalent in contemporary art, mainly by those whose aim is to (re)shape the memory/history of the Holocaust. These photographic images, taken either from public archives or personal photo albums, are being transformed, modified, and embedded in new contexts, thus giving an individual interpretation to the void, the absence, and the feeling of loss. Similarly, Lightman makes sense of her life through her creative work based on family photos, tying her work to that of contemporary artists who employ postmemory. In giving an historical overview of how other contemporary Jewish artists engage in postmemory, we can see how Lightman positions herself within this genre. I will first consider the works of other Jewish artists, Christian Boltanski, Shimon Attie, Haim Maor, Ruth Kestenbaum Ben-Dov and Daniela Rosenhouse-Ben Zion. I will then discuss Lightman's work and her influences.

Salient examples of postmemory can be seen in the works of the oeuvres of the French artist Christian Boltanski, who created various installations using pictorial images based on photographs, which create a "Holocaust Effect"[2] in order to trace its victims. In one of the installations in his series *Lessons of Darkness*, he built an Altar to the Chajes High School in 1987, based on a photograph of the 1931 graduation class of a Jewish high school in Vienna. Boltanski:

> intensifies the effect of absence by enlarging the photos so much that most [of the] details disappear. The eyes, noses, and mouths become dark holes, the faces, white sheets. These blow-ups produce [...] a "Holocaust Effect." They remind us of pictures of survivors of the Holocaust, just after they were released.[3]

When the American artist Shimon Attie visited the *Scheunenviertel* Quarter, also known as the Barn Quarter, in Berlin in 1991, he was intrigued by the lack of any remembrance of its past Jewish inhabitants. After searching in the city's archives, he managed to trace photographs of some of the occupants, their houses and shops, and other evidence of Jewish community life. In his installation "Writing on the Wall" (1991–1993), these photographs were enlarged and projected onto the walls of the very houses where the pictures had been taken some 60 or 70 years earlier. This juxtaposition created layers of memory, and through blending the past with the present, he erected a living memorial to this persecuted population, bringing them out of oblivion.[4]

Haim Maor, an Israeli artist, dug through his own personal archive to create his 1988 installation, "The Faces of Race and Memory"; part of it, a table covered with glass, was entitled *Shulchan Aruch*, meaning both a written manual of Jewish law as well as a set table, described thus:

> A heavy transparent glass plate lies on the wooden surface of my desk. As through a transparent tombstone, one clearly sees who lies underneath. Under the glass I place photos, reproductions, postcards and notes, as was done at my father's house. Nowadays, one layer of memories covers its predecessors, conceals and obstructs it [...]. The memories become ghosts. The photos on the desk make a partial, broken mosaic, an incomplete jigsaw puzzle that hardly manages to join together to form a story, due to the black holes between the islands of memory.[5]

The installation is linked to his previous works, which are an ongoing and ceaseless research into his family's history, a story that cannot be fully traced and reconstructed due to lacunae—"the black holes between the islands of memory."

In the drawings and paintings that comprise the series "The Painter and the Hassid" (2007–2010), the American born Israeli artist Ruth Kestenbaum Ben-Dov formed an imaginary encounter between Rabbi Kalonymus Shapira, the Grand Rabbi of Piaseczno, Poland (1889–1943), the Czech Jewish painter Malva Schaleck (1882–1944) and herself. She was deeply moved and impressed by the spiritual resistance of Rabbi Shapira and Schaleck during the Holocaust. Kestenbaum Ben-Dov based her series on an archival photograph of Rabbi Shapira and a self-portrait done by Schaleck while interned in Terezin. Kestenbaum Ben-Dov depicted both protagonists either by themselves or together and with her own self-portrait. She culminated her series with an imagined, virtual encounter between the Rabbi and the Czech artist, taking place while both are immersed in their respective activities: the Rabbi is writing a sermon while the painter is working on a portrait.[6]

Daniela Rosenhouse-Ben Zion desired to fulfill her father's last wish. She summoned to his deathbed members of his family who perished in the Holocaust many years earlier, in the series of paintings "In the Name of the Father."[7] The artist called upon her paternal and maternal family members, whose deaths preceded her birth, and evoked their presence through the only memorabilia left to her: a box of old, black-and-white family photographs. Thus the ten oil paintings that comprise the series are based on small familial photographs, colored and enlarged, accompanied by painted images of the living members of her family.

By doing so she managed to assemble the past and present generations, to fill the gap the victims left behind, and to re-create a virtual reunion, that could only be possible through art.[8]

Although each of the artists makes different use of photographs and embeds them in different media, they all share a common denominator: the photographs serve as a bridge to the past and provide a tool for "postmemory." Lightman's *The Book of Sarah* is not related directly to Holocaust memory, but it is deeply connected to it. The British Jewish artist not only fashions her drawings on works of familial postmemory but also claims that her artwork is linked to the illustrated diary of Charlotte Salomon, a Holocaust victim.

From Salomon to Lightman

It is not in vain that a paraphrase of Charlotte Salomon's illustrated diary *Life? or Theatre?* (1998) appears in the title of Sarah Lightman's *The Book of Sarah. Life? or Theatre?* is formed of over 800 pages of text and images and is a powerful and beautiful visual autobiography by a German Jewish artist who was later killed in the Holocaust. Not only is Salomon's moving legacy a crucial keynote, a fundamental code to decipher Lightman's oeuvre, but it is, as the contemporary artist herself attests, her primary source of inspiration, the one that motivated her to dwell in this medium.[9] Yet, while Salomon depicted her story, with broad ink and color strokes, almost impasto-like, and narrated her personal and familial biography with expressive, almost true-to-life images, Lightman's fragmented minute pencil drawings, partly concealing, partly disclosing, require a considerable effort in order to decode her life story, to force the reader/viewer to reconstruct the fragments so as to recreate the whole text/image of *The Life of Sarah* [Fig. 13] which is "partially unrolled, as life yet unread, undrawn and unwritten."[10] Lightman's visual biography is a multilayered artwork; though Salomon's diary is the undeniable muse, it is nevertheless also founded on Biblical structure, as well as on various artistic sources derived from Western and Eastern cultures—all melting and merging in her "life project."[11]

The Book of Sarah/The Life of Sarah: A *Megillah* (Scroll) of Her Own

The Book of Sarah charts the search for an interlocking of traditional Jewish forms and autobiography, as I seek my own identity [...] I was committed in re-engaging Judaism with the visual, and not just the textual to make my book, *The Book of Sarah,* full of narrative self-portraits, and studies of family photographs and diary drawings.[12]

There is no *Torah* book or Scroll dedicated to Sarah, the first and the foremost of the four Jewish Biblical Matriarchs. This does not seem to be an oversight or anti-feminist gesture, since Esther, the Jewish girl who became the Queen of Persia, and Ruth the Moabite, who converted into Judaism and became the great-grandmother of King David, have Scrolls (or *Megillots*) named after them. Hence Sarah Lightman's illustrated diary remedies Sarah's lack of literature by creating a Scroll of her own with remarkable artistic fidelity to the Jewish tradition. The Book(s) of *Torah* or Scroll(s) is a handwritten copy of the *Torah* (Pentateuch), created as a scroll, and read during Jewish services, by unrolling and exposing part of it at a time, from right to left, as Hebrew is written (otherwise it is kept in a synagogue in the Holy

Ark/*Aron Kodesh*). Thus, a constant movement accompanies the procedure of its reading: one portion is unrolled, its text is revealed, and so forth. Lightman herself in 1996 turned her single sheet diary pages into a "real" *Torah* Scroll, therefore not only "animating" it but also contextualizing it within her religious sphere:

> In 1996 I created a scroll from pages of tracing paper sewn together, *The Scroll of Sarah*. On it I wrote the story of my family's origins of my name, and I performed reading this scroll in my undergraduate seminars. In my religious world this was a creative and self-expressive overflow.[13]

Even though Lightman's text/image retracement of (her) story is done on separate sheets of paper, the process of deciphering it is similar to the scroll's reading. Her "fragmentary" images can be fully deciphered only by a careful and slow "rolling" and "re-rolling." The viewer is asked to participate in the process of unveiling her biography, folding and unfolding it—going back and forth—just like the Scroll reading, and thus the complete familial portrayal can be reconstructed and retrieved. Moreover, *Torah* reading is a perpetual/cyclical process; every year, on *Simchat Torah* (the Jewish Holiday of the Joyous Celebration of the Torah) on the eighth day of *Sukkot* (Feast of Tabernacles) its reading is resumed—just like Lightman's ongoing diary, whose *modus operandi* is a never-ending one.

Sarah Lightman's text/visual Scroll evokes not only her own religious roots but also another artistic tradition—Japanese horizontal illustrated narrative hand scrolls. The *emakimono* (or *emaki*)—literally "picture scroll"—created during the 11th to 16th centuries, combine both text and pictures; they were drawn or painted on paper or silk, while the writ-

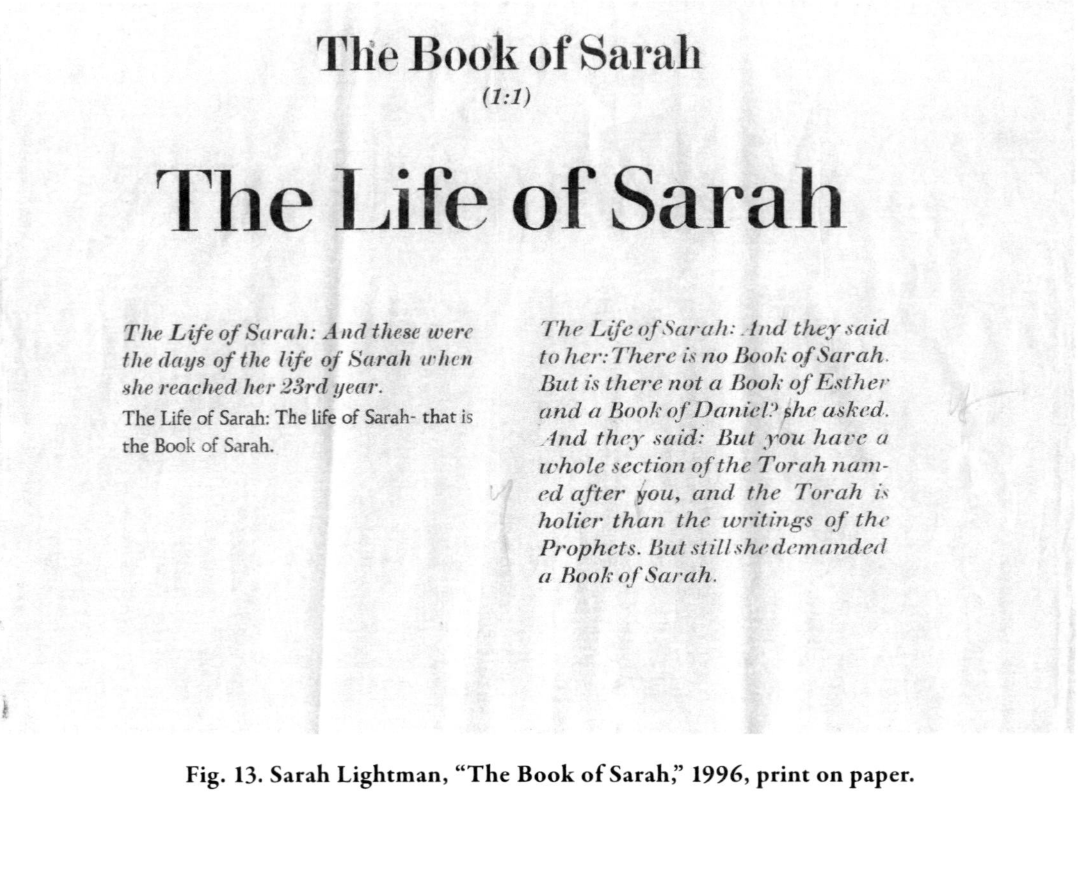

The Book of Sarah

(1:1)

The Life of Sarah

The Life of Sarah: And these were the days of the life of Sarah when she reached her 23rd year.

The Life of Sarah: The life of Sarah- that is the Book of Sarah.

The Life of Sarah: And they said to her: There is no Book of Sarah. But is there not a Book of Esther and a Book of Daniel? she asked. And they said: But you have a whole section of the Torah named after you, and the Torah is holier than the writings of the Prophets. But still she demanded a Book of Sarah.

Fig. 13. Sarah Lightman, "The Book of Sarah," 1996, print on paper.

ten account either appeared at the start of the scroll, or was interspersed between the pictures. The most well known are the *Genji Monogatari* (*The Tale of Genji*), c. 1130, narrating the amorous life of the Heian period Prince Genji, based on Murasaki Shikibu's 10th century novel and *Chouujuu Giga* (*Scroll of Frolicking Animals*), a visual allegory of Japanese 12th century society. The scrolls, whose height may reach 51 cm. while their length is usually 9–12 meters, are read by exposing an arm's-length of them at a time, from right to left.[14] Hence, "reading" *emaki* reminds one both of winding a film and viewing comic strips. The reader/viewer is the one that animates the oeuvre—s/he is the one that "dictates" its rhythm, who accumulates the images and makes an entirety out of them. On one hand, literally, the reader advances the story and on the other hand s/he seals it. Although the content is the summation of the accumulative process, each of its individual "fragments" stands for itself, similar to Lightman's diary.

Lightman's artistic/personal heritage is multifaceted as much as she is embedded in her Jewish roots, which she explores unceasingly.[15] She is also linked to the world of contemporary autobiographical comics, as manifested in her activity as artist and curator as well as her academic/scholarly research. These seemingly dual poles—"how to marry religious life and art school"[16]—that preoccupy Lightman are not as opposed as one might think at first glance, but complete each other and lay beneath her time-space expedition as found in *The Book of Sarah*.

The Expulsion from Eden:
Families like glass. See yourself and reality through them

I found myself, in my art studio at the back of my parents' garden, looking through family photographs and hoping this might give me a sense of who I was and where I came from and what art I wanted to make [...] Every day when I opened my sketchbooks, I entered a quiet and protected space away from the outside noise and complex events taking place.[17]

Sarah Lightman explores her origins, as in the Book of Genesis, and looks into the origin of the world. She emerges from her own familial Garden of Eden, bites the apple of the Tree of Knowledge, in quest of her identity as the youngest child in her family. "To be born last, into a pre-existing structure of a family of four, brings its own dynamics: 'Constructing yourself in an already established community.'"[18] In the series *Family* (1996–2012) as well as in previous chapters of *The Book of Sarah*, the artist depicts an amazing familial portrait:

These drawings show myself, and my siblings as we pose, push and squabble in our photograph—I lean on my sister, and also stand on her toe. In looking backward to old photos, and capturing everyone with my pencil, I controlled the external transitions in my life.[19]

The opening image of the series *Family* [Fig. 14] depicts a trinity, whose identities we gradually decipher. One can deduce that the left side silhouette represents Sarah's brother Daniel, since he is the only one wearing trousers; the height of the two other outlined figures and length of their skirts indicate that Esther—the elder sister—is the one in the middle, thus Sarah is the one to the left. The image, like the whole series, is based on "riddles" to be carefully decoded, similar to the painstaking process of constructing and reconstructing undergone by the artist. "My own personal archeology is a balance between creation and revelation."[20]

The pencil illustration, which seems as if drawn on tracing paper placed over a photograph, depicts the threesome in harmonious unity, not only due to the flowing line that binds them, but also by the composition that forms a very solid oval-like triangle of a huddled

Fig. 14. Sarah Lightman, *Family*, 1996–2012, pencil on paper.

group. The trio is outlined in contour lines—resembling a scientific, schematic, silhouette-like illustration, or a drawing that accompanies a photograph, which serves to identify the photographed persons, as well as children's picture booklets that encourage youngsters to color in the empty space. The amalgam of identification vs. anonymity, revelation vs. eradication, is the scarlet thread woven throughout Lightman's work.

The following "pages" entitled *like glass* and *See yourself*, respectively, in which the void is gradually filled with the protagonists' details—their facial features and part of their clothes—are deliberately inconsistent. One of the images is rapidly sketched while the other one depicting Sarah's very detailed bust-like "close up" image is meticulously done, contrary to the voided silhouettes of her siblings. Thus each step leads to a new revelation, nothing is to be taken for granted. The viewer needs to be constantly alert and vigilant, while being led by Sarah's footsteps.

After undergoing a deliberately disoriented deconstructive process, the viewer is prepared for a further reduction [Fig. 15]. However the next "paragraph," entitled "and reality

Fig. 15. Sarah Lightman, "and see yourself and reality, through them" from the series _Family_, 1996–2012, pencil on paper.

through them," does not follow those expectations. Not only do the threesomes appear again, but they are "doubled" in a mirror-like image; the penciled trio appears in the "mirrored" version to the left. Contrary to their previous position, the trio's mirrored left image is done in ink and is thus darker and more accentuated. Sarah's doubled left hand, which serves both as a bonding/separating element of the two groups, seems chained, creating a triangle, and apexes between her "doubled" head, culminating in her fingers. This composed/reflective image is quite intriguing—mainly due to the unease one feels while being exposed to the ambiguous left hand(s). From ancient times the left hand has been associated with defiance and enmity, as is manifested in the vocabulary of various languages—Latin/Italian: _sinistra_ (sinister); French: _gauche_, which means in English "awkward" or "tactless." Yet, the Biblical left-handed judge, Ehud ben–Gera, became famous for his resourceful use of his "deficiency": he attacked the Moabite King Eglon with his sword, concealed on his right thigh, where it was not expected, thus delivering the Israelites from Moabite domination.[21] The discomfort and the awkwardness that Sarah's left hand confers on the double image may well reflect both the sinister insignia as well as the Biblical resourcefulness, a virtue so skillfully used by the artist while depicting the _Family_ de-reconstruction.

Constructing Yourself in an Already Established Community

After the double-gazed image, which brings to mind Lewis Carroll's _Alice in Wonderland_ (1865), and its sequel _Through the Looking-Glass, and What Alice Found There_ (1871), whose protagonist constantly wonders who she is, Lightman pursues her fragmented quest-like "adventures" in order to decipher the identity of the semi-contoured silhouette. One has to re-roll the scroll back, to look for clues in the first "key image." By deciphering the two pairs of hands that surround the central figure and left shoe standing on her toe, it is understood that the almost transparent figure is Esther. Sarah's stepping on her elder sister's foot can be regarded as a mischievous childish act, yet it could also be interpreted as the "newcomer" transgressing the already established space of her elder siblings. Her struggle to conquer a place of her own might explain Sarah's attempt to almost "efface" her elder sister from the picture, though she is undeniably present.

Moving Pictures

The following images, which have no caption, involve a similar strategy: the artist hints at the existing people by revealing parts of them—be it their coiffures, their eyes or their very detailed clothing; each of the images resembles a preparatory drawing, usually done by artists while wishing to achieve perfection in one of those aspects. Yet, while those image-sequences are rapidly rolled, one can capture a different image—the complete one—as is done in animated movies. They are rolled, wound, and unwound—in constant movement and involvement by the viewer who tries to grasp their coherence. If we copy them on transparent paper and put one layer above the other, then, like in a kaleidoscopic puzzle, we manage to re-create the whole from its components. In order to complete the figures one has to "add" the following images, depicting their garments: Sarah's blue-striped short dress accompanied by her "mischievous" shoes, Esther's long red teenager's garment, and Daniel's solid outfit—shirt, trousers and shoes. The images that move from side to side are full of rhythm and resemble cartoons.

And I still squash Esther

After exploring the various possibilities of effacing and adding constantly, Lightman culminates the series, attesting, "Put us all in the same room and nothing's changed. I still need propping up," allusively depicting Esther and Sarah, identified by their metonymic outfits, embracing/leaning on each other. The final image/text "And I still squash Esther"—visualized by the two girls' legs, while Sarah's right one is stepping on her sister's left leg—creates a triangle that opposes the one created previously by Sarah's mirrored image hands and together form a diamond-shaped rhombus. Thus the *Family* chapters' dialogue is between themselves: they are bonded yet autonomous, they can be read from left to right or from right to left; they are constantly on the move, adding and removing/erasing layers to the intimate and complex familial structure.

A Language of Her Own

The *Family* series, which can be considered as a chapter of the *Book of Sarah*, narrates a complex, yet tender story of brother-sister relationships, as seen from an "intruder's" point of view. It unfolds, discloses and conceals, in constant and perpetual movement, the stirred familial agitation, the elder brother's/sister's resentment toward the new "invader" that breaks the already established cell, as well as the mutual dependence. Forcing the viewer to go back and forth not only accelerates the rhythm of the mini-saga but also traces Lightman's voyage in her consciousness. It is an expedition that never reaches its terminus—a perpetual process in each chapter, due to a constant alteration, depending on changing circumstances. This route is vividly veiled and unveiled in the enigmatic, yet very clear, *The Book of Sarah*; once the reader/viewer is ready to follow Lightman's operative instructions, s/he is rewarded with a most challenging image/text adventure.

Lightman, despite being rooted and inspired by past traditions and contemporary artistic currents, is not pacing a paved road; she is constructing *The Book of Sarah* by a pattern of her own, obeying its rigorous rules:

> While my work both belongs and doesn't belong in comics, it is a world I feel comfortable and welcomed in. Admittedly my work looks different, I don't use paneling in my drawings as I prefer to work over a whole uninterrupted page, and my style of drawing is very labored and careful, without the loose graphic style of many artists.[22]

Thus we see that Lightman not only follows her forerunner and spiritual guide, Charlotte Salomon, by creating a comics-diary, but she also bases her retracing work on one of the major devices that is used while memorializing and re-creating the 20th century Jewish catastrophe. Her "postmemory" multilayered *The Book of Sarah,* which reveals a strong affinity to the artists who are trying to fill this haunting-phantasmagoric void, pays, through her own artistic ingenuity, homage and tribute to all the Charlotte Salomons of the world.

Notes

1. Marianne Hirsch, *Family Frames: Photography, Narrative, and Postmemory* (Cambridge: Harvard University Press, 1997) 22.

2. Ernst Van Alphen, "Nazism in the Family Album: Christian Boltanski's *Sans Souci,*" in *The Familial Glaze,* ed. Marianne Hirsch (Hanover, NH: University Press of New England, 1999) 38.

3. Van Alphen, "Nazism in the Family Album: Christian Boltanski's *Sans Souci,*" 38.

4. See James. E. Young, *At Memory's Edge: After-Images of the Holocaust in Contemporary Art and Architecture* (New Haven: Yale University Press, 2000) 62–73; Hirsch, 264–265.

5. Haim Maor, "Forbidden Stories," in *The Faces of Race and Memory from the Forbidden Library* (Kibbutz Tel Itzhak, Israel: Masua, 2005) 52.

6. Pnina Rosenberg, "Portrait of a Family Album: Re-Collection—The Paintings of Daniela Rosenhouse," *Prism: An Interdisciplinary Journal of Holocaust Educators* 3 (2011): 84.

7. Daniela Rosenhouse-Ben Zior, *In the Name of the Father* [2007–2008]. http://drosenhouse.com/. Accessed April 7, 2010.

8. Rosenberg, 85–89.

9. Sarah Lightman, "Life Drawing: The Visual Autobiography of Jewish Women Artists" (draft). The final version is published in *The Routledge Handbook of Contemporary Jewish Cultures* (London: Routledge, 2013).

10. Lightman, 18.

11. Lightman, 4.

12. Ibid.

13. Ibid.

14. See Robert Treat Paine and Alexander Soper, *The Art and Architecture of Japan* (New York: Penguin, 1985) 133–157; and Noma Seiroku, *The Arts of Japan: Ancient and Medieval* (Tokyo: Kodansha, 1987) 140.

15. Lightman, 4.

16. Ibid.

17. Lightman, 5, 18.

18. Lightman, 18.

19. Ibid.

20. Ibid.

21. *Judges* 3: 12–18.
22. Lightman, 18.

BIBLIOGRAPHY

Boltanski, Christian. *Lessons of Darkness.* Jerusalem: The Israel Museum, 1989.
Carroll, Lewis. *Alice in Wonderland.* London: Macmillan, 1865.
_____. *Through the Looking-Glass, and What Alice Found There.* London: Macmillan, 1871.
Hirsch, Marianne. *Family Frames: Photography, Narrative, and Postmemory.* Cambridge: Harvard University Press, 1997.
Lightman, Sarah. *Family.* PowerPoint Presentation, 1996–2012.
_____. "Life Drawing: The Visual Autobiography of Jewish Women Artists" (draft). The final version is published in *The Routledge Handbook to Modern Jewish Cultures.* London: Routledge, 2013.
Maor, Haim. "Forbidden Stories." In *The Faces of Race and Memory from the Forbidden Library.* Kibbutz Tel Itzhak, Israel: Masua, 2005. 52–56.
Noma, Seiroku. *The Arts of Japan: Ancient and Medieval.* Tokyo: Kodansha, 1987.
Paine, Robert Treat, and Alexander Soper. *The Art and Architecture of Japan.* New York: Penguin, 1985.
Polen, Nehemia. *The Holy Fire: The Teachings of Rabbi Kalonymus Kalman Warsaw Ghetto.* London: Jason Aronson, 1994.
Rosenberg, Pnina. *Images and Reflections: Women in the Art of the Holocaust.* Kibbutz Ghetto Fighters, Israel: Ghetto Fighters House Museum, 2002.
_____. "Portrait of a Family Album: Re-Collection—The Paintings of Daniela Rosenhouse." *Prism: An Interdisciplinary Journal for Holocaust Educators* 3 (2011): 83–89.
Rosenhouse, Daniela. *In the Name of the Father.* Daniela Rosenhouse, 2010. http://drosenhouse.com/. Accessed April 7, 2010.
Salomon, Charlotte. *Leben? oder Theater?—Life? or Theatre?* London: Royal Academy of Arts, 1998.
Van Alphen, Ernst. *Caught by History: Holocaust Effects in Contemporary Art, Literature and Theory.* Stanford: Stanford University Press, 1997.
_____. "Nazism in the Family Album: Christian Boltanski's *Sans Souci.*" In *The Familial Glaze,* ed. Marianne Hirsch. Hanover, NH: University Press of New England, 1999. 32–50.
Young, James. E. *At The Memory's Edge: After-Images of the Holocaust in Contemporary Art and Architecture.* New Haven: Yale University Press, 2000.

Mi Yimtza?

Finding Jewish Identity Through Women's Autobiographical Art

Evelyn Tauben

In a 1975 essay, renowned modern art critic Harold Rosenberg writes: "Works ... [that] represent the Jewish experience are likely to belong to a bypassed style or to be, in a significant sense, outside the art of the twentieth century."[1] This proclamation from a Jewish man and art world arbiter is treacherous terrain on which to begin a close examination of a body of work by women artists that represents the Jewish experience in the 20th and 21st century. Yet this is precisely the inhospitable domain in which these women have been operating: an art world skeptical of narrative art and dominated by men. Furthermore, as Jewish artists they enter into a cultural milieu that remains heavily patriarchal, often marginalizing women.

This essay will explore how through their work Jewish women comics artists question and engage with tradition, faith and community while reflecting on shapers of identity ranging from family to sexuality. Through compelling and revealing comic art that draws upon their own experiences, Miriam Libicki, Liana Finck, Sarah Glidden, and Miriam Katin prod their connections to their Jewishness. We will see how their work reflects the modern-day tension between Judaism as a religion, Judaism as a nation state, and Judaism as a peoplehood. Some strive to encompass all three dimensions in their lives, some relate to only one aspect, while others do not find any facet of Jewish life today compelling.

The second part of this essay will consider the artistic output of other Jewish women visual artists who pull heavily from their own personal narratives while probing Jewish experience, including Andi Arnovitz, Helène Aylon, Jacqueline Nicholls, Rochelle Rubinstein, Melissa Shiff and Joan Snyder. We will discuss their art in relation to the autobiographical work of the specific comic artists considered in this essay. We will explore both shared and divergent notions of Jewish identity as expressed through women's art and what is similar and distinct in the approaches of the comic artists. The focus here will be on how these women navigate organized Jewish life and tackle the spectrum of contemporary experience, ranging from identifying as culturally Jewish, to living a life informed by religious observance. It is powerful artwork that explores a vacillation between alienation and affiliation, and between resignation and reclamation.

Coming Home? North American Jews and Israel

Modern Jewish life in North America is punctuated by many organizing structures, ranging from social to spiritual: synagogues, schools, summer camps, youth groups, federations, community centers, to name several. These institutions have been refined over the last century to help mold and define diasporic Jewish consciousness. By and large the personal journey to understand one's own Jewish identity inevitably involves navigating Jewish institutions, which can offer community, support, knowledge and context but also the greater challenge of fitting in, or feeling distinct in, a larger homogenizing structure. The State of Israel itself might be counted amidst the list of institutions of modern Jewish life. This is where two young American women locate their graphic novels—Miriam Libicki and Sarah Glidden. Organizational structures mediate their experiences in the ancestral Jewish homeland: the Israeli Defense Forces in Miriam Libicki's *jobnik!* (2008); and in Sarah Glidden's case, a Birthright Israel trip[2] in *How to Understand Israel in 60 Days or Less* (2010). In *jobnik!*, Libicki writes about being an American in the Israeli army just as the second Intifada is beginning. As the story unfolds, we learn that Miriam grew up in a Modern Orthodox home in Ohio and made *aliyah* at age 17.[3] While her relationship to Israel is evidently central to her understanding of herself as a Jewish person, Miriam is an outsider in every situation— even in religious circles, like the ones in which she was raised. She describes how the program for new *olim* (immigrants) was divided into secular and religious Israelis: "I was in the religious group, but I showed up wearing shorts, which no Orthodox Israeli girl does. I roomed with the secular girls, but maintained I was religious, nobody was quite sure."[4] In each respective scene on that page, the other teens—whether religious or secular—are portrayed contemplating her with mild puzzlement.

With paltry Hebrew skills and a lack of familiarity with the culture, Miriam is even more incongruous in the Israeli army. She feels insignificant in her clerical assignments and physically inferior to the "hot Israeli female soldiers." In the drawn essay "Towards a Hot Jew: The Israeli Soldier as Fetish Object," Libicki expands on the disjuncture between the self-image of North American Jews and their perception of Israeli soldiers as erotic embodiments of the "New Jew."[5] Above a drawing done in a photorealist style of a male and female Israeli soldier canoodling, Libicki pronounces: "The Jew in North American consciousness is curiously unsexy, especially in Jewish eyes." In *jobnik!*, Miriam's feelings of alienation are compounded by curt, exploitative sexual encounters with men. The narrative vacillates uncomfortably between illustrated re-creations of jarring actual television and radio news reports of the political situation and mundane quotidian scenes on the army base, where Miriam either thinks about men, or angles to get their attention. Beneath those unfulfilling thoughts and needy gestures is a desire to connect to another person and to elicit feeling in an otherwise numb emotional state, impelled by the overwhelming surrounding political reality and frightening media onslaught.

Sarah Glidden's experience of Israel is also as an outsider, recorded in devoted detail in *How to Understand Israel in 60 Days or Less* (2010). Sarah sets off on her Birthright trip like a citizen-journalist, looking for essential truths; seeking to reaffirm through first-hand experience her understanding of Israel as a place whitewashing past and present. Preparing for her trip, Sarah tells her Muslim boyfriend Jamil: "I'm ready to go there and discover the truth behind this whole mess once and for all."[6] This early scene establishes the possibility of being fed propaganda over truth. When Sarah begins to feel a connection to the place and the people, she assumes this must be the so-called Birthright brainwashing machine at work. She experiences an emotional breaking point prompted by a visit to Independence Hall, where her guide concedes to the complexities of Israeli life while continuing to speak to the group about Israel being *their* country, *their* home: "You came here to feel the State of Israel. You came here because you have come home." With this Sarah tells herself: "I am not going to let this get to me... This whole speech is designed to make me emotional."[7] Yet despite her best efforts at self-soothing, Sarah flees from the group to get some air with a frenzy of images streaming through her mind, drawn over multiple panels as if she is actually passing these scenes on the streets of Tel Aviv: Nazi soldiers attacking emaciated concentration camp prisoners; distressed Palestinians running in all directions under gunpoint; the site of an Israeli bus bombing with armed militia men. Through sniffles and sobs she proclaims to one of the Israeli group leaders, Nadav:

> So you win! I feel a connection, okay? I hope you're happy. How can I feel a connection to a place that causes so much suffering? Or maybe I don't really feel this connection. Maybe it's just impossible not to, after someone talks to you about Holocaust refugees and teenaged soldiers![8]

Thus, Sarah grapples with the tension between her previous understanding of Israel in comparison to her slowly shifting and expanding perspective. She is confronted by the inherent challenges of synthesizing aspects of Israeli policy and military actions with her liberal worldview. Meanwhile, she is also contending with the weight of the meta–Jewish narrative of Israel as a homeland to all Jewish people, while trying to resolve her place within that collective.

Since Sarah's personal journey is set in the framework of a group trip, the reader glimpses an array of Jewish experiences of young Americans. Some have had an immersive Jewish upbringing, while others are confronted by their Jewishness only upon arriving in Israel, and there are those in her group who have converted to Judaism. These varying affiliations become particularly apparent in facilitated group activities that are typical of these sorts of identity-building trips. In one scene, the facilitator asks the participants to complete the sentence: "I am a Jew because..." and the various answers include: "I am a Jew because my parents are Jewish, I guess" and "I am a Jew because half my blood is Jewish and half is Protestant, but my mom's side is Jewish so I, like, am officially a Jew."[9] A young woman shares with the group that as a teenager she immigrated to the U.S. from the Ukraine, where she was raised as a Christian: "One day I went to synagogue with a friend and felt that I really belonged there. A few years later, I converted." While Sarah dreaded the forced group-bonding activity, the range of perspectives she is exposed to is in fact surprising and intriguing. A conversation with her friend Melissa after the activity underscores an ambivalence among many American Jews, the influential role of the family in mediating Jewish identity, and even the ongoing effects of anti–Semitism. Growing up, Melissa intuited from her family's behavior that there was something shameful or fearful about being Jewish, something "that people shouldn't know about."[10] As a result, her family seemed to avoid engaging with their Jewishness altogether. Melissa is envious of the very experiences that Sarah takes for granted and even derides: going to Sunday school, learning Shabbat songs, having a Bat Mitzvah.[11]

Glidden's book does not offer the reader any image of a young person with a robust Jewish identity or inspired upbringing. Rather, we are presented with an underlying picture of insufficient or lack-luster exposure in their youth to Jewish tradition and education. Additionally, the people Glidden portrays lack the tools to interact with and understand Jews with different experiences and backgrounds from their own. These characters soon discover that essential concepts about Jewish life and community presented to them in their youth may in fact be highly unstable. For example, at one point during the trip, Glidden's group crosses paths with a Birthright group of Russian-Jewish participants. Melissa encounters blank stares upon greeting them enthusiastically. Sarah proclaims: "So much for Jewish unity."[12] This brief exchange calls the notion of Jews as one nation into question. Both Glidden's and Libicki's graphic novels tease out contemporary Jewish identities replete with complexity and uncertainty and yet both books highlight the inextricable and often inexplicable link between Jews in the Diaspora and Israel.

Synagogue and the City: One Woman's Quest and Inquest

The organized Jewish community has long heralded immersive Israel experiences as an essential benchmark in identity formation for young people—indeed, their "birthright." Another key entry point into Jewish life for diasporic Jews is through the synagogue, which has evolved over the last half century into the multipurpose facility we know today. In the online comic series *The Shul Detective* (2007), on the Lilith Magazine blog,[13] Liana Finck explores the landscape of Jewish life for a young woman living in New York who, through the guise of a detective character, sets out to find "the perfect *shul* or *shuls*" (Yiddish for synagogue). She recounts in Part One of the eight-part series: "For no reason, at one point, I stopped going to synagogue. I think I will start again. For no reason."

An erratic narrative and drawing style, mixed with absurd scenes and disjunctive visuals, seems to mirror a chaotic association with Judaism mixed with the inherent distractions and interferences of New York City [Figs. 16–17]. The Shul Detective is not terribly committed to her project: by the third installment she is already skipping *shul*. She stays home and Googles *"shuls"* instead, only fully returning to the subject at the end of Part Five, promising: "More next week about my experience at *Ramat Orah*." A promise unfulfilled in subsequent installments. A lackluster detective, perhaps, but her half-hearted quest is nevertheless grounded in a bastion of organized Jewish religious life. And, when she does go to *shul*, she appears to have meaningful experiences and is often inspired by the surroundings and the people.

Equally apparent in this series are the abundant options for a young Jewish person in a place like New York. One can even have a devotional encounter at a concert. In Part Five, the main character goes to a Sway Machinery show, featuring Jeremiah Lockwood's pseudo-cantorial stylings. However, she is suspicious whether the offering on stage is sincere or ironic. Seemingly skeptically the following statement is scrawled above an image of a non-descript figure wildly flapping his arms, with colorful orbs emitting from his middle: "If it is not ironic, it is definitely a novel view of God and prayer." Below the figure, Hebrew letters drawn freely using computer illustration software spell out: *"kadosh, kadosh, kadosh,"* a particularly performative part of the daily prayer service, where the words "holy, holy, holy" are chanted with feet together and heels lifted at each repetition of the word to evoke the angels in heaven.

Perhaps it is precisely the dizzying array of options for "plugging into" public Jewish life that sets the Shul Detective off course. City life is so over-stimulating that it is easy to stop living Jewishly for "no reason." It does after all involve effort and interaction to go to synagogue. Yet we cannot dismiss Finck's narrative meandering and *shul* dodging as mere ambivalence. Rather, there is a deep underlying fear about what self-discovery will look like. In Part Two, she sits down at a café, sharing: "I need time to think about this most recent,

Fig. 16. Liana Finck, sequence from *The Shul Detective: Part 2*, 2007. The Lilith Blog of *Lilith Magazine*, November 21, 2007.

most dangerous project I've taken on. I mean, *shul*. Anything can happen when you make an effort to follow the vector of your birth and upbringing." The artist stresses "anything" and "sadly" in highlighted star bursts around the detective's body. What follows in the next panel is an ominous abstract image like a black cloud surrounding red, diseased cells, suggesting a foreboding visual landscape, seemingly triggered by contemplating her exploration of Jewish roots [Fig. 17]. It's no wonder that the detective character does not embrace her mission with exuberance. The comment about attempting to explore the context in which one is born is a reminder that there is a critical turning point when a young person seeks to define his/her own identity, as opposed to simply grafting family values and practices onto one's self. Finck, Glidden and Libicki all situate their stories within that turning point, writing of experiences in their twenties and creating their work shortly after the described

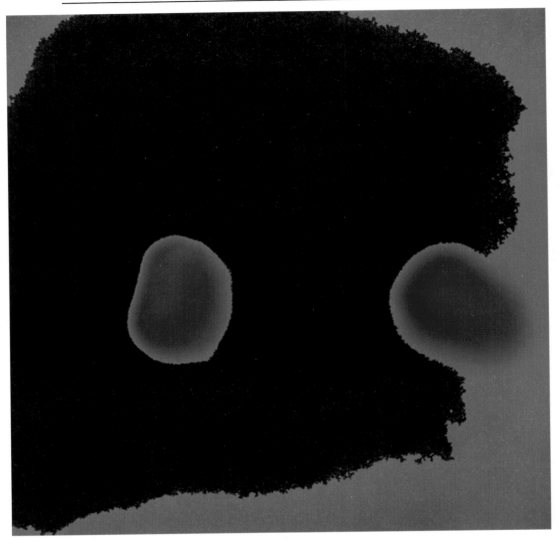

Fig. 17. Liana Finck, sequence from *The Shul Detective: Part 2*, 2007. The Lilith Blog of *Lilith Magazine*, November 21, 2007.

experiences. By contrast, Miriam Katin's graphic memoir looks back on a time much earlier in her life.

Belonging—and Showing It

The story of *We Are on Our Own* (2006) unfolds primarily from the perspective of Miriam Katin's mother, while Katin, who was very young at the time, appears as a little girl. The mother character is called Esther while the character that represents Katin is called Lisa. Several flash forward scenes show Lisa as an adult in the United States with her own small child. This poignant memoir reveals a woman who is at odds with North American Jewish life, and left with a crisis of faith following her experiences after hiding with her mother during World War II. A conversation about whether or not to send her son to Hebrew school reflects Lisa's struggle to accommodate her own sense of herself as a Jew with the mainstream mode of Jewish life in America. Her husband stresses his desire for their son to be surrounded by other Jewish children. As a secondary thought he notes the significance of studying Jewish heritage and practice. He answers Lisa's question about why their son has to go to Hebrew school simply with "To be with our own kind," adding "He must learn the Bible and prayers the way I did."[14] Lisa's reaction to the former statement made by her husband is that Hebrew school merely serves to separate the Jews into "us" and "them." In Glidden's book, in particular, one observes the unstable trajectory of a Jewish education driven by the parents' diffuse xenophobic desire for Jews to unite and be socialized together, rather than by passionate affiliation supported by Jewish practice at home. Several pages later in *We Are on Our Own*, the "success of the system," and the disjuncture between Lisa's beliefs and her son's schooling, is revealed when he is assigned to read "My First Bible." He says: "Mom, the teacher told us all about God." After Lisa reads him the abridged creation story, her son asks: "Did he Mom? Did God really make all those things in just six days?" Trapped between her own atheism and the teachings from school, Lisa deflects the conversation replying: "Well no [...]. This is just sort of a story. We will talk about it. Soon."[15] The color of the "present-time scenes" is used to its full effect. A cool blue shadow cast over her face highlights feelings of worry and sadness.

At the end of her graphic novel, Katin outlines her life after the war through pure prose, describing the challenge of maintaining her brand of Jewishness in the U.S. in contrast to her own upbringing in Israel, after her family left Hungary in 1956:

> I absorbed my father's atheism at home and the secular education in school. My father, however, never denied being a Jew and held pride in the ethical and literary nature of our background. I was always comfortable with this. Living in Hungary and in very secular Israel was no problem. In New York, however, I had to allow a more conservative approach to Jewish lifestyle. You had to belong and show it. I agreed reluctantly but had trouble with it.[16]

"Belonging" and "comfort" as a Jew are varyingly accessible or remote throughout Miriam Katin's life depending on the context. Katin lays out the distinction between a largely secular, broad-based Jewish identification informed by ethics and cultural influences and "a more conservative approach," which she experienced as the dominant approach in a place like New York. This highlights the dual conundrum and opportunities of contemporary Jewish life: seemingly endless possibilities to define one's identity and affiliation in a very personal and individual manner, set against a wider narrative rooted in religious tradition and informed by collective, communal practices.

Sarah Glidden's character also faces the question of belonging throughout her Israel trip. She is loath to acknowledge the very real feelings of kinship that being in Israel inspires in her. Her reticence at embracing this aspect of her identity as a Jewish person is also tied to her abhorrence at the notion of being lumped in with a whole group of people. This is a group that in the eyes of her social circle (such as her boyfriend's Pakistani father) is narrow-minded, conservative and blindly supportive of Israel. Indeed a thematic current that runs through all of the graphic works discussed in this essay is a hesitancy to accept oneself as part of the group and an inability to self-identify as a fully-fledged member of the Jewish people. Sarah's friend Melissa does not feel she belongs due to her lack of Jewish education. Meanwhile in various different works, Miriam Libicki repeatedly portrays herself as a "defective" Jew despite a substantive Jewish education. Rather Miriam perceives that her actions and personal choices set her apart and alienate her from the Jewish mainstream: "Though I have had both of the most cited vaccinations (going to Israel and attending Jewish private school) it is looking as if I will marry out."[17]

Ultimately, for all these artists, the process of navigating Jewish life is a search for belonging and a question about how to "show it." The delineated way to reach this space of comfort and belonging is often so circumscribed that it barely feels like a personal choice. After a moving montage through five years of memorial days for the assassinated Israeli Prime Minister Yitzhak Rabin, Miriam concludes: "I don't belong **in** Israel as much as I belong **to** Israel. Every year on Rabin's yahrzeit I know it's not even a choice"[18] [Fig. 78]. This kind of deterministic belonging can be difficult to embrace as one's own. It is not a simple undertaking to be a part of such an immense narrative, full of loss and trauma. Naturally, one might be compelled to turn away from it. Artist Joshua Neustein once responded to a question about whether he considers himself a Jewish artist: "My Jewishness is a shadow that follows me no matter how hard I try to run from it."[19] The ominous visual conjured by Neustein resembles the dark blot created by Finck in *The Shul Detective* series [Fig. 17].

Sarah Glidden's first inklings of belonging in Israel creep in when the group's participants are permitted to wander alone during a parade for the holiday of *Purim*. Even amidst the hubbub, with people of all ages decked out in costumes, she realizes how she feels more at home in the crowd than in her other travels to foreign places around the world. On those trips, Sarah felt evidently foreign and visibly out of place. By contrast, in this bustling Israeli crowd, she realizes "I could easily be one of these people," recognizing that only by chance she is not, since her great-grandparents fled Eastern Europe for the United States instead of Israel.[20] Incongruously, she feels a part of that anonymous mass of people and the festivities. By the end of Sarah's time in Israel, her feeling of belonging is heightened when she further senses that she is a part of something bigger than herself, leading to an unsettling comfort. Post-Birthright trip, Sarah and Melissa spend the day exploring the Old City's Muslim and Christian quarters and unexpectedly ending up in East Jerusalem. It is a day of feeling profoundly like an outsider. That evening, Sarah and Melissa go to see a play in Hebrew, and despite sitting in a Jerusalem theatre where Sarah can barely understand the production, she is overcome with a sense of kinship with the audience:

> Almost everyone in this room is Jewish [...]. They like intellectual theater which means they probably like contemporary art and translated novels [...]. We probably have so much in common. I'm ashamed to admit to myself that I like this feeling of being in this room. I'm even more ashamed at how much I didn't like being outside of it.[21]

Absorbing this feeling, she "let[s] the shame and comfort wash over" her. The final panel on the page reveals that Sarah's imagination has turned the entire audience into young Israeli soldiers, signaling an acceptance of her allegiance and affection for them that had begun to set in earlier in the trip.

Even within the difficult-to-decipher Jewish journey, which Liana Finck portrays, one intuits a desire for community and connection, for belonging and acceptance. The Shul Detective character states: "What I like at shul is the people." At the services of *B'nai Jeshurun*, an initial instinct to disconnect and to shut herself out quickly turns to belonging, participation, and even joy: "I want my headphones on! But suddenly I'm having fun." Her subsequent observations focus on the people at *shul* and on their faces, rather than accounts of the practices or the prayer experience. Of the services at *Romemu*, she proclaims: "The people are great. By the way they dance you can tell they are the real thing." The first *Shul Detective* installment is filled with descriptions of random people and sites observed on the Upper West Side on her way to Friday night services, and concludes with noticing the amount of people in synagogue: "People upon people." Before the services, Jewish life and city life are described as separate realms. Leaving her electronic gear at home in preparation for the Sabbath creates a sense of alienation from herself: "Without these things, alone in NYC, I am scattered [...]. Who am I, even?" After services, the Jewish world merges unselfconsciously with the city: "Afterwards they all spill out onto the street."

In an illustrated essay on autobiographical comics, "Jewish Memoir Goes Pow! Zap! Oy!," Miriam Libicki expands on the dual challenge of and yearning for belonging, detailing the transgressions of a "nice Jewish girl" after a childhood of "Judaism done right." She lives with a non–Jewish partner; she made *aliyah* but then left Israel; and while all her artwork is about Israel, it does not offer an exclusively positive picture of the Jewish state, so the Jewish community center where she lives will not exhibit it. Miriam proclaims: "I live in a very non–Jewish town with few Jewish friends, and feel Jewish, and want to be Jewish, more than ever before."[22] This expression of longing is an essential element to the journeys which these comic artists take the reader on, as they grapple with a yearning for belonging, while resisting descent into alienation. Yet there remains the perennial dichotomy between feeling Jewish and doing Jewish. The noted scholar Barbara Kirshenblatt-Gimblett has said: "Jewish is as Jewish does."[23] What does it mean to stay at home and google *shuls*? What does it mean to live in a non–Jewish community and feel Jewish? What does it mean to be conflicted about Israel? These comic artists reveal the subtle ways in which North Americans have been implicitly taught that there is a particular way to be a Jew. As discussed earlier, Katin writes: "You had to belong and show it." The imperative in itself is daunting and possibly even repellant; while defining what it might look like to demonstrate belonging can be even more foreboding.

Taking the Texts to Task: Jewish Women Artists Reimaging Ritual and Re-Evaluating Tradition

The tension between alienation and affiliation in contemporary Jewish life is compounded for women who are explicitly excluded through *halachah* (Jewish law) and custom from multiple arenas of Jewish life. We will now consider the projects of the Jewish women comics artists discussed in this essay alongside work by other Jewish women artists equally engaged in personal, visceral examinations of how the wider sphere of Jewish life and history informs their understanding of themselves as people, as women and as Jews. Much of the work by these artists is spurned by a conscious desire to break the prescribed mold of traditional Jewish practice and belief.

Melissa Shiff is a multimedia and performance artist from Toronto, whose work asks critical questions about Jewish practice and tradition, often inventing new ritual infused with contemporary relevance. In 2003, she staged her own wedding as a multimedia performance piece re-appropriating Jewish practices. One part of the ceremony addressed what she and her partner, Louis Kaplan, perceive as offensive Biblical writings about marriage laden with patriarchy. They rewrote a problematic passage of Deuteronomy, rearranging the text into a poem through the use of digital animation projected onto their "new media *chuppah*" (marriage canopy). For the processional, a text about the veiling of Rebecca was projected onto the bride; the measured lines of black Hebrew script make for a compelling image upon her white gown and long white veil. Upon reaching the *chuppah*, Shiff turned to face the gathering and by unveiling herself, she subverted the text from Genesis that was projected onto the *chuppah* overhead: "She took the veil and covered herself." This subtle gesture is a potent enactment of transformation, revealing the challenge of tradition and embracing it all in the same moment.

Helène Aylon has co-opted a similar visual strategy to create striking self-portraits as part of a larger series called *The Liberation of G-d*, a project she describes as "'rescu(ing)' G-d from the Patriarchy"[24] in which she highlighted in pink all of the misogynist, vengeful language in the *Tanach* (the complete texts of the Hebrew Bible) as well as the spaces between the words where a female presence is omitted [Fig. 18]. In the photographic portraits, the traditional texts wash over the artist's face, which she has described as similar to the way in which the teachings of the *Torah* were projected onto her in her Orthodox upbringing in Borough Park, Brooklyn. Art critic Savannah Schroll Guz writes of this work:

> Ultimately, Aylon's examination does not challenge the sacred, but seeks to rescue it from imperfect human understanding and profane encumbrances. Such re-evaluation suggests the possibility of overcoming ingrained, text-perpetuated intolerances.[25]

Thus, the milieu of art making for Jewish women is not only a place for voicing fear, frustration, anger and resentment but also for re-evaluation, as Guz describes, for reinvention and for reclamation. Shiff and Aylon use very personal gestures to make Jewish tradition their own, drawing upon their own bodies and stories.

In taking on tradition, Melissa Shiff and Helène Aylon literally take on the foundational texts of Jewish belief and practice. The physical properties of the text, not just its messages and meanings, become a part of the work. Shiff and Kaplan explain the significance of this act within the context of their "Post-Modern Jewish Wedding":

> We felt it was important and crucial to integrate the *Torah*[26] into our processionals both as a marker of our Jewish inheritance and our interpellation as Jewish subjects. The goal was to transform this sacred scripture from its static form as a book into new media via video projection and moving bodies. In this way, the *Torah* was animated in space and time.[27]

Even as these artists seek to subvert traditional modes and thinking about Jewish practice, the centrality of the texts which define Jewish thought and law is preserved. By taking up the substance and graphic properties of the text rather than dismissing the tradition outright, the works of art become imbued with the potency of centuries of textual debate and analysis. This practice also demands a measure of rigor and textual understanding. These artists are not integrating the canonical material in a superficial, cursory manner. This cleaving of text and incorporating it into a visual art experience draws this body of art nearer to the domain of comic art, defined by its unique and clever blending of image and word.

Many other Jewish women artists use the physical properties and inherent meanings of the traditional texts in their work. Originally from Missouri, Andi Arnovitz lives in Jerusalem where she creates garments out of paper that is rolled, cut, torn and sewn. She works with discarded prayer books and facsimiles of Jewish texts or prints words and letters onto the surfaces of her unwearable clothing. A striking example is *Coat of the Chained Woman* (2008), referencing the plight of the *agunot*, literally "chained women" who are not free to remarry because of their husbands' refusal to grant them the legal Jewish divorce proceedings and specifically the *get*, the document required to authorize a separation of husband and wife. Arnovitz's coat resembles a samurai cloak suggesting a woman readying for battle,

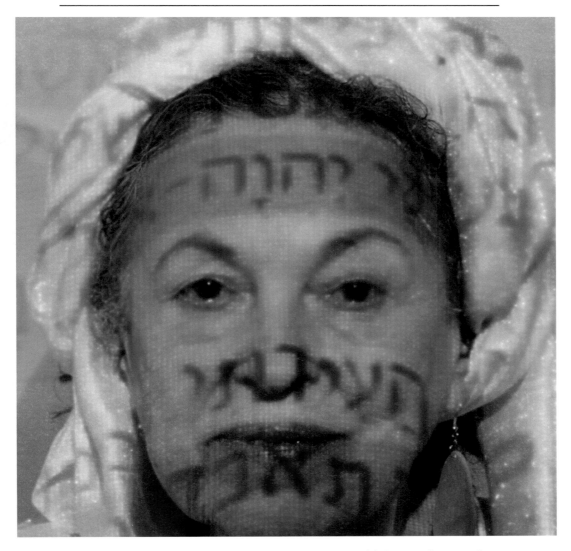

Fig. 18. Helène Aylon, "Self Portrait: The Unmentionable," 2011, photograph.

made of tiled fragments of reproduced antique *ketubot*, the Jewish wedding contract. The materiality of the text becomes the substance of the work as well as its symbolic framework. The *ketubot*, the very documents that enter women into a marriage contract, are also the fabric of their imprisonment in the case of *agunot*.

A series of paper cut works by British artist Jacqueline Nicholls recalls both dainty doilies and the Jewish tradition of paper cutting to adorn traditional texts. Begun in 2009, in *The Ladies Guild Collection* (the Ladies Guild being the British version of synagogue Sisterhood groups), Nicholls paired texts propagating misogynist attitudes with sexualized images of women to interrogate and play with the tradition. For example, in *Don't Talk to Women*, an elaborate border encircles a line from *Pirkei Avot* (Ethics of our Fathers) included in Hebrew and English: "A man who talks too much with women brings trouble upon himself, neglects the study of *Torah*, and in the end will inherit *Gehinnom* [Hell]." The imagery is suggestive of the bold, edgy graphics found in comic art with pared-down and sexualized types. Women are rendered in various poses of idle talk: one whispers gossip and one who lounges while chatting on the phone is a sex line operator. Another woman is shown bound and gagged. Nicholls's combination of disjunctive visuals with writings that are particularly jarring to the contemporary ear such as the *Talmud* and *Mishnah*, as well as from blessings, points to the challenge for women navigating the traditional Rabbinic texts. This work shines a light on inherent hypocrisies and patriarchies. A practicing, observant Jew, Nicholls does not turn away from this tradition but takes it on and transforms problematic language and practice into powerful political statements.

Like Nicholls, Toronto artist Rochelle Rubinstein was raised in an Orthodox home. In her work, she often incorporates colloquial Jewish language in addition to Biblical text and liturgy. In one piece, the Hebrew words *"bruchim habaim"* (welcome) repeat in measured rows as if pushing past the edges of the canvas. But the dark palette is decidedly unwelcoming. In a similar rhythmic fashion, the despairing and ubiquitous sigh of the Jewish people—"oy"—appears in several of her prints. In a piece of the same name, a cluster of people are huddled together at the bottom third of the print, while the block letters "OY" repeat hundreds of times forming a patchwork of letters like an endless chant. The text is in the same red as the people, seemingly representing their bleeding cries; and the placement of the letters hovering above the figures is akin to a comic book text bubble. Rubinstein has also created artist-made books, including *Genesis*, *Song of Songs*, and *the Book of Esther*, referencing books of the *Tanach*[28] featuring prominent female figures and revising the traditional text.

Of the first generation of self-proclaimed feminist artists, Joan Snyder's work is characterized by vigorous, expressive brushstrokes. In recent years her art has become increasingly abstract but it also contains identifiable markings and more figurative subject matter. When commissioned to make an artwork for the Jewish Museum, Snyder turned to words and to language to embody all of the women mentioned in the Bible, both Jewish and non–Jewish, in creating *Our Foremothers* (1995). In this piece, she includes the women's stories as well, conveying much emotion through gestural script and vibrant color. Snyder's family and her partner, Molly, join the chorus of canonical female figures. Here, as with the other artists we have looked at, the personal marries with a universal Jewish woman's narrative. The self is central yet shouts out a story bigger than one person.

Ritual, Belief and Observance in Glidden, Libicki, Finck and Katin

As we have seen, Jewish women who turn to comic art as their medium often also create highly personal work where their own identities, their self-image and the details of their lives are central to a larger conversation about the Jewish experience. Jewish religious practice—ritual, belief and observance—is touched upon in the comic art of Miriam Libicki, Sarah Glidden, Liana Finck and Miriam Katin but their stance is less defiant than in the work of the feminist Jewish artists just discussed. Rather their position often borders on resignation.

In Glidden's graphic novel, Sarah is generally sarcastic and skeptical about religious Judaism. She dismisses outright the Birthright group activity of welcoming in *Shabbat* on Friday night. She paints Orthodox Jews as a monolithic, small-minded group with hypocritical, dated perspectives. Early scenes in her travelogue show Sarah observing Hasidic Jews in the airport with befuddlement: "I'm not used to seeing them doing mundane things like waiting for luggage."[29] This observation implies that these ultra–Orthodox Jews operate in an interior world consumed by prayer and void of everyday activities. As the narrative unfolds, a modest adjustment to her perception of Orthodox Judaism mirrors the widening of her perspective with regard to Israel over the course of her trip. Through an unexpected series of events, Sarah and her friend, Melissa, attend a talk at the Shalom Hartman Institute given by Rabbi Hartman himself. As he lectures on the necessity of going beyond the strict letter of the law to a place of feeling and compassion, Sarah's resistance to listening to an observant Jew slackens, much to her own surprise. The illustrations show the Rabbi's lecture unfolding over a series of several panels, concluding one thought with: "The difference between Jew and non–Jew does not exist. We are all members of the human condition." These lines are transcribed in a text bubble that enters the rectangular panel isolated from any representation of the Rabbi and beneath these words is simply an image of Sarah seated in a chair. The rest of the audience has dissolved away. She looks ahead in delight and a small, red heart-shaped symbol floats over her head, signaling a little Jewish crush forming for this open-minded, intellectual Rabbi. As they leave the talk she proclaims: "It almost makes me want to be religious [...]. Okay, not really. But he's **almost** that good."[30] This quip to Melissa reveals once again the tension in Sarah's Jewish identification. She feels drawn to aligning herself with an ideology that will resonate with her core values while struggling with the notion that there is a Jewish collective experience that she can feel an allegiance to. This ongoing inner struggle is measured by her cynicism and fears.

While Sarah's limited perspective on religious Judaism is a result of equally restricted first-hand experiences with observant Jews, as we have seen, Miriam Libicki was raised in a Modern Orthodox community and is well versed in religious practice albeit uncertain of her connection to it. Her story of army life and sexual exploits is punctuated by moments of Jewish observance: attending High Holiday services, going to an army friend's family for *Shabbat*, reciting morning prayers. Each instance is colored with a strange mixture of reverence and ambivalence. Does the practice give meaning to her life and connect her to a larger sense of herself as a Jew, or is it performed out of obligation, nostalgia or guilt? Can all of these factors be operating at once? Miriam attends *Kol Nidre* services on *Yom Kippur* with her sister and just as they recite the words "Then they will be one community," her cell phone rings. Beset by embarrassment, she nevertheless runs out of the synagogue to take the call.[31] After an especially hurtful and difficult end to an ongoing dalliance with one of the soldiers, Miriam starts praying every morning in the base's chapel. She indicates a particular affection for this routine and illustrates herself making connections between the language of the prayers and her own experiences.[32] The scene has a touching quality suggesting solace in prayer and a meaningful return to practices of religious observance learned in her youth. Yet at the same time, throughout Libicki's comic work it is evident that the construct of Jewish religious life has given her the self-image that she is both defective and corrupt. One flashback scene in *jobnik!* shows Miriam at age five walking down an aisle at synagogue and ten years later as a developed teenager, while women in frumpy suits glare at her disapprovingly. The accompanying narration reads:

> Ever since I was five, I knew that I was the biggest slut on the earth. I went to Jewish private school in Ohio, and we belonged to a strict synagogue. But neither my mother nor I could ever get the hang of dressing me right. We didn't have the Orthodox-girl sixth sense of *tzniut*.[33]

Libicki points to the challenges of Jewish life for a modern woman in North America without offering a corrective or an alternative approach, as the artists we have seen with more prominent activist leanings do, such as Hélène Aylon and Melissa Shiff.

In *The Shul Detective*, Liana Finck focuses the detective's inquiry on a central institution of organized Jewish life—the synagogue. However, the reader is left wondering about the main character's position on Jewish practice and the role of feminism in her Jewish identification. Over a manicure in the second installment, she muses: "I don't know whether I'm a traditional feminist or what." Several panels in the series show egalitarian synagogue communities with women wearing the *kippa* and *tallit*[34] and taking a lead role in the service while another depicts a sanctuary with separate seating for men and women, without articulating an allegiance or preference for either setting. She is emphatic, though, in her admiration of the exuberant faith exhibited by some *shul*-goers, such as in her report on the independent community *Romemu* at the end of Part Two: "With most people, definitely with me, *IT* is not an issue of God. With these people, 'I' think it *IS* and you gotta respect this." Just as the question of God's mystery and existence forms the leitmotif of Katin's memoir, so too does a conversation about God weave in and out of *The Shul Detective* series, between increasingly tangential and nonsensical musings. This early installment establishes that the quest for a perfect *shul* is not related to a search for God, yet later parts in the series contain rather intimate, profound and revealing meditations on the divine. For example, Part Three in the series speaks of God being in the little things in life and later in the installment she states: "The point of God is that he cannot express himself on his own. He can be accessed through visual things—through faces, animate and inanimate. When we look at them, we provide the spark that lights them into life."[35] The existentialist conversation continues into Part Four, suggesting that understanding the relationship between the individual and God is indeed at the heart of this detective's investigation and signaling that the notion of God cannot be easily dismissed, even with a liberal, urban, modern, potentially feminist worldview.

Finally, while Miriam Katin's graphic memoir unfolds as an atheist's confession, it begins with the word of God. A dramatic yet minimalist opening sequence blends the message of a canonical Biblical text with the visual corollary to the words. The first page of Katin's book is a black square with the darkness inked in via sketchy markings. In the center, an empty square revealing the white of the page contains the lines from Genesis: "In the beginning darkness was upon the face of the deep."[36] A turn of the page lurches the reader from the abstract moment of creation into the darkness of Nazi-occupied Europe [Figs. 19–20]. The first panels contain the enlarged shape of the first letter of the Hebrew alphabet—the *aleph*—which is so massive that a point of its curvilinear form pushes out of the circumscribed box. The shape of the letter *aleph* is eerily echoed on the other page in the interlocking form of the swastika on a red Nazi flag. On the left page, the mother reads to the little girl from the Bible [Fig. 19]. In this sequence, Katin has faithfully copied out the words of *Bereshit* (Genesis), adorning the Hebrew letters with their many particular vowel markings and fanciful flourishes. Both the meaning of the words and the inherent beauty of the typography are celebrated, paired with the accompanying narration: "And God said: Let there be light, and there was light ... and it was good." On the next page, Katin launches into recounting her personal narrative and inverts the traditional words of the Bible with the caption: "And then one day, God replaced the light with the darkness"[37] [Fig. 20]. This opening sequence uses Jewish text to its maximal effect: honoring it, questioning it, ultimately subverting it; and sets up Jewish faith and teachings as the foundation upon which the story is built, a foundation that becomes increasingly unstable. This approach is ultimately more compelling than erasing all markers of traditional Judaism while also signaling the nature of Jewish education and discourse that informed Katin's youth.

Fig. 19. Miriam Katin, *We Are on Our Own* (Montreal: Drawn and Quarterly, 2006) 4.

Conclusion: Who Can Find a Woman of Strength?

The title of this essay borrows from the first line of *Eshet Chayil* (Proverbs 31:10–31) traditionally sung by a man to his wife at the Friday night dinner table. Many women today shun this practice, having difficulty relating to the proceeding description of an idealized woman gracefully attending to her household. However, referencing it in this context draws upon a similar gesture of reclamation seen in the many forms of art of Jewish women artists taking on traditional modes of Judaism and transforming them. *"Mi Yimtze"*—"Who will find...?"—implies a quest for a particular Jewish female self. Indeed, through their richly detailed drawings and revealing writing, the Jewish women graphic artists go on a quest for

AND THEN ONE DAY, GOD REPLACED THE LIGHT WITH THE DARKNESS.

Fig. 20. Miriam Katin, *We Are on Our Own* (Montreal: Drawn and Quarterly, 2006) 5.

self-definition, self-expression and connection to community. "*Eshet chayil mi yimtze*?" Who can find a woman of strength, a woman of valor? The answer is a given. These women with their fragility and fears know their own strength and the validity of placing themselves at the center of their stories and their art. They undeniably belong and they show it.

With thanks to Sarah Lightman and Michael Kaminer for introducing me to the wonderful world of "Graphic Details" and to Ida Ferdman and Sarah Ferdman Tauben for editorial support and assistance with key terminology.

NOTES

1. First published in *The New Yorker*, December 1975.

2. Birthright Israel was launched in 2000 by leading philanthropists and Jewish organizations under the premise that it is the birthright of every Jewish person to visit Israel. With some stipulations, Jewish youth between the ages of 18 and 26 are eligible for a free ten-day guided trip to Israel.

3. To "make *aliyah*," literally meaning "to go up" or "to ascend," is the Hebrew expression for immigration of a Jewish person to Israel under the Law of Return. Here, the author is referred to by her family name (Libicki) while the drawn version of herself is referred to by her first name (Miriam). This approach applies to all of the comics artists discussed in this paper except for Miriam Katin whose graphic novel memoir uses pseudonyms for herself and her mother and for Liana Finck whose protagonist—*The Shul Detective*—remains nameless.

4. Miriam Libicki, *jobnik! An American Girl's Adventures in the Israeli Army* (Coquitlam, BC: Real Gone Girl Studios, 2008) 108.

5. Miriam Libicki, *Towards a Hot Jew: The Israeli Soldier as Fetish Object* (Coquitlam, BC: Real Gone Girl Studios, 2008) 1.

6. Sarah Glidden, *How to Understand Israel in 60 Days or Less* (New York: DC Comics, 2010) 8.

7. Glidden, 99–100.

8. Glidden, 104.

9. Glidden, 66.

10. Glidden, 68.

11. The coming of age ceremony for Jewish girls, modeled on the traditional *bar mitzvah* ceremony for boys at age 13, which involves reading a portion of the *Torah* in synagogue.

12. Glidden, 114.

13. The eight-part series *The Shul Detective* can be read on the Lilith Magazine blog.

14. Miriam Katin, *We Are on Our Own* (Montreal: Drawn and Quarterly, 2006) 84.

15. Katin, 101–102.

16. Katin, 126.

17. See Libicki, *Towards a Hot Jew*. 6.

18. See Libicki, *jobnik!*, 73. Stress is in the original. The *yahrzeit* is the time of remembering a departed loved one on the annual anniversary of their passing, per the Hebrew calendar.

19. In conversation with the author, 2010.

20. Glidden, 83.

21. Glidden, 192.

22. Miriam Libicki, "Jewish Memoir Goes Pow! Zap! Oy!," in *The Jewish Graphic Novel*, eds. Samantha Baskind and Ranen Omer-Sherman (New Brunswick, NJ: Rutgers University Press, 2010) 272.

23. See exhibition catalogue for *Melissa Shiff: Reframing Ritual*, 10.

24. From Aylon's artist statement in an online exhibition: "Jewish Women and the Feminist Revolution," Jewish Women's Archive, New York.

25. Guz in *Pittsburgh City Paper*, May 26, 2011.

26. The *Torah*, as texts, contains the Five Books of Moses, the Pentateuch, which comprise the Written Law. But the concept of *Torah* also includes the Oral Law, which came to be written as the *Talmud*, which is a complex compendium of commentaries and discussions of Jewish law and practice.

27. Melissa Shiff and Louis Kaplan detail the thinking behind the various components in their wedding ceremony in the exhibition catalogue for *Melissa Shiff: Reframing Ritual*, 16.

28. The *Tanach*, the Jewish bible, refers to the *Torah* plus the books of the Prophets and the books known as Writings.

29. Glidden, 13.

30. Glidden, 198–99.

31. Miriam Libicki, *jobnik!*, 41.

32. Libicki, *jobnik!*, 106.

33. Libicki's own note defines *tznitut* as "modesty of dress," see *jobnik!*, 100.

34. A *kippah* (skullcap) and a *tallit* (Jewish prayer shawl) are both traditionally worn just by men but in some progressive communities, Jewish women have also taken on the practice of wearing them.

35. Liana Finck, *The Shul Detective*, Lilith Blog, n.p.

36. Katin, 3.

37. Katin, 4–5.

BIBLIOGRAPHY

Glidden, Sarah. *How to Understand Israel in 60 Days or Less.* New York: DC Comics, 2010.

Guz, Savanah Schroll. "At the Warhol, an artist delves into the patriarchal limits of the Torah." *Pittsburgh City Paper*, Pittsburgh, May 26, 2011.

Finck, Liana. *The Shul Detective.* New York. Lilith Magazine, The Blog, 2007.

Katin, Miriam. *We Are on Our Own.* Montreal: Drawn and Quarterly, 2006.

Libicki, Miriam. "Jewish Memoir Goes Pow! Zap! Oy. " In *The Jewish Graphic Novel.* Eds. Samantha Baskind and Ranen Omer-Sherman. New Brunswick, NJ: Rutgers University Press, 2010, 253–74.

_____. *jobnik! An American Girl's Adventures in the Israeli Army.* Coquitlam, BC: Real Gone Girl Studios, 2008.

_____. *Towards a Hot Jew: The Israeli Soldier as Fetish Object.* Coquitlam, BC: Real Gone Girl Studios, 2008.

Rosenberg, Harold. "Jews in Art." *The New Yorker*, 22 December 1975. 64–8.

Shiff, Melissa, Louis Kaplan, and Michaela Hájková. *Melissa Shiff: Reframing Ritual.* Prague: Jewish Museum in Prague, 2006.

Fetal Attractions

Diane Noomin's "Baby Talk: A Tale of 3 4 Miscarriages" (1995) and My Journal of a Miscarriage, 1973

JOANNE LEONARD

Central to this essay are two autobiographic artworks about miscarriage, a rare subject in visual art, though a common occurrence in the lives of women. There are 4.4 million confirmed pregnancies in the U.S., and 900,000 to 1 million of those end in pregnancy losses, each year.[1] I first met Diane Noomin, and discovered "Baby Talk: A Tale of 3 4 Miscarriages," during her visit to the University of Michigan in 2004 when I was on the faculty there.[2] I was excited then, and re-examining "Baby Talk" now, I'm all the more intrigued by this complex work and its parallels to, as well as differences from, my own *Journal of a Miscarriage, 1973*.[3]

My *Journal* and Noomin's "Baby Talk" are not precisely comparable. The two works come from different eras (the 1970s, the 1990s) and different genres (fine arts, underground comics). They also have different "centers." "Baby Talk," set against the background of an ongoing relationship, is the story of one pregnancy loss after another and the discovery, after the rollercoaster journey of "baby, no baby, baby, no baby," in the end to a "fetal attraction."[4] My *Journal* is the story of one miscarriage against the background of romantic loss, and the regaining of hope along with the reimagining of a future with or without a partner and a child. In this essay I present overviews of both "Baby Talk" and *Journal* and then I provide various additional points of comparison between the two works.

"Baby Talk": A Reading

The very appearance of the title text block that heads "Baby Talk," Noomin's remarkable 12-page comic, foretells the story, like a stage set visible to an audience before the performance begins[5] [Fig. 83]. The words "Baby" and "Talk" are spelled out in letters formed from drawings of safety pins. The "Y" of "baby," for example, is drawn as if an open safety pin is dangling a closed safety pin from its hinge; the "L" of "talk" resembles a safety pin standing with the length of its clasp side upright and its pin side resting along the base line. Thus, the phrase

"Baby Talk" is visually "barbed" by all the pointed ends of the safety pins depicted, and it contains a verbal barb as well, since the story of "Baby Talk" is "all talk and no action"— that is, lots of words but, ultimately, no baby. The subtitle continues this visual punning. The words of the subtitle, "A Tale of 3̸ 4 Miscarriages," are written with dark-filled, Halloween-like, blood-dripping letters, suggesting the blood of miscarriage; by contrast, the safety pin letter shapes are mere outlines with nothing but the white of the paper "inside," signaling the motif of emptiness in the story to come. These signifying visual "passages" are impressive, and Noomin's command of inventive artistic strategies starts in the opening pages and continues throughout the piece.

Noomin maintains the theater analogy suggested in the title text block by setting the scene on the first page to music. The readers are first introduced to the characters Glenda and Jimmy, who are stand-ins for—or "playing"—Diane and her husband, Bill Griffith. Later in the comic, it is the drawn version of the artist herself, Diane,[6] appearing with her alter ego DiDi Glitz, who continues the narrative. But in this first scene, we have Glenda and Jimmy in bed, discussing names for their baby. This scene allows the reader to grasp that Glenda is pregnant. By the third frame, Glenda gasps, "Omigod Jimmy ... what if it's **twins?!?**" and Jimmy immediately offers the solution: "**no problem**, Hon ... we'll call them Toody and **Muldoon!**" [All emphases in the original]. Jimmy and Glenda then begin to sing "Car 54, Where Are You?"[7]—a song and TV series from the 1960's that was resurrected from 1987 to 1990 by Nickelodeon and thus played for decades. Unnoticed by me, and possibly by other readers, until many rereadings, the lyrics from the Rolling Stones's "You Can't Always Get What You Want"[8] float in the background of a panel of the fourth page, "setting up" the story of loss yet to unfold. The sense of theater mixed with everyday life recalls a precursor autobiography in graphic novels: the text, image, and music of the Berlin artist, Charlotte Salomon's *Life? or Theatre?* (1942), a Holocaust-era work comprised of 1,400 drawings, along with the artist's explicit notations for musical accompaniment.

All in all, Noomin had four miscarriages in what she thought of as her miscarriage decade, beginning with her first in 1980, when she was 33. About the inception of her comic, she wrote to me: "I'd made a stab at it earlier—(thus the crossed-out "3" in the title) but didn't get very far."[9] Throughout the 12 pages of "Baby Talk," several visual devices, like the crossed-out number (an × is written over the "3," and "4" is substituted above the "3" in the subtitle) contribute to a subtle underlying commentary about the nature of self-writing. The cross-out in the subtitle of "Baby Talk" points to the flow of the life and the story, to its mutability (and possible unreliability) over time, and to the acts of including and excluding information that are necessary parts of creating a story from a life. Noomin's cartoon characters never utter a word of "literary theory," yet by the third page of "Baby Talk" a central problem in self-narration is explored—the problem of putting what is "private" into a public space through published or exhibited works of autobiography. Noomin has established an alter ego, DiDi Glitz, Diane's romance-starved, glamorous, sexy friend and purveyor of tough love. It is in exchanges between Diane and DiDi that the reader experiences Diane's reluctance to give her miscarriage experiences a public forum. DiDi climbs through the surface of the page, dragging with her a figure who evidently represents a resisting Diane Noomin being brought from behind the "cover" of her fictional characters [Fig. 85].

DiDi Glitz pulls Diane (the drawing of herself) out from behind her comics characters while asking, "Are you gonna let some **cartoon yuppies** cry **cartoon tears** over **your lost babies**?"—maybe arguing both for and against the power of "cartoons" with respect to deep emotion. Diane, attempting to climb back through the torn page to get out of sight, admits:

"I feel so exposed" and "I'm used to protecting my private life." She also expresses her reluctance to give the fans of her "semi-famous" husband (cartoonist Bill Griffith) any behind-the-scenes gossip [Fig. 86]. The problems of privacy as well as of telling another's story while narrating one's own are ones that affect all autobiographic writers/narrators—with potential consequences ranging from lawsuits to critiques that trivialize intimate revelation as "over-sharing."

Other problems/challenges of life writing, such as capturing the culture and class surroundings of the story one tells, abound in Noomin's "Baby Talk." One marvelous example occurs in a doctor's office where Diane goes for more advice and help in getting pregnant.[10] [Fig. 21] Noomin draws details of the doctor's office, including very clearly the titles on the magazines prominently displayed in the waiting room. Titles such as *Elle, Money, Vogue,* and *Baby* read like locations on the map of a middle-class woman walking a path through gender, economics, cultural norms, and birthing clinics toward her own motherhood. On one side of the doctor's office is a rack containing two copies of *People,* so that the right side of the image seems to be shouting: "People, People," which can be read as either a workers' rallying cry or a statement about multiplying and populating the world.

The last page of "Baby Talk" begins with a frame headed "Last stop..."[11] After her fourth miscarriage, Diane has arrived at a "feminist clinic that specializes in artificial insemination" and is being told that, should she become pregnant again, she is likely to have another miscarriage, given her age and history. In the next frame (under some of the largest lettering in the entire story) Diane stands—and screams [Fig. 22]. Tellingly, she stands in the middle of a street, thus signaling Noomin's refusal to make this turn in her story represent a merely personal, private moment of anguish behind closed doors. The setting resembles that of Edvard Munch's *The Scream* (1893). It has a receding street and landscape as background; figures of others on the street hover at the left edge; and the weather (a blood-red sky in Munch's painting, rain in Noomin's comic) creates atmosphere. Noomin's use of rain in her scene is also a possible substitute for (or magnification of?) tears. Certainly it is meant to invoke high drama through reference to *"Sturm und Drang,"* a phrase in German, loosely translated as "storm and stress," that suggests high emotion. In this setting, a wild-eyed Diane yells: **"I CAN'T DO THIS!"**

Earlier alter ego DiDi showed little sympathy for Diane: "You're not the **first** person in the world to **lose a baby!!**"[12] However, on this final page she seems to offer counsel and comfort by saying: **"You're right**, you know... You've gotta stop **sometime!"** Here, the refrain "You can't always get what you wa-a-ant" returns, drawn as a ribbon of song words and musical notes that float across the page under the frames, echoing the theme introduced on the first page of the story. Perhaps there is also the implied further refrain from the Rolling Stones's consolation that you may not get what you want, but...[13] And DiDi drives home the message with "You **know** the **song**, Toots...." In fact, Noomin provides an epilogue where Diane is shown on the phone to her boundary-testing adolescent niece, who has come to live with Bill and her. We are, thus, allowed a hint of how the "cure" for "baby-wanting" came partly through "adolescent-getting"—an unexpected arrival of something that was needed, if not all that was wanted. The two-frame epilogue continues with an additional crucial scene: friends, Diane and DiDi, nude, companionably shower together. And the text has Diane declaring: **"It's gone** ... the **fetal attraction** is **gone!!** It's like a **cancer** was **removed! Suddenly I feel lighter!!"** Like the cleansing bath of Jewish tradition, a *mikveh,* Noomin's shower setting has helped her signal a profound change, if not precisely a purification.[14] However, DiDi is shown swivelling her head to glance at Diane's belly and saying: "Honey, don't kid yourself." DiDi is completely in character here as the voice of the tough-

Fig. 21. Diane Noomin, "Baby Talk: A Tale of 3̶ 4 Miscarriages," 1993, from *Glitz–2-Go* (Seattle: Fantagraphics, 2012), 99 (detail).

Fig. 22. Diane Noomin, "Baby Talk: A Tale of ~~3~~ 4 Miscarriages," 1993, from *Glitz–2-Go* (Seattle: Fantagraphics, 2012), 101 (detail).

love friend and representative of women policing their bodies, their size, and their sex appeal.[15] Moreover, Noomin may be acknowledging here the heaviness of the new responsibility— the care of an adolescent. She is almost certainly also suggesting that, while you might "get what you need," there will be no complete curing of the cancer or shedding of the sadness about unfulfilled maternity. "Don't **kid** yourself" are the last words of "Baby Talk."[16]

Journal of a Miscarriage, 1973: An Accounting

I had not set out to make an artwork about miscarriage but rather to keep a journal using collage as my form of notation, an ordinary bound black sketchbook for the pages on which to work, and my new pregnancy as my subject. As I began, I found a photograph of a pear. Using collage, I added legs to the pear, giving it a joyful, pregnant, dancing appearance [Fig. 23]. But within days of this happy start, I was having a miscarriage. Scared and uncertain, I put blood on some pages of my new book and then left for the hospital. For weeks, even as I cried and struggled to recover from the despair at my sudden loss, I continued my visual journal. I stopped after about a month, in which time I'd created nearly 30 pages of collage—the work that I came to call *Journal of a Miscarriage, 1973*.

What was really exciting was the intensity of my work during the period when I created the pages of *Journal*; I'd felt exhilaration as I rushed to secondhand bookstores and other sources to look for what pictures might be useful in making the collages I envisaged. In my earlier photo collage work, I had incorporated photographs from my darkroom. Here, as I created the pages of *Journal*, I used only images I could find in books, magazines, and other printed sources. As I worked, I felt I was gaining spontaneity and command over the photo collage medium, and using my skills in new ways. I felt a kind of certainty about what I was doing that was not common for me, and I sensed that what I was accomplishing was something important. The initial pages of *Journal* were made using clippings from obstetrical texts, some in combination with the blood that I'd placed on some of the pages [Fig. 24]. By the middle of the work, the pages were no longer only reflecting sadness, anger, and reproductive loss. I had begun to imagine a future with a new pregnancy leading to a birth. Though no match for the humor in "Baby Talk," *Journal* even has pages that are light-hearted, if not "comic." On one such page, Santa gives birth—a humorous extension of my wish for "the gift" of a child.

Journal's final page combines the two themes of loss: romantic love and motherhood. A horse ridden by a damsel and knight in shining armor (representing the romantic myth of happily-ever-after love) tramples a baby. The horse-and-riders image uses an N.C. Wyeth book illustration I'd also used in "Romanticism is Ultimately Fatal," which had been part of an earlier collage series, *Dreams and Nightmares*, and, for me, symbolized deep romantic disappointment.[17]

Like "Baby Talk," *Journal* had an epilogue, a set of collages I called the *Post Journal Series* (1973–1975).[18] The images in the *Post Journal Series* accumulated slowly over the next two years. They resemble the *Journal* images—same size pages made with collage and an occasional penciled title. "Celebration"[19] is the title of the last *Post Journal Series* image, a collage with a series of concentric circles (white, blue-bordered, saucer and teacup, seen from above) and sperm afloat in this intentionally female space: conception. The *Post Journal Series*, ending with "Celebration," forms a bridge between *Journal* and the *Julia Series*, which begins with my picture of Julia on the day of her birth and marks the divergence of parallels between Noomin's story and mine.[20]

When, in 2008, I published *Journal of Miscarriage, 1973* in *Being in Pictures*, I included all 30 pages of the journal I had made. Yet two of the pages I reproduced appear with "X's" through them, and in nearby text, I write (40 years after the making of *Journal*) about the self-censorship and revised perspective these crossings-out represent. Little did I realize that this very gesture of crossing out, late in the story of *Journal*, would link my work to the visual

Fig. 23. Joanne Leonard, from *Journal of a Miscarriage, 1973,* collage and pencil on paper.

strategy employed by Noomin, the "X" at the very beginning of her work, described above. We were both visually revising our still-unfolding lives, as we attempted to narrate our stories. Finding these points of comparison has been a gratifying task for someone like me who enjoys coincidence and parallels. Below, point-by-point, are some additional parallels, comparisons, and contrasts between "Baby Talk" and *Journal*.

Fig. 24. Joanne Leonard, "Reproduction" from *Journal of a Miscarriage, 1973*, collage and pencil on paper.

While "Baby Talk" is made entirely with drawings, Noomin has both earlier and later work that uses photography and collage. Her "Coming of Age in Canarsie: A Sociological Study of Primitive Youth in Western Civilization" (it's actually Brooklyn) has two photos of Noomin in the title block.[21] In a sense, these photos mock the use of photographic images of "natives" in ethnographic studies in those collaborations between Margaret Mead and Gregory Bateson.[22] A more recent work, "I Was a Red Diaper Baby," also uses collage and photography.[23] This work includes pasted-in copies of telegrams and other documents. I mention these works to underscore the choice Noomin made *not* to include photographs in "Baby Talk." Without the photographs, Noomin's "Baby Talk" carries, perhaps, an intended degree of ambiguity between fiction and autobiography. The inclusion of *any* photographs (with their oft-ascribed evidentiary nature) might have given this account more emphasis on the autobiographic than Noomin wished it to have.

Since I was a photographer who had already carved out an autobiographical approach in photography, the choice of photography for my *Journal* about miscarriage might have seemed obvious, but photo collage is a medium I seem to have turned to repeatedly in times of crisis and change. Photography itself has some odd drawbacks for autobiography and some definite hindrances for intimate or traumatic revelation—among these, the intrusiveness of the camera, the improbability of photographing during traumatic moments, the impossibility of creating a photograph after a crucial moment has passed. In many ways, collage was the perfect medium for me at the moment I began my journal. Hillary L. Chute considers Lynda Barry's use of collage in her autobiographical comics work *One Hundred Demons*.[24] Chute maintains that collage is particularly apt for memoir since it is, or at least can be, a form of re-collecting—suggesting a firm connection between collage's gathering of materials on one surface and the process of remembering.[25] My collages in *Journal* depend on analogy and juxtaposition: a pear signals a pregnant woman; the prickly trunk of a tall cactus suggests the phallus of an uncaring sexual partner; a child playing with dolls is disconcertingly juxtaposed to an image of a woman, feet in stirrups, giving birth: placed, in the collage, like a thought balloon, the birthing woman's image hovers over the girl's head, suggesting, instead of the child's thoughts, something the child herself simply cannot yet imagine [Fig. 25].

There are few words in *Journal,* a work that took form on sketchbook pages, not in a typical journal or writing book—I conceived my journal from the beginning as a visual enterprise to be worked out through collage. Some of the pages have lightly penciled titles, but the occasional titles do not create a narrative. A few pages use language in a way that might be called "punning" or, perhaps, word-collage: one of the pages with blood on it depicts a bleeding woman draped as if ready for giving birth. This image is titled "Miscarriage/Ms. Carnage." Another image, with torn paper and teardrops, bears the penciled title "tears/tears" layering onto the image, in collage fashion, two pronunciations of the word "tear."[26] "Reproduction" is the title of a *Journal* page with a baby "developing" in a tray of darkroom chemicals. In later work, I made much more use of text than in *Journal*. In *Not Losing Her Memory* from the 1990s I used text to give "voice" to photo subjects by writing their own words directly onto photographic images.[27] *Journal*, having so little text, lacked explicit context until it was published at the center of *Being in Pictures: An Intimate Photo Memoir*, my book from 2008 containing more than 200 images and text of 30,000 words.

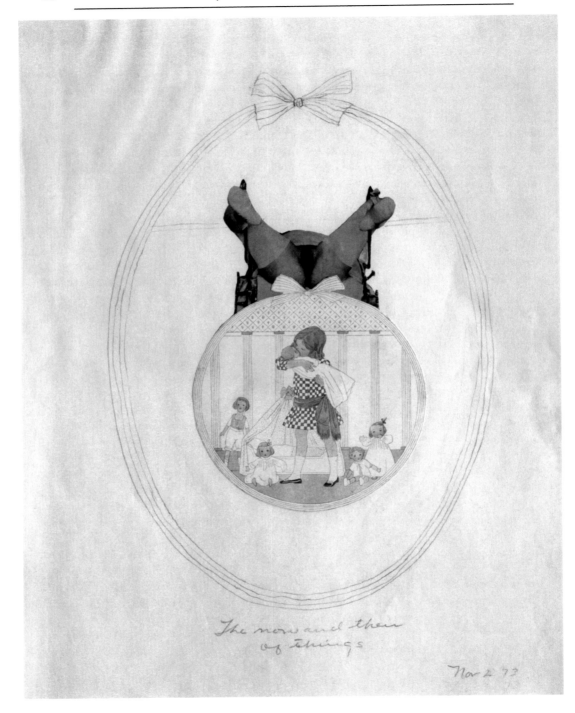

Fig. 25. Joanne Leonard, "Now and Then" from *Journal of a Miscarriage, 1973,* collage and pencil on paper.

Putting the Unmentionable on View

It was a tenet of the burgeoning feminist movement of the 1970s that women's stories mattered, and that the rarer these stories had been in the past, the more important it was at that moment to begin bringing them forward. The general idea was to create a gathering of voices and visions that would make the unmentionable, and unseen, a part of shared conversation, part of the visual universe. I think that this background of openness and permission forms part of the history of "Baby Talk" and *Journal*. The self-help manuals (particularly *Our Bodies, Ourselves*, first published in 1971) made by women's health collectives, pictured women, during self-exams (with a speculum, with a mirror) and natural childbirth among other explicit images, as a way, through publishing, for women to educate each other about their bodies.[28] Noomin's work (not only "Baby Talk" but her earlier work in comics that dates to 1974[29]) and my *Journal* may have been, in some part, engendered by an atmosphere of openness about frank and bold images of bodies, sexuality, and reproductive life that existed in the 1970s after the advent of the women's alternative health movement.[30]

Almost as early as *Our Bodies, Ourselves*, Abigail Heyman's *Growing Up Female* (1974) was full of wonderful photographs made to capture the texture of women's everyday lives.[31] In the most startling photograph of the entire book Heyman captures her surgical abortion, or D&C (dilation and curettage). Noomin's depictions of her D&C after her miscarriage not surprisingly perfectly mirror Heyman's viewpoint in her abortion photo. In abortion, D&C surgery removes the pregnancy; in miscarriage, a D&C prevents hemorrhaging and/or infection when the fetal tissue has not been completely expelled in the miscarriage itself. In "Baby Talk" we see Diane's own upraised knees from her own (the patient's) perspective.[32] Of course Noomin may never have seen Heyman's photograph and didn't need to have done so in order to draw what she herself saw. I'm suggesting, rather, that all of these images are quite rare depictions by women of their own experiences—Noomin's from the 1990s nearly as rare as Heyman's from the 1970s.

In a note to me, Noomin commented on the loneliness she felt when making "Baby Talk." "At the time it was a topic rarely mentioned in books [...] I remember feeling quite isolated."[33] Noomin may have felt *less* isolated (certainly I did) when she discovered Frida Kahlo's 1934 painting about her own miscarriage.[34] But the vacuum Noomin experienced, of other work she could turn to about miscarriage, persists to this day. There is virtually no literature of such images, so each woman artist is inventing her own idiom. Part of my excitement about Noomin's work is the opportunity it provides to begin to think of our miscarriage images together as part of a literature of women's visual self-representations from the stories of their reproductive lives.

The Politics of Miscarriage Imagery

Both Noomin and I created images based on our devastation and loss when the hope of a baby turned into miscarriage. We imagined the baby as we longed for it, pictured the baby we hoped we were about to have, or, after the miscarriage, that we missed and longed for. A wrenching frame in Noomin's account has Diane's baby (drawn oddly, somewhere between baby and fetus in appearance) floating above her in a dream, foreshadowing the miscarriage about to happen.[35] This fetus/child speaks through a thought bubble: "**Sorry mom**, I'm **outta** here," as Diane, eyes closed, utters: "**NO!**" in outsized lettering. Most miscarriages happen during the first three months of pregnancy. But when an artist's imagination turns a barely formed fetus into the image of a baby or child, the image may join the visual rhetoric of the Right to Life movement and risk co-optation, even as the artist may hope to claim such an image for her own purpose. When I had my miscarriage in the 1970s and made the *Journal*, I was not self-conscious about my use of the image of a baby to represent my desires and losses. But when my daughter was a teenager and fiercely insisting on separation, I made "Letting Her Go with Difficulty" in the early 1990s[36] using one of Lennart Nilsson's famous photographs from *A Child Is Born: The Drama of Life Before Birth*, of a baby looking like a small astronaut floating in space.[37] I wrote about that use:

> I had conflicts about the use of the photograph of an unborn fetus, so often used as an anti-abortion image by the right-to-life movement. I risked that association, hoping to claim the image for my own purpose here. I wanted to show new life emerging into the battle for connection and autonomy.[38]

The tug of war about meanings of images of the unborn is, even today, a likely force suppressing expressions by women artists who want to depict miscarriage and other matters of women's reproductive lives.

Psychological Predispositions

Later in this essay, I ruminate on cultural and historical factors that may have permitted Noomin and me to create images that were unusually frank, if not unprecedented in art, for their time. The questions about predispositions (who would make personal revelations and why?) might seem odd to a generation that has grown up with widely available personal blogs and intimacies, so it's important to think of a moment, from the 1970s through to the 1990s, unconnected to a "memoir boom," cell phone exchanges of nude photos, and the clear hunger today for daily confessionals with video-camera accompaniment. Michael Kaminer wrote in *The Jewish Daily Forward* about Diane Noomin and her female colleagues in comics circles:

> While women have been writing frank confessional cartoons since the early 1970s, the context has changed. Brutal sexism defined underground comics back then, with females mostly depicted as fawning objects for a largely male readership. Blunt confessional comics were a throat-grab from women who dared male readers to confront real, unvarnished female characters.[39]

Today's autobiographical comics come as less of a cultural jolt. For one thing, women have become a formidable presence in comics. Personal problems have also supplanted gender politics as a dominant theme. But these young artists are just as ruthlessly honest, presenting their bodies as nakedly as their emotions. They're also finding a new crop of audiences, weaned on blogs and tell-all Facebook pages, even hungrier for first-person intimacy.

In my case, I can trace a few factors that may have launched me very early on toward the autobiographical path in my photo and collage work. These include growing up in Hollywood (even being in a Hollywood movie when I was a baby) and seeing myself and my life as if on a screen before a public; knowing the story of Anne Frank from the time I was 12—a young girl's diary that was quickly taken seriously as literature as well as history; having a psychoanalyst for a mother—someone who listened to everyday people's stories about their innermost thoughts and actions; and having a twin sister as a "mirror"—a sensation of looking at my sister and being able to observe (and objectify?) a parallel version of myself.

Another question raised by autobiographies of trauma, and one that comes up in Noomin's work and my own, is the notion of catharsis. Is the very making of such a work an act of self-therapy? I've resisted the question, feeling that it tends to shift the work out of its realm of artistic accomplishment into a vehicle for healing—thereby diminishing the artistic achievement the work may represent. Certainly the excitement I felt in making *Journal* carried me through weeks in which I felt nearly entirely bereft. If making the work actually helped Noomin to end her "fetal attraction," as she records, then it is no less an artistic accomplishment for being such a record of resolution. Moreover, "Baby Talk" is, importantly, a version of a survival story for women—a story that Lynda Layne, in her book *Motherhood Lost*, describes as, usually, painfully off limits for most women to tell.[40] The typical response, which disallows mourning in women who miscarry, goes something like: "Don't cry—you are young and healthy and can get pregnant again." While this may seem reassuring, even one such loss, especially when followed by further miscarriages, can create a nearly overwhelming feeling of isolation and despair. There are a number of references in "Baby Talk" to "hiding out" from friends, wanting not to speak of her miscarriage in the moment.[41] It is the strength of "Baby Talk" that makes these losses part of a story told with self-parody and humor as well as poignancy and power.

Medical Profession

In our miscarriage works, Noomin and I are each commenting on intersections of women's reproductive lives and the medical profession.[42] Noomin's explorations of confrontation with medical practices in "Baby Talk" are some of the most biting, funny, and at the same time powerful comments. They are likely to elicit a sense of identification between many readers and the character of Diane, nearly as much for women who've never had a miscarriage as for those who have. There are a number of instances in "Baby Talk" when Diane comments about the doctors, male and female, she encounters. For one thing, she picks up the office language in which receptionists and nurses refer to "doctor" (not "the doctor" or "doctor so and so"), using "doctor" as one might say "God." Receptionist: "Doctor has scheduled you for a **myomectomy**." Diane: **"Nurse" please tell "Doctor"** I'll need a **2nd opinion…**"[43] Just a few frames before this, the doctor is telling Diane that he can't detect a heartbeat, but "**we might be okay**."[44] Diane utters a frightened "might???" while a rectangle of text (and arrow pointing to a framed picture on the desk) provides a visual space for Noomin's comment: "Perhaps it's the photo of the doc with Princess Di that compels him to use the 'royal we' …" This visual aside from author/narrator creates, all in the same moment and image, humor as well as critical and class analysis of the doctor's locution.

In an earlier frame, a doctor is shown above Diane, operating.[45] The doctor's hair is hidden in a medical skullcap; a surgical mask covers all but her eyes. A text block narrates: "The doctor **finally** shows up—an ice maiden who seems to have contempt for everyone with an **iota** of emotion. She does a 'D and C' with **no** pain killers and refuses to analyze the fetus." The four text balloons of this frame are even more chilling: "This won't **hurt**. C'mon you can **take** it," "It'll be over in a minute … **RELAX!**" and "You don't **need valium**," while the one balloon that conveys Diane's words is filled with "**AIEEE!!**" In the next frame Diane makes an essentializing comment: "You'd **THINK** a **woman doctor** could cough up a little **compassion!!!**" In an attached/adjacent frame, Diane is shown wild-eyed, gasping: "At **that** point I would have **licked** her *!@#!*© **stethoscope** for an **aspirin!!**"—an example of the kind of self-deprecating humor that at one and the same moment conveys the abjectness of "letting it all hang out" and the humor in a pronouncement so extreme. Later pages offer a contrast to this unfeeling doctor. In these, Noomin represents her last miscarriage, beginning the episode with words that might seem to underscore the expected sameness of medical trauma: "Another loss, another hospital, a different doctor and a familiar pain." Yet in the frame adjacent to this text, a doctor, now clearly female—with wings and a halo!—appears at Diane's bedside. A block of text with an arrow pointing at this new doctor says: "The doctor just drove 20 miles in the middle of the night to get to the hospital!!" The angel-winged doctor is saying: "You should feel **some relief from pain now**..." and Diane, drawn with an I.V. tube running to her arm, sighs: "**Valium!!**"[46]

For my collages in *Journal* where I used images from obstetrics textbooks, several of my collage works show birthing positions as seen from the doctor's perspective, and others make use of photographs that show profile views as the baby is born, especially photos that have the physician's hands placed as they would be in the case of a breech birth. Describing a collage, I once wrote:

> The bird-like form, actually a sea shell, represents the mother's body during birth, struggling for possession of her infant against the world, symbolized here by the pulling hands of the doctor and the medical management of birth."[47]

Of course, Noomin and I were lucky to have medical assistance at the time of our miscarriages to prevent any complications that might have made the next opportunity for fertilization impossible. But each of us, in our work, expresses ambivalence toward doctors. Perhaps it's inevitable to feel doubt about a surgical procedure that follows a miscarriage. Irrational fears may have overtaken Noomin as they did me; as the doctor takes away the final material from the lost pregnancy, did she too wonder: "Had it not been for the doctors, might the pregnancy have gone forward?"

Access to Publication

"Baby Talk" and *Journal* each headed for publication after completion, but "Baby Talk" was published a few years after Noomin finished it in *Twisted Sisters* in 1994, while my *Journal*, though exhibited twice after its creation, was published only in fragments in the 1990s and never published in full until *Being in Pictures*.[48] Access to publication for Noomin was particular to her location in the realm of underground comics. In a history of her own work she describes her entry into comics-making: "It was sort of a circle of friends and a lot of the women who were rooming with men cartoonists who decided that they [the women] wanted to be cartoonists."[49] What seems especially important to me is the way these women took power and agency for themselves. In 1976, Aline Kominsky-Crumb and Diane Noomin published the first issue of *Twisted Sisters* as an underground comic book. Their "low art" or counterculture approach seems to me to have been liberating and enviably challenging to the terms of debate over the representation of women's bodies, even though few had attained, until recently, the star power their intrepid work deserves as compared with some of their male partners, like Robert Crumb and Bill Griffith.

Noomin wrote in reference to the publication of the first *Twisted Sisters* anthology, *Twisted Sisters: A Collection of Bad Girl Art*[50]:

> I got a deal with Penguin (Viking-Penguin as they say). It was really a big thrill. It meant we were getting out of the Underground. It was the illusion that we were getting out of the

Underground and into the shopping malls and we did—for a very brief time—manage to do that. Penguin heaved a sigh of relief when they sold the first print run and they didn't run another. I think they sold out in eight months, and I was very naive and shocked when they wouldn't reprint it. I thought maybe the advantages of a big publisher weren't quite as much as I thought they were."[51]

For *Twisted Sisters 2: Drawing the Line*, Noomin returned to underground publishing with Kitchen Sink Press of Northampton, Massachusetts.

Noomin and her women comics-writer colleagues gave themselves a sense of independence with respect to publishing, to a degree I had not dreamed of. They edited and published, included and supported each other in the underground publishing world—something women in the fine arts generally did not do, with the possible exception of the Heresies Collective and their journal.[52] Because the comics medium has a history of humor and fantasy, and existed as so-called "low art" counterculture work, it seems to have traveled below the radar, less threatening to audiences or vulnerable to censorship than, say, the art that ran into overt censorship during the culture wars of the 1980s and 1990s. For women working in the fine arts, access to publication was changing too. By the mid–1980s the Guerrilla Girls were publishing their wonderful posters, including: "Do women have to be naked to get in to the Met. Museum?"[53] The Guerrilla Girls were arguing—through street theater—the need to open the doors of museums and publications to women's work. The feminist movement put pressure on Abrams, the publisher of Horst W. Janson's famous *History of Art*, which had been published for 20 years without a single example of art by women.[54] As a result, later editor Anthony Janson took the initiative to add work by women for the first time to his father's book.[55] Also pushed by the impetus of the feminist movement, the San Francisco Museum mounted the exhibition "Women of Photography: An Historical Survey" at the San Francisco Museum of Modern Art.[56] Anthony Janson, while looking for women to put in his revised *History of Art*, spotted my work in the San Francisco Museum's *Women of Photography* catalogue which led to my work's inclusion in the 1986 revision of Janson's *History of Art*. I was, therefore, a beneficiary of the arts' women's movement.

Yet, like many other women artists, I sometimes waited too politely outside the gates, so to speak, of institutions like publishing houses, gates that the women comics artists were walking through or around. It is perhaps significant that among my collage works, the earliest published work was "Romanticism is Ultimately Fatal," the image of my mourning the loss of oft-represented (heterosexual) love and romance.[57] My *Journal*, on the other hand, a work about loss that had to do with women's hidden, traumatic, bloody experiences from bedroom, bathroom, and medical arenas—one that millions of women the world over experience and no less "universal" than the images of male experiences that overflow museums—waited 20 years more to be published in the powerfully regulating realm of fine-art publishing.

Truth vs. Fiction

Diane Noomin's *Glitz-2-Go: Diane Noomin Collected Comics* was published in 2012 by Fantagraphics. "Baby Talk" is included in this anthology as well as many other comics with DiDi Glitz. When I asked Noomin about DiDi's role, she replied that DiDi is

part alter ego, part satire and a way of discussing things with myself from an antithetical point of view. She can take over easily—I am drawn in by the tension between us when I do autobiographical or quasi-autobiographical work.[58]

As well as being an artist's story on the topic of miscarriage, "Baby Talk" can also be read as an exploration of autobiographical narrative and the challenges of the genre.

Claiming an autobiographic voice is a fraught and difficult step in the early pages of "Baby Talk." I suspect Noomin started her story with the fictional characters Jimmy and Glenda as a result of an actual ambivalence and uncertainty, as she began the account of her miscarriages, about the mode in which she'd tell her story—as fiction or autobiography? The cleverness of the visual device she hit upon, having her self-representing cartoon–Diane climb through the page, is also one of the things one must consider in a discussion of "Baby Talk" as an autobiographical work. When DiDi punches a hole through the page and, thus, into the space of autobiography from the land of comics, she insists Diane, the artist, follow. Diane declares: "O.K. DiDi, you **dragged** me **out here** ... **NOW** what?" and DiDi replies: "Why ask **me**? I'm 'fictional' ... what do **I** know?!"[59] [Fig. 85].

After her third miscarriage, in a moment Noomin marks as "sudden infantile regression," Jimmy and Glenda stage a brief return.[60] But these cartoon yuppies are noticeably absent for most of the pages and, importantly, do not reappear at the conclusion. Thus, the reader is invited to experience as autobiographical the story of four miscarriages and the long-lasting but eventually vanquished "fetal attraction." Similar to Christian Boltanski, in the book *Art Works: Autobiography*, Noomin, through the presence of the fictional DiDi, continually reminds readers that so-called autobiographical truth is itself difficult, if not impossible, to create without added bits of fiction.[61] These days, Noomin writes that she is working on an anthology of her work and a memoir of her childhood "that resembles a jigsaw puzzle with many missing pieces."[62] She describes the process as "daunting," yet it is clear from these upcoming publications that Noomin has continued to engage (and perhaps progressively overcome) her reluctance with respect to autobiography in the years since "Baby Talk."[63]

In conclusion, there have been clear cultural, historical, and social forces that prompted and supported, hindered and undermined the development of the body of frank and often sexually graphic works of which "Baby Talk" and *Journal* are a part. Works about miscarriage are a special subset of autobiography, especially interesting today because they represent a common event of loss and trauma in women's lives around which there is virtually no artistic literature, whether visual or textual. My main purpose in writing this essay will have been fulfilled if other works about reproductive loss are retrieved from history, revealed in present-day exhibition and publishing, or made in present or future moments.

NOTES

1. Statistics taken from "Loss and Grief," www.Marchofdimes, October 2008, and "Miscarriage Statistics," www.Hopexchange, 2004. Accessed April 8, 2012.

2. Diane Noomin, "Baby Talk: A Tale of 3 4 Miscarriages" was first published in 1995 in *Twisted Sisters 2: Drawing the Line*, ed. Diane Noomin (Northampton, MA: Kitchen Sink Press) 164–175. Throughout this essay I will be using the page numbers from the most recent publication of "Baby Talk," *Glitz–2-Go Diane Noomin Collected Comics* (Seattle: Fantagraphics, 2012) 90–101.

3. *Journal of a Miscarriage, 1973*. Exhibited at the San Francisco Art Institute, Diego Rivera Gallery (1974) and Laguna Gloria Art Museum, Austin, Texas (1980) and published in *Being In Pictures: An Intimate Photo Memoir*, with foreword by Lucy R. Lippard (Ann Arbor: University of Michigan Press, 2008).

4. Noomin, 95.

5. Noomin, 92.

6. I will use "Diane" hereafter when I'm referring to the self-like character in the drawings of *Baby Talk* and "Noomin" when I'm referring to the author more generally. "Baby Talk" 92–101.

7. *Car 54, Where Are You?* ran on NBC from 1961 to 1963. The theme song lyrics were written by series creator, writer, and director Nat Hiken, with music by John Strauss.

8. "You Can't Always Get What You Want " by The Rolling Stones, written by Mick Jagger and Keith Richards and released on the album *Let It Bleed* (1969).

9. Diane Noomin, email, March 24, 2011.

10. Noomin, "Baby Talk," 99.

11. Noomin, 99.

12. Noomin, 93.

13. "You Can't Always Get What You Want," The Rolling Stones (1969).

14. Here I'm indebted to an observation made by Margaret Lourie.

15. "I remember feeling quite isolated and vaguely embarrassed when someone would ask if I was pregnant and I wasn't—I had gained weight..." Email from Diane Noomin, March 24, 2011.

16. Though "Baby Talk" is filled with irony and wit, in correspondence Noomin gave me a sense of her state of mind when she first attempted to create it: "I remember sobbing my way through a timeline as a way to get started." Email from Diane Noomin, March 24, 2011.

17. "Romanticism is Ultimately Fatal" reproduced in *Ms. Magazine* (June 1974): 92–93. The image I used was from *The Boy's King Arthur: Sir Thomas Malory's History of King Arthur and His Knights of the Round Table Edited for Boys* (New York: Scribner's, 1945), illustrated by N.C. Wyeth. See "Romanticism is Ultimately Fatal" at www.beinginpictures.com.

18. The *Post Journal Series* is a small set of collages containing imagery that furthers the themes of the desire to be pregnant again, sleeping and dreaming, windows and veiled (barely revealed) images of babies.

19. "Celebration," *Being in Pictures*, 125.

20. *Julia Series* is a set of black and white photographs made between 1975 and 1997, illustrated in *Being in Pictures*, 129–161.

21. Diane Noomin, "Coming of Age in Canarsie: A Sociological Study of Primitive Youth in Western Civilization," 1989.

22. Gregory Bateson and M. Mead, *Balinese Character: A Photographic Analysis* (New York: New York Academy of Sciences, 1942).

23. "I Was a Red Diaper Baby," 2002, published in *Glitz-2-Go*, 122–123.

24. Lynda Barry, *One Hundred Demons* (Seattle: Sasquatch Books, 2002).

25. Hillary L. Chute, "Materializing Memory: Lynda Barry's *One Hundred Demons*," in *Graphic Subjects: Critical Essays on Autobiography and Graphic Novels*, ed. Michael A. Chaney (Madison: University of Wisconsin Press, 2011) 282–309.

26. If the rain surrounding Diane when she declares "I can't do this" signalled tears (crying) for Noomin as I suggested, then my use of tears in "Tears/Tears" provides one more coincidence and comparison between "Baby Talk" and *Journal*.

27. "Not Losing Her Memory, Stories in Photographs, Words and Collage" is formed of 60 works made from 1991 to 1992 (*Being in Pictures*) 190–207. "Not Losing Her Memory, Stories in Photographs, Words and Collage" was exhibited at the University of Michigan Museum of Art, Ann Arbor, Michigan, and Schlessinger Library, Radcliffe University, Cambridge, Massachusetts, all in 1995.

28. Women's Health Book Collective, *Our Bodies, Ourselves* (Boston: New England Free Press, 1971).

29. "Wimmin and Comix." http://www.english.ufl.edu/imagetext/archives/v1_2/noomin/. Accessed April 8, 2012.

30. Chadwick Lee Roberts, "Consuming Liberation: Playgirl and the Strategic Rhetoric of Sex Magazines 1972–1985." Dissertation, Bowling Green State University, 2011, Chapter 5.

31. Abigail Heyman, *Growing Up Female* (New York: Holt, Rinehart and Winston, 1974).

32. Noomin, "Baby Talk," 96.

33. Diane Noomin, email, March 24, 2011.

34. Frida Kahlo is known to have made the painting *Henry Ford Hospital* in 1934 after a miscarriage. By the mid–1970s, Kahlo's work had begun to be known (thanks to the women's movement in the arts), but I had never seen it until shortly after I made my own miscarriage collages, which became *Journal of a Miscarriage, 1973*.

35. Noomin, "Baby Talk," 92.

36. Joanne Leonard, "Letting Her Go with Difficulty," *Being in Pictures*, 217–219.

37. Lennart Nilsson, *A Child Is Born* (New York: Dell, 1965).

38. Joanne Leonard, "Photography, Feminism, and the Good Enough Mother," in *The Familial Gaze*, ed. Marianne Hirsch (Hanover, NH: University Press of New England, 1999) 293–310.

39. Michael Kaminer, "Graphic Confessions of Jewish Women: Exposing Themselves through Pictures and Raw Personal Stories," *The Jewish Daily Forward*, December 12, 2008. http://www.forward.com/articles/14657/.

40. Linda Layne, *Motherhood Lost* (London: Routledge, 2002).

41. Noomin, "Baby Talk," 96, 98.

42. Jo Spence's important work *Putting Myself in the Picture* (1986) lies chronologically between "Baby Talk" and *Journal*. Her story centers on both class struggle and the struggle against the medical profession's authority over her body. In some of her work Spence wrote directly on her breast ("property of Jo Spence") and then photographed

herself, showing a way she found to blend a visual and text-based artistic practice. See Jo Spence *Putting Myself in the Picture: A Political, Personal and Photographic Autobiography* (London: Camden Press, 1986).

43. Noomin, "Baby Talk," 99.

44. Ibid.

45. Noomin, "Baby Talk," 96.

46. Noomin, "Baby Talk," 97.

47. "Miscarriage/Ms. Carnage and Other Stories: A Visual Essay," in *Discourses of Sexuality: From Aristotle to Aids*, ed. Domna Stanton (Ann Arbor: University of Michigan Press, 1992) 297–311.

48. Parts of *Journal* have appeared in the following publications: Laurence Goldstein, *The Female Body: Figures, Styles, Speculations* (Ann Arbor: University of Michigan Press, 1991); Domna C. Stanton, ed., *Discourses of Sexuality: From Aristotle to AIDS* (Ann Arbor: University of Michigan Press, 1992); Marianne Hirsch, ed., *The Familial Gaze* (Hanover, NH: University Press of New England, 1999); Sandra Matthews and Laura Wexler, *Pregnant Pictures* (New York: Routledge, 2000).

49. Diane Noomin, "Wimmin and Comix," *ImageTexT: Interdisciplinary Comics Studies* 1.2 (2004). http://www.english.ufl.edu/imagetext/archives/v1_2/noomin/ Accessed November 5, 2011.

50. Diane Noomin, ed., *Twisted Sisters: A Collection of Bad Girl Art* (New York: Penguin Books, 1991).

51. Diane Noomin, "Wimmin and Comix."

52. "The Sex Issue," *Heresies: A Feminist Publication on Art and Politics* (New York: Heresies Collective Publication, No. 12, 1981).

53. "Less than 5% of the artists in the Modern Art sections are women, but 85% of the nudes are female." Guerrilla Girls, "Conscience of the Fine Art World," c. 1988.

54. H.W. Janson, *History of Art*, 1st ed. (New York: Harry N. Abrams, 1962).

55. H.W. Janson and Anthony F. Janson, *History of Art*, 3d ed. (New York: Harry N. Abrams, 1986).

56. "Women of Photography: An Historical Survey," San Francisco Museum of Modern Art, 1975–1976.

57. Before "Romanticism is Ultimately Fatal" was published in *History of Art* it was published in *Women of Photography: An Historical Survey*, Margery Mann and Anne Noggle (San Francisco: San Francisco Museum of Art, 1975).

58. Diane Noomin, email, March 24, 2011.

59. Noomin, "Baby Talk," 166.

60. Noomin, "Baby Talk," 98.

61. Barbara Steiner and Jun Yang have assembled a set of works by artists particularly bent on questioning what, if anything, is true in autobiographical art works. The authors provide this description of Boltanski's work: "In 1968, artist Christian Boltanski started to reconstruct his childhood. However, as he could not or would not always recall certain things and events with any clarity (if at all) and did not have any photos (or pretended he did not have any photos) he bridged the gaps in the reconstruction by using 'foreign material' or by manufacturing scenes." *Art Works: Autobiography* (New York: Thames & Hudson, 2004), 68.

62. Diane Noomin, email, March 24, 2011.

63. Diane Noomin, email, March 24, 2011.

BIBLIOGRAPHY

Bateson, G., and Margaret Mead. *Balinese Character: A Photographic Analysis.* New York: New York Academy of Sciences, 1942.

Chute, Hillary, "Materializing Memory: Lynda Barry's *One Hundred Demons.*" *Graphic Subjects: Critical Essays on Autobiography and Graphic Novels.* Ed. Michael A. Chaney. Madison: University of Wisconsin Press, 2011. 282–309.

Goldstein, Laurence, ed. *The Female Body: Figures, Styles, Speculations.* Ann Arbor: University of Michigan Press, 1991.

Heresies: A Feminist Publication on Art and Politics. No. 12, "The Sex Issue." New York: Heresies Collective Publication, 1981.

Heyman, Abigail. *Growing Up Female.* New York, London, and San Francisco: Holt, Rinehart and Winston, 1974.

Hirsch, Marianne, ed. *The Familial Gaze.* Hanover, NH: University Press of New England, 1999.

Janson, H.W. *History of Art.* 1st ed. New York: Harry N. Abrams, 1962.

Janson, H.W., and Anthony F. Janson. *History of Art.* 3d ed. New York: Harry N. Abrams, 1986.

Kaminer, Michael. "Graphic Confessions of Jewish Women: Exposing Themselves through Pictures and Raw Personal Stories." *The Jewish Daily Forward*, December 12, 2008. http://www.forward.com/articles/14657/.

Layne, Linda. *Motherhood Lost.* London: Routledge, 2002.

Leonard, Joanne. *Being in Pictures: An Intimate Photo Memoir.* Foreword by Lucy R. Lippard. Ann Arbor: University of Michigan Press, 2008.

_____. *Journal of a Miscarriage, 1973.* Exhibited San Francisco Art Institute, Diego Rivera Gallery, 1974, and Laguna Gloria Art Museum, Austin, Texas, 1980.

_____. "Miscarriage/Ms. Carnage and Other Stories: A Visual Essay." In *Discourses of Sexuality: From Aristotle to Aids.* Ed. Domna Stanton. Ann Arbor: University of Michigan Press, 1992. 297–311.

_____. "Photography, Feminism, and the Good Enough Mother." In *The Familial Gaze.* Ed. Marianne Hirsch. Hanover, NH: University Press of New England, 1999. 293–310.

_____. "Portfolio, 'Romanticism is Ultimately Fatal' and 'Lost Dreams'" (reproductions of photo collages). *Ms. Magazine* (June 1974): 92–93.

"Loss and Grief." www.Marchofdimes. October 2008. Accessed April 8, 2012.

Malory, Thomas. *The Boy's King Arthur: Sir Thomas Malory's History of King Arthur and His Knights of the Round Table Edited for Boys.* Illustrated by N.C. Wyeth. New York: Scribner's, 1945.

Mann, Margery, and Anne Noggle. *Women of Photography: An Historical Survey.* San Francisco: San Francisco Museum of Art, 1975.

Matthews, Sandra, and Laura Wexler. *Pregnant Pictures.* New York: Routledge, 2000.

"Miscarriage Statistics." www.Hopexchange 2004. Accessed April 8, 2012.

Nilsson, Lennart. *A Child Is Born.* New York: Dell, 1965.

Noomin, Diane. "Baby Talk: A Tale of 3 4 Miscarriages." In *Twisted Sisters 2: Drawing the Line.* Ed. Diane Noomin. Northampton, MA: Kitchen Sink Press, 1995. 163–175.

_____. "Coming of Age in Canarsie." http://www.adambaumgoldgallery.com/telling_tales/Noomin_Diane/coming_of_age_in_canarsieWB.jpg. Accessed April 8, 2012.

_____. *Glitz-2-Go.* Seattle: Fantagraphics, 2012.

_____. "I Was a Red Diaper Baby." Adam Baumgold Gallery, 2002.

_____. "Wimmin and Comix." *ImageTexT: Interdisciplinary Comics Studies* 1.2 (2004). Dept of English, University of Florida. http://www.english.ufl.edu/imagetext/archives/v1_2/noomin/index.shtml. Accessed May 10, 2011.

_____, ed. *Twisted Sisters: A Collection of Bad Girl Art.* New York: Penguin, 1991.

Nilsson, Lennart. *A Child Is Born: The Drama of Life Before Birth.* Text by Axel Ingelman-Sunberg and Claes Wirsén. Trans. Burt and Claes Wirsén and Annabelle MacMillan. New York: Delacorte Press, 1966.

Roberts, Chadwick Lee. "Consuming Liberation: Playgirl and the Strategic Rhetoric of Sex Magazines 1972–1985." Dissertation. Bowling Green State University, 2011.

Salomon, Charlotte. *Life? or Theatre? An Autobiographical Play.* New York: Viking, 1981.

Spence, Jo. *Putting Myself in the Picture: A Political, Personal and Photographic Autobiography.* London: Camden Press, 1986.

Stanton, Domna C., ed. *Discourses of Sexuality: From Aristotle to AIDS.* Ann Arbor: University of Michigan Press, 1992.

Steiner, Barbara, and Jun Yang. *Art Works: Autobiography.* New York: Thames and Hudson, 2004.

Women's Health Book Collective. *Our Bodies, Ourselves.* Boston: New England Free Press, 1971.

Graphic Lesbian Continuum

Ilana Zeffren

HEIKE BAUER

Tel Aviv-based cartoonist and graphic artist Ilana Zeffren publishes a weekly column in the entertainment magazine *Achbar Hair*. Entitled *Rishumon*—or "little sketch"—it is autobiographically inspired, featuring Zeffren, her girlfriend and their two speaking cats, Rafi and Spageti.[1] My way into the work is led by the fact that Zeffren is an out lesbian[2] who takes the everyday lesbian as the starting point for exploring other issues such as, in her own words, "life in the city [Tel Aviv], current affairs, cat stuff and the process of making the column."[3] The *orientation* of the cartoons—their lesbian starting points for considering, to borrow the words of Sara Ahmed, "how we come to find our way in a world that acquires new shapes, depending on which way we turn"—lends Zeffren's work a particular critical currency.[4] She traces the shape of lesbian becoming, which, as Ahmed points out, "still remains a difficult line to follow in a world organized around the heterosexual couple," an organization, that forms "the very point of how life gets directed [but which] is often hidden from view."[5] According to Annamarie Jagose, the "hidden" heterosexual direction of life causes a distinct "problem" for lesbian representation—the fact that unlike male homosexuality "it" has been ambivalently constituted in relation to the logics of vision: it is less the subject of prohibition than of an incredulousness that would deny the space of its possibility."[6] Comics provide an apt medium for making space for lesbian representation and dispelling any lingering doubts about lesbian life. As Hillary Chute, author of *Graphic Women* (2010), has pointed out, the "complex visualizations" afforded by graphic art lend themselves particularly well to addressing "tropes of unspeakability, invisibility, and inaudibility."[7] "The force and value of graphic narrative's intervention," Chute argues, "attaches to how it pushes on conceptions of the unrepresentable [by asserting] the value of presence, however complex and contingent."[8]

In what follows, I will examine how Ilana Zeffren draws out the value of lesbian presence, using her own life as the point from which to decenter the cultural and critical imperatives to overlook female-identified sexuality. Ahmed argues that the shared experience of desire for other women helps to create a particular "lesbian landscape, a ground that is shaped by the paths that we follow in deviating from the straight line" of heterosexuality.[9] Zeffren's comics, similar to Alison Bechdel's work, which had a considerable impact on both Anglo-American lesbian culture and the genre of autobiographical graphic narratives, make visible this landscape.[10] They are both evidence of and a contribution to what I call a "graphic lesbian continuum": a visual language of lesbianism that gives centrality to female same-sex life. The term "graphic lesbian continuum" is inspired by the work of theorist and poet Adrienne Rich who developed the notion of the "lesbian continuum" to challenge what she called the "compulsory heterosexuality" that structures our lives.[11] Where Rich's primary concern was with how all women's lives are connected through shared experiences, I make a case for the "graphic lesbian continuum" specifically to consider how lesbian lines of orientation are drawn across space and time, and across cultural and linguistic boundaries.

My analysis of Zeffren's work, then, is also partly an attempt to trace the transnational shape of lesbian presence in the 21st century. I want to problematize the fact that the identity-related terminology of "the lesbian" has become so unfashionable in Anglo-American critical discourse even as representations of lesbians have increased in literature, film, TV, cartoons and graphic art. The critic Elizabeth Freeman has called this phenomenon the "deadweight effect" of the lesbian in critical theory where she has been relegated "to the zone of the gender-normative [...] the conceptually rearguard to a queer enlightenment dated to around 1990."[12] Yet this negative critical image of the lesbian does not reflect her role in contemporary cultural life. Zeffren's cartoons show, I argue, how transnational lesbian affinities emerge out of localized contexts and in conjunction with other modes of identification, such as nationality, language, education, ethnicity and religion, without negating them.

The Comics Stripper

Fig. 26 indicates some of the main themes in Zeffren's cartoons. The pun of "The Comics Stripper" emphasizes the close link between verbal and visual content and gestures toward the intimate aspects of her work—the task of stripping bare the self and others in comics format—as well as alluding to the fact that this kind of stripping is tied in to the economics of making a living. The combination of reflections on subjectivity and observations of the main (human and feline) subjects that feature in her life is a key concern of Zeffren's work. Here the naked—or blank—autobiographical self holds on to an oversized pencil that rises from the girlfriend's shoulder, symbolizing the lesbian beginnings and queer direction of Zeffren's work, which is further underlined by the representation of the two speaking cats who are both commentators and separate stars of the scene. The pencil further gestures toward the process of creating the cartoons—their distinct "physical reality," which, according to Alison Bechdel, comes from the fact that cartooning involves "not just writing, but designing and then drawing—manually laboring—over each page."[13] Here the efforts of Zeffren's labor—she draws the images with a pencil before scanning them and completing the layout and coloring on the computer—are indicated by the pencil shavings. Hovering like butterflies and reminiscent of the fans strippers use to cover up parts of their body, one of the shavings is distinguished by its proud display of rainbow colors. The rainbow colors, which are a well-known symbol of LGBT activism in different countries, add a particular political note to "The Comics Stripper," connecting Zeffren's representation of the specifics of her own life and work to a visual register that forges queer transnational affinities.

"The Comics Stripper" was first published in a special issue on translation of the U.S.-based journal *Sh'ma: A Journal of Jewish Ideas* which has as its stated aim to "create a 'conversation-in-print.'"[14] It was produced in response to the question: "How do you translate your life into comics?"[15] Translation is a useful metaphor for describing the conscious and

Fig. 26. Ilana Zeffren, "The Comics Stripper," *Sh'ma*, December 2010.

unconscious processes by which our sense of self emerges in relation to a wide range of social, material and cultural contingencies. It helps conceptualize how the experience of this process and the feelings it produces are transcribed into a verbal-visual format in autobiographical comics. In Zeffren's work, issues of translation feature most prominently in relation to her move between Hebrew, the language in which most of it is produced, and English, the language into which she translates some of her comics together with her American girlfriend. Most theorists concerned with translation focus on the metaphorical, cultural and social significance of language.[16] Fig. 27 illustrates that the process of translation also has particular spatial qualities, which become evident in the comics genre. Featuring Me, Rafi and Spageti

When that time of the month arrives, even a tough girl like me breaks down

Rafi: You're not going to basketball practice?

Me: Nope

Spageti: What kind of lesbian are you?

Fig. 27. Ilana Zeffren, *"Rishumon,"* *Achbar Hair*, 2006.

in a reflection on menstruation, the panel's humor relies fairly heavily on text, which is why its rendering into English illustrates particularly well how translation from one language to another requires specific decisions about visual representation. English tends to occupy more space on the page than Hebrew. For example, the English word "nope" on its own would occupy more space than the small speech bubble that contains its Hebrew counterpart. To deal with these issues, Zeffren discards in-panel translation in favor of a rendering that retains the original Hebrew text and adds English "subtitles" below the panel. If the "subtitles" preserve the original shape of the panel and its caption, the spatial effect of translation is found elsewhere. It becomes visible in the location of the panel on the page where the English words extend its overall shape vertically, thus visualizing the decision-making process that constitutes the task of the translator, including, as is the case here, if the translator renders her own work into another language.

The "subtitles" subtly alter the perspective of the original drawing. As the Hebrew reader is directed to look down on the scene after reading the commentary, the English reader's gaze is directed upward from the subtitles with the effect that the Hebrew speech bubbles become part of the visual language of the panel. While this cements the sense of encountering a work in translation, the panel's subject matter of menstruation draws familiar connections. Historian Valerie Traub has made the case that cultural representations of female sexuality are characterized by "forms of intelligibility whose meanings recur, intermittently and with a difference, across time," as well as, we might add, across space.[17] Menstruation is one such trope by which female life is demarcated culturally, socially and politically. In 1970, Germaine Greer famously picked up on its significance in *The Female Eunuch* when she urged women to taste their own menstrual blood in a bid to reclaim the female body from an oppressive patriarchy that habitually denigrated it.[18] In contrast, Zeffren's depiction of the unpleasant experience of menstruation, together with Spageti's wry question "What kind of a lesbian are you?" queries the alignment of menstruation with a celebration of the female body. The work allows for political and personal recognition of this aspect of female embodiment without purporting that menstruation defines a collective experience of womanhood.

Issues of translation are written directly into Zeffren's work in Fig. 28, "Everything Was Brand New." This is taken from her graphic novel *Pink Story* (2005), an autobiographically inspired account of Israel's lesbian and gay community. It was published not long after Zeffren first turned to cartooning in 2004, when, following what she calls "the dramatic break up" with her first girlfriend, she turned to word and image to work through the experience.[19] The panel is from a page in the novel that deals with the experience of adolescence including tropes—such as studiousness versus social exclusion—which are familiar in coming-of-age narratives across cultural contexts (Zeffren herself cites Marjane Satrapi's autobiographical graphic novel *Persepolis*, published in 2000 as one of her key influences).[20] Sara Ahmed has argued that "accounting for the 'pull' of lesbian desire is important" as it "puts her in contact with others and with objects that are off the vertical line."[21] "Everything Was Brand New" interrogates the experience of first beginning to feel "the pull of lesbian desire" without yet fully understanding its direction.

That the picture is about lesbian becoming is indicated by the inclusion of another panel on the same page in the novel, which depicts the autobiographical younger self as an

Opposite: Fig. 28. Ilana Zeffren, "Everything Was Brand New," *Pink Story* (Tel Aviv: Mapa Publications, 2005).

As far as schoolwork went, everything was fine

Socially, not so much

47

outsider to a gathering of implicitly heterosexual girl-boy couples. Yet "Everything Was Brand New" also makes clear that the process of becoming is subject to a multitude of influences. The picture lays a queer feminist claim to the male dominated cultural archive by reworking Leonardo da Vinci's famous drawing "Proportions of the Human Figure" (1485–1490), which is also known as the "Vitruvian Man" as it was inspired by the work of the Roman architect Vitruvius.[22] Da Vinci's drawing of the "perfect" male body is framed by text above and below, which, in mirror writing, gives further information about the body's architecture. Zeffren redraws this iconic picture into a multilayered image that centers on the female body. Her image queers da Vinci's focus on physical geometry by including words and objects on, around and behind the main female figure. This representational strategy helps to indicate some of the influences by which the body gains cultural signification. The autobiographical avatar, featuring devil's horns, is depicted against a background of Hebrew script and surrounded by visual references to school (the teacher figure) as well as home (the cat). It is noteworthy that both the speech and caption are translated into English, yet the background remains in the original languages. This picks up on the fact that language within graphic novels has a visual as well as a verbal function. The untranslated background includes part of a school report card, part of an ad for tampons, the logo of a column about sex from a popular teen magazine and personal pronouns in Arabic.[23] The Arabic words are written on the naked body, thus conceptualizing the body as a foreign language to the adolescent self. While the rich detail of the background and its focus on matters of sex is lost in the decision not to translate the Hebrew into English, the panel's place on the page nevertheless retains the sense that lesbian becoming takes place at least in part as a process of deviation and alienation from hetero-centric culture.

"Everything Was Brand New" exemplifies how Zeffren plays with words and image as well as with issues of shape, size and positioning on the page to reflect on the multiplicity of influences that accompany the event of lesbian becoming. Zeffren's engagement with the processes of translation and representation here not only allows her to visualize the gaps that show up when translating between Hebrew and English, but it is crucial to her (re)tracing the lines that have shaped her sense of self.

Sign: It's good to live with two moms

Rafi: But it's not easy

Fig. 29. Ilana Zeffren, "*Rishumon*," *Achbar Hair*, 2009.

PolitiCats

While Zeffren explores issues of subjectivity through autobiographical reflection, her work negotiates much of the political terrain of living as a lesbian in Israel through the depictions of Rafi and Spageti. The cats, whom she calls her "feline alter egos" have become more and more central to the strip over the years.[24] Drawing on the long tradition of animal-human relationships in cartoons, their role as core members of the household also adds a queer dimension to the strip as it plays with assumptions about whose voices make up a "family." The cats allow Zeffren to pursue what she calls her "non-militant attitude," a strategy of intervening in political debate by representing different points of view.[25] Figs. 29 and 30 aptly illustrate this method, both of them by making use of the placard, a central form of the visual language of political activism. In Fig. 29 Spageti's placard asserts that "it is good to live with two moms." The affirmative political message is brought into tension with a speech bubble in which Rafi proclaims "But it is not easy," offsetting by humor the political and the private. It is worth noting that the Hebrew words also allude to Israeli animal rights discourse.[26] This is lost in translation, indicating the un-translatability of certain aspects of cultural life, at least if they are to be rendered in the same format in which they were originally produced.

Fig. 30 depicts Spageti holding a placard which announces in bold typescript: "Yehuda and Samaria, the story of every Jew." This is followed by a handwritten scrawl that proclaims: "And what can you do? Of every Arab too." Yehuda and Samaria are Israel's official names for the West Bank and Jewish settlements hence aligning that part of the placard with Israeli state politics. But the different kinds of writing—the formal typescript versus the graffiti style handwriting—also reflect on the unequal

Yehuda and Samaria,
the story of every Jew.
And what can you do?
of every Arab too

Fig. 30. Ilana Zeffren, "*Rishu-mon*," *Achbar Hair*, 2008.

power relations between Israel and Palestine, which is further nuanced by the coloring of the letters, which opposes a cool "official" palette of blue and green with the hot red of political resistance. The two visual parts of the placard are held together by language. They are linked by the use of rhyme, which bridges the different sections and suggests that these lands are part of a shared story that inextricably connects Jews and Arabs.

Zeffren's reflection on life in Israel from within the country adds a fresh dimension to some of the political debates about Israel-Palestine within the Anglo-American academy. It importantly emphasizes the distinction between Jewishness and Israeli citizenship as well as interrogating how they are linked.[27] Zeffren was brought up in a conservative Jewish environment by American parents who raised their four children (she has a twin sister and two older brothers) in Ashkelon, a small town in the south of the country. She turned her back on the conservative lifestyle after her *bat mitzvah*, or, in her own words, "the minute I could," and left Ashkelon after completion of her army service to study at an art college in north Israel. On graduating in 1998, she moved to Tel Aviv where she has lived since. When I asked Zeffren to comment on her Jewishness in relation to her sexuality she replied: "Other than the fact that Orthodox rabbis don't accept or respect lesbian identity, I don't really see a relationship between my Jewish and lesbian identity. I feel more Israeli than Jewish, and my life as an Israeli is reflected in my comics more than the fact that I'm Jewish."[28]

Fig. 31 illustrates how the different concerns meet in her work. It depicts the autobiographical avatar in dialogue with Rafi, who asks: "Why isn't this week's column about the gay pride parade?" The response, which is like Rafi's question translated into English as a

Rafi: Why isn't this week's column about the gay pride parade?

Me: Because I don't want Rabbi Ovadya Yosef to stop reading it

Fig. 31. Ilana Zeffren, *"Rishumon," Achbar Hair*, 2007.

subtitle, reads: "Because I don't want Rabbi Ovadya Yosef to stop reading it." This is a witty intervention in the ongoing political debates about gay rights and visibility in Israel.[29] While Tel Aviv has been hosting "Gay Pride" events since 1998, they remain a contentious issue in Israel, coming under regular, virulent and sometimes violent attack from influential right-wing religious figures such as Rabbi Ovadya Yosef.[30] Yosef, leader of the ultra–Orthodox Shas party, is famous for his anti-feminist, anti–Arab and anti-LGBT attitudes, so the suggestion that he is a regular reader of Zeffren's column shrewdly uses his object of hate to turn him into the subject of scrutiny.

Working Through the Lesbian, Working Through Me

Asked if she was happy to be labeled a "lesbian artist," Zeffren replied as follows:

> I'm very proud to be a lesbian artist. I present lesbian lifestyle as an obvious thing, as a non-issue. I present my girlfriend and me as any other couple dealing with life in the city. On the other hand, I put an emphasis on gay issues and use the word "lesbian" as much as I can. But I always do it with humor.[31]

By using "the word 'lesbian' as much as I can," Zeffren tacitly acknowledges the significance of naming, which forms a crucial part in personal orientation and political organization as well as in the critique of the normative ways in which the subject is constituted discursively.[32] However, discourse alone is not enough to explain the process of becoming. Or, as Ahmed has argued: "It is not that one is simply a lesbian before the very moment in which one speaks of oneself as 'being' a lesbian at the same time that it is not that one is 'not' a lesbian before the act of naming ... If lesbianism was generated by the word 'lesbian,' then lesbian politics might be easier: it would just be a matter of spreading the word!"[33] Zeffren's comics help to make visible the frequently opposing forces of discourse, desire, material reality and socio-cultural contingency that contribute in unequal measures to our articulation of self. They also remind us, I suggest, that the event of becoming is often articulated at least in part through the encounter with verbal, visual and other forms of culture.

Comics hold a special place in this process. In an article on what they call "self-regarding art," Gillian Whitlock and Anna Poletti have argued that what distinguishes critiques of "autographics"—or "life narrative fabricated in and through drawing and design using various technologies, modes, and material"—from textual criticism is the "deliberate attention to 'what happens as I perceive this.'"[34] Reading autographics demands, they argue, "that you look for yourself, and that you enter the field of representation that is indicated not in a conventional quotation but something more substantial—a graphic specimen drawn from the body of the text itself."[35] These words speak closely to my own experience of encountering Zeffren's cartoons and writing about the autobiographical self in her work, a process which has its own critical particularity: the central character in her works is "Me." Of course the "Me" is not I who live and work some thousand miles away with my own girlfriend and two cats who would not like to share their territory with Rafi and Spageti. But my encounter with Zeffren's "Me"—or Me in Zeffren's work—is at least in part shaped by a particular kind of lesbian recognition.

Critically speaking, this kind of affinity describes what I have called the graphic lesbian continuum, a concept that seeks to expand the 21st-century critical and cultural landscapes by turning to the lesbian to think afresh about issues of visibility, politics, representation and the transnational attachments of female-identified intimate lives. Zeffren's cartoons allow us to trace some of the queer lines that demarcate lesbian becoming. By using lesbian life as its *point of orientation*, her work destabilizes hetero-centric ways of seeing—or rather, of *not* seeing—female-identified sexuality. She creates a visual landscape which shows that the critical anachronism of the 21st-century graphic lesbian continuum is not a return to a narrowly defined identity politics but the opening up of a conceptual and creative space which values a lesbian presence.

NOTES

1. This and other Ilana Zeffren quotations are taken from an email exchange we had during August 2011. I am extremely grateful for Ilana's generosity in responding to my questions.

2. I am using the term "lesbian" to describe women who have intimate relationships with other women whereby "woman" is understood as a cultural signifier that can include biological and non-biological identifications.

3. Ilana Zeffren, email, August 2011.

4. Sara Ahmed, *Queer Phenomenology: Orientations, Objects, Others* (Durham: Duke University Press, 200) 1.

5. Ahmed, 20.

6. Annamarie Jagose, *Inconsequence: Lesbian Representation and the Logic of Sexual Sequenc*e (Ithaca: Cornell University Press, 2002) 3.

7. Hillary L. Chute, "The Texture of Retracing in Marjane Satrapi's *Persepolis*," *Women's Studies Quarterly* 36, 1.2 (2008): 93.

8. Hillary L. Chute, *Graphic Women: Life Narrative and Contemporary Comics* (New York: Columbia University Press, 2010) 2.

9. Ahmed, 20.

10. See Alison Bechdel's *Are You My Mother?* (Boston: Houghton Mifflin Harcourt, 2012); *The Essential Dykes to Watch Out For* (Boston: Houghton Mifflin Harcourt, 2008); *Fun Home: A Family Tragicomic* (Boston: Houghton Mifflin Harcourt, 2006). For an account of Bechdel's place in queer studies see Valerie Rohy, "In the Queer Archive: *Fun Home*," *GLQ: A Journal of Lesbian and Gay Studies* 16.3 (2010): 341–361; and Heather Love's "The Mom Problem," *Public Books*: http://www.publicbooks.org/fiction/the-mom-problem. Accessed October 23, 2012.

11. Adrienne Rich, "Compulsory Heterosexuality and Lesbian Existence," reprinted in Henry Abelove, Michèle Aina Barale and David Halperin, eds., *The Lesbian and Gay Studies Reader* (New York: Routledge, 1993) 239.

12. Elizabeth Freeman, "Sacramentality and the Lesbian Premodern," in Noreen Giffney, Michelle M. Sauer and Diane Watt, eds., *The Lesbian Premodern* (New York: Palgrave Macmillan, 2011) 179.

13. Alison Bechdel in an interview with Anne Crémieux, *Transatlantica* 1 (2007): http://transatlantica.revues.org/1220. Accessed April 12, 2012.

14. On its website, the journal lists list two alternative titles: *Sh' ma: A Journal of Jewish Ideas* and *Sh'ma: A Journal of Jewish Responsibility*, http://www.shma.com/about/. Accessed April 11, 2012.

15. Josh Rolnick, *Sh'ma*, December 2010. This can be accessed online via the Berman Jewish Policy Archive: http://www.bjpa.org/Publications/results.cfm?PublicationName=Sh%27ma%3A%20A%20Journal%20of%20 Jewish%20Responsibility&VolumeIssue=Vol.41%2Fno.675. Accessed April 11, 2012.

16. See, for example, Walter Benjamin's foundational observations in "Die Aufgabe des äbersetzers" in Walter Benjamin, *Gesammelte Schriften*, 4.1, ed. Tillman Rexroth (Frankfurt: Suhrkamp, 1972), 9–21.

17. Valerie Traub, "The Present Future of Lesbian Historiography," in Giffney, Sauer and Watt, eds., *The Lesbian Premodern*, 23.

18. Germaine Greer, *The Female Eunuch* (New York: Farrar, Strauss & Giroux, 1970) 57.

19. Ilana Zeffren, email, August 2011. See also Leah Berkenwald's interview with Ilana Zeffren, Jewish Women's Archive: "Jewesses with Attitude," March 14, 2011. http://jwa.org/blog/graphic-details-interview-ilana-zeffren. Accessed April 11, 2012.

20. She lists as her other influences Art Spiegelman, Joan Sfar, Gerald Durrell, *The Muppet Show*, *Sesame Street* and "the colorful streets of Tel Aviv," August 2011.

21. Ahmed, 94.

22. Vitruvius, *The Ten Books of Architecture*, trans. Morris Hicky Morgan (Cambridge: Harvard University Press, 1914). See especially 72–76 on the symmetry of the (male) human body.

23. Special thanks to Ilana for translating this for me.

24. Ilana Zeffren, email, August 2011.

25. Ilana Zeffren, email, August 2011.

26. Thanks to Maya Barzilai from the University of Michigan who has pointed out to me that the Hebrew words "*tov lichyot im shtey imahot*" (it is good to live with two mothers) allude to Israeli animal rights discourse, as the word "*lichyot*" could also be read as "*la-chayot*" (for the animals). This recalls the slogan for animal rights in Israel: "*Tnu la-chayot lichyot*" (Let the animals live). The double meaning in Hebrew strengthens the focus on queer family in Zeffren's work.

27. Judith Butler dissects the issues at stake in her *Precarious Life: The Power of Mourning and Violence* (London: Verso, 2004) 101–127.

28. Ilana Zeffren, email, August 2011.

29. Israel's affirmation of its gay rights legislation—homosexuality was decriminalized in 1988; the age of consent is the same for heterosexuals and homosexuals—has recently become a point of critical contention as some critics accuse Israel of "pinkwashing" by which they mean that Israel uses gay rights to direct attention away from Palestine. For a summary of debates see David Kaufman, "Is Israel using gay rights to excuse its policy on Palestine?" May 13, 2011: www.time.com, accessed April 11, 2012; and Stephen Gray, "Tel Aviv best gay city destination of 2011," January 12, 2012: http://www.pinknews.co.uk, accessed April 12, 2012.

30. Events came to a head in 2006 when the World Pride Festival was to be held in Jerusalem but was met with violent opposition by certain members of the Jewish, Christian and Muslim communities. See Nitzan Giladi's excellent documentary film *Jerusalem Is Proud to Present* (2008). In 2009, Israel's LGBT community suffered the fatal shooting of two people at a center for gay teens. Ilan Lior, "Pink on the Outside/ Gray on the Inside," January 13, 2012: http://www.haaretz.com, accessed April 12, 2012. The "Tel Aviv Pride" continues as a successful annual event, which attracts an international crowd.

31. Ilana Zeffren, email, August 2011.

32. See Michel Foucault's *The History of Sexuality Volume 1: An Introduction*, trans. Robert Hurley (London: Penguin, 1990) and J.K. Simon, "A Conversation with Michel Foucault." *Partisan Review* 38 (1971): 192–201.

33. Ahmed, 92–93.

34. Gillian Whitlock and Anna Poletti, "Self-Regarding Art," *Biography* 32.1 (2008): v and vii.

35. Whitlock and Poletti, vii.

BIBLIOGRAPHY

Ahmed, Sara. *Queer Phenomenology: Orientations, Objects, Others*. Durham: Duke University Press, 2004.

Bechdel, Alison. *Are You My Mother?* Boston: Houghton Mifflin Harcourt, 2012.

_____. *The Essential Dykes to Watch Out For*. Boston: Houghton Mifflin Harcourt, 2008.

_____. *Fun Home: A Family Tragicomic*. Boston: Houghton Mifflin Harcourt, 2006.

_____. Interview with Anne Crémieux. *Transatlantica* 1 (2007). http://transatlantica.revues.org/1220. Accessed April 12, 2012.

Benjamin, Walter. *Gesammelte Schriften*. 4.1. Ed. Tillman Rexroth. Frankfurt: Suhrkamp, 1972.

Butler, Judith. *Precarious Life: The Power of Mourning and Violence*. London: Verso, 2004.

Chute, Hilary L. *Graphic Women: Life Narrative and Contemporary Comics*. New York: Columbia University Press, 2010.

_____. "The Texture of Retracing in Marjane Satrapi's *Persepolis*." *Women's Studies Quarterly* 36 1.2 (2008): 92–110.

Freeman, Elizabeth. "Sacramentality and the Lesbian Premodern." In Noreen Giffney, Michelle M. Sauer and Diane Watt, eds. *The Lesbian Premodern*. New York: Palgrave Macmillan, 2011.

Giffney, Noreen, Michelle M. Sauer, and Diane Watt, eds. *The Lesbian Postmodern*. New York: Palgrave Macmillan, 2011.

Greer, Germaine. *The Female Eunuch*. New York: Farrar, Strauss & Giroux, 1970.

Jagose, Annamarie. *Inconsequence: Lesbian Representation and the Logic of Sexual Sequence*. Ithaca: Cornell University Press, 2002.

Rich, Adrienne. "Compulsory Heterosexuality and Lesbian Existence." In Henry Abelove, Michèle Aina Barale and David Halperin, eds., *The Lesbian and Gay Studies Reader*. New York: Routledge, 1993. 227–254.

Traub, Valerie. "The Present Future of Lesbian Historiography." In Noreen Giffney, Michelle M. Sauer and Diane Watt, eds., *The Lesbian Premodern*. New York: Palgrave Macmillan, 2012.

Vitruvius. *The Ten Books of Architecture*. Trans. Morris Hicky Morgan. Cambridge: Harvard University Press, 1914.

Whitlock, Gillian, and Anna Poletti. "Self-Regarding Art." *Biography* 32.1 (2008): v–xxiii.

Zeffren, Ilana. Interview with Leah Berkenwald. Jewish Women's Archive: "Jewesses with Attitude." March 14, 2011. http://jwa.org/blog/graphic-details-interview-ilana-zeffren. Accessed April 11, 2012.

Traces of Subjectivity

The Embodied Author in
the Work of Ariel Schrag[1]

NATALIE PENDERGAST

At Ariel Schrag's March 27, 2011, animated[2] performance and Creating Comics Step-by-Step master class in Toronto,[3] the New York cartoonist asked her audience why they thought comic book dialogue is typically written in uppercase lettering. After a few moments of silence, she offered her answer: uppercase letters fit better into tight rows of speech balloon text. The writing must be considered first as an image that meets the reader's eye in conjunction with the iconographic language of pictures, and thus uppercase lettering offers a square neatness that prevents the cumbersome overlaps in lowercase scrawl, created by letters such as "g," "y," and "p," which hang into and poke at the letters in the line directly below.

Schrag herself prefers to use lowercase lettering, in order to reserve uppercase letters for emphatic statements or insinuations of a louder volume of speech or noise. In her distinct approach to lettering, every aspect of the letter's body is a crucial performative element of the word it helps to form. Thus, in Schrag's comics, the handwritten lettering embodies and enacts the abstract meaning of the words it composes. Similarly, in her four-part autobiocomics[4] series, little is symbolic—the work is less a representation than it is a presentation or an expression of selfhood, a staged re-enactment of the author's four momentous high school years.

Circumventing clichéd categories of gay identity and established generalizations about the "subculture" of lesbianism,[5] Schrag offers a tell-all confessional graphic narrative in which being sexually attracted to other girls is simply another fact of her life, on a par with her parents' divorce, losing her virginity, and never-ending chemistry homework. During the summers from 1995 to 1998, Schrag wrote and drew an autobiographical graphic novel for each of her four years of high school at Berkeley High. Like her childhood favorite, Toronto-based Lynn Johnston, creator of the *For Better or For Worse* strip (1979–2008), Schrag endeavored to write her comic chronicles in real time as both a document of and a testament to her teenage firsts.

Schrag's stories are richly detailed; the chronicles are literally chronic in the sense that they wontedly reveal all that goes on in the life of the author. Little, gratuitous episodes that seemingly contribute nothing to the central narrative appear frequently, along with sequences of self-reflexive internal monologue. Small, serial episodic events, each rarely more or less significant than the next, make up the *stuff* of these graphic novels, removing any possibility of chipping away at the story to arrive at some nucleus of what it is "about." Indeed, the chronicles have no climax but rather prioritize the ongoing development of a character—the narrator—over the development of plot. Every detail, every moment narrated serves the purpose of allowing the reader a heightened level of intimacy with the narrator; the reader gets to know this character and the reader partakes in this character's development.

Schrag's autobiography thus reads like a diary. In its constant reportage of her train of thoughts, her comics resemble the genre coined by Ross Chambers, "loiterature."[6] According to Chambers, loiterature, like the diary, "relies on techniques of digression, interruption, deferral and episodicity [...] to make observations of modern life that are unsystematic, even disordered, and are usually oriented toward the everyday, the ordinary and the trivial."[7] Loitrature embraces what would be deemed a failure of a published novel to edit out any details unnecessary to the plot, character construction or "message" of the story. Contrasting the "aesthetic sublimity"[8] that is the aim of traditional novelists, loiterateurs' ambling is a comment on and rejection of the literary ideal. Though the diary does not necessarily transgress the standards of life writing, it does resist, or at least precede editing. French literary critic and specialist in autobiography Philippe Lejeune views the diary as an antifiction,[9] since, unlike the autobiography, which must be written with no foreseeable origin to the story, the diary is kept with no foreseeable end.[10] Schrag's comics preserve pre-textual writing and drawing, while also containing her re-enactments of events from memory.

The meandering style of the diary allows for a more automatic and immediate transcription of the writer's thoughts. In a visual autobiography like Schrag's, the language of drawing renders unedited thoughts into dramatic and iconic images. This essay explores the possibility of Schrag's oeuvre embodying the author through the performativity of her iconic self-portrait, her diaristic drafting process, and the metaphor of her ink as a bodily fluid, which adds a sense of indexicality to her text. I argue that Schrag achieves a certain presence of the author that is evident not only in the voice of the narrator, but also in the texture of the words and images that form the story. This description stems from the particular type/genre of autobiographical narrative that literary historian Irene Gammel terms: "Visual and performance diaries, a serial form of life writing that allows [authors/artists] to represent their multiple selves in their full complexity, producing an interfacing of artistic, domestic and sexual selves."[11] I would forego Gammel's choice of the term "representation" in favor of "expression," "manifestation," or simply "presentation," given that "representation" implies a distancing of the creative work from its creator. However, I contend that Schrag's volumes could be categorized as visual and as performance diaries that mediate the author's life story through an iconic character who resembles her physically and a visual language that preserves her expressive gestures. Schrag's chronicles function as does performance art, albeit by way of different means, just as the "body on stage appears to be the 'thing itself,' incapable of mimesis, afforded not only no distance between sign and referent but, indeed, taken for the referent."[12] Her graphic novels form a body of work that brings the sign (her drawn autobiography) closer to the referent (her actual life and body).

I shall demonstrate how Schrag's work embodies the author/narrator by first discussing Schrag as an icono/typographic, autobiographical "performer" in the anatomic or formal design of her work. However, she also demonstrates this immediacy—this closeness between the author and the text—through her work's genesis and through thematic and metaphorical devices. I shall thus also focus on her process of art-making, which gives her text an uncensored quality by preserving traces of the original draft of her drawings. Finally, I will compare

Schrag's development of Ariel's sexual subjectivity to that of Proust's, by emphasizing the role of masturbation in and of the text. In these ways, Schrag's graphic novels perform the life, the body and the subjectivity of the author.

Although readers of Schrag's graphic novels do not always have the privilege of viewing a live performance of her stories, her cartooned characters sustain in print the performative quality she evokes on stage. Although they are always based on "real" people in Schrag's life, she transforms their images into what she calls a "cartoon version of themselves" in the comics ("Creating..."). In this way, the exaggerations in facial expressions—indeed the caricaturizations of people—make visual all the emotions they feel on the inside.[13] The outward cartoonish stylings of their faces and body positions reflect in an overt way all that the characters might be thinking or feeling and that would be—in real life—invisible from the outside. In Schrag's chronicles, she most often characterizes and dramatizes herself in order to express to the reader, in the form of a soliloquy, her most personal feelings. The theatrical self-expression in her comics and her stage performances resembles her early experiences of storytelling while playing with family members. In my interview with Schrag from April 25, 2011, she explained, "when I was younger I did a lot of drawing [...] my sister and I would sit at this drawing table that was in the kitchen and we would both be drawing the picture and we'd tell the story of what was happening [...] and I think that was the first [seque] into comics." In her high school chronicles, Schrag translates this voice that dramatically "tells the story" into a visual style. In Fig. 32—page six of *Definition*—Ariel expresses rage at the notion of her older male friend seducing her younger, twelve-year-old sister. The page is constructed as an intimate storytelling sequence between Ariel and the reader only. Although the story she tells us is about her sister, the real story is the anger Ariel feels and reveals to us. The development of her character is the most important event in this sequence, and what she tells us becomes only a means to demonstrating or performing her emotions. The caricatured drawings of her own, frequently changing facial expressions reflect a type of portraiture that not only exaggerates her appearance, but also demonstrates characteristics of her personality and identity. In this way, the caricature contains a performative quality that projects the image of not just Ariel's outward appearance, but her essential character.

Although Schrag's personality is preserved in the body language and facial expressions of her character, her cartoonish appearance is iconic rather than identical to her "real" self. According to semiotician Charles Sanders Peirce, "an *icon* is a sign which would possess the character which renders it significant, even though its object had no existence; such as a lead pencil streak as representing a geometrical line."[14] As an iconic portrait that possesses Schrag's characteristic fair hair and casual dress, but no details of her appearance, the drawn figure of Ariel is simplistic in appearance, with features so minimal—aside from abnormally large eyes[15]— that her hairline is hardly discernible from her face. In black and white, with no shading or perspectival depth, we readers are called upon to interpret more from the exaggerated eyebrow arches, the twisted mouth containing disproportionate, clenching teeth, eyes that can grow ever wider with psychedelically mad pupils, sweat, and tears than from any imagined physical likeness. The written text bears much of this dramatization as well, whether Schrag uses devices such as the occasional underlined or darkened word, or, as mentioned above, all-uppercase lettering, which, when used sparingly, accentuates a particular word. Hand-drawn lettering can sometimes ooze out of the speech balloon or the narrator's caption in an effort to extend and emphasize the meaning of the enlarged word in question. This occurs to great effect in the middle-right frame of figure 32. Ariel says: "well one day I felt sick at art camp so I came home. I wandered innocently into my sister's room ONLY

Fig. 32. Reprinted with the permission of Scribner Publishing Group from *Awkward and Definition* by Ariel Schrag, 6. *Awkward* copyright © 1995 Ariel Schrag. *Definition* copyright © 1996 Ariel Schrag.

to DISCOVER!!" which is followed by an image of her sister's diary page that, legible to the reader, describes her late night phone calls with an older boy. Both of the words "only" and "discover" are capitalized for emphasis, but this is not enough to convey Ariel's anger, so "discover" is also stretched until the bottom half of the word extends beyond the boundary of the caption box that holds it. In this very subtle extension, Schrag uses the freedom of the hand-drawn comic book medium to direct or design a textual language that goes beyond the symbolic meaning of the words. According to Peirce, "[a] *symbol* is a sign which would lose the character which renders it a sign if there were no interpretant. Such is any utterance of speech which signifies what it does only by virtue of its being understood to have that signification."[16] The presence of Ariel's and Schrag's emotion in the form of the drawing precedes any agreed upon signification of her words.

    This style of drawing favors the expression of the artist at the time of the drawing act and the movement of the artist's hand, the lettering and the characters' bodies on the page. French comics theorist Philippe Marion discusses two categories of drawn lines in his 1993 book, *Traces en cases, Travail graphique, figuration narrative et participation du lecteur*. The *ligne-contour* is the outline of a drawn shape and it marks the distinction between it and all other objects or background in a frame. The *ligne-expression* is the line that creates movement and depth, sometimes extending beyond the confines of the contour. Media scholar Paul Atkinson contends that the *ligne-expression* "attests to the capacity of the line to signify outside of the contour of the subject and maintain some of its internal force or compulsion."[17] The way that Schrag spreads the lines of words or shading beyond the contouring line denotes the action of her hand moving the fill of her shapes beyond their representational limits. They are not "frozen" into place like the drawings of many *ligne-claire* comics, such as Hergé's *The Adventures of Tintin* (1929–1976), but rather escaping the grip of the contour.

    Indeed, the text becomes a character or a performer in the story, as it moves alongside Ariel or acts as an extension of the bodies of Ariel, her sister, and her friends. Again, in the bottom right frame, Ariel's speech balloon conveys her anxiety in questioning her sister's whereabouts: "well well where are you going?!" she asks. This time, both the wavering lettering and the dripping speech balloon itself add meaning or intonation to her words. In these ways, the reader quickly learns the iconographic language of Schrag's own design. The words are images that contain several dimensions of meaning: they are signs of referential value and they play the role of making visual the effects given to words in oral/spoken situations.

    Schrag's presence is evoked by this indexical quality of her drawings. According to Peirce, this is the third category of signs: "[the] *index* is a sign which would, at once, lose the character which makes it a sign if its object were removed, but would not lose that character if there were no interpretant."[18]

    Given that Schrag's unique musculature and technique are contained in her lines, the drawings give substance to her physical movements. They signify that her presence caused them to be etched onto the page, like how smoke signifies fire. The indexicality of drawing means its marks are always a trace of the artist's bodily movement. Art theorist Edward Hill has argued that the conjunction of the artist's body and materials involved in the act of drawing creates a kind of performance: "Together ink and paper become the substance of a visual expression as formed by a complex, sustained performance."[19] Due to the unique musculature of the artist's body, the creative act is irreproducible. We readers get a sense not only of the story being told to us in the graphic novel, but also of the cartoonist's own sweeping motions. In the very texture of the drawn panels, the stylized words, the scribbled hair of a character and the frayed lines that shade a cartoon face, we experience the process of the drawing act and the artist's dexterity in commanding his or her pencil.

The traces of Schrag's process are built into her finished drawings. Schrag described her most common working method as follows: she draws out her frames in pencil in the "rough draft" of each sequence and sketches in each image in its most raw and immediate conception. From these originals she gradually perfects the drawings and eventually inks them into permanence.[20] Compared to the process of other cartoonists such as Bryan Lee O'Malley (*Scott Pilgrim*, 2004–2010) and Chester Brown (*Louis Riel*, 2004, *Paying For It*, 2011), this is a rather revolutionary way of working. In the back pages of *Scott Pilgrim Vs. The Universe:* Volume 5,[21] O'Malley offers a step-by-step tutorial on how to make comics like him. After writing a script, he commits the story to miniature, "thumbnail" versions of his comic book frames and loosely outlines the composition of the images. After deciding on the sequence and content of the story frames, he then redraws the narrative in larger panels and, after refining the drawings, adds ink and color. Chester Brown uses a similar, multi-draft process in his art-making.[22] Schrag, however, prioritizes the original conception and technique of drawing over the edited versions of her art. There is thus a degree of immediacy and performativity that remains unobscured by the self-correcting act of revision or redoing. Furthermore, the process of Schrag's cartooning again removes the distance between the reader and the cartoonist, for the reader is permitted access to a level of intimacy with the cartoonist's thoughts and artistic process. The drawing over the drawing allows Schrag to prolong the initial creative moment in which the birth of her concept for the image took place, while also giving a sense of a closer proximity and connection to the events narrated.

The self-caricature of Ariel allows for a further, more metaphorical palimpsest of the artist through image. Not only are the drawings of Ariel both the product and the process of her creativity because they include the stages of artistry and of the artist's development, they are also figments of Schrag's self/body-image. Schrag's initial, rather crude drawings from the ninth grade are included in the same series as her later styles, and her own "becoming" as both subject and artist is performed and formed directly on the page. In this way, the process of art-making, for Schrag, becomes the praxis for her own coming out and coming into subjectivity. The graphic novels each depict the preceding year, and as she grows up, so does her style of cartooning, making the form of her comics match their content in a self-reflexive practice of self-definition. The graphic novels are thus in their very form indicative of her own developing body, undergoing the same changes over the course of her adolescence as does her self-image.[23]

As discussed above, the performativity of Schrag's comics is in many ways what separates them from drawings that strive for verisimilitude. As stated, the cartoon versions of the people in her life include exaggerated effects of the emotions they are feeling at particular moments; therefore, the illustrations bear both the outward appearance and the inward thoughts of the characters in one figure. As Scott McCloud writes in *Understanding Comics* (1993): "Through traditional realism, the comics artist can portray the world without—and through the cartoon, the world within."[24] The de-emphasized physical appearance of the character, in favor of a more iconic image, invites readers to identify more personally with the character, by interpreting or completing the image mentally.

In addition to Schrag's use of iconic simplification and indexicality to convey a deeper (emotional/psychological) reality beyond that which is possible with a purely physical/photo-iconic illusionism, the images and frames also work together to add meaning to the language of the comics. In their juxtaposition from one frame to the next, the characters show a wide range of emotions, and during dream sequences, Schrag adopts an entirely new method of drawing in order to portray a different, subconscious dimension of the character's life story. On page 154 of *Potential* [Fig. 33], for example, Schrag demonstrates, by way of form, the transition in the narrator's consciousness as she falls asleep. The stylized cartoon images gradually shift with each frame to more photorealistic drawings with greater amounts of detail, shading and depth, thereby denoting Ariel's now sleeping/dreaming state of mind. Schrag drew many of the dream sequences from photographs, unlike the other drawings which she drew from memory or from her imagination. These two methods have very different effects on the reader. For one thing, as Schrag pointed out in her "Creating Comics" class, the illustration from the photograph conveys its "stillness" or the static immobility. The photographic drawing also shows a more realistic physical appearance of the characters and less of Schrag's own creative interpretation, iconicity, or caricaturization of their personalities in visual form. This sequence is the last of three extensive dream narratives in *Potential*, and comes directly after a devastating rejection of Ariel by her girlfriend, Sally. Over the course of the graphic novel, the dreams increase in both length and intensity, matching the climactic progression of Ariel's anti-romance. In the first dream sequence,[25] Ariel and Sally are kissing, nude in bed, and Ariel is thinking of performing oral sex on Sally. Instead, they move to the floor and ask Sally's mother, who, oddly, is seated in the next room and facing them, why sex is important. In this scenario, Ariel feels the pressure to pleasure Sally as much as her previous boyfriends had, but rather ends up questioning the source of her anxiety itself: romantic sex and what it means. In the second dream sequence, Ariel's fears of losing Sally come true and Sally, who is first shown standing behind Ariel, eventually joins an unknown man in laughing at Ariel, and finally is shown cuddling up to him with her head in his lap.[26] Ariel is upset, but meets what looks like a younger version of herself with a different, dark face. This person asks if she can "eat Ariel out," which Ariel then contemplates, guiltily. Finally, the last dream scene [Fig. 33] shows Ariel feeling trapped between a desire to help her father steer the car and wiping sand from the beach off her shoulders. She does not have enough hands to do both and feels conflicted. The scene continues in the kitchen as Ariel feels intense hunger but cannot give in to the tempting chicken before her because of her promise to Sally to remain vegetarian. Again she feels guilty for her desire, and, after taking one bite, races to the bathroom to purge.

The progression of the narrative is punctuated by these three dream sequences which all follow Sally's increasing resistance toward Ariel in "real" life. In each dream, Ariel's anxiety escalates as she identifies ways in which she may fail her girlfriend, through being unable to please her sexually, by betraying her with another girl or by renouncing her vegetarianism. Conflicted by the need to compromise her desires in order to keep her girlfriend, Ariel expresses feeling constricted in her dreams. That these sequences are copied from static photographs emphasizes their fixity and lack of performative flexibility. Since these dreams are narrative manifestations of her anxieties—they did not actually occur—Ariel cannot reenact them or filter them through her own interpretative storytelling as narrator. Indeed, the narrator is completely absent as Schrag's ability to control how these sequences are told is now missing. Ironically, the fact that the dreams came from her subconscious and not from "real life" makes them less of a subjective, reconstructed account of Ariel's life, and, by extension, they warrant a more photorealistic style of illustration.

Some cartoonists, like Alison Bechdel (*Dykes to Watch Out For*, 1983–2008, *Fun Home*, 2006) and Shannon Gerard (*Unspent Love, or Things I Wish I Told You*, 2011), endeavor to

Fig. 33. Reprinted with the permission of Scribner Publishing Group from *Potential* by Ariel Schrag, 154. *Potential* copyright © 2000 Ariel Schrag.

preserve a more mimetic style of drawing and therefore trace figures from photographs more often than not. For Bechdel, photographing herself in every pose of her characters in her comics allows for what she calls a more "realistic" illustration.[27] In an interview with ArtSync, Gerard reveals that she photographs her subjects in various positions and then traces directly over the photos to arrive at the drawings in her comics. She says:

> I get models to kind of substitute in for me. We have these sort of improvisational photo shoots where I kind of tell them a little bit about what the narrative's about, but it's pretty critical to me to not let them read the text because I don't want them to kind of enact it or interpret it.[28]

In both cases, the artist is again doing all the interpretation of the characters by either acting out their role for them, as Bechdel does, or having them follow instructions without knowing why, so that the artist can add interpretive value later to their positions, as Gerard does. Although these cartoonists demonstrate the importance of performativity to the process of drawing, they do not impress the semiotics of performance or body language onto the image with the same level of indexicality as does Schrag. For Bechdel and Gerard, likeness of the drawing to the live figure is of priority; whereas for Schrag, the re-enactment of live gestures, tone and emotions is more important.

Like her photographic drawings of the dream sequences summarized above, Schrag sometimes experiments with other drawing methods besides her distinctive palimpsest process of layering or darkening over her original illustrations. However, she is very precise about using different styles and methods to create formal effects. In her fourth and final volume, *Likewise*, she especially codifies certain visual devices according to what she terms specific "modes of reality."[29] As a writer, she keeps a diary, tape records conversations, photographs friends, has memories and has fantasies. At the time of drawing *Likewise*, Schrag relived her year through all of these different media and mental states. In order to stay true to her rather immediate and earnest process, she developed different visual styles to distinguish one way of experiencing life from another: "I wanted to express all of those modes of reality through [different styles of] drawing the comic. So that's why, in the book, there are different styles for each mode of experience."[30] Most of the book conforms to her original method of cartooning with layered, crosshatched drawings and stream-of-consciousness narration, but she fills in flashbacks with a computer gray tone and gives them no narration. Fantasies, like dreams, are drawn with stippling pointillism and also have no narration. She illustrates her diary entries with quick, rough, loose drawings on lined paper; there are typed, computer font narration sections that are paired with ink wash drawings; there is tape-recorded dialogue drawn in heavy black and white and there are illustrations drawn from photographs that make certain moments with her girlfriend Sally inanimate. These photographic drawings are purposely juxtaposed against her usual style in order to emphasize Ariel's and Schrag's feeling of being "stuck" or trapped in situations over which she feels she has no control.

Since being true to an objective reality is most often not Schrag's goal in cartooning, and performativity takes precedence over mimetic drawings of her characters, she usually draws directly from concept as opposed to drawing from a concept that is first rendered into photographic form and finally copied. Even when she experiments with more mimetic styles, she does so in order to emphasize the restrictions she felt in relation to certain experiences while re-creating them in comics. In this way, Schrag's process again removes the distance between artist and artwork by limiting technical refinement and reducing characters to her most performative and emotive interpretations of them. A drawing from a photograph will appear more "realistic," but drawings from memories or from abstract ideas are "real" in other ways. Indeed, they depict not only the events of the story, but also what the cartoonist herself has added to the events—her own interpretive re-enactments of them. The cartoonist's subjectivity can thus be found in each drawing, whether her own narrating character is present or not. As Charles Hatfield writes:

> The cartoon self-image [...] seems to offer a unique way for the artist to recognize and external-ize his or her subjectivity. In this light, comics autobiography may not be alienating so much as radically enabling.[31]

In Schrag's case, the comics offer her a venue for controlling her self-image even as it is still developing. Another way in which Schrag inserts herself into the narrative is by discussing the act of drawing her graphic novels within her chronicles. They become a part of her life on a par with all other major events. In my interview with Schrag, she described her creative output and self-fashioning:

> It started out as this fun project that I did, but it became more and more of my identity and pretty soon it was the only thing that mattered to me. And that was partly because I was proud of it and enjoyed doing it and it felt important. It was also because it became sort of an escape. It was like I didn't have to really care about what was actually happening if I could think that what would really only matter was how I portrayed it in the comic.... The reality of the comic became more important than my present reality.[32]

The meta-fictional and anti-fictional writing, which is especially apparent in the final comic book, *Likewise*,[33] for example, resembles the self-reflexive cartoonist in other works such as "Caricature" (1998) by Daniel Clowes, as well as the *Journal* series (1996–2002) by Fabrice Neaud. Ariel/Schrag evolves over the course of narrating her detailed life story, to the point where the story comes to supersede the life. The act of writing and drawing is so important to the life of Schrag that it becomes the subject of the narrative being written. In this *mise-en-abyme* of writing, art and life merge, thereby removing distance once again between the work and the work's creator.

At one point in *Likewise*, Ariel's love interest, Sally, expresses anxiety and resentment about Ariel's constant prioritizing of her comics over relationships in her life.[34] This accusation is confirmed when Ariel later tells her mother the following:

> ... I think the thing is that love is like the thing you can be totally obsessed with and your life revolves around it, but *only* if art is like this stable thing that's kept behind it, which means it's *really* the most important thing, because without the art, if you lost the love, which you don't have control over, then you'd really be completely desperate with nothing, so art *has* to remain the most important.[35]

Here, Ariel articulates what Schrag has already demonstrated in her chronicles: her art has eclipsed many of the other events in her life that were once, in *Awkward* and *Definition*, the central parts of her story. Ariel balances the constricting love she feels for Sally with the liberating feeling of expressing herself through comics art. The increased desire to control her "reality," demonstrated first by the stylistic juxtaposition between her iconic storytelling of "real" life and her more photographic and static renditions of her dreams, is now more than just a formal gesture. In *Likewise*, the last graphic novel in the series, the character Ariel and the cartoonist Schrag become one person as Ariel explicitly refers—in both image and text—to her art as inseparable from herself. In this way, Schrag's comics resemble the work of Marcel Proust, who also chronicled a life that gradually came to converge with his own. The narrator in *À la Recherche du Temps Perdu* (1913–1927) eventually reveals his desire to become a writer, which leads to his progressively becoming obsessed and overwhelmed by his growing writing projects and their value in his life.

Despite their common narrative voice, Schrag and Proust explore the culture and discourse of queer sexuality in different ways. In *Within a Budding Grove* and *Cities of the Plain*, Proust's narrator becomes fascinated with the homosexual relationship between his friend's uncle, Monsieur de Charlus, and Jupien, to the point where he finds himself watching them having sex and then discussing it at length and explicitly with the reader. Despite his interest in sexuality, he only ever discusses his own desire by way of metaphor. His long-term relationship with Albertine is much less about eroticism than it is about jealousy and possessiveness. Literary and queer theorist Eve Kosofsky Sedgwick writes:

> Charlus's closet is specularized so that the erotics around Albertine (which is to say, around the narrator) may continue to resist visualization; it is from this inchoate space that will include Albertine, and to guarantee its privileged exemption from sight, that the narrator stages the presentation of Charlus; it is around the perceptual axis between a closet viewed and a closet inhabited that a discourse of the world takes shape.[36]

By creating two closets, Proust constructs a cultural discourse around homosexuality. The closet viewed and described by the spectator will only ever be understandable to others by way of the interpretation of this viewer. This Proustian spectacle then serves as a metaphor for the heterosexist perspective of closeted homosexuality—the straight person can only ever perceive homosexuality from outside the closet, which evidently limits the ability of the viewer to fully know or understand queer subjectivity. To demonstrate this difference in observing and fully experiencing, Proust's narrator never describes his own closeted experience, for that would remove the distance necessary for the reader to understand that the socially constructed closet is only a description of closeted homosexuality. Proust wanted his readers to recognize that as spectator, his narrator can only ever interpret the closet for us, and not invite us inside.

Schrag does not feel cultural pressure to secretly reside inside a closet, though she presents the closeted space of her subjectivity openly. When she does "come out" as a lesbian it is as much a discovery to herself as it is to others. In her first graphic novel, *Awkward*, she has a boyfriend and describes sexual experiences with boys, but by the time she writes *Definition*, at the age of 15, she speaks freely of her attraction to girls and considers defining herself as bisexual, but inevitably decides she prefers the "straight" label.[37] Although she tries to shelve her interest in women, by page nine of her third graphic novel, *Potential*, she gives up her resistance [Fig. 34]. After a friendly hug with a pretty girl—who later becomes her girlfriend—Ariel remarks: "I do believe that's one of the nicest things I've ever felt... I suppose this pretty much finalizes it. Well it's not like being bi was some prize to hold on to! So with a final fling—reality reared forth. DYKEDOM HERE I COME! No pun intended!"[38] Coming out by way of a performative and direct address in her graphic novel demonstrates that the closet is not only a constructed space that hides a part of one's identity from others, it can also hide one's sexual identity from oneself. Furthermore, she does not create a spectacle for the readers to experience from a mediated distance as Proust does, but rather speaks directly to the reader, walks the reader through her own self-discovery, and therefore invites the reader to share in her coming out.

Ariel performs several similar self-affirming statements over the course of her graphic novels, including her soliloquy on page 152 of *Likewise* when, by herself, she proclaims into

Fig. 34. Reprinted with the permission of Scribner Publishing Group from *Potential* by Ariel Schrag, 9. *Potential* copyright © 2000 Ariel Schrag.

the night air: "Homosexuality definitely exists!" These performed lines appear to be directed inward (to herself) or toward the reader only, but as we read on, some of the events in the now very self-reflexive story depict rather an ongoing quest for subjectivity between the cartoonist Schrag and her self-constructed character, Ariel. In this way, the reader is further invited to share Ariel's experience by entering particularly private spaces in her life and by experiencing performed speech that visually maintains a connection between the body of the character and the words she says. The reader is a witness to the re-enactment by Ariel of Schrag's self-affirmation.

Like Proust's narrator, Ariel returns frequently to her bedroom as a space of solitude, work, sleep and masturbation. In this way, although Proust indeed constructs the spectacle of the closet with explicit reference to gay sex while not allowing his reader access to his narrator's own sexual experiences with Albertine, he does invite the reader to share other layers of his sexual subjectivity. The writing done by Proust and cartooning done by Schrag become their own, closeted spaces of confession, in the same way that diaries are private, for "diarists make secret spaces within a larger social world."[39] Schrag does not deconstruct the closet itself, but rather demonstrates the bedroom and the autobiocomic as closeted spaces that can be shared with or presented to a straight reader. Thanks to the proximity of the sign to the referent and her distinctive visual language, Schrag's comics lie formally in contradistinction to universal and heteronormative discourses on queer identity.

Proust's narrator repeatedly speaks of his room as a setting in which his confusion and general malaise could expand to fit the walls, like an extension of his body: "At Combray ... long before the time when I should have to go to bed and lie there, unsleeping ... my bedroom became the fixed point on which my melancholy and anxious thoughts were centered."[40] This quotation foreshadows the role of his bedroom in subsequent novels when his sexuality and writing feature more prominently. On the cover of *Likewise*, Ariel is shown in her bedroom as well, working at her desk. The space of the bedroom in this graphic novel picks up from where the bed-ridden dream sequences of *Potential* left off and becomes a common setting for her anxieties, sleepless nights, writing and masturbating, as demonstrated on page 259 [Fig. 35]. In this silent page, Ariel is shown first at her desk working on her comics, and then masturbating on her bed shortly thereafter. This room comes to visually represent the book that contains the life story, and that readers are also invited to share with the cartoonist. I equate the bedroom with both the closeted subjectivity of the cartoonist and the manifestation of this closet in book/graphic novel form because of the ways in which the walls/lines/frames are blurred in the narrative between consciousness and corporeality. In Schrag's chronicles, the books themselves become two walls of a four-walled closet/room— the other two walls being comprised of the reader and the cartoonist. Just as the expression "breaking down the fourth wall" in theater studies denotes the inclusion of the audience as characters in the play being performed,[41] so too does the bedroom stage blend the cartoonist's internal and external configurations of self. Indeed, the work comes to embody its creator in its repetitive staging of the private mental and physical space of the bedroom.

Perhaps most intriguing is the trope of masturbation *as self-expression* in both Proust's and Schrag's works. In the introductory pages of *À la Recherche du Temps Perdu*, Proust's narrator first describes masturbating in bed: "Sometimes, too, ... a woman would be born during my sleep from some strain in the position of my thighs. Conceived from the pleasure I was on the point of consummating, she it was, I imagined, who offered me that pleasure...."[42] The narrator would fantasize that it was a woman who caressed the "strain" or the erection between his thighs, and abandon all other thoughts. Masturbation becomes a

Fig. 35. Reprinted with the permission of Scribner Publishing Group from *Likewise* by Ariel Schrag, 259. *Likewise* copyright © 2009 Ariel Schrag.

recurring theme throughout the novels and in *The Captive*, in the third volume of *À la Recherche*, the narrator unites the act of writing with the act of masturbating. He first describes a common element between "two sensations" of the philosopher's art and what he calls his "little manikin": "I know how selfish this little manikin is; I may be suffering from an attack of breathlessness which only the coming of rain would assuage, but he pays no heed, and, at the first drops so impatiently awaited, all his gaiety is forgotten, he sullenly pulls down his hood."[43] He often is powerless to this "manikin," which serves as a metaphor for his penis, and the asthmatic narrator's breathlessness, aggravated by the manikin's "selfish gaiety," is thus an instance and formal presentation of masturbation.

In his book, *Proust in Love*, William C. Carter discusses the link between the narrator's masturbation and that of Proust. In a letter to his friend Bizet, Proust states: "This morning, dearest, when my father saw me ... he begged me to stop masturbating for at least four days."[44] His compulsive masturbation becomes so present in his writing that inversely, his writing *becomes* masturbatory. Like the "breathlessness" the narrator feels, the passage reads breathlessly, impatiently. The sentence builds to a climactic end by starting with a hesitating semicolon, followed by a series of rhythmic commas and finally, a period, after the "little manikin [...] sullenly pulls down his hood." Writing for Schrag, as well as Proust, is self-serving because, like masturbation, at certain times, there is no other person who can satisfy one's desire—whether sexual or subjective—than oneself. Schrag's drawings of Ariel masturbating are formally fluid, with looser contouring lines that allow for more emphasis to be placed on the emotional expression of the character. Compared to the more photorealistic sequences in which she is in a sleeping, dream-state, these wakeful daydreams or sexual fantasies are drawn in a more iconic style that prioritizes movement and gesture over a fixed, mimetic representation. As quoted above, Ariel links love and art when she tells her mother: "Without the art, if you lost the love, which you don't have control over, then you'd really be completely desperate with nothing." Like her art, masturbation allows for a solitary release of either emotional or sexual tension. Furthermore, as a form of self-expression in both Schrag's and Proust's work, the increasing episodes of masturbation with the progression of the narratives parallel the increasing acts and discussions of writing and art-making taking place in the life stories.

This connection between masturbation and life-writing/self-portraiture is most explicit between pages 224–225, on a set of unpaginated pages in *Likewise* [Fig. 36]. Just as Proust's narrator related the two sensations of the philosopher's art and (coded) masturbation, so too does Ariel make visual and explicit the connection between her self-pleasing writing and her masturbation. In this example from *Likewise*, Ariel is shown writing about a past experience with her love interest Sally. Schrag then shows this flashback visually as Ariel leaves her desk to join Sally on the bed. The middle frames on the page denote a shifting back and forth from the present situation of Ariel narrating her flashback from memory, alone in her room, to the bottom left frame that again shows the re-enacted event of Ariel and Sally being intimate on the bed. All the while, present-day Ariel is narrating the scene through typed text: "I'm talking about my favorite fluids—blood, ink, and down there all mingled together preferably." The following frame depicts a story Ariel is telling Sally and shows Ariel at her desk, thereby confusing the story with the reality of the present-day, working Ariel, only she blends the acts of drawing and masturbating:

> I was working on my comic and my rapidograph was leaking, but it was leaking in like these pulses, and I couldn't get it to stop. So I'm just sitting there watching it pulse out and all of a sudden I was stricken with the need to join along in the pulsing, and so I put my hand down my

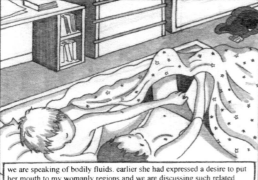

Fig. 36. Reprinted with the permission of Scribner Publishing Group from *Likewise* by Ariel Schrag. *Likewise* copyright © 2009 Ariel Schrag.

pants, my fingers covered in the ink, and I did it with my eyes kept open watching the ink pulse as I masturbated. That's the only time I've come sitting up.[45]

Rather than go to her bed where she is normally shown masturbating, Ariel remains seated at her desk and combines the motions, bodily position, and writing tool (the ink and rapidograph) with bringing herself to orgasm. "Coming" can mean both arriving at a conclusion in creating her comics and climaxing sexually. The boundary between body and body of work is blurred by the pulsating pen, the ink of which flows uncontrollably onto both page and vagina. By blending ink with her bodily fluids, she explicitly gestures toward the indexicality of her comics. The ink now mixes her "down there" into the drawings, making them signs that not only represent her thoughts and memories, but also present her body—they are a sign of her once being there.[46] Ariel's body becomes a metaphor for the comics and vice versa, concretized by the next frame on the following page, in which Sally responds to her thoughts and says: "I want to lick ink out of you."

For both Proust and Schrag, the text becomes masturbatory as it gradually gleans, shapes, and strikingly sculpts the subjectivity of its author/artist into being. By continuously inviting the reader to watch or experience the otherwise solitary act of masturbation, Ariel and the Proustian narrator demonstrate that their sexualities are much like their art: the self is both the means and the end to these acts. Queer sexual identity for Proust and Schrag is not just about having closeted gay sex lives, but also about an engagement with oneself, a self-discovery/knowing over the course of creating either novels or graphic novels. Furthermore, the body is not only *not* separate from consciousness, but the work serves to embody the author/artist in its very re-enacting of masturbation both on the level of the content of the narrative and on the formal level of the text itself as masturbatory. The work, then, performs or plays the same role as its creator, mimicking life events unique to the subject in question; but also, by way of process and form, the act of coming into sexual subjectivity.

Despite the common theme of masturbation in Schrag and Proust, Schrag's cartoon character Ariel does not create the distance between reader and closet that the Proustian narrator does with his elaborative voyeurism of Charlus and Jupien. Rather, Ariel comes out to herself and her readers simultaneously in *Potential* as the narrator shifts roles from representing a queer subjectivity to presenting or acting it out by way of the character Ariel's declaration of "DYKEDOM HERE I COME!" The comic book medium allows for the shift in perspective from Schrag the narrator describing past events from a (temporal) distance, to Ariel the character performing these same events in real time. The visual component of the graphic novel thus sustains the performativity of the main character as an embodiment of the cartoonist. In the case of Schrag, drawing her life story involves a process that both preserves (narrates) and presents (acts) herself.

To conclude, Schrag's graphic novels are in some ways expressive of queer subjectivity in their form alone. The life story embodies its creator in its performative re-enactments and in each stroke of her pen; the hand-drawn lettering, lines and illustrations are extensions of her particular musculature. Schrag's creative process sets her apart from her contemporaries by preserving the initial conception and draft of her life-writing in the final, published volumes because she works over the top of the original. She preserves the unedited drawings of her first drafts in her comics, which reflects the honesty and privacy of the diary genre. The reader then intimately experiences as layered palimpsest all the stages in the work's becoming and Schrag's own coming into being.

Although, as Sedgwick explains, Proust creates a distance between the reader and the homosexual closet of Charlus and Jupien, by way of his spectatorship and interpretation of the gay sexual relationship, there are other ways in which Proust removes this distance. The self-reflexive, metafictional writing and narrator in both Schrag's and Proust's work create a *mise-en-abyme* of self-referentiality. These autobiographical texts then become performative, not only thanks to Ariel's declarative soliloquies, but also because the text that refers to itself erases the line between sign and referent: the body of work becomes a metaphor for the body of the author and indeed, "stands in for" or supersedes the real life being narrated.

In addition to containing a self-preserving process and an embodiment of the author, Schrag's chronicles, like Proust's novel, also perform her singular subjectivity by gradually becoming a masturbatory text. Schrag's pulsating pen makes explicit and visual the overlap in both her sexual desire and her creative endeavors. The references to the connection between the physical act of masturbating and the subjective exploration of selfhood by way of life writing/drawing in these works extend also to the very structures and forms of the narratives. Proust's constructed closet resembles Schrag's graphic novel architecture. Furthermore, his long-winded sentences structurally match his narrator's breathless and masturbatory physical state, while Schrag's drawing style shifts from fixed and constrained to loose and fluid in order to formally parallel her emotional and sensorial feelings. Therefore, Schrag and Proust do not only "represent" themselves in their work, they also demonstrate and manifest their consciousness and corporeality in the very physicality and anatomy of the book objects.

Schrag's presence in her graphic novels is made explicit by her prioritizing of the development of Ariel and her interpretations of the events and people in her life over the narrative *fabula*. The progressive formal development of each graphic novel mimics the character Ariel's eventual growth into the cartoonist Schrag. It is thus not specific enough to call these chronicles a representation of her life—they are both a representation and a performative presentation of a blended present and past self-image.

NOTES

1. Over the course of the essay, I shall refer to the author as Schrag and the narrator/character as Ariel in my descriptions of scenes.

2. Schrag animates her comics by projecting pages onto a large screen and simultaneously acting out the voices of characters and the sounds or music in the background. She uses body language to bring life and movement to her stationary panels. This very physical performance resembles her description of drawing in comparison to writing: "drawing [is] a much more immediate, visual, inclusive thing because somebody can watch you while you do it and sort of experience it while you do it." Interview with Natalie Pendergast, 2011.

3. This event was facilitated by the Koffler Centre of the Arts between the hours of 2 p.m. and 5:30 p.m. at the Gladstone Hotel.

4. Here, I am applying the term "autobioBD" to Anglo-American comics which, I contend, warrants the translation of the abbreviated *Bande Dessinée* from "BD" to "comics." Ann Miller and Murray Pratt first coined "autobioBD" in an article published in Dalhousie University's *Belphegor* in 2001: Ann Miller and Murray Pratt, "Transgressive Bodies in the Work of Julie Doucet, Fabrice Neaud and Jean-Christophe Menu: Towards a Theory of the 'AutobioBD'," *Belphegor* 4, no. 1 (November 2004). http://etc.dal.ca/belphegor/vol4_no1/articles/04_01_Miller_trnsgr_en_cont.html#note2.

5. Schrag's evolving self-characterization constantly disrupts the fixity of gender stereotypes and gay archetypes. In Rob Cover's article entitled "Bodies, Movements and Desires: Lesbian/Gay Subjectivity and the Stereotype," he explores the "mass-circulated, reductive media images of lesbians and gay men," namely stereotypes from which Schrag distances herself, like the "aggressive lesbian," or the "butch and femme lesbians," 83, 82 and 81.

6. Loiterature is a predominant subgenre of both gay literature (though Chambers views it as "anti-Proustian") and the graphic novel. Theresa M. Tensuan considers Lynda Barry's graphic novel *One! Hundred! Demons!* (2002) and Marjane Satrapi's graphic memoir *Persepolis* (2000) works of loiterature, stating that "vignettes ... linger on seemingly inconsequential details," 951.

7. Ross Chambers, "Messing Around: Gayness and Loiterature in Alan Hollinghurst's *The Swimming Pool Library*," in *Textuality and Sexuality: Reading Theories and Practice*, eds. Judith Still and Michael Worton (Manchester: Manchester University Press, 1993) 207. An example of a diarist who succeeded in "loitering" in his writing is Rousseau, whose endless details about what James Olney calls "the trivial, the shameful and the puerile" in his *Confessions* (1782–1789) would have been considered unnecessary were it not for the urgency with which Rousseau insisted upon their importance. Indeed, as Olney notes: "Rousseau ... assumed that his correspondents cared whether he pissed well or badly because Rousseau cared so very deeply himself. The bizarre and incomprehensible thing is that those correspondents did care—or feigned to—about Rousseau's urinary problems, so successful was he in making his concerns the only ones that should matter to anyone," 406.

8. Chambers, 208.

9. Lejeune calls the diary antifiction because since the writer is not relying on memory, but rather recording thoughts and events in the present, it is, as he puts it, "hooked on truth," 201.

10. Philippe Lejeune, "The Diary as Antifiction," 2007, in *On Diary*, eds. Jeremy D. Popkin and Julie Rak, trans. Katherine Durnin (Manoa: University of Hawaii Press, 2009) 201–202.

11. Irene Gammel, "Mirror Looks: The Visual and Performative Diaries of L.M. Montgomery, Baroness Elsa von Freytag-Loringhoven, and Elvira Bach," in *Interfaces: Women/Autobiography/Image/Performance*, eds. Sidonie Smith and Julie Watson (Ann Arbor: University of Michigan Press, 2002) 290.

12. Lynda Hart, "Introduction I, " *Acting Out: Feminist Performances* (Ann Arbor: University of Michigan Press, 1993) 5.

13. Derived from the Italian *carico* or *caricare*, the etymological roots of the word "caricature" literally mean "to load" or "to exaggerate" and denote an added value or meaning onto what would have been a photorealistic image of an object, person or scene (*Caricature* 5). They are expressive because they exaggerate physical features to emphasize and materialize the personality of the subject.

14. Charles Sanders Peirce, *Peirce on Signs: Writings on Semiotic*, ed. James Hoopes (Chapel Hill: University of North Carolina Press) 239. This definition differs from Scott McCloud's use of the word "icon," which collapses the categories of symbolic and indexical signs into sub-categories of the icon, 24–31.

15. Schrag's style resembles that of her influences Walt Disney and Bill Watterson (*Calvin and Hobbes*, 1985–1995), and she purposely tried to mix a child-like quality of drawing with heavier, controversial autobiographical stories, like the ones she had read in the mini-comics of a later influence, Ariel Bordeaux (*Deep Girl*, 1995), in order to create irony. Interview with Natalie Pendergast, 2011.

16. Peirce, 240.

17. In his 2009 article, "Movements Within Movements: Following the Line in Animation and Comics," Atkinson analyzes Paul Karasik and David Mazzucchelli's adaptation of Paul Auster's 2004 novel *City of Glass*. In it, the outline of a drawn object or person is sometimes colored over by the fill of the outline, just as expressive lines in manga often spread past the boundaries of the frame to emphasize emotion or action. On page three of *City of Glass*, the cartoonists use shading to depict a fire, but "the drawn lines barely describe the outline of a building and the shading exceeds even this flimsy boundary," 272. In this way, the image contains not only the representations of a fire and a building, but also the motion of the fire, which therefore releases the image from the fixed hold of representation and demonstrates the manifestation of the artist's hand in the gestures of objects/characters on the page. See Atkinson 274.

18. Peirce, 239.

19. Edward Hill, *The Language of Drawing* (Englewood Cliffs, NJ: Prentice-Hall, 1966) 7.

20. Schrag explained this process to me during a casual conversation at the Gladstone Hotel, Toronto, on the evening of March 27, 2011.

21. Bryan Lee O'Malley, *Scott Pilgrim Vs. the Universe*, Vol. 5. (Portland: Oni Press, 2009) 180–184.

22. Chester Brown spoke on a panel with cartoonists Seth, Adrian Tomine, and Chris Ware at the Toronto Reference Library on May 6, 2011, as part of the Toronto Comic Arts Festival.

23. This likeness between the graphic novel form and the content of the character development is evident also by way of the increasingly slower pace, darker tone, and move into subgenres such as tragicomedy and metafiction. The last two graphic novels in the series, *Potential* and especially *Likewise*, embody Ariel's growing anxiety and cynicism created by the experiences presented in the earlier comics.

24. Scott McCloud, *Understanding Comics: The Invisible Art* (New York: HarperPerennial, 1993) 41.

25. Ariel Schrag, *Potential* (New York: Simon & Schuster, 2008) 113–116.

26. Schrag, *Potential*, 138–140.

27. Hillary L. Chute, *Graphic Women. Life Narrative & Contemporary Comics* (New York: Columbia University Press, 2010) 200.

28. Shannon Gerard, *Women in Comics*, dir. Nicole Bazuin and Heather White, web video: http://vimeo.com/22171768. Accessed April 9, 2011.

29. Interview with Natalie Pendergast. Recording. April 25, 2011.

30. Interview with Natalie Pendergast.

31. Charles Hatfield, "'I made that whole thing up!' The Problem of Authenticity in Autobiographical Comics," in *Alternative Comics: An Emerging Literature* (Jackson: University Press of Mississippi, 2005) 115.

32. Interview with Natalie Pendergast.
33. See Ariel Schrag, *Likewise* (New York: Simon & Schuster, 2009) 39–42, 76–77, 95, 111–112, 154.
34. Schrag, *Likewise*, 217.
35. Schrag, *Likewise*, 270.
36. Eve Kosofsky Sedgwick, *Epistemology of the Closet*, 1990 (Berkeley: University of California Press, 2008) 231.
37. Ariel Schrag, *Awkward* (New York: Simon & Schuster, 2008) 1, 3.
38. Ariel Schrag, *Potential*, 9. Schrag notably switches verb tenses from present to past depending on whether Ariel is narrating or talking in speech balloon. The two modes of storytelling blend the present with the past to create a re-enactment of coming out.
39. Julie Rak, "Dialogue with the Future: Philippe Lejeune's Method and Theory of Diary," in *On Diary*, eds. Jeremy D. Popkin and Julie Rak (Manoa: University of Hawaii Press, 2009) 18.
40. Marcel Proust, *Swann's Way. À la Recherche du Temps Perdu*. 1913–1927, *Remembrance of Things Past*, vols. 1–3, trans. C.K. Scott Moncrieff and Terence Kilmartin (New York: Random House, 1981).
41. Bertolt Brecht considers the breaking down of the "fourth wall" to be unusual in Western theater and thus alienating to the audience when it does happen. But in Chinese theater, "the [actor] never acts as if there were a fourth wall besides the three surrounding him. He expresses his awareness of being watched," 91–92. Furthermore, he self-reflexively acknowledges that there is a performance/a staging taking place, thereby breaking the illusionism of a fourth wall that an unseen audience can see through (voyeuristically).
42. Proust, *Swann's Way*, 4.
43. Proust, *The Captive. À la Recherche du Temps Perdu*, 4.
44. William C. Carter, *Proust in Love* (New Haven: Yale University Press, 2006, 4.
45. Schrag, *Likewise*, 220.
46. Joshua W. Cotter also uses the ink as authorial blood metaphor in his autobiocomic, *Skyscrapers of the Midwest* (2008). Pages 135–136 show his alter ego's yearbook spread with black ink blotches obscuring some classmate names. Only later, on page 138, does he reveal that the blotches are bloodstains from his nosebleed.

BIBLIOGRAPHY

ArtSync. *Women in Comics*. Dir. Nicole Bazuin and Heather White. Web video. April 9, 2011. http://vimeo.com/22171768.
Brecht, Bertolt. *Brecht on Theatre: The Development of an Aesthetic*. Ed. and trans. John Willett. New York: Hill and Wang, 1992.
Caricature and Its Role in Graphic Satire. Dir. Daniel Robbins. Providence: Museum of Art Rhode Island School of Design, 1971.
Carter, William C. *Proust in Love*. New Haven: Yale University Press, 2006.
Chambers, Ross. "Messing Around: Gayness and Loiterature in Alan Hollinghurst's *The Swimming Pool Library*." *Textuality and Sexuality: Reading theories and practice*. Eds. Judith Still and Michael Worton. Manchester: Manchester University Press, 1993.
Chute, Hillary L. *Graphic Women. Life Narrative & Contemporary Comics*. New York: Columbia University Press, 2010.
Cotter, Joshua W. *Skyscrapers of the Midwest*. Richmond, VA: Adhouse Books, 2008.
Cover, Rob. "Bodies, Movements and Desires: Lesbian/Gay Subjectivity and the Stereotype." *Continuum: Journal of Media & Cultural Studies* 18, no. 1 (March 2004): 91–97.
Gammel, Irene. "Mirror Looks: The Visual and Performative Diaries of L.M. Montgomery, Baroness Elsa von Freytag-Loringhoven, and Elvira Bach." *Interfaces: Women/Autobiography/Image/Performance*. Eds. Sidonie Smith and Julie Watson. Ann Arbor: University of Michigan Press, 2002. 289–313.
Hart, Lynda. "Introduction I." *Acting Out: Feminist Performances*. Ann Arbor: University of Michigan Press, 1993. 1–12.
Hatfield, Charles. "'I made that whole thing up!' The Problem of Authenticity in Autobiographical Comics." *Alternative Comics: An Emerging Literature*. Jackson: University Press of Mississippi, 2005. 108–127.
Hill, Edward. *The Language of Drawing*. Englewood Cliffs, NJ: Prentice-Hall, 1966.
Jonnes, Dennis. *The Matrix of Narrative: Family Systems and the Semiotics of Story*. Berlin: Mouton de Gruyter, 1990.
Kilmartin, Terence. "Note on the Translation." *Remembrance of Things Past*, vol. 1. New York: Vintage, 1981.
Lejeune, Philippe. "The Diary as Antifiction." 2007. *On Diary*. Eds. Jeremy D. Popkin and Julie Rak. Trans. Katherine Durnin. Manoa: University of Hawaii Press, 2009. 201–210.
Marion, Philippe. *Traces en Cases: Travail graphique, figuration narrative et participation du lecteur*. Louvain-la-Neuve: Academia, 1993.

Mavor, Carol. *Reading Boyishly: Roland Barthes, J.M. Barrie, Jacques Henri Lartigue, Marcel Proust, and D.W. Winnicott*. Durham: Duke University Press, 2007.

McCloud, Scott. *Understanding Comics: The Invisible Art*. New York: HarperPerennial, 1993.

Miller, Ann, and Murray Pratt. "Transgressive Bodies in the work of Julie Doucet, Fabrice Neaud and Jean-Christophe Menu: Towards a Theory of the 'AutobioBD'." *Belphegor* 4, no. 1 (November 2004). http://etc.dal.ca/belphegor/vol4_no1/articles/04_01_Miller_trnsgr_en_cont.html#note2.

Olney, James. *Memory and Narrative: The Weave of Life-Writing*. Chicago: University of Chicago Press, 1998.

O'Malley, Bryan Lee. *Scott Pilgrim Vs. The Universe*. Scott Pilgrim Vol. 5. Portland: Oni Press, 2009.

Oxford English Dictionary. Second edition, 1989; online version, March 2011. http://www.oed.com.myaccess.library.utoronto.ca/Entry/27973. Accessed May 30, 2011. Earlier version first published in *New English Dictionary*, 1888.

Peirce, Charles Sanders. *Peirce on Signs: Writings on Semiotic*. Ed. James Hoopes. Chapel Hill: University of North Carolina Press, 1991.

Phelan, Peggy. "Reciting the Citation of Others; or, A Second Introduction." *Acting Out: Feminist Performances*. Ann Arbor: University of Michigan Press, 1993. 13–34.

Proust, Marcel. *À la Recherche du Temps Perdu*. 1913–1927. *Remembrance of Things Past*, vols. 1–3. Trans. C.K. Scott Moncrieff and Terence Kilmartin. New York: Random House, 1981.

Rak, Julie. "Dialogue with the Future: Philippe Lejeune's Method and Theory of Diary." Philippe Lejune. *On Diary*. Eds. Jeremy D. Popkin and Julie Rak. Manoa: University of Hawaii Press, 2009.

Schrag, Ariel. *Awkward and Definition: The High School Comic Chronicles of Ariel Schrag*. New York: Simon & Schuster, 2008.

_____. "Creating Comics Step-By-Step with Ariel Schrag." Koffler Centre of the Arts, The Gladstone Hotel, Toronto. March 27, 2011.

_____. Interview with Natalie Pendergast. Recording. April 25, 2011.

_____. *Likewise: The High School Comic Chronicles of Ariel Schrag*. New York: Simon & Schuster, 2009.

_____. *Potential: The High School Comic Chronicles of Ariel Schrag*. New York: Simon & Schuster, 2008.

Sedgwick, Eve Kosofsky. *Epistemology of the Closet*. Berkeley: University of California Press, 2008.

Sewell, Edward H., Jr. "Queer Characters in Comic Strips." *Comics & Ideology*. Eds. Matthew P. McAllister, Edward H. Sewell, Jr., and Ian Gordon. New York: Peter Lang, 2001. 251–274.

Tensuan, Theresa M. "Comic Visions and Revisions in the Work of Lynda Barry and Marjane Satrapi." *MFS Modern Fiction Studies* 52.4 (Winter 2006): 947–964.

The Turd That Won't Flush

The Comedy of Jewish Self-Hatred in the Work of Corinne Pearlman, Aline Kominsky-Crumb, Miss Lasko-Gross and Ariel Schrag

DAVID BRAUNER

"Hey, I may loathe myself, but it has nothing to do with the fact that I'm Jewish."—Larry David[1]

"There's nothing I'm ashamed of."—Miss Lasko-Gross[2]

Surveying the pieces of comic art that comprise the "Graphic Details: Confessional Comics by Jewish Women" exhibition, what immediately struck me (apart from the rich diversity of the material) was that two of the artists had chosen to contribute strips revolving around recalcitrant stools. Ariel Schrag's story, simply titled "Shit" (2003) [Figs. 100–101], deals with a brief but intense friendship that the author's autobiographical self has with a schoolmate. On the opening page, Schrag depicts the burgeoning relationship between Ariel[3] and Samantha, "the new girl" who quickly becomes her "best friend," representing a redemption of sorts for Ariel, who had "recently been ostracized from the rest of the class" by her previous best friend, Norica.[4] The new friendship is formally recognized by Samantha's invitation to Ariel to accompany her on a family trip on their houseboat, which they subsequently moor next to a large house owned by friends of the family. Text-rich, in the small, neat hand that characterizes Schrag's work, it is nonetheless primarily through imagery that the artist emphasizes the intimacy between the two girls on this first page of the story. The pair are repeatedly shown in symmetrical arrangements: facing each other, seated on the branch of a tree; side by side on Samantha's houseboat; sitting opposite each other in the houseboat, talking and playing cards; sitting together watching television in their shared bedroom; making a "best friends" pact, sealed by a meeting of hands, in the wood. The central panel seems to be another example of the girls' synchronicity, as they are depicted with their heads at identical angles, looking at the toilet on the boat. However, the symmetry obtained elsewhere is disrupted here by the fact that only Samantha is given a speech bubble, in which she informs Ariel that she "can piss in there, but if you need to shit, do it in the big house." It is this ostensibly innocuous, incidental moment that precipitates the crisis of the story. In the final panel of the first page, we see Ariel, seated at a large dining table, face partly obscured, grimacing, thinking "need to go," while in the top half of the panel the explanatory text amplifies her predicament, clarifying that "the pressure in my colon began to build" during the course of dinner but that "I *could* not do it, everyone would know."

On the first panel of the second page the girls are back on the house boat, Ariel now "starting to sweat profusely" and sitting in "a cramped, bent position" but still finding the prospect of confessing to Samantha that she needs to go back to the house to defecate "embarrassing beyond belief." The next panel demonstrates visually the scenario that Ariel fears: it depicts Ariel running into the house, explaining to its owners that "I'm just coming into your house at this late hour for no other purpose than to go shit on your toilet thanks!" but the next panel makes it clear that she has rejected this option in favor of going to the house boat, ostensibly to pee. Returning hurriedly, before she is able to ascertain whether or not her stool has been flushed away, the first tensions between the girls appear, as Samantha asks Ariel "did you shit?" and Ariel denies having done so, the text below disclosing that Samantha "seemed suddenly mean and bossy" and that this "scared" Ariel. Later Samantha herself goes to the house "to take a shit" and Ariel rushes back to the houseboat toilet, where she is dismayed to see that the evidence of her earlier visit remains. She tries flushing again to no avail, then tries shoving it down the hole manually but is forced to abort her efforts when she hears Samantha return. For the rest of the evening, Schrag tells us: "All I could think about was the shit." The thought of her shit being discovered by Samantha or her parents "was death" [Fig. 100], but she is at a loss as to how she can "make my shit disappear." Finally, she goes back to the bathroom, removes the shit from the toilet, wrapping it in layers of toilet paper, and puts it in her backpack, which she wears throughout the following day since "the risk of leaving it unattended was too great." On returning home, she "rid[s] [her]self of the evidence forever," flushing it down her family toilet [Fig. 101]. The last two panels of the story tell us that two weeks after the boat trip, "Samantha dumped me for Norica" but that, by this time, Ariel was looking forward to graduating and "was ready for anything."

This short graphic narrative bears close resemblance to one of the submissions of Schrag's contemporary, Miss Laski-Gross. Entitled "The Turd" (2009) [Figs. 37–38], this strip relates an incident in which Melissa (Lasko-Gross's autobiographical self) and her friend Terry visit a local coffee shop, which they are dismayed to discover has been taken over by Starbucks. Having lamented the growing market dominance of large corporations, the girls sit down to drink their coffees and chat. Melissa asks Terry if she wants a bagel and then Terry exclaims "Oooh Yoy!," to which Melissa replies "Der Yoy!": the phrases are both asterisked and glossed in a window at the bottom of the respective panels, as "check out the hottie" and "you're *so* right, he's totally fine."[5] The turd makes its belated appearance in the final section of the story, which is introduced with a vertical window at the top of the third page of the strip with the words: "3 hours later." The second panel on this sixth page depicts Melissa grimacing and clutching her stomach (which emits a cartoon "gurgle"), thinking to herself "I think I had like 5 coffees too many." We then see her sitting on the toilet and trying repeatedly to flush away her stool, before finally wrapping toilet paper around her hand, gingerly lifting her feces from the water-bowl and depositing it in the rubbish bin, all the while averting her gaze [Figs. 37–38].[6] Lasko-Gross tends to use text much more sparingly than Schrag, but the previous sequence of nine panels is particularly striking in that it features no writing at all except the single word "c'mon" and some sound effects. Only after Melissa has disposed of the turd, in the first panel of the final page, is there a thought bubble ("What have I done?") and, just visible over her head, amid the scratched graffiti of the toilet wall, the words "new low." The next panel, again textless, shows Melissa gazing down sadly at her hand, with curved lines above the waste bin signifying the smell of her excrement. In the final panels, she exits the toilet with affected nonchalance, grabs Terry and runs out of the cafe. A mystified Terry asks "What? Did you steal something?" but Melissa just says "It's nothing. Just run."

On the face of it, Schrag's and Lasko-Gross's stories are about the feelings of self-consciousness, awkwardness, embarrassment and shame that teenagers (arguably female teenagers in particular) often associate with their bodies and its functions. Yet the intensity of the feelings aroused in the autobiographical surrogates of Schrag and Lasko-Gross seems at times to lack an objective correlative: unpleasant and malodorous though ordure may be, the extremity of their responses seems disproportionate. To put it another way: there is a peculiar intensity about these pieces that imbues them with something of the power of parables. It follows, then, that shit in these stories is not simply shit but rather functions as a metaphor. But for what, precisely? To address this question, it is helpful to explore the contexts of these pieces: the immediate context of the "Graphic Details" exhibition, the forum in which they were first published, the social milieu in which the stories take place, and their relationship to the larger tradition of confessional female Jewish comics.

To begin with the obvious, most of the contributors to the "Graphic Details: Confessional Comics by Jewish Women" exhibition chose, reasonably enough, to submit pieces that engaged with Jewish identity, in one way or another. Schrag and Lasko-Gross were no exceptions. Of the three other pieces that Schrag contributed, one advertises her lesbian sexuality ("Dyke March"[2005] [Fig. 6]), another was originally published in an anthology of lesbian comics authors (*Juicy Mother*) and one, entitled "The Chosen" (2008) [Fig. 102] and originally published in an alternative Jewish cultural magazine (now website), *Heeb: The New Jew Review*, deals with her ambivalent sense of her own Jewishness. "The Chosen" represents something of a departure for Schrag, as her *High School Comic Chronicles of Ariel Schrag* series—*Awkward* (1995), *Definition* (1996), *Potential* (2000) and *Likewise* (2009)—foregrounds her sexuality but rarely mentions her ethnicity. The probable reasons for this are the subject of "The Chosen." Ariel and her sister are looking for an apartment to rent, when they are asked by a Hasidic real estate broker whether they are Jewish: Ariel's sister explains that "our dad is Jewish and our mom isn't, but we celebrate Hanukkah and Passover, so—," trailing off as her interlocutor turns his back on the sisters, muttering "Not Jewish" to himself.[7] Years later, when Ariel decides to move out, this situation is reprised when a Hasidic broker asks Ariel if she is Jewish, but this time Ariel answers in the affirmative as she "wanted him to like me." However, when her friend Mandy visits, she tells Ariel that "you're not even really Jewish." Ariel protests half-heartedly "but ... yes ... I am...," but Schrag's insertion into the panel of a box with the words "Real Jew" and an arrow pointing toward Mandy undermines Ariel's Jewish credentials. Moreover, when Mandy notices Ariel's toothbrush, decorated with a series of Stars of David down the length of its handle, Ariel decides that "the toothbrush's absurdity seemed proof that I WASN'T REALLY JEWISH."

Lasko-Gross's other contributions to the exhibition consist of two brief excerpts from her first book, *Escape from "Special"* (2006), one of which shows Melissa responding to taunts about her name ("Hey Gross! You're gross") with the realization that she can "use words to manipulate other kids," while the other, entitled "The Gruswerk's Sabbath"(2002) [Figs. 73–75], recounts an episode in which Melissa attends a Sabbath meal at the house of a friend.[8] During the meal, Melissa parodies the Hebrew litany (rendered in untranslated Hebrew characters), thinks "This is *so* boring" and entertains Vera, her friend, by playing about with

Fig. 37. Miss Lasko-Gross, "The Turd," *A Mess of Everything*, 2009, ink on paper, 76.

Fig. 38. Miss Lasko-Gross, "The Turd," *A Mess of Everything*, 2009, ink on paper, 77.

a *yarmulke* [skullcap].[9] The father of the family rebukes her twice ("If you cannot speak it correctly, say nothing" [Fig. 74]; "Sit quietly, or leave the table" [Fig. 75]) and the final panel shows Melissa sitting glumly, thinking: "I'm glad my family isn't Orthodox and has a sense of humor" [Fig. 75].[10]

In the context of *Escape from "Special,"* "The Gruswerk's Sabbath" is just one of a number of episodes in which Melissa displays a vehement hostility toward Judaism. The first of these occurs when Melissa protests at being made to go to temple with the rest of her family: she ends up vomiting in the car park, at which point her mother says that she can stay in the car and wait until the service is over. The final panel of this episode shows a smiling Melissa, eyes shut, reclining in the driver's seat, one foot resting on the steering wheel, happily listening to music on the car stereo.[11] Later, in an episode entitled "Of Little Faith: Jew School," Lasko-Gross shows Melissa, in the full-page opening panel, sitting in a classroom, fists clenched, thinking to herself "This is total horse shit!' ... how DARE they tell us how to think!," while her Jewish education teacher talks about moral decisions.[12] On the next page, Melissa brandishes the Jewish Studies textbook she has been given and screams "This means nothing to me! NOTHING!"[13] In this panel, Lasko-Gross draws Melissa with her teeth bared, specks of saliva being spat out of her open mouth and a series of dark lines apparently emanating from her body, all indicating her fury.

On the one hand, Melissa's resistance to Jewish tradition and dogma can be seen as part of a larger rebellious refusal to conform to social conventions. She herself certainly rationalizes it in this way, claiming to be "too old and too smart to fall for any of it [religion]"[14] and complaining that worshipping the god of your ancestors is "so fucking automatic and primitive and unspiritual."[15] Melissa repeatedly constructs herself as a misfit, someone who stands "outside of some mass cult of social agreement"[16] and who is "missing something that makes people feel the right way about certain things."[17] This alienation also manifests itself visually, for example when Lasko-Gross draws Melissa's arrival at a new school, representing her classmates all wearing cheerful clothes with corporate logos, while Melissa sports a dull T-shirt with a skull on it.[18]

What is particularly striking, however, about her hostility toward Judaism is its visceral nature: it is one thing to create mischief during a tedious family dinner ("The Gruswerk's Sabbath"), quite another to work yourself into such a frenzy that you actually vomit ("Psychosomatic Refusal"), or become so agitated that you are literally spitting with rage ("Of Little Faith: Jew School"). Moreover, the language that Lasko-Gross uses in this last episode suggests that Melissa's resentment of what her mother calls her "heritage"[19] is not purely a matter of intellectual principle: Melissa's repeated use of the word "they" when referring to her Jewish teacher ("How DARE they tell us how to live!"; "How *dare* they give us homework!") and, in particular, her use of the word "Jew" adjectivally (instead of the grammatically correct "Jewish") seems to implicate her in the long history of anti–Semitic discourse. That Melissa wishes to reject not just Judaism but Jewish ethnicity is suggested by a conversation that she has with a child therapist, in which it emerges that Melissa has told the kids at her new school that her name is Roas because "I don't want people to know my identity."[20] When the therapist asks her what her "identity" is, she answers his question with a question: "Is that a trick question?"[21] Although it remains unclear what Melissa means by "identity," in the light of the other episodes I have been discussing, it seems likely that it is her distinctively Jewish surname that Melissa wishes to conceal, hence her adoption of a Hispanic-sounding alternative. It is perhaps relevant in this context that the episode in which Melissa is teased about her surname ends with her witnessing the class bully turning his attentions toward another classmate with a Jewish name ("Mehndik likes men dick!"); but rather than coming to his aid, Melissa simply observes his humiliation, thinking "sucker."[22]

There are fewer references to Melissa's Jewishness in *A Mess of Everything* (2009) (the sequel to *Escape from "Special"*), but most of them are clustered in and around "The Turd" episode. In fact, the first mention of it is made in the "the cross," which immediately precedes "The Turd," in which Melissa, sporting a crucifix that she had bought on a school French trip to Quebec earlier in the book, is confronted by two of her classmates, who tell her that "it's disrespectful for you to wear that as a Jew."[23] Melissa informs them that "Jesus was a Jew" but the girls dismiss this, one of them boldly contradicting her ("No he *wasn't*") while the other sneers ("Don't be so stupid").[24] The episode ends with a panel in which Melissa is shown walking home alone, a thought-bubble with the single word "ha?" floating above her.[25] Whether her classmates are offended by Melissa's appropriation of a Christian symbol or by her implied apostasy is unclear. Either way, the issues raised by this incident are implicitly explored further in "The Turd." Ostensibly, Melissa's invocation of bagels and her use of a private Yiddish-inflected language with Terry (which, unlike the Hebrew in "The Gruswerk's Sabbath," she translates) seem to suggest that she is comfortable with her Jewish ethnicity. However, her near-hysterical reaction to the turd that won't flush hints at anxieties about her Jewishness that uncannily echo those in the corresponding episode in Schrag's "Shit." This is particularly evident on a page that was cut from the version of "The Turd" that appears in the "Graphic Details" exhibition, in which Melissa's unsuccessful attempts to flush her stool lead initially to mounting panic ("I can't just leave it here"/"Everyone will know it was mine"), then a brief acknowledgement that her anxiety may be excessive, which is itself then overwhelmed by renewed dismay (represented by a thought-bubble in which Melissa reflects, "Maybe I'm over-react" before the thought is interrupted with an emphatic "NO!" that displaces the "ing" that would have completed the word) [Fig. 37].[26] Although Melissa attaches her anxiety to the specific fear that Henri, her current object of desire, may be "out there" and that "one of his friends [might] ... tell him,"[27] it is clear that this is an *ex post facto* rationalization, since she has already decided that she "can't just leave it there" and that "everyone will know it was mine."

On one level, Melissa's and Ariel's anxieties about their bodily waste are clearly expressions of insecurity about their adolescent sexuality: they feel that they will not be attractive to Henri and Samantha if their bodies are contaminated by an association with shit. However, the specific diction of these incidents may also signify a fear connected with their ethnicity. Like Ariel in "Shit," who determines to "rid [her]self of the evidence," Melissa's experience is couched in terms more usually encountered in the context of illegal activities ("What have I done?" Melissa asks herself, while her friend, Terry, assumes that she has stolen something as they flee the scene of the crime). Could it be that, on a subconscious level, the crime for which both Ariel and Melissa fear being indicted is the crime of being Jewish? Certainly, in both cases, their paranoid fear of discovery seems to be exacerbated by their sense of themselves as social outcasts. In the opening panels of *A Mess of Everything* Melissa observes life in her home town, commenting, "This is probably one of the best places to live in the history of mankind"[28] before asserting, with perfect comic timing, that "I hate it here."[29] Her ennui and frustration is represented not just verbally, but visually, in the image of her face pressed up to the window-pane of a sandwich bar, mouth open, eyes shut, as if drowning, receiving a hostile look from one of the diners inside.[30] Although her sense of difference is never explicitly linked to her Jewishness, this image is inverted at the end of the book. When she arrives in New York (the quintessentially "Jewish" city and a place that Melissa loves because "no

one is startled by 'strange'"),[31] a boy presses his face to the other side of the windowpane of
Melissa's incoming train carriage,[32] reciprocating her gesture, which reinforces the sense that
it is Melissa's ethnicity that underlies her sense of herself as "a self-effacing non-conformist,"
as the blurb at the back of the book puts it (n.p.).

Similarly, one of the sub-texts of Schrag's "Shit" seems to concern social class and, by
extension, ethnicity. "Shit" is bookended with images of Ariel's exclusion from her peer
group: in the second panel of the story, a group of her former friends are gathered in a huddle
in the foreground, agreeing that she is crazy, while Ariel herself is visible in the background,
standing alone; in the final panel, the image is reversed, with Ariel sitting alone in the foreground with her classmates assembled in a semi-circle in the background. Ostensibly, Ariel's
ostracization has more to do with her sexuality than her ethnicity (Norica tells her classmates
that Ariel has been rifling through the other girls' underwear drawers), but the two are often
intimately linked. Certainly, there is a strong suggestion that Samantha's family and their
friends are affluent, country-club Gentiles (Curtis, Samantha's surname, is a quintessentially
WASP name)[33] and that Ariel feels ill at ease in their presence because of her Jewishness (as
Jackie Mason liked to say: "There's no bigger schmuck than a Jew with a boat"). As "The
Chosen" makes clear, Ariel's self-identification as a Jew is not straightforward. Although she
tells the Hasidic broker that she is Jewish, and observes some of the Jewish holidays, the
implication of her friend Mandy being labeled a "real Jew" is that Ariel is not one (the point
being that as Judaism is a matrilineal religion, and Ariel's mother is not Jewish, Ariel cannot
be Jewish according to Orthodox doctrine). On the other hand, in the very act of labeling
Mandy "a real Jew" Ariel paradoxically testifies to her own status as a Jew in the sense that
arguably only a Jew would be able to make the distinction that Ariel is making here between
different kinds of Jewishness. At any rate, it is quite possible to feel inauthentically, tenuously
Jewish in the presence of other (more religious or biologically unequivocal) Jews, and conspicuously and irrevocably Jewish in the presence of non–Jews. Ariel's conviction that "everyone would know" if she uses the toilet in the Curtis's friends house and that it would be
"death" if the Curtis family discover that she has defecated in their houseboat toilet, like
Melissa's belief that "everyone will know" unless she finds a way of disposing of the turd, certainly seems to invoke the history of anti–Semitism, with the concomitant imperative for
Jews to hide their real identities.

This analogy is reinforced by the fact that one of the staples of anti–Semitic discourse,
from the medieval period through to the early 20th century, was the belief that Jews could
be identified through their characteristic (unpleasant) odor—which became known by the
pseudo-scientific term *"foetor judaicus."* Furthermore, as Sharon Achinstein points out, this
traditional belief extended to "mak[ing] a strong correlation between Jew and excrement"
as in "the German folktale in which a Jewish mother tries to bring her converted daughter
back to Judaism by undoing the baptism—'washing off' the holy water by a three-fold immer-
sion in human excrement."[34]

I should make it clear at this point that I am not accusing Lasko-Gross and Schrag of
anti–Semitism or indeed of unwittingly implicating themselves in anti–Semitic discourse.
Rather, I am suggesting that their work is part of a Jewish tradition of self-conscious, confessional work in which self-hatred is exploited for comic purposes and that "Shit" and "The
Turd" take on additional resonance when read in the context of that tradition. In this respect,
it is vital to make a distinction between the author and her autobiographical self. As the
Canadian-Jewish comics author Miriam Libicki puts it:

When comics take on semi-autobiography, they are both more and less revealing than fictionalized autobiography. More, because not only are you recording your most shameful moments, the moments themselves are made graphic, over the page, where any kids in a comic shop can flip right to them. But the stylized drawings of comic books are also an extra membrane of mediation between the creator and the reader's experience of her.[35]

In the work of Schrag and Lasko-Gross it is not just their stylized drawings of themselves however, but the texts and contexts that accompany them that complicate the relationship between author and reader, and also between author and protagonist. The Ariel of Schrag's comics and the Melissa of Lasko-Gross's are no more identical to their authors than the fictional protagonists of several of Philip Roth's novels who share his name are identical to Philip Roth the author.[36] They may share many characteristics with their creators but they are ultimately fictional constructs—a means for their authors to implicate themselves in their fiction while at the same time maintaining an ironic distance between themselves and their comics surrogates. Crucially, "Shit" and "The Turd" are funny because of the incongruity between the desperate seriousness with which Ariel and Melissa try, literally, to grapple with their shit, and the sense of absurdity with which Schrag and Lasko-Gross imbue their representations of their predicaments. It is because of this ironic distance that Schrag and Lasko-Gross are not complicit with their heroines' self-hatred but are able to present it (self-) satirically.[37] This is not to suggest, either, that the feelings expressed by Ariel and Melissa about themselves are irredeemable. On the contrary, as sociologist Keith Kahn-Harris has suggested, the term self-hatred is more complex than has often been acknowledged, and may be "worth reclaiming."[38] In the context of this essay, at any rate, I am using the term Jewish self-hatred primarily to indicate not an unthinking, internalized anti–Semitism but rather a process of satirical self-interrogation and self-criticism that is paradoxically most Jewish when it is most adversarial toward Jewishness. In the remainder of this essay, I will explore further this tradition of Jewish female-authored self-satirical confessional comics by looking at the work of Aline Kominsky-Crumb and Corinne Pearlman, who, I argue, respectively, created and extended a visual and verbal language in which to express the comedy of Jewish self-hatred.

As well as alluding to the "*foetor judaicus*," the toilet scenes in "Shit" and "The Turd" may also be read as homages to Aline Kominsky-Crumb, whose famous cover for the first issue of *Twisted Sisters* in 1976 (an underground comics series founded by Kominsky-Crumb and her fellow Jewish-American confessional artist, Diane Noomin), featuring her comics self sitting on the toilet, thinking: "What if someone comes while I'm making??" while a "grunt!!" noise issues from her rear, inaugurated a new era of taboo-breaking self-revelation in female-authored comic[39] [Fig. 69]. Marrying a confrontational, deliberately rough-and-ready, aesthetically unappealing drawing style with subject matter that Hillary Chute calls "the complex terrain of lived sexuality that includes both disgust and titillation,"[40] Kominsky-Crumb created an alter ego, The Bunch, whose name, with its objectifying definite article, she felt encompassed the qualities of the character herself: "strong, obnoxious, repulsive, offensive."[41] Kominsky-Crumb has described her work as exhibiting "a certain kind of Jewish fatalistic humor ... anecdotal, self-deprecating,"[42] but Harvey Pekar may be closer to the mark when he writes, in the introduction to Kominsky-Crumb's *Love That Bunch* (1990)— a collection of semi-autobiographical episodes featuring The Bunch—that "her work is full of self-loathing."[43] Pekar goes on to explain that the "Long Island Jewish community in which she grew up was and is full of people capable of turning a sensitive young person's stomach," before defending himself against potential accusations of anti–Semitism by pointing out that "I'm not anti–Jewish; in fact, I'm Jewish myself."[44]

Pekar's strategy here—making deliberately provocative comments that court accusations of anti–Semitism—before anticipating such charges and defending himself against them by identifying himself as Jewish, is echoed in an episode entitled "Grief on Long Island" in *Love That Bunch* itself. Accompanying her grandmother on a long walk "thru the old hometown of Hebrewhurst," The Bunch is derided for her dress sense by a group of three "snobby teenage Jewesses"; in the following panel she is depicted with two boxes of text pointing at her, the first saying "The Bunch has no tolerance for these Jewish shit-brats!" and the second "She usta be one herself!"[45] Here the revelation that she was once also a "snobby teenage Jewess" both bestows on her a certain immunity to the charge of anti–Semitism (being an insider arguably entitles her to invoke the Jewish American Princess stereotype for comic effect in the same way as African-American comedians use the word "nigger"), and at the same time further implicates her in the charge of self-hatred (since her intolerance for "Jewish shit-brats" implicitly extends to her younger self). In fact, it becomes clear later in the book that Kominsky-Crumb continues to identify her surrogate self with this stereotype, when she depicts a domestic disagreement between The Bunch and her husband, Robert, in which she places a box with an arrow pointing to Robert, containing the text: "Still hasn't learned how to handle Jewish brat girls!!"[46] There are other references to Jewishness scattered throughout *Love That Bunch*, some unequivocally anti–Semitic (such as the scene in which The Bunch's father calls her mother a "lousy kike cunt" before raping her),[47] and some invoking more positive Jewish stereotypes at The Bunch's expense (such as when she lists a number of other things she can't do, including "play music," illustrated by an image of her playing the violin, saying "Jews are suppose [*sic*] to be good at this!").[48]

The most explicit manifestation of The Bunch's Jewish self-loathing, however, is to be found in an episode entitled "The inner voice screams," which features a panel with a flow chart beginning with "Life of the Jewess" and ending with "Death," via "Guilt," "Food, Caddilacs [*sic*], Condos" and "Yelling Fat."[49] At the bottom of the flow chart is The Bunch, naked apart from a large Star of David necklace, sweating under the burden of the boxes of text, the last of which ("Death") is balanced on her head. On the next page there is a panel depicting a series of happy passengers boarding a flight to Mexico, while The Bunch, who has a pathological fear of flying, announces that the doorway to the aircraft "looks like the door to the gas chamber!"[50] Kominsky-Crumb's work is always uncompromising and unsettling formally, in its refusal to conform to the aesthetic conventions of comics (her drawings are not only "loaded with ugliness,"[51] as Pekar puts it, but also inconsistent in their representation of the Bunch and other characters). It is also unsentimental, unsparing and often unsympathetic in its treatment of the Bunch herself. "The inner voice screams" episode exemplifies all these aspects of her art. The opening panel consists of a grotesquely distorted image of The Bunch's face and hands, surrounded by swirling, asymmetrical, jagged lines and hundreds of small black crosses. In the second panel Kominsky-Crumb draws attention to the comic incongruity between the banality of her everyday life and the anguish with which she imbues it, aptly describing her internal debate as to whether or not to get rid of her collection of dolls and toys as "a moral dilemmer [*sic*] in my pitiful little soul." The "Life of the Jewess" panel, directly below, exploits this tension further, by juxtaposing profound, universal preoccupations such as guilt and death with the Bunch's personal trivial concerns with Cadillacs and condos. Anatomizing The Bunch's deepest fears and desires under the generic label "Life of the Jewess," Kominsky-Crumb simultaneously situates the Bunch's neuroses in the context of a larger ethnic heritage, and mocks such self-mythologizing tendencies. Her absurd analogy between the perils of flying and the fate suffered by six million European Jews in the Nazi death camps—serving only to highlight the disparity between The Bunch's phobia and the grand narrative of historical suffering which she invokes—reinforces the comic nexus between self-pity, self-satire and self-hatred that lies at the heart of Kominsky-Crumb's work and that has provided a template for what the Anglo-Jewish comics artist Corinne Pearlman calls the "Jewish confessionistas" who have followed her [Fig. 2].[52]

Pearlman is herself one of these "confessionistas" and her very coinage of the humorously self-deprecating term demonstrates the affinities that she has with Kominsky-Crumb, as well as Schrag, Lasko-Gross, Diane Noomin and Phoebe Gloeckner, all of whom she names and draws in the strip entitled "Show & Tell" [Figs. 1–2]. Closer in age to Kominsky-Crumb and Noomin, Pearlman nonetheless didn't find a regular showcase for her work until 2002 (when she began publishing a strip entitled "Playing the Jewish Card" in the *Jewish Quarterly*) and in this sense is a contemporary of Schrag and Lasko-Gross, who began publishing in the late 1990s and 2000s, respectively. Like these younger writers, Pearlman uses a graphic version of herself to create an ongoing autobiography in comics form, but hers is a serial narrative that deals even more self-consciously and explicitly—even more self-reflexively—with the comedy of Jewish self-hatred. This self-reflexivity manifests itself not just in examinations of her own motivations for, and methods of, working, but also extends to discussions of the invitations given to her to contribute to the *Jewish Quarterly* and to the "Graphic Details" exhibition.

In the former case, in a strip entitled "The Non-Jewish Jewish Female Cartoonist and Other Confusions" (1992) [Fig. 39], Pearlman begins by depicting Corinne "wandering in life's dark wood" (a metaphor literalized in her drawing), asking herself: "Who am I? Where do I belong? Should I have a child? Shall I go to Waitrose?"[53] The debt to Kominsky-Crumb that is implicit here—in the juxtaposition of grand existential questions with the trivial one of whether or not to visit the supermarket—is made explicit in the panel directly below, in which Pearlman reproduces the "Life of the Jewess" panel, alongside one from Art Spiegelman's *Maus*. The text that accompanies these panels reads: "You see, the truth is—I'm neither the child of a survivor ... nor a Long Island émigré JAP like Aline Kominsky-Crumb." Ostensibly, Pearlman's purpose is to highlight how unqualified she is for the job that she has just been offered (to contribute to the *Jewish Quarterly*) but of course the knowledge and skill she demonstrates in doing so actually establishes the very credentials that she claims not to possess. She then draws Corinne in tears, her head in her hands, saying: 'In fact, m-my parents are **assimilated**!!" while her parents, visible in the background, discuss horticulture in their garden[54] [Fig. 39]. Here Pearlman pays homage to—and at the same time parodies—the self-dramatizing tradition of which Kominsky-Crumb is the grandmother, and which was institutionalized in the "Kvetch" issue of *Wimmin's Commix* (1992) to which, Pearlman points out in the preceding panel, she (Pearlman) did not contribute.[55] If the use of the bold type and double exclamation mark, combined with the sob-induced stammering repetition of the first letter of "my," and the contrast with the serenity of the scene behind Corinne, suggests her (self-)satirical agenda, the rest of the strip certainly confirms it.

In a variation on the themes of Schrag's "The Chosen," a Chinese friend first questions Corinne's authenticity as a Jew by accusing her of "playing the Jewish card" (the phrase which becomes the title of Pearlman's *Jewish Quarterly* strip), and then reaffirms it by issuing a playful command, "Make me a cup of tea, Jew!" which onlookers denounce as anti–Semitic but which Corinne herself welcomes, smiling broadly and looking directly at the reader, while thinking: "An identity! I have been labeled!" Her moment of euphoria is short-lived, however, as she wonders whether her embrace of the "Jewish" label might be self-serving ("perhaps I'm just trying to exploit my identity") while a speech bubble issues from her parents' house with the text, saying: "How could she?" and the strip finishes with Corinne resuming her self-interrogation in the dark wood: "Who am I? What is a Jew? Perhaps I will go to Waitrose after all?"

The issues raised by this strip (does Corinne's identity as an assimilated Jew somehow make her less entitled to deal with Jewish issues than the American-Jewish counterparts whom she cites? Is anti–Semitism in the eye of the beholder? Is Corinne appropriating a spurious Jewishness in order to profit from it? Is she betraying her family by using autobiographical material in her strips?) recur repeatedly in the "Playing the Jewish Card" series. "In Valhalla" (2004), for example, dealing with Corinne's love of Wagner, begins with a panel in which she is holding her head in her hands (echoing the image from "The Non-Jewish Jewish Female Cartoonist") and reproaching herself for having "betrayed my people (again)."[56] It also includes an incident in which Corinne imagines herself being labeled as an anti–Semite: when a man she meets at a concert responds to her confession that she is "a bit of a Wagner fan" by saying that he "never go[es] to Wagner," Corinne rapidly moves from speculating that he might be Jewish to becoming convinced that he believes her enthusiasm for Wagner to be evidence of her anti–Semitism, prompting her to deliver an impassioned monologue which ostensibly seeks to exonerate her but ends up reinforcing the sense that to be a Jewish fan of Wagner is an irreconcilable position to maintain: "I'm no anti-semite! ... Just because he preached the FINAL SOLUTION ... and his music was appropriated by the Nazis ... and neo–Nazis ... It's still part of our culture!" Here again, Pearlman's diction and typographical effects provide an ironic subtext that undermines Corinne's intentions: the cumulative effect of the bold typeface of "anti-semite," the capitalization of "final solution," and the supernumerary addition of "the neo–Nazis" is to make the final, unemphatic line of Corinne's speech seem half-hearted.

In "Whatever happened to Great Grandma?" (2005), Pearlman reveals how Corinne discovered "a few months ago" during a meal with her parents that her paternal great-grandmother had killed herself, having been rejected by her son on the grounds, as Corinne's father puts it, that "she was HUGELY fat" and "spoke only Yiddish."[57] Rather than take her with him to the hotel where the family lived during the war after their flat was commandeered, Corinne's grandfather persuades his business partner to take her into his home where she found herself "among strangers" who "weren't even Jewish" and where, having "no-one to cook for any more, nothing to do" she cuts her throat "with an axe! In the henhouse!" The clear implication of this story is that the great-grandmother was sacrificed by her family because of their embarrassment at her old-country appearance and customs—in other words because of their internalized anti–Semitism—but the self-hatred that Corinne focuses on in the second half of the strip is her own. In the first panel of the second page, Corinne is shown looking at a photograph of her father who has a thought-bubble with the single word "JUDAS!" while the text at the top of the panel informs us, "In a strange way, it felt rather LIBERATING ... my capacity for betrayal was a family inheritance!" In the final panel of the story, Pearlman shows Corinne's mother complaining to a neighbor of how her daughter "invites herself for the weekend ... then SPIES on us and SHOPS us to some Jewish mag!!" while her friend suggests that she could perhaps "try KEEPING HENS??"

Once more, Pearlman treats the subject of self-hatred comically: she juxtaposes the horrific revelation of her great-grandmother's suicide with an absurd image (in a thought-bubble emerging from Corinne's head) of a prone, large body, of which the only distinct feature is a foot, protruding from a shapeless smock. The body is hemmed in by three hens (more clearly drawn) and has an axe embedded somewhere in its amorphous upper folds. The accompanying debate between Corinne's parents ("NO, darling, NOT with an AXE ... "; "Yes, darling! With an AXE! You've forgotten! With an axe, with a knife, whatever ... it was terrible") amplifies the sense of absurdity, making the fact of the death (and its origins in her family's disowning of her for fear of being tainted by association with her conspicuous old-world Jewishness) subsidiary to the method by which it was accomplished. Whether Corinne's father genuinely cannot remember how his grandmother killed herself or whether he wants to spare Corinne the gory details, is left ambiguous, but in any case his airy dismissal of the subject ("With an axe, with a knife, whatever"), combined with his earlier implicit attempt to mitigate the betrayal of his father (in response to Corinne's query "Didn't they take her too?" he says: "You should have SEEN her! They couldn't have!"), actually exacerbates it. Equating Corinne's betrayal of her parents in exposing this dark family secret in the pages of "some Jewish mag" (the abbreviation "mag" and generic "some" implying derisive dismissal of the importance of the journal and of Pearlman's work) with the original betrayal, Pearlman implicates herself in a sort of vicious circle of self-loathing, in which exposing self-hatred becomes in itself evidence of self-hatred. Yet the essential disparity between the behavior of Corinne and her grandfather's family is implied, again comically, by the final line of the strip, in which the neighbor reminds Corinne's parents (and Pearlman's readers) of the real

Fig. 39. Corinne Pearlman, "The Non-Jewish Jewish Female Cartoonist and Other Confusions," 1992, ink on paper (detail).

crime, by suggesting (ironically?) that they should try "keeping hens" as a way of deterring future visits from their treacherous daughter.

In "Your Global Community Needs YOU" (2007), Pearlman represents Corinne's serial refusal to affiliate herself with various associations, movements, campaigns and causes, which she traces back to her response, as a child, to visiting a *Habonim* Jewish youth group meeting ("PLEASE don't make me go back again! They're all Jewish!" she implores her mother).[58] On the first page of the strip, she draws a facial portrait of Sarah Lightman—one of the curators of, and contributors to, the "Graphic Details" exhibition—above a text message on a mobile phone that reads: "Would you be interested in signing up to Jewish Angst-ridden Cartoonists Kvetching Self-." Leaving the final word incomplete is perhaps Pearlman's self-reflexive joke about the taboo that still exists for Jewish artists exploring questions of self-hatred. The (parodic) self-censorship is temporary, however: on the following page she accuses herself of "wallow[ing] in my status as a Jewish Angst-ridden Cartoonist Self-Hating Introspective Tripe [*sic*]."

Pearlman returns to this theme in "Show & Tell" (2009), in which she explicitly interrogates the relationship between Jewishness, confessional art, comedy and self-hatred [Figs. 1–2]. Asserting that "it is surely true that we Jews do PRIDE ourselves on our ANGUISH!" Pearlman asks whether it is "in our genes," a cultural phenomenon ("Are we all followers of Woody Allen? Philip Roth?"), or the legacy of the Holocaust ("do we just feel BAD that we SURVIVED?"), concluding that "it's easier to give voice to internalized guilt than it is to take responsibility for what happens 'in our name'" (a reference to the Israel/Palestine situation, illustrated with a reference to the graphic novel *How to Understand Israel in 60 Days* (2010), by Sarah Glidden, another Jewish-American "confessionista"). Pearlman also includes a note referring readers to an article by Michael Kaminer (co-curator of the "Graphic Details" exhibition), "Graphic Confessions of Jewish Women" (published in the Jewish-American publication *The Jewish Daily Forward*), which deals with many of the same issues.

In the article, Kaminer argues that in the work of the confessionistas "even if the content of the work isn't especially Jewish, it reflects the kind of unfiltered sharing that Jews do especially well."[59] Yet this seems to me to raise two fundamental problems. First, while it is certainly true that one of the defining characteristics of the work of these artists is their willingness to present their autobiographical selves warts and all (sometimes literally), this rejection of conventional self-censorship does not necessarily mean that the experiences they represent are "unfiltered." The internal evidence of the comics is contradictory on this point. All of Ariel Schrag's books are described as "autobiographical" (n.p.) and on the back cover of *Potential* it claims that it is "a true account of Ariel Schrag's junior year of high school" (n.p.). However, on the inside cover of *Likewise* there is a note informing readers that "certain names and identifying characteristics have been changed" (n.p.). The blurb on the back of both of Miss Lasko-Gross's books refers to them as volumes in a "semi-autobiographical trilogy" (n.p.); the back cover of Kominsky-Crumb's *Love That Bunch* features a series of photos of the author, some in the company of other family members who appear in the book under their own names (notably her husband, Robert Crumb). Yet The Bunch, as her name suggests, is clearly a persona, not an "unfiltered" self-portrait. Whether or not Philip Roth is right to suggest that autobiography is "probably the most manipulative of all literary forms,"[60] it is clear that even the most ostensibly uncensored, authentic account of autobiographical experience is a mediated, selective, constructed version of that experience. If this is true of prose memoirs, it is arguably even more so of autobiographical comics, since visual self-portraits in comics are invariably stylized and simplified (Schrag often draws Ariel without a mouth, for example), while text and image often offer implicitly divergent information or even explicitly conflicting narratives.

Secondly, the idea that "sharing," whether "unfiltered" or not, is something that Jews "do especially well" is rather contentious. It does seem to have widespread currency, not least among Jewish comics writers themselves. Lasko-Gross claims, "We're willing to be open about things that aren't necessarily flattering ... we've got lots of problems, and we like to talk about them." Schrag cites Woody Allen as "a big influence," explaining that "my comics are very Jewish in that sense" (both quoted in Kaminer) and T.J. Waldman, the author of *Megillat Esther* (2005), argues that "it is no wonder that Jews possess a distinct and profound affinity to commix [*sic*]," since "Jewish people ... have a historic propensity toward communication."[61] Even Art Spiegelman, when presenting a Lifetime Achievement Award from the National Foundation for Jewish Culture to Will Eisner, claimed that "the comic book" is a "specifically Jewish contribution to American culture."[62] Many critics have also suggested that there is an intrinsic connection between comics and Jewishness. According to Paul Buhle, there is a distinctively Jewish sensibility which finds a natural outlet in confessional comics: "there's a Jewish self-identification in these artists' sense of humor, their unashamed discussion of personal lives, their dealings with angst and unhappiness through a pop-culture form."[63] For Baskind and Omer-Sherman, the genre of the graphic novel "is uniquely suited to the quintessential narrative themes of the Jewish imagination: mobility, flight, adaptation, transformation, disguise, metamorphosis and much else that has inspired memorable explorations both visually and textually."[64] In a similar vein, Simcha Weinstein suggests that successive generations of Jewish comics creators have been drawn to the form because it offered them the opportunity to explore "the ambiguities of assimilation, the pain of discrimination, and the particularly Jewish theme of the misunderstood outcast, the rootless wanderer."[65] Finally, Danny Fingeroth identifies "some kind of perhaps historically driven impetus for Jews to absorb, reflect, and express idiosyncratic visions of the world around them" in the form of comic books.[66]

It is difficult to argue with most of these statements, but equally they tend to rely on rather vague generalizations. While most critics would agree with Paul Gravett's claim that "the impact of Jewish creativity and intellect on the foundation of the comic book as an art form ... is well attested,"[67] Laurence Roth sounds a salutary note of caution when he warns against a "triumphalist reading" of the history of American comics that aims to "lend cultural legitimacy and social prestige to Jewish identity,"[68] as does Derek Parker Royal, who points out that though "Jews have contributed greatly to the history of comic art, one must resist the temptation to define the medium solely or even primarily through this involvement."[69] Whereas within the male-authored genre of superhero comics there is arguably a well-established, self-perpetuating tradition at work, with one generation of Jewish artists being inspired by another, as well as by their peers, the "confessionistas" are working in what is still a relatively new field, whose progenitors include not just the first generation of Jewish women artists such as Kominsky-Crumb and Noomin, but also male Jewish-American filmmakers (Woody Allen) and novelists (Philip Roth). The "Graphic Details" exhibition makes clear that this emergent field is marked as much by the diversity of its practitioners as by their affinities, but in this essay I have identified a characteristic that is shared by at least some of these artists: namely, the comic treatment of Jewish self-hatred. In particular, the graphic narratives of Kominsky-Crumb, Schrag, Lasko-Gross and Pearlman constitute a body of confessional art that redefines Jewish self-hatred, exploiting its comic potential by ironizing the relationship between their autobiographical selves, the authors of those selves, and their implied readers.

NOTES

1. Cited in Keith Kahn-Harris, "Why We Are All Worth a Mix of Self-Love and Self-Hate," *The Guardian*, June 11, 2011. http://www.guardian.co.uk/commentisfree/belief/2011/jun/11/self-love-and-self-hate. Accessed August 4, 2011.

2. Cited in Michael Kaminer, "Graphic Confessions of Jewish Women: Exposing Themselves Through Pictures and Raw Personal Stories," *The Jewish Daily Forward*, December 12, 2008. http://www.forward.com/articles/14657/. Accessed July 7, 2011.

3. To distinguish between the author and her presentation of her self in her comics, I will refer to the former by her surname and the latter by her first name. I will follow the same practice with Miss Lasko-Gross and Corinne Pearlman.

4. Ariel Schrag, "Shit," 2003, 1.

5. Miss Lasko-Gross, "The Turd, " in *A Mess of Everything* (Seattle: Fantagraphics, 2009) 70–78.

6. Lasko-Gross, "The Turd," 76–77.

7. Ariel Schrag, "The Chosen," 2008.

8. Miss Lasko-Gross, *Escape from "Special"* (Seattle: Fantagraphics, 2006) 106.

9. Lasko-Gross, *Escape from "Special,"* 63.

10. Lasko-Gross, *Escape from "Special,"* 63–64.

11. Lasko-Gross, *Escape from "Special,"* 56.

12. Lasko-Gross, *Escape from "Special,"* 80.

13. Lasko-Gross, *Escape from "Special,"* 81.

14. Lasko-Gross, *Escape from "Special,"* 81.

15. Lasko-Gross, *Escape from "Special,"* 55.

16. Lasko-Gross, *Escape from "Special,"* 137.

17. Lasko-Gross, *Escape from "Special,"* 153.

18. Lasko-Gross, *Escape from "Special,"* 77.

19. Lasko-Gross, *Escape from "Special,"* 81.

20. Lasko-Gross, *Escape from "Special,"* 69.

21. Lasko-Gross, *Escape from "Special,"* 70.

22. Lasko-Gross, *Escape from "Special,"* 106.

23. Lasko-Gross, *A Mess of Everything*, 69.

24. Ibid.

25. Ibid.

26. Lasko-Gross, *A Mess of Everything*, 76.

27. Ibid.

28. Lasko-Gross, *A Mess of Everything*, 4.

29. Lasko-Gross, *A Mess of Everything*, 5.

30. Lasko-Gross, *A Mess of Everything*, 2.

31. Lasko-Gross, *A Mess of Everything*, 218.

32. Lasko-Gross, *A Mess of Everything*, 219.

33. Hence its adoption by the Jewish actor Tony Curtis, who was born Bernard Schwartz but was advised, like many of his contemporaries from ethnic minorities, that he would be more likely to succeed in show business if he changed his name to something more redolent of WASP America.

34. Sharon Achinstein, "John Foxe and the Jews," *Renaissance Quarterly* (Spring 2001). http://www.thefreelibrary.com/John+Foxe+and+the+Jews+%5b*%5d-a074523889. Accessed July 14, 2011.

35. Miriam Libicki, "Jewish Memoir Goes Pow! Zap! Oy!" in Samantha Baskind and Ranen Omer-Sherman, eds., *The Jewish Graphic Novel: Critical Approaches* (New Brunswick, NJ: Rutgers University Press, 2010) 253—274.

36. See David Brauner, *Philip Roth* (Manchester: Manchester University Press, 2007) 80.

37. Here again, Roth is a key influence, cited repeatedly by Libicki, 254, 261, 266, 268, 269.

38. Kahn-Harris, "Why We Are All Worth a Mix of Self-Love and Self-Hate."

39. Reproduced in Hillary L. Chute, *Graphic Women: Life Narrative and Contemporary Comics* (New York: Columbia University Press, 2010) 25.

40. Chute, 29.

41. Hillary L. Chute explains that "this name was initially inspired by a sexy adolescent character, 'Honeybunch Kaminski,' which Robert Crumb [her future husband and one of the most influential "underground" comics artists] drew before he ever met Kominsky," 39.

42. Chute, 57.

43. Aline Kominsky-Crumb, *Love That Bunch* (Seattle: Fantagraphics, 1990) iii.

44. Kominsky-Crumb, iii.

45. Kominsky-Crumb, 59.

46. Kominsky-Crumb, 111.

47. Kominsky-Crumb, 43.
48. Kominsky-Crumb, 68.
49. Kominsky-Crumb, 64.
50. Kominsky-Crumb, 65.
51. Kominsky-Crumb, iii.
52. Corinne Pearlman, "Playing the Jewish Card: Show & Tell," *Jewish Quarterly*, December 11, 2009. http://jewishquarterly.org/2009/12/playing-the-jewish-card-show-tell/ Accessed August 4, 2011.
53. Corinne Pearlman, "The Non-Jewish Jewish Cartoonist and Other Confusions," *Jewish Quarterly* 147 (Autumn 1992): 57.
54. An image that provides a neat visual shorthand for Jewish assimilation (see David Brauner, *Post-War Jewish Fiction: Ambivalence, Self-Explanation and Transatlantic Connections* [Basingstoke, Hampshire: Palgrave, 2001], 73–76).
55. "The Kvetch Issue," ed. Caryn Leschen, *Wimmin's Comix* 17 (1992).
56. Corinne Pearlman, "Playing the Jewish Card: In Valhalla," *Jewish Quarterly* 195 (Autumn 2004): 4–5.
57. Corinne Pearlman, "Playing the Jewish Card: Whatever happened to Great-Grandma?" *Jewish Quarterly* 193 (Spring 2004): 4–5.
58. Corinne Pearlman, "Playing the Jewish Card: Your Global Community Needs YOU!," *Jewish Quarterly* 206 (Autumn 2007): 4–5.
59. Kaminer, "Graphic Confessions of Jewish Women: Exposing Themselves Through Pictures and Raw Personal Stories."
60. Philip Roth, *The Facts: A Novelist's Autobiography* (London: Jonathan Cape, 1988) 172.
61. T.J. Waldman, "Foreword: Comix, Judaism, and Me," in Samantha Baskind and Ranen Omer-Sherman, eds., *The Jewish Graphic Novel: Critical Approaches* (New Brunswick, NJ: Rutgers University Press, 2010) ix–xiii.
62. "Art Spiegelman presents Will Eisner with a lifetime achievement award," *Jewish Quarterly* 186 (Summer 2002): 6.
63. Kaminer, "Graphic Confessions of Jewish Women: Exposing Themselves Through Pictures and Raw Personal Stories."
64. Samantha Baskind and Ranen Omer-Sherman, eds., *The Jewish Graphic Novel: Critical Approaches* (New Brunswick, NJ: Rutgers University Press, 2010) xvii.
65. Simcha Weinstein, *Up, Up, and Oy Vey! How Jewish History, Culture, and Values Shaped the Comic Book Superhero* (Baltimore: Leviathan, 2006) 18.
66. Danny Fingeroth, *Disguised as Clark Kent: Jews, Comics and the Creation of the Superhero* (New York: Continuum, 2007) 19.
67. Paul Gravett, "After *Maus*: Graphic novels confront the Jewish experience," *Jewish Quarterly* 184 (Winter 2001–02): 23.
68. Laurence Roth, "Contemporary American Jewish Comic Books: Abject Pasts, Heroic Futures," in Samantha Baskind and Ranen Omer-Sherman, eds., *The Jewish Graphic Novel: Critical Approaches*, 7.
69. Derek Parker Royal, "Jewish Comics; Or, Visualizing Current Jewish Narrative," *Shofar* 29. 2 (2011): 5–6.

BIBLIOGRAPHY

Achinstein, Sharon. "John Foxe and the Jews." *Renaissance Quarterly*, Spring 2001. http://www.thefreelibrary.com/John+Foxe+and+the+Jews+%5b*%5d-a074523889. Accessed July 14, 2011.
"Art Spiegelman presents Will Eisner with a lifetime achievement award." *Jewish Quarterly* 186 (Summer 2002): 6–7.
Baskind, Samantha, and Ranen Omer-Sherman, eds. *The Jewish Graphic Novel: Critical Approaches*. New Brunswick, NJ: Rutgers University Press, 2010. xvii.
Brauner, David. *Philip Roth*. Manchester: Manchester University Press, 2007.
Chute, Hillary L. *Graphic Women: Life Narrative and Contemporary Comics*. New York: Columbia University Press, 2010.
Fingeroth, Danny. *Disguised As Clark Kent: Jews, Comics and the Creation of the Superhero*. New York: Continuum, 2007.
Gravett, Paul. "After *Maus*: Graphic novels confront the Jewish experience." *Jewish Quarterly* 184 (Winter 2001–02): 21–8.
Kahn-Harris, Keith. "Why We Are All Worth a Mix of Self-Love and Self-Hate." *The Guardian*, Saturday, June 11, 2011. http://www.guardian.co.uk/commentisfree/belief/2011/jun/11/self-love-and-self-hate. Accessed August 4, 2011.
Kaminer, Michael. "Graphic Confessions of Jewish Women: Exposing Themselves Through Pictures and Raw

Personal Stories." *The Jewish Daily Forward*, 12 December 2008. http://www.forward.com/articles/
14657/. Accessed July 7, 2011.

Kominsky-Crumb, Aline. *Love That Bunch*. Seattle: Fantagraphics, 1990.

Lasko-Gross, Miss. *Escape from "Special."* Seattle, WA: Fantagraphics, 2006.

_____. *A Mess of Everything*. Seattle, WA: Fantagraphics, 2009.

Leschen, Caryn, ed. "The Kvetch Issue" *Wimmin's Comics* 17 (1992).

Libicki, Miriam. "Jewish Memoir Goes Pow! Zap! Oy!" in Samantha Baskind and Ranen Omer-Sherman,
eds., *The Jewish Graphic Novel: Critical Approaches*. New Brunswick, NJ: Rutgers University Press, 2010.
253–274.

Parker Royal, Derek. "Jewish Comics; Or, Visualizing Current Jewish Narrative." *Shofar* 29.2 (2011): 1–12.

Pearlman, Corinne. "The Non-Jewish Jewish Cartoonist and Other Confusions," *Jewish Quarterly*, 147,
Autumn 1992. 57.

_____. "Playing the Jewish Card: In Valhalla." *Jewish Quarterly* 195 (Autumn 2004): 4–5.

_____. "Playing the Jewish Card: Show & Tell." *Jewish Quarterly*, December 11, 2009. http://jewishquarterly.
org/2009/12/playing-the-jewish-card-show-tell/. Accessed August 4, 2011.

_____. "Playing the Jewish Card: Whatever happened to Great-Grandma?" *Jewish Quarterly* 193 (Spring
2004): 4–5.

_____. "Playing the Jewish Card: Your Global Community Needs YOU!" *Jewish Quarterly* (Autumn 2007):
4–5.

Roth, Laurence. "Contemporary American Jewish Comic Books: Abject Pasts, Heroic Futures," in Samantha
Baskind and Ranen Omer-Sherman, eds. *The Jewish Graphic Novel: Critical Approaches*. New Brunswick,
NJ: Rutgers University Press, 2010. 3–21.

Roth, Philip. *The Facts: A Novelist's Autobiography*. London: Jonathan Cape, 1988.

Waldman, T.J. "Foreword: Comix, Judaism, and Me," in Samantha Baskind and Ranen Omer-Sherman, eds.,
The Jewish Graphic Novel: Critical Approaches. New Brunswick, NJ: Rutgers University Press, 2010. ix–
xiii.

Weinstein, Simcha. *Up, Up, and Oy Vey! How Jewish History, Culture, and Values Shaped the Comic Book
Superhero*. Baltimore: Leviathan, 2006, 18.

The Comedy of Confession

Judy Batalion

The Setup

Upon entering the "Graphic Details" exhibition at the Yeshiva University Museum, I was pleasantly surprised to find myself confronted with an image of a porn shop. In Vanessa Davis's "Toys in Babeland" (2005) [Fig. 7], two females browse at a sex store and notice that one of their fellow shoppers is a Hasid. "I wanted to tell my mom about seeing him there but I didn't want to tell her about me being there," one of the women declares.

I laughed at first, because the piece was edgy, surprising; it felt subversive and fresh. But I laughed a second time, because it reminded me of an old Yiddish jibe my father used to relay about a Rabbi who is so obsessed with golf that he couldn't resist frequenting the course even on Yom Kippur, between *musaf* and *mincha* [the morning and afternoon services at synagogue]. Lo and behold, that's the day he hits a hole-in-one! But, how dreadfully annoying, he can *never* tell anyone. My father told this joke when the situation demanded some sympathy for the agonizing and seemingly unfair way that life works out, and how we need to treat fate with an accepting sigh. That same sentiment struck me in Davis's work. What luck! The Hasid sighting would have made a great story, and perhaps proved a point to her mother.

Here, in this unique, feminist, confessional collection of works about online shopping and being dumped, I began to find various humor tropes, including those of old Jewish jokes. The works in the exhibition represent and build on the Jewish traditions not only of auto-biography and confessional writing, but of comedy.

Scholars and thinkers have analyzed and outlined different types of Jewish jokes—of which there are many. I am thinking along the lines of "Two Jews, three opinions on what Jewish humor is...." Those who have pontificated on the topic—including Freud, the humor expert, Avner Ziv, and the Yiddishist Ruth Wisse—have focused mainly on the verbal realm and have identified several strategies at work within Jewish comedy: self-deprecation, anti–Semitic stances, obsession, paralogic, caricature and attack.[1] As graphic comics, how-ever, the pieces in this exhibition blend the verbal with the visual, merging words with images. In so doing, they twist Jewish humor, creating their own versions of each of these six tropes.[2]

Fig. 40. Lauren Weinstein, "Last Dance," *Girl Stories* (New York: Henry Holt, 2006) 94, ink on paper.

The Many Selves of Self-Deprecation

Most scholars agree that Jewish humor frequently involves self-deprecation. From Woody Allen's "My one regret in life is that I'm not someone else,"[3] to Joan Rivers's "Rapists tap me on the shoulder and ask: 'have you seen any girls?'"[4] Jews have often belittled themselves for a laugh.[5] Self-disparagement is, indeed, one of the most common forms of humor in these memoir works. In Miss Lasko-Gross's "The Turd" (2009), the protagonist is flustered by her unflushable feces, especially since she is at a coffee shop checking out a crush [Figs. 37–38]. In Lauren Weinstein's 2006 *Girl Stories*, she arrives at her school dance in a ripped up used prom dress and fishnet stockings with runs, realizing that she looked "like an idiot. Like I tried way too hard to be different" [Figs. 40–41]. In the narration and images, these works show the body to be a site of shame, and in relaying that shame honestly, it is somewhat owned and overcome. Humor helps lead to, and demonstrates, a degree of self-acceptance.

In Diane Noomin's work, however, the body is not shamed for being unlady-like or awkward, but probed for being medically and maternally dysfunctional; she uses the comic form with its visual element, to take self-deprecation to another level. In "Baby Talk: A Tale of ~~3~~ 4 Miscarriages" (1993) [Figs. 21–22, 83–86], she addresses the taboo subject—and her harrowing experience of repeated miscarriage—in graphic form. The work is *a priori* humorous by juxtaposing the seriousness and untalked-about-ness of the subject matter with the lighthearted and ephemeral comic form. As articulated by Freud, humor is often created by juxtaposing unexpected components; and the more the unexpected the components, the funnier the joke.[6] This version of a joke is apparent in many of the works in this show, based on their use of the fleeting cartoon form imbued with child connotations and their heavy adult content.

Fig. 41. Lauren Weinstein, "Last Dance," *Girl Stories* (New York: Henry Holt, 2006) 95, ink on paper.

But Noomin's combination of visual and verbal storytelling takes this juxtaposition, and self-disparagement, further: she presents three contrasting versions of herself, three different bodies. In this case, the protagonist of the story is, at first, the primped Glenda who is pregnant and discusses baby names with her husband Jimmy. Glenda has a nightmare about losing her baby, and the darker side of the story emerges. DiDi, a sassy blond character who is Noomin's alter-ego, enters dragging a bespectacled character that looks like Noomin the artist to the front of the comic: "It's your story ... are you gonna let some cartoon yuppies cry cartoon tears over your lost babies?" [Fig. 85]. In having DiDi accuse the comic artist of hiding behind a fictional character, Noomin questions her own experience of her emotions, and her reaction to and management of her life: "DiDi, I can't tell the story without using Glenda and Jimmy as stand-ins!!" she mocks herself for her what she lacks. "Besides, Glenda and Jimmy are doin' a good job! So if you don't mind I'm in the middle of a tragic saga here and I'd like to get back to it!" [Fig. 86]. The tale then goes on to feature the bespectacled Noomin who suffers numerous failed pregnancies, and who visits many doctors and emergency rooms.

Three different characters play Noomin: DiDi Glitz wears fishnets and is sexy, impulsive and speaks her mind; Diane, a drawn version of the artist at work who later re-enacts her experiences, looks intellectual and scared; and Glenda who is a naïve and optimistic yuppie. The comic medium enables the author to present all these versions of the self, and to have them merge and converse in a way that is direct and unmediated. By demonstrating different sides of the same person in one moment and in the same frame—as in the aforementioned Noomin/DiDi altercation—Noomin shows internal ambivalence and the various sides of oneself that often contradict each other, as well as the way that inner experience exists in two time frames: the past and the present. The mature narrator who tells the story of past events is still perturbed, as represented by DiDi who has anxieties as the artist crafts her tale

(DiDi asks: "I'm scared... What happens to me if you crack up!"). Personal history is never completely resolved. Noomin is always there represented as a third person (as two different third people), providing distance from the intensity of the true story, thereby allowing viewers to feel closer to Glenda—and allowing for humor.

The humor of the piece also includes a family dinner of lobster juxtaposed with the tragic termination of a pregnancy and a reaction to a dead fetus in the toilet bowl with the simple: "It looks like liver." Furthermore, there is humorous anger at the doctor that helps relieve sorrow and make sense of negative experience: "You'd think a woman doctor could cough up a little compassion." / "Or at least a mega-hit of valium!" Drawing on the visual/verbal combination, the self-disparagement is self-conscious. The artist shows awareness, not just of her emotions, but of the very art she is making about them and the fact that she needs that art. We might also ask whether humor, which includes various drawings of the fetuses, including one that is a mini bespectacled version of Noomin, helps avoid dealing with feelings of loss.

A similar multilayered narrative perspective emerges in Aline Kominsky-Crumb's "Wiseguys" (1995) [Figs. 71–72], in which she exposes her background—a Jewish family with drug dealers and Mafia connections. As part of her tale, she presents herself from the viewpoint of another: that of her male character, who is based on Robert Crumb, her non–Jewish husband and collaborator. This character says of Kominsky-Crumb: "She's so ethnic and exotic! And a mind reader" [Fig. 72]. Including his analysis of her mind in "Wiseguys" shows that her self-concept includes others; "I" is dynamic and complex. Kominsky-Crumb has said that she feels "exotic" and sexy with non–Jewish men, and here she might be projecting this feeling onto her husband's voice.[7] If he were not her husband, and if we did not know about her proclivities, we might consider that she was taking on the underdog role of "the ethnic and exotic." And by mocking herself for it in the male voice, she takes ownership of it; or rather the "you can't hurt me by calling me that if I call myself that first" attitude. This type of role reversal parody enables control and assuages anxiety. By coining herself a mind reader, in someone else's mind, she adds a layer of self-consciousness to her self-disparaging humor. The comic medium enables Kominsky-Crumb to switch perspectives, shedding light not only on how others see her, but how she envisions them seeing her. The combination of visual and verbal allows for the expression of multiple versions of self-deprecation and a more holistic form of self-acceptance.

"Anti-Semitic" and Surreal Jibes

Corinne Pearlman's work is also self-consciously self-deprecating, but she uses the visual and verbal mix in a different way, and to different ends. In her 2009 piece "Playing the Jewish Card: Show & Tell" [Figs. 1–2] her character explains: "I've always had a soft spot for confession... People with self-respect take their feelings to a therapist... But I like to share my negative emotions!"[8] She is aware of her self-doubt, critical of herself for it, and cartoons about this very matter. Her images, however, illustrate this sentiment in the surreal: she portrays herself at a mental health show-and-tell fair, where she sells anxiety bookmarks. Though Pearlman makes herself the "butt of the joke," the piece ultimately reflects on Jewish culture as a whole, probing whether it is simply easier to be neurotic than to take responsibility and change (she implies it might be). I am reminded of Henny Youngman's "Why don't Jews drink? It interferes with their suffering."[9] In this way, self-deprecating humor can also be a strategy for offering palatable social critique, by making one's self the object of criticism, as well as for acknowledging and coming to terms with one's imperfections.

In other works the artists use humor to critique Jewishness, without making themselves a stand-in for the religion and culture.[10] In Miss Lasko-Gross's "The Gruswerk's Sabbath" (2002) [Figs. 73–75], she is a child, deeply bored at an observant friends' *Shabbat* dinner where she cannot act as she wants and must adhere to a strict code of behavior which she undermines. "I'm glad my family isn't Orthodox and has a sense of humor," she boldly declares. In *How to Understand Israel in 60 Days or Less* (2010) [Figs. 45–47, 61–64], Sarah Glidden is critical of Birthright and the Zionist sentiment. She inwardly refers to the country as "Palestine" and from the start of her trip she is self-aware about her readiness to "pass judgment on it." She even finds the safety requirements bizarre: "It's hard for me to imagine what this guy would be able to protect us from, especially with a gun that looks like the rifles we used at summer camp."[11]

Like Pearlman, Glidden uses the comic medium to levy critique through flights-of-fancy. In Glidden's memoir, her graphics jump into the surreal, casting herself in historical scenes and conversing with fantasy figures. Her nights are peopled by imagined characters—from prehistoric men and women to Ottoman tax collectors—who had once slept in the same Israeli spot where she now lies. In more overt political ways, she debates with the pioneers who came to build up Palestine ("Wait, but what about the people who live there already?"); she listens cautiously as Ben-Gurion explains to her how he never wanted to infringe on Arab rights. In these surreal and imaginative moments, Glidden offers new possibilities for critiques of and questions about Israel's narrative and politics.

Jews sometimes take on Jewish-critical, and even anti–Semitic, stances in order to downplay Jews' achievements and help them "fit in"—if Jews make themselves look inferior, or even take on stereotypes, perhaps they will be less intimidating and more accepted by others. Alternately, and perversely, by adopting and expressing anti–Semitism, Jews may come to terms with or control a fear of that very same anti–Semitism, and can debunk this attitude by showing how inane it is. This is demonstrated in Lenny Bruce's joke about Christ: "All right, I'll clear the air once and for all, and confess: Yes, we did it. I did it, my family. I found a note in my basement. It said: 'We killed him, signed, Morty.'"[12] Or Sarah Silverman's version: "I hope the Jews did kill Christ. I'd do it again. I'd fucking do it again in a second."[13]

In Pearlman's and Glidden's works, however, the self-deprecating stance about Jewish identity allows for the experience of ambivalence, and leaves a place to express difficult and controversial, or seemingly disrespectful, ideas and feelings. The merger of text and image enables surreal imaginative scenes, opening the discussion up for conversation and distance. The resultant humor enables real-world possibility and creativity, by providing alternative ways to view a situation. (I am for some reason compelled to include here Woody Allen's "Not only is there no God, but try getting a plumber on weekends.")[14]

OCD (Obsessive Comic Depictions)

Jewish humor might emerge from a self-conscious anxiety about potential danger and a resulting sensitivity to the surroundings; it can be very observational, obsessing over minutiae. Think, for instance, of a Seinfeld routine about Swiss Army knives where every element and angle of the object and its use is prodded, pun intended: "The Swiss have an interesting army. Five hundred years without a war. Pretty impressive. Also pretty lucky for them. Ever see that little Swiss Army knife they have to fight with? Not much of a weapon there. Corkscrews. Bottle openers. 'Come on, buddy, let's go. You get past me, the guy in the back of me, he's got a spoon. Back off. I've got the toe clippers right here.'"[15]

In Ariel Schrag's "The Chosen" (2008) [Fig. 102], she tries to rent her apartment and her real estate agent turns out to be a Hasid. This coincidence and his inquiry about whether she is Jewish make her very conscious of her half–Jewishness (the wrong half). She notices that she has Judaica-type objects scattered in her house, including her toothbrush, which is adorned with Stars of David, an item which receives its own relatively empty frame and stands out as the core illustration of the piece. The narrator obsesses about the brush: Will the agent think she painted the stars on purpose, thus making her seem even less Jewish? Will he sense her pretense? The humor of the comic centers around the obsession with the toothbrush that becomes a marker of identity. You can almost hear the Seinfeld routine about the Zionist toothbrush—what if the bristles are Zionist, and the handle hates Jews?

A similar obsession is at the core of Schrag's 2005 work "Home for the Holidays," a (very relatable) piece that reflects her holidays, which consist of going to doctor's appointments: the skin doctor, the breast doctor, the physical therapist, and the throat doctor who tells her: "I'm sorry to say, but you have both tuberculosis and cystic fibrosis" [Fig. 42]. She is neurotically obsessed with one thing, her physicality (and mortality) and is aware of it, mocking it and herself. While the verbal story is about health and home, the visual narrative centers around beds. At the beginning of the story, she is covered up and alone in her bed. Then as she visits the doctor, she shows herself, always covered by her dark suit, in various positions on or near examining tables. At the end of the story she seems more comfortable, covered still, but splayed across her bed, talking on the phone, indicating connection and relief. She repeats the bed motif with slight alterations throughout, making it become the visual focus of the neurosis. Lying down stresses her sense of vulnerability. Her insecurities are recognizable and expressing them humorously and openly leads to catharsis for herself and for the viewers as well.

One might consider Lauren Weinstein's 2009 piece "Different Combinations of Me and Tim," an exploration of pregnancy, to have "obsessive" qualities in that it is a probing and repeated exploration of a topic. This piece is not organized by frame, and does not relay a tale with straight chronology, but is more abstract and meandering across the page, with thoughts, experiences and questions occurring all in one time. The circular (like a cycle) visual organization evokes the worried thought process about these issues, and along with the black background and bright red "Pain!" repeated at the top of the page, enhances the artist's senses of urgency, anxiety and excitement. (As such, it differs from the "The Turd" in which Gross places scatology in a social context to show up the shame that it invokes.) The coloring is inexact and thin, making these thoughts seem raw, and the artist more exposed. The child-like font and doodle-like images feel vulnerable and intimate, and serve as a softener for the taboo subjects that are addressed: her fear of "bloody show," the mucous plug, meconium, placentas, hemorrhoids, bodily object that is rarely even discussed, let alone illustrated. The visual presentation enables a humor of juxtaposition that in turn allows the author to expose taboos. Visual and verbal combos allow the artists to be non-linear and repetitive, thereby revisiting the same ground in different and surprising ways, and ultimately creating humor that helps address the forbidden and achieve catharsis.

Fig. 42. Ariel Schrag, "Home for the Holidays," 2005, ink on paper.

Word Play Plus

Sometimes this obsession over minutiae might appear to be faux Talmudic-style reasoning—logical, but then para-logical, twisting situations and parameters. For instance, Henny Youngman's reasoning: "When I read about the evils of drinking, I gave up reading,"[16] or "What's the use of happiness? It can't buy you money."[17] This is the kind of humor at work in Vanessa Davis's piece "Toys in Babeland" [Fig. 7]. The situation almost makes sense but then it is skewed: Not only is this a crazy thing to see, but I can't even tell anyone about it. One can imagine the Talmudic discussion: if you see a Hasid somewhere illicit, can you then tell your mother about it? What if you yourself are involved in the same illicit thing? What if you were *considering* being involved. In Davis's piece she draws on an old Jewish joke trope, but turns it around. Now the Rabbi-figure, instead of golfing on the Day of Atonement, is being spotted by a woman in an illicit place. *She* now carries the burden of silence, making the woman the subject of the conundrum. If Davis were aware of the Jewish joke, this piece might also be seen as self-conscious, in that she playfully questions not just the roles and meanings of Jewish jokes but also Jewish cultural tradition. All this paralogical humor might be related to the Yiddish humor of wishing someone the worst, when it sounds like you are wishing them the best. ("May you have a sweet death, and be hit by a sugar truck.")

Pearlman plays with language in her work, and creates humor from puns in both the visual and verbal realms. "Losing the Plot" is a story about a cemetery and we see a tombstone. The title of her series "Playing the Jewish Card" reappears as text written on playing cards. In Canadian Bernice Eisenstein's book *I Was a Child of Holocaust Survivors* (2006), she relays how as a child she noted that the kosher tags on the chicken read as "Jew" when turned on their sides [Fig. 59]. She used them to make bracelets, though complained that her relatives never wore them. "They had their own tags."[18] She then illustrates them wearing kosher tags and concentration camp tattoos. The humor here is one of turning language upside down, literally, accomplished only in this visual medium, and of the child misinterpreting adult behavior in a way that almost makes sense, reflecting a "Talmudic" humor. The inclusion of the word as image intensifies the twist of the joke, adding layers of meaning. One can question whether this sort of intellectual play serves as a defense mechanism, steering us away from what is at the bottom of all the layers: pain.

From Characters (Letters) to Characters (People)

The characters' tendency to hyper-analyze things is also applied to people. While, as the popular myth goes, "Eskimos have 20 words for snow," Yiddish has 20 words for idiot, each one related to a very particular type of idiocy. A *shmendrik* is less slick than a *shmuck*. A *shlemiel* is the guy who has bad luck by falling out the window; a *shlemazel* is the type of guy he falls upon.[19] Yiddish, arguably the original language of Jewish comic attitudes, is replete with words that describe nuances of personality. A Jewish humor of caricature also appears in these works, which—both verbally and visually—poke fun at dispositions and domestic situations; this humor serves to tackle the intensity of family links and to embrace the paradox of feeling both strangled and nurtured.

Alongside her word play, Bernice Eisenstein's *I Was a Child of Holocaust Survivors* considers and pokes fun at her immigrant family members, subtly unveiling their characters. In a frame, she visually portrays a mother holding an Eiffel Tower lamp and her father with a

Birth of Venus saltshaker. Her complementing text reads: "This is not what my parents looked like when they originally arrived in Canada."[20] From just this one unexpected and thus funny line and the knowledge of the conditions of their immigration, a viewer can imagine a mother who is modest in dress, unworldly and unpretentious and a father who is the opposite of the bon vivant. The mix of text and words presents not just portrayals of the parents, but of the writer's knowing voice and sense of non-belonging.

Trina Robbins's 1989 piece "Big Sister Little Sister" [Fig. 89] is about how, as a young girl, she idolized her older sister, who (as the older Robbins realizes) was actually a staunch anti-feminist and even misogynist (the younger Robbins is a feminist). This touching tale of ambivalence about a loved one is also a visual and verbal character study of the sister: full hair, big bust, and curves, and she responds to the bespectacled narrator who is reading the book *Great Ladies* with "Amelia Earhart? A lesbian! Just look at her short hair and slacks!"

In Pearlman's "Playing the Jewish Card: The Gap Year" (2004) [Figs. 87–88], she presents various caricatures of students who take a gap year before going to university, including the peace protestor's gap, the royal gap, and the Oxbridge gap: "I'm planning to ride round China on my bicycle, introducing Wagner's lesser operas to the peasants! Here's my book contract!" She parodies these characters each in one line and frame, sometimes using metaphorical and fantastical images to enhance the concept (i.e., the cultural "apology form"). Because her tirade is humorous (through exaggeration), and because she equally makes fun of many types, her critique appears to be positive. The type of person to whom she refers might not take offense, but instead, agreeably sees herself as sharing some of these characteristics.

Similarly, Noomin parodies types in her miscarriage piece. Her yuppie alter ego Glenda suggests naming her baby Jedidiah or Jessica. Glenda's husband Jimmy responds: "Too normal!" [Fig. 83]. With subtle details, she lovingly evokes a familiar kind of idiocy. Glidden also portrays some comic characters, like the girl from Orange County, who wears enormous sunglasses and a scarf. When Glidden says she's excited to find out the political, religious and moral reasons for her fellow travelers' participation on the trip, the girl says: "Um, I came here to meet hot Israeli soldiers." And in "The Turd," Lasko-Gross includes her mouthy friend who is appalled by the artist's crush and says: "He has no fucking chin." This commentary adds humor to the piece, reflecting on the banal realities of physical attraction. A funny line of dialogue due to its terseness, it is even funnier in the graphic comic form, where it's followed by an image of this guy's amorphous facial feature. We see what the friend sees, and chuckle in recognition at her apt and blunt description. Overall in these works, the visual and verbal work together to create slightly exaggerated versions of characters that are recognizable—and funny—in an instant. Their humor enables a sense of mutual social experience, a comfort of recognition.

Attack of the Vulnerable

Jibing about character and dysfunctional family relations can be seen in Laurie Sandell's *The Impostor's Daughter* (2009) [Figs. 95–99]. In this case, Sandell uses the comic form to expose a grave tale of taboo; her work is a troubling story of emotional abuse by her father, who has porous boundaries with his daughter. In one frame she is a nerdy girl going to the prom with "a nice Jewish boy"; in another, she is naked as her father walks into her room [Fig. 95]. In her work she critiques her father's behavior, but it never reads as an ambush.

This is partially due to her self-portraiture, which presents a vulnerable protagonist. Having a physical body—and one that is awkward, thin, and seemingly uncomfortable in its own skin—endows the narrator with vulnerability, and allows viewers to empathize. She sees her own faults as well. Sandell put herself in frames with her father, sharing space with him, acknowledging that they are ultimately united. Because we feel empathy with Sandell's representation, she is able to "attack" in a way that presents a complex, mature and multidimensional relationship.

The self-deprecating humor of Sandell's voice (and image) makes the tale palatable, as it suggests that the narrator has some distance from the events. Humor functions as a form of attack: it is through joking about her father that Sandell can get back at him. Scholars, such as Ruth Wisse, have suggested that Jewish humor is part of a coping mechanism for dealing with trauma and making dangerous situations seem less frightening.[21]

Another form of attack, satire, is seen in Sarah Lazarovic's "Abstained" (2007) and "Shop til you Stop" (2008), which both critique capitalist consumer culture [Figs. 76–77]. Lazarovic's comic editorial work is idea-driven, and contains chunks of explicatory text, but her images soften the blow. Her critique is presented as a narrative voice (*not* in text bubbles) but the female protagonist (we assume herself) is represented as a wiry-haired, bespectacled, sympathetic woman who is trying to do her best, even if she is a little bit hypocritical. For instance, her character says that because we are in a recession, she must make her possessions look less expensive: she is painstakingly "exfoliating my bag—removing it of all vestiges of ostentatiousness"[22] [Fig. 77]. In another scene, she challenges herself to give up shopping. She begins to barter, humorously portraying the details of the exchange by exaggerating desire and highlighting her seemingly disordered way of valuing objects: "You need some peanut butter and I need a hybrid." / "Is it crunchy?" / "Yes." / "Deal"[23] [Fig. 76]. Viewers empathize with the humorous character who is both aware of the right thing to do, but struggles to do it. The artist critiques the sorts of objects we obsess over by exaggerating them—a customer ogles a laser guided i-phone toothbrush—but the i-brush is presented as a small object, much smaller than the text and not threatening. These visual/verbal strategies soften the attack by making it more complex and funny, enabling readers to engage with the message. Again, word and text are intertwined to softly highlight discomforts.

The Punchline

In conclusion, the works in "Graphic Details" are personal memoir pieces, and, like humorous pieces of visual art and literature, they use and combine satire, parody, linguistic twists, logical upheavals, obsessive observation, role reversal, self-deprecation, and self-consciousness to help relay their emotional, harrowing, and uncomfortable tales. In these cases they merge text and image, adding their own punch to Jewish comedy. Humor makes their traumas less frightening, provides distance, helps give value to negative experiences, and leads to and stems from an ability to distance from difficulty. Humor assuages anxiety and manages hypersensitivity; it mollifies the experience of extreme emotions. Comedy can be a means of non-violent attack and retaliation, but also, a way to avoid or side-step experiencing negativity or conflict. Humor functions to confront taboo and discomfort; to make strong statements palatable to a wider audience; to reduce interpersonal conflict; and to offer playful alternatives to traditional assumptions: humor offers the possibility for creativity and invites alternative modes of thinking. On the whole, humor is granted the function of social catharsis, offering group solidarity and belonging, by showing that, as Jews, as women, as Westerners, we share a particular world experience.

NOTES

1. I have selected these subheadings as categories, as they frequently appear in this order in writing on Jewish humor. See for instance Avner Ziv and Anat Zajdman, eds., *Semites and Stereotypes: Characteristics of Jewish Humor* (Westport, CT: Greenwood, 1993) and Ruth Wisse, *Some Serious Thoughts About Jewish Humor* (New York: Leo Baeck Institute, 2001).

2. I wrote a piece for the *Jewish Quarterly* in which I articulated the ways in which Jewish humor plays out in the visual realm: juxtaposition, domestic caricature and logical twists. In the case of graphic comics, however, the visual is blended with the verbal, creating humor in unique ways. See Judy Batalion, "Seeing Shlock: Jewish Humour in Visual Art," *Jewish Quarterly* 211 (Autumn 2008).

3. "Woody Allen," Wikiquote. http://sv.wikiquote.org/wiki/Woody_Allen. Accessed October 1, 2012.

4. Joan Rivers, *Still Talking* (London: Random House, 1992), 156.

5. Other examples of self-deprecating jokes include: "I refuse to join any club that would have me as a member."—Groucho Marx; "My parents hated me. All I ever heard was, 'Why can't you be like your cousin Sheila? Why can't you be like your cousin Sheila?' Sheila had died at birth."—Joan Rivers; "I have flabby thighs. But fortunately, my stomach covers them."—Joan Rivers.

6. Sigmund Freud, *Jokes and Their Relation to the Unconscious*, Penguin Freud Library, volume 6, trans. James Strachey (London: Penguin, 1991, orig. 1905).

7. Ilana Arazie, "Drawn Together: R. Crumb's Beloved Aline Kominsky," *Heeb* (February 1, 2007). Accessed October 1, 2012.

8. Corinne Pearlman, "Playing the Jewish Card: Show & Tell," *Jewish Quarterly* 214 (December 11, 2009).

9. Searchquotes. http://www.searchquotes.com/quotation/Why_don't_Jews_drink%3F_It_interferes_with_their_suffering./21816/. Accessed October 1, 2012.

10. Examples of "anti-Semitic" jokes include: "I'm Jewish. I don't work out. If God had wanted us to bend over, He would have put diamonds on the floor."—Joan Rivers; "I'm very proud of my gold pocketwatch. My grandfather, on his death bed, sold it to me."—Woody Allen; "A lot of people say to me, 'Why did you kill Christ?' I dunno, it was one of those parties, got out of hand, you know."—Lenny Bruce; "Why do Jewish men die before their wives? They want to."—Henny Youngman.

11. Sarah Glidden, *How to Understand Israel in 60 Days or Less* (New York: DC Comics, 2010) 22.

12. As cited in Christie Davies, *The Mirth of Nations* (New Brunswick, NJ: Transaction, 2002) 180.

13. *Sarah Silverman: Jesus Is Magic*, director Liam Lynch, performed by Sarah Silverman, Laura Silverman, Brian Posehn, Bob Odenkirk, Roadside Attraction, 2005.

14. "Woody Allen," Wikiquote. http://sv.wikiquote.org/wiki/Woody_Allen. Accessed October 1, 2012.

15. "Jerry Seinfeld Quotes," Goodreads. http://www.goodreads.com/quotes/9890-the-swiss-have-an-interesting-army-five-hundred-years-without. Accessed October 1, 2012. Additional examples of obsession jokes are: "I don't want to achieve immortality through my work. I want to achieve it by not dying ... I'm not afraid of death. I just don't want to be there when it happens."—Woody Allen; "Are there keys to a plane? Maybe that's what those delays are sometimes, when you're just sitting there at the gate. Maybe the pilot sits up there in the cockpit going, 'Oh, I don't believe this. Dammit ... I did it again.' They tell you it's something mechanical because they don't want to come on the P.A. system, 'Ladies and gentlemen, we're going to be delayed here on the ground for a while. I uh ... Oh, God this is so embarrassing ... I, I left the keys to the plane in my apartment. They're in this big ashtray by the front door. I'm sorry, I'll run back and get them.'"—Jerry Seinfeld.

16. "Henny Youngman Quotes," Goodreads. http://www.goodreads.com/author/quotes/82949.Henny_Youngman. Accessed October 1, 2012.

17. "Henny Youngman Quotes," Brainy Quote. http://www.brainyquote.com/quotes/quotes/h/hennyyoung141786.html. Accessed October 1, 2012. More examples of "paralogical" jokes include: "It's amazing that the amount of news that happens in the world every day always just exactly fits the newspaper."—Jerry Seinfeld; "My grandfather always said: 'Don't watch your money; watch your health.' So one day while I was watching my health, someone stole my money. It was my grandfather."—Jackie Mason; "I have enough money to last me the rest of my life, unless I buy something."—Jackie Mason.

18. Bernice Eisenstein, *I Was a Child of Holocaust Survivors* (New York: Riverhead Books, 2006) 52.

19. Idiot = *Shlemiel, Shlemazel, Shmegegee* (a less important *shlemiel*), *Shmendrick* (spineless *shlemiel*), *Shmuck, Shmekeleh* (small *shmuck*), *Shlepper* (a tag-along), *Shluch* (slob), *Shlump* (bad postured), *Shtunkener, Shnorrer* (cheap), *Shtinker, Shikker* (drunk), *Shvitzer* (braggart), *Zhlob* (serious slob), *Shmo, Shrek* (a fright).

20. Eisenstein, 74.

21. Other samples of attack jokes might be: "The more I think of you, the less I think of you."—Henny Youngman; "May God bless and keep the Czar ... far away from us."—*Fiddler on the Roof*; "Elizabeth Taylor has more chins

than the Chinese telephone directory."— Joan Rivers. For a summary of Ruth Wisse's discussion of Jewish humor as a coping mechanism, and the potential problems of it being so, see her lecture "God Forbid You Should Laugh" given at Melbourne University, October 4, 2003, extracted in *The Sydney Morning Herald*. http://www.smh.com.au/articles/2003/10/03/1064988390639.html. Accessed October 1, 2012.

    22. Sarah Lazarovic, "Abstained," print on paper, 2007.

    23. Sarah Lazarovic, "Shop til you Stop," print on paper, 2008.

BIBLIOGRAPHY

Arazie, Ilana. "Drawn Together: R. Crumb's Beloved Aline Kominsky." *Heeb*, February 1, 2007. Accessed October 1, 2012.

Batalion, Judy. "Seeing Shlock: Jewish Humour in Visual Art." *Jewish Quarterly* 211 (Autumn 2008): 6–23.

Davies, Christie. *The Mirth of Nations*. New Brunswick, NJ: Transaction, 2002.

Eisenstein, Bernice. *I Was a Child of Holocaust Survivors*. New York: Riverhead Books, 2006.

Freud, Sigmund. *Jokes and Their Relation to the Unconscious*. Penguin Freud Library, volume 6. Trans. James Strachey. London: Penguin, 1991 (orig. 1905).

Glidden, Sarah. *How to Understand Israel in 60 Days or Less*. New York: DC Comics, 2010.

"Henny Youngman Quotes." Goodreads. October 1, 2012.

Lazarovic, Sarah. "Abstained," print on paper, 2007.

_____. "Shop til you Stop," print on paper, 2008.

Pearlman, Corinne. "Playing the Jewish Card: Show & Tell." *Jewish Quarterly* 214 (December 11, 2009): 14–15.

Rivers, Joan. *Still Talking*. London: Random House, 1992.

Sarah Silverman: Jesus Is Magic. Dir. Liam Lynch. Perf. Sarah Silverman, Laura Silverman, Brian Posehn, Bob Odenkirk. Roadside Attraction, 2005.

Wisse, Ruth. "God Forbid You Should Laugh." Melbourne University, October 4, 2003. As extracted in *The Sydney Morning Herald*, October 1, 2012.

_____. *Some Serious Thoughts About Jewish Humor*. New York: Leo Baeck Institute, 2001.

"Woody Allen." Wikiquote. October 1, 2012.

Ziv, Avner and Anat Zajdman, eds. *Semites and Stereotypes: Characteristics of Jewish Humor*. Westport, CT: Greenwood, 1993.

Part III:
Interviews

Bernice Eisenstein and
the Persistence of Memory

Michael Kaminer

Bernice Eisenstein uses words and pictures to accomplish the impossible in *I Was a Child of Holocaust Survivors* (2006), her award-winning debut graphic novel. With her lush, sensuous style, pitch-perfect ear for dialogue, and magical-realist approach to storytelling, she manages to address the horror of the Holocaust head-on without depicting the war itself. Instead, her evocation of the melancholy richness of her parents' circle of survivors tells us all we need to know about the world they lost, and the lives they built from the scraps they could save. Michael Kaminer interviewed artist, illustrator, and author Bernice Eisenstein by email in February 2012.

You've talked a lot about the fact that working on *I Was a Child of Holocaust Survivors* enabled you to have a dialogue with people who were no longer with us. Did the graphic novel form, where characters are actually visible on the page talking or thinking, enhance that experience?

I'm not sure how to begin to answer the question, since it takes me back to remembering how I actually felt while drawing or painting both people that I missed—such as my father, who had already been dead for a number of years when I began the book—and those that I had never known, family members who had died in the war. Sometimes only a portrait was made, and with others, words were added to the page. So, my experience of placing them on the page meant having that private and reflecting time spent in their company. I was listening to conversations that arose and trying to sort out my relationship to their past, and its effect and hold on me. The graphic novel form, very simply, is words and pictures on a page, and that structure, or shape, not only enhanced the experience, it was essential.

Which comic artists have influenced your art?

I think of the word "influence" as also implying encouragement, and then from that there is company. So, I'm rephrasing your question for myself: Charlotte Salomon's *Life? or Theatre?* struck a deep emotional chord. Her work consists of over 800 paintings—often with text overlaid—that brought together music, poetry, memoir and memory. The German word that defines her work is *Gesamtkunstwerk*, an all-embracing art form. I realize this is something of an inadequate, if not reductive, description, but perhaps, by my saying not enough about Salomon's beautiful expressionist paintings and text, which tell the story of her life and of her family, it might lead someone reading this to discover her for themselves, and be personally moved and influenced as well.

The book *Art of the Holocaust* (1981) had a great impact—filled with the works of artists who were in the camps, and of many who did not survive. Drawings, paintings, sketches, some made on canvas, and others on scraps of paper, scenes of what was witnessed. That book led me to look more closely at the surrealist paintings of Felix Nussbaum, who when he hid his paintings in Brussels in the house of a friend was reported to have said: "If I go down, do not let my paintings die. Show them to the people." And *The Book of Alfred Kantor* (1971). Kantor had been in several concentration camps, and had drawn what he had seen and experienced. Many of those drawings had been lost or destroyed, but after the war he recreated those images from memory, with briefly written descriptions. In *I Was a Child of Holocaust Survivors,* I wrote about bringing the book to show to my father, and what we both had felt. He found it too difficult to look beyond a few pages and I then understood the visceral power of art and memory. And of course, Art Spiegelman's *Maus,* which I first read in issues of RAW magazine, and then again later when it was published by Pantheon.

Some readers disconnect when they see that the Holocaust—or any element of it—has been examined through the lens of a graphic novel or comic book, as if the gravity of the subject matter precludes a treatment they consider less serious. How would you respond to them?

I might say something like, if the Holocaust had occurred in the 18th century, then a young boy named Isaac Newton (renamed Itzik Newton) wouldn't have needed an apple to fall on his head to discover the universal law of gravity. By proposing the seriousness of the subject had become scientific fact, I wonder if that would have settled the subject once and for all. Probably not. The world was once thought to be flat, that if you came to its edge, you'd fall off. And now we know that the world is round. But there are perspectives—lines of vision—that once again have you fearful of falling off the edge.

We all have a value system, with our tastes and dislikes, and as such we are, whether consciously or not, keepers at the gate. And on the ground before the Holocaust's gate is a sign firmly planted—Whoever Goes Here, Beware. The gravity of the subject does not preclude, nor should it limit, the form in which an artist or writer responds. But what is offered, and experienced, from that work—whether a novel, a poem, an essay, a cartoon, a graphic novel—is what matters. Words are never easily found, nor paintings or drawings casually brushed.

Can you talk about your stylistic choices for the book? There's an innocence and openness about the drawings that almost stand in counterpoint to the weight of the subject matter.

The very nature of pen and ink drawings helps define the balancing act—using black and white to mirror the coexistence of dark and light. There are some drawings in the book that are clear in their stylistic references to other artists. A fiddler on the roof playing his violin next to my aunt who was a Yiddish singer[Fig. 43], and then another of my parents enfolded in an embrace, floating—it's Chagall, for his lyricism and for the sense of the past, of memory and loss, that is imbued in his work. And there's also a portrait of myself *à la* van Gogh[Fig. 44]. Their influence has been a presence long before the book.

But as for "openness," the word describes the whole process in which I was immersed. There is something that happens when doing portraits. It's not easy to put into words—but

Fig. 43. Excerpted from *I Was a Child of Holocaust Survivors* by Bernice Eisenstein, 54–55. Copyright © 2006 Bernice Eisenstein. Reprinted by permission of McClelland & Stewart.

you paint until you come to a moment when that person's image finally holds all the thoughts and feelings you've been able to find, or unearth. And in that instance of recognition, you are released. It can't happen without being open. And with each new painting, you keep discovering this over and over again.

The different presentations of "Graphic Details" have drawn a straight line between autobiographical comics and other forms of Jewish art and literature. How do you see your own work in relation to those traditions?

I'm Jewish, I draw and I write. Tradition?—Just add a few bars of familiar music...

Did you draw yourself different than you'd expected?

I realized early on that what I was creating was initiated through remembering myself at different ages. Sometimes I'm five years old, or ten, or twenty, or older. Whatever the age and the feelings that belong to that time, they reside and float inside the older person—me—reflecting and commenting, either in words or drawings, or both. It's more than split personalities appearing—it was a movement through past and present, forwards and backwards, accompanied with the full range of rollercoaster emotions. Funny, sad, confused, ironic, serious, all layered one on top of the other. I needed to draw myself, have a visual persona that was not specific to a particular age. The cartoon self-portrait became a comfortable "voice" that mirrored my sensibility.

Would your experience with *I Was a Child of Holocaust Survivors* encourage you to create more autobiographical work in this format?

Lust for Life

3 Faces of Eve

Bridge Over a River Kwai

Uhuru

Diary of Anne Frank

The Pawnbroker

Fig. 44. Original art for *I Was a Child of Holocaust Survivors*. Copyright © 2006 Bernice Eisenstein.

I don't think I'd want to do another autobiographical book, but if you consider any work that's made as coming from an individual's way of seeing and thinking ... of responding—then there is always an autobiographical element. And in doing that—finding ways of putting words and drawings together—always.

You created such a vivid evocation of your parents' Yiddish milieu. Can you talk about how the comic/cartoon elements enhanced that aspect of the book?

Perhaps it has to do with coming to the point where words are not enough, and then a drawing, a cartoon, is able to continue the evocation of the past—not only my own, which was infused with Yiddish in our household when I was growing up, but also the life that was shared by my parents with their group of friends. The drawings are intended to have that past come to life, just as the door was opened for me to remember them; the drawings are there for their life to be seen.

BIBLIOGRAPHY

Blatter, Janet, and Sybil Milton. *Art of the Holocaust.* New York: Routledge, 1981.
Eisenstein, Bernice. *I Was a Child of Holocaust Survivors.* New York: Riverhead Books, 2006.
Kantor, Alfred. *The Book of Alfred.* New York: McGraw-Hill, 1971.
Salomon, Charlotte. *Leben? oder Theater? Life? or Theatre?* London: Royal Academy of Arts, 1998.
Spiegelman, Art. *Maus.* New York: Pantheon, 1986.

How to Understand Sarah Glidden in 2,000 Words or Less

Michael Kaminer

The simplicity of Sarah Glidden's drawing style belies the raw honesty, weight, and power of her stories. *How to Understand Israel in 60 Days or Less*, which started life as a self-published 'zine in 2007—and became one of 2012's most acclaimed releases after prestigious DC Comics imprint Vertigo picked it up—reflects everything that makes Sarah's work so potent. Stark compositions, clean lines, and masterful composition bring both poignancy and energy to her account of a Birthright Israel trip. Throughout, Glidden voices the same uncertainties, fears, and hopes we bring as readers. Sarah earned a place in the *2012's Best American Comics* anthology (Houghton Mifflin Harcourt, 2012) for the "Golan Heights" segment of *How to Understand Israel in 60 Days or Less* (Vertigo, 2010). Michael Kaminer interviewed Sarah Glidden by email in January 2013.

How unfiltered were the experiences and thoughts we saw in *How to Understand Israel in 60 Days or Less*? How much was Sarah a character vs. you?

I tried to keep the book as honest, as close to the experience and my thoughts surrounding it as possible. I had a lot of material to help me with this, as I kept a journal during the trip and was pretty diligent about recording everything as it was happening (conversations, worries, thoughts, etc.). But there's no such thing as an unfiltered memoir. Researchers who study how memory works are pretty sure that each time you "remember" something, you're actually recreating it; it's not just some file stored somewhere in your head that you can pull out and read. We all go through our lives creating characters of ourselves. Making a memoir or an autobiographical comic is just a way of putting that character down on paper.

How to Understand Israel in 60 Days or Less is full of ambiguities. Why do you think an autobiographical comic was an effective vehicle for that?

The book was meant to be a retelling of my own personal experience and not some sort of objective guide to the conflict. It follows my thoughts as we travel through the country, and I was constantly weighing what we were being told against what I already knew and what I was gleaning from conversations with other people. Of course, nothing is going to be clear-cut when it comes to a place like Israel, which has had such a complicated history, and ambiguities were constantly present. When we think about anything, whether it be a political issue, our own past, a conversation we had yesterday, we're not thinking in just words or images, it's some combination of those things that shift constantly. Comics are perfect for representing this process because they include both elements (words and pictures) and you can control how much of each you use. I tend to daydream a lot and comics work well with daydreams [Figs. 45–47].

Can you give us some insight into stylistic choices you made in *How to Understand Israel in 60 Days or Less*? **The drawing style is so straightforward, but the content is so full of inner conflict and turmoil.**

The drawing style is straightforward because that's how I draw! I studied oil painting at a very traditional art school [Boston University College of Fine Arts], so I learned how to reproduce what I saw in front of me. That means I can draw from a model or a photograph well ... but that's not really useful for comics. You're using a whole different skill set when you're creating a panel or a character, and it's one that I'm still learning. I doubt I'll ever get to a point where I'll be satisfied with my drawing skills. But at the same time, I'm comfortable with my limits. The style I use is just me working within them and challenging myself without pretending I can draw in a way that I can't.

I also just draw what I like to look at. The comics that tend to draw my eye, grab my attention, are ones that are drawn with a clear and somewhat delicate line. I love the work of Gabrielle Bell, Anders Nilsen, and the old Franco-Belgian artists like Hergé. Their drawings breathe and I feel comfortable staying with them for a long time, so I was naturally trying to emulate that feeling a little when I started making my own comics. It's just a question of personal taste [Figs. 61–64].

What kinds of responses did the book receive from the Jewish establishment, which generally doesn't appreciate anything but unbridled enthusiasm for Israel?

That idea, that the Jewish establishment doesn't accept criticism of Israel, is a belief that I held while I was working on this book, and I was very nervous about how it would be received. I was expecting hate mail. But that turned out to be a huge misconception on my part. I got a very enthusiastic response from the American Jewish community and a lot of invitations to come talk about the book at Jewish community centers, Hillel Houses, and synagogues all over the country. This is not to say that everyone who I spoke to at these places (or the organizers who invited me) agreed with all of the thoughts I outlined in the book. But there's a growing recognition among U.S. Jews of all stripes that this is an issue that should be open to discussion. People want to talk about it and they want to be able to do so without being called a "self-hating Jew" because they criticize Israel. This has become increasingly urgent in the past decade as the Israeli government has become more and more conservative, I think. [This move more to the right] isn't sitting well with liberal American Jews and there's a hunger for conversation about it.

What's the connection you see between autobiographical comics and newer work you've been calling "graphic journalism?"

The connection is that at their root, these are very similar things. I'm going somewhere, talking to some people, and then making a comic about it. But the Israel book was never intended to be journalism, and I didn't go into that trip thinking of myself as a reporter. I was going on a Birthright trip, having feelings, and writing down what happened. I didn't know what I was doing, really. It was after the trip, when I was working on the book, that I became interested in the journalistic process and started thinking about moving more in that direction. The difference may seem subtle, because journalism can still be very subjective and include elements of autobiography. I think it has a lot to do with intention. What am

52

Fig. 45. Sarah Glidden, "Sleep," *How to Understand Israel in 60 Days or Less* (New York: Vertigo/DC Comics, 2010) 52. © 2010 Sarah Glidden. Used with permission of DC Comics.

Fig. 46. Sarah Glidden, "Sleep," *How to Understand Israel in 60 Days or Less* (New York: Vertigo/DC Comics, 2010) 53. © 2010 Sarah Glidden. Used with permission of DC Comics.

Fig. 47. Sarah Glidden, "Sleep," *How to Understand Israel in 60 Days or Less* (New York: Vertigo/DC Comics, 2010) 54. © 2010 Sarah Glidden. Used with permission of DC Comics.

I trying to explore here? In the Israel book, it was the experience of struggling with one's own relationship to a political conflict. In the work I've done since, the focus is on people and ideas that are much more outside of myself. One memoir was enough; I'm much more interested now in finding out more about other people's thoughts.

Did your autobiographic work in *How to Understand Israel in 60 Days or Less* open you up to confront other political subjects in cartoons such as "State of Palestine" and "The Waiting Room"?

I think, more than the Israel book, it was the move into journalism that opened up my work. The day before *How to Understand Israel in 60 Days or Less* came out in bookstores, I was getting on a plane with two friends of mine who are journalists in order to follow them on a two-month-long reporting trip to Turkey, northern Iraq, Lebanon and Syria, the idea being that my next book would be about these reporters and how they work. I was learning about journalism by watching journalists at work, but also because I was being a journalist in the process of doing so. The reporting for "The Waiting Room," which is about Iraqi refugees in Syria, was actually done during that trip. By the time those two months were up, I was addicted to journalism. The idea that you can just talk to people, ask them questions about their lives and experiences, and then pass that on to other people ... it's intoxicating. Behind every political subject are people living their lives who have stories to tell. I'm not really interested in researching these things at a deep foreign policy level, I just want to listen to and tell those stories.

BIBLIOGRAPHY

Glidden, Sarah. *How to Understand Israel in 60 Days or Less.* New York: Vertigo, 2010.
_____. "State of Palestine," *Cartoon* Movement, 2011. http://www.cartoonmovement.com/comic/.15.
_____. "The Waiting Room," *Cartoon Movement*, 2011. http://www.cartoonmovement.com/comic/.10.
Mouly, Françoise, Jessica Abel, and Matt Madden. *The Best American Comics 2012.* Boston: Houghton Mifflin Harcourt, 2012.

Sarah Lazarovic: On Politics, Big Glasses and Not Shopping

Michael Kaminer

It's impossible to pigeonhole Sarah Lazarovic's prodigious output as an illustrator, filmmaker, visual artist, conceptual prankster, and newspaper commentator. But her work does carry common threads: sly, subversive humor, a sensual drawing style, and a knowingly self-mocking overlay that reveals complete control of whatever medium she's exploring. Her autobiographical work also stands alone in "Graphic Details: Confessional Comics by Jewish Women"; no other artist portrays herself through editorial cartoons, as Sarah did in her "Another Week" series for Canada's *The Ottowa Citizen* from 2005 to 2010 and *Vancouver Sun* from 2006 to 2009. With her and her husband as characters, Sarah uses the minutiae of daily life to confront bigger questions around politics, consumerism, and identity. Michael Kaminer interviewed Sarah from her home base of Toronto by email.

You made yourself a character in editorial strips that ran in several Canadian newspapers. What do you think that allowed you to do that a conventional editorial cartoon wouldn't?

A conventional editorial cartoon has pretty strict parameters—large noses, crosshatching, big text labels for things that may be otherwise too obtuse. I was lucky there was no rulebook for my weekly cartoon, as it wasn't an editorial cartoon but more of a column in cartoon form that my first editor generously helped me concoct. Though the characters I drew were pretty much my husband and myself, I never explicitly referred to them as such. Instead, we were proxies for two sides of whatever issue of the week I was tackling. By giving us outlandish views (okay, usually me), and funny physical characteristics (Ben had a spring for a neck, which he protested weekly, and I had glasses the size of my face, which I coveted weekly), I also created some distance between the comic strip and us [Figs.76–77].

Through your personal issues and conflicts, you brought up resonant truths about consumerism, religion, relationships, and politics. Did you start from the outside in—beginning with an issue—or from the inside out, choosing a topic from personal experience?

Each week's column was almost always pegged to an issue in the news or something extremely *Zeitgeist*. The comic was meant to poke at these ideas with humor, and hopefully provide thoughtful commentary as well. I just became the filter for making fun of the inherent absurdity of so much of what passes for news.

Your work's unusual in "Graphic Details" because it's not a narrative autobiography, like much of the work. Is your cartooning autobiographical? How would you characterize it?

The work in the show is perhaps less autobiographical and I do a lot of straightforward illustration and reportage comics as well, but I also have a part of my comics practice that is more traditional autobiography. I do comics for *Tablet Magazine* that are narratives about my personal experiences. And I've just started a monthly comic for *Bunch*, an online Jewish magazine that is autobiographical. I'm also working on a book about my experiences *not* shopping (PLUG: out with Penguin Viking 2014!) that is a completely personal illustrated tale [Figs. 48–49].

Your husband, Ben Errett, wrote *Jew and Improved* (2010), a terrific book about becoming Jewish. He also appears in your work. Did having his perspective affect the Jewish "content" or perspective of your work in any way—not just overtly, but even in terms of sensibility?

Definitely not overtly, but we really like working together, and often act as each other's editor, so there's certainly some idea seepage between us. When one of us is working on something the other can't help but have it smushed into their brain, and having read his book approximately 35 times I'm not sure where his sensibility ends and mine begins. Also, for a new Jew he has old soul Borscht Belt wit, which lends itself very well to comics.

In 2006 I didn't buy any clothes. I felt I was buying absentmindedly, sauntering into a boutique and walking out with a 'find.' In 2012 I decided to not shop again, after noticing I was buying too much crap on the Internet. It's not that I'm a crazy shopaholic*—I'm just really good at finding amazing stuff to buy. Amazing stuff to buy that I totally do not need. Except for that adorable sweater.
*GROSS WORD ALERT

Saint James cream/navy crew neck knit Breton jumper, £85.00

Fig. 48, *left*; fig. 49, *right*. From *A Bunch of Pretty Things I Didn't Buy* by Sarah Lazarovic © 2014 by Sarah Lazarovic. Used by permission of Penguin, a division of Penguin Group (USA) Inc.

Your work doesn't fit neatly in any boxes; you've tackled cartooning, installations, illustration, film, and more. Does that become a challenge? Do comics geeks embrace your work, since it's so hard to categorize?

I've always wished I could focus on one thing and aim for virtuoso status at it (accruing Gladwell's 10,000 hours and a MacArthur Genius Grant or seven), but I've slowly come to the realization that I'm just not built that way. Luckily, I feel equally uncomfortable at film fest industry gatherings, art openings and comics conventions, so it all works out.

Do you think your work has anything in common with other women in "Graphic Details?" Were you comfortable getting grouped this way as part of the show?

I was beyond flattered to be included with such an amazing line up of ladies, and while there is a huge range of style and subject, I think together there's a nice cross-section of issues and ideas that dominate the Jewish female experience. I recognize that my work tends towards the outward and light, and I really appreciate that so many of the other artists in the show tackle much deeper and tougher issues.

You're now a mother, which you weren't when a lot of this work was created. Has that changed the content and style of your work?

I refuse to exploit my personal life for subject matter... Hey, have you checked out my web comics about my daughter and me?

BIBLIOGRAPHY

Errett, Ben. *Jew and Improved.* Toronto: HarperCollins, 2010.
Lazarovic, Sarah. "Another Week." *The Ottawa Citizen* from 2005 to 2010 and *Vancouver Sun* from 2006 to 2009.

"A portrait of the world through my eyes"

An Interview with Miss Lasko-Gross

TAHNEER OKSMAN

Published in 2006, *Escape from "Special"* is Miss Lasko-Gross's debut graphic memoir, and it is followed by a second memoir that continues the story chronologically, entitled *A Mess of Everything*, and published in 2009. The "semi-autobiographical" books trace the main character, Melissa, from her earliest memory to her high school years. Lasko-Gross is currently working on a fictional graphic novel, *Henni*, which explores religious fundamentalism.

In the following interview, conducted on Manhattan's Lower East Side on April 15, 2011, Tahneer Oksman speaks to Miss Lasko-Gross, who discusses the impetus behind her creation of these memoirs, as well as the importance of the themes of identity and Jewishness both in her works and in her own life. Lasko-Gross points out, not once but twice, in the interview that the memoirs are a portrait of the world through her eyes—or works that hold, over and above the importance of maintaining verifiable particular truths, the cardinal concern of representing the more universal "Truths" of human experience—those embedded not in any definitive or ultimate location, but instead in the winding and often painful pursuit of the unanswerable.

In a recent interview on the Jewesses with Attitude blog you said you didn't think your Jewish identity influences your work—is this true?[1]

It [my work] reeks of Jewishness, but I didn't set out to do anything [like that]. I'm non-religious, very much secular. But at the same time, I'm such a Jew. I especially notice that in relation to my husband, who's not a Jew.

On the back cover of *A Mess of Everything*, it says that the book is part of a semi-autobiographical trilogy. Is there a third book in the works?

I never said I was doing a trilogy. Somewhere along the line, someone decided that it was a trilogy, but it was not. I always planned to continue doing books up until old age. I thought it would be great to have a series that starts from my very earliest childhood memories, which are kind of sketchy and flash memories that make no sense, and going up to when I'm horribly old and cranky and just miserable. But at the same time, I would never have said that I was doing a trilogy because I want to do the whole life. And also, as much as people have asked me to do the third one, I want to be, probably, forty before I do a book about my twenties. You need the time to have perspective about what was actually significant.

A lot of autobiographies get into minutia, where it's not interesting, it's more self-indulgent, and you don't really see the themes. You're still so close to the perspective you had at the time [that you are writing about] you can't laugh at yourself in the same way that you can ten years later. You have to understand that [certain events are] not significant in order to write about them. Otherwise, it's a bit too much like a diary.

You work has been compared to Harvey Pekar, which seems an unlikely comparison.

I think someone probably thought they're both Jewish and they're cranky—go! It's a nice comparison. But at the same time, I don't think it's apt.

What does semi-autobiographical mean to you? Did you use that term to describe your work?

No. I would have said it's an autobiography. But now, in retrospect, I'm glad that they put it on [the cover] because it gives you this kind of plausible deniability when it comes to people.

Now, all of a sudden, all of these people I went to school with have realized [I wrote these books]. Someone told someone else and now I'm getting emails from people who are randomly wanting to catch up, and they say to me: "Oh! I haven't read the book or anything, but I heard this exists..." It makes some people really angry. They say: "It didn't really happen like that *or* your personal view of things is not what mine was *or* you had that thing happen then, and it really happened then." It's people who don't understand that you need to edit, otherwise it's just a long-winded conversation with a very boring person.

Some characters are basically a composite. If you're trying to be literally 100 per cent true-to-life, then you'll constantly be introducing characters who show up for a week and then disappear. There are so many people who come in and out of your life that it would be unwieldy. The names are all changed. And appearances are changed too, but there were still some complaints. People ask: "Why didn't you put me in the book? And, why did you put me in the book?" No matter what, you'll never please everyone. There will always be some who will be angry and hate you, and there's nothing you can do about it.

Is Miss your legal name?[2]

No, it's Melissa. But Miss is short for Melissa.

Which do you prefer?

Miss. Only my family calls me Melissa.

Do you consider Melissa—the character in the book—an alter ego or a character?

Just me ... I think I'm pretty fair in showing the bad and the good. Lots of female artists draw themselves a lot prettier than they are, a lot younger than they are. I think I'm pretty honest with the physicality of the character and the personality.

Why do you think female cartoonists have a tendency to draw themselves as less attractive than they are, for example Aline Kominsky-Crumb or Julia Wertz?

With Kominsky-Crumb, I think she's intentionally exaggerating the giant ass and big Jew nose... It's a totem, more than it's meant to be her.

The opening of *Escape from "Special"* feels like it has a different tone from the rest of the book, almost like it's a prelude. There's a close-up of Melissa with what looks to be a tear or a drop of sweat rolling down her face, and her thought bubble reads: "I always want to know everything true" [Fig. 50]. Is this your impetus behind writing both these books? Is it about capturing the truth?

I don't know whether it's something I set out to do. But you can see yourself more clearly when the book's done. You can see things about yourself that you didn't know ahead of time. I wouldn't say I set out to do that. I want to tell entertaining stories, to make good artwork. It's not so self-indulgent that it's really about me and a personal exploration. It just happens to be that I am my own source material. I think in the end it's more of a portrait of the world through my eyes than of me as a person.

Do you have to go back to source materials for your memories, like journals and photos, or was it more of a cerebral experience?

I tried to make it organic. I've actually been a lot more truthful than I set out to be. When my mother looked at the book, she said: "Oh, that's so-and-so." Whereas, I was thinking that this is just a woman who was like the one I remembered. But she can look at it and say: "Oh yeah, that was so-and-so." Or: "That's the wallpaper at so-and-so's house." It's a little fuzzy with the younger memories. Everything is a little bit less specific because I didn't want to make things up and I didn't want to tie things up with a beginning, middle, and end for all of the vignettes. I wanted it to be just pure memories... So they kind of begin and end the way your own childhood memories do. Very few people remember what happened when they were five or can pinpoint *the day started out like this, I was doing this, and I was wearing this.* I don't think those details are important ultimately. If this was the biography of an important historical figure, then it's important to know the details—the temperature was this, they were wearing plaid... But it's not really about me. It's a portrait of the world through my eyes, so it doesn't really matter.

So, it's more about tone than about the actual events?

Yeah. And it ends up being more true when you don't research something to death.

Alison Bechdel did a lot of archival research to produce *Fun Home*.

I love that book and it was the opposite [of what I do] because it was very literal. Everything was well researched, well written. She narrates the hell out of it... For that book, it works. It's a masterpiece.

Your work is reminiscent of Vanessa Davis's journalistic and autobiographical comics, especially the way you piece your story out of seemingly unrelated vignettes.[3]

It's what's unsaid. There's an unspoken philosophical point behind every one of those short stories. I didn't just put the most interesting things that happened, or the most horrible, or the best. But there's a meaning behind every story. One review said, the stories just begin and end for no reason. When someone says that, I know that they don't really understand what the books were about.

You mean like with the turd story from the "Graphic Details" exhibit?[4] [Figs. 37–38.]

That's a good example. The point of that story is that you can look at that and it's a scatological story. It's funny. Or you can think: Oh that story's really about how as a teenager everything seems so intensely important. And then you read it as an adult and you realize it didn't matter. There was a giant log in the toilet and you left it, and so what? It's so clearly not important when you put it into the perspective of adult existence.

Why does the theme of institutional religions and organizations come up so often in your work? In *Escape from "Special"* Melissa experiences her parents putting her in different schools, feeling like an outsider and being told she's an outsider [Fig. 51].

For so much of my life—and I'm sure a lot of people feel this way—your identity is revealed to you in relation to your struggles with whomever or whatever you're coming up against. And for me, it was always whatever order I was rebelling against, where there was a rule, it didn't seem reasonable to me, and I didn't see why I had to do it. Whether it was wanting

Fig. 50. Miss Lasko-Gross, "Kidnapped," *Escape from "Special"* (Seattle: Fantagraphics, 2006) 5.

Fig. 51. Miss Lasko-Gross, "Of Little Faith II," *Escape from "Special"* (Seattle: Fantagraphics, 2006) 115.

to graduate early from school, or having to go to religious services or classes when that's not really what I wanted to do and I thought it was a ridiculous waste of my time... As a kid, you don't really have any control over your life. You go to school where your parents put you in school. You can only wear, for the most part, what they give you. You can only read what's around you. So it's about those kinds of conflicts with rules, and it just happens that I organized my childhood as a struggle against religion, school, and buffoonish authority figures.

In the comic entitled "Of Little Faith II" (*Escape from "Special"*) Melissa sits next to her friend in Hebrew school. Her friend says to her that the miracles in the Bible "are all crap," which perks Melissa up. But then she adds: "But of *course* I believe in God!" and Melissa thinks to herself: "I really am alone" [Fig. 51].

That's something I actually still feel. For example, when you're having a very rational conversation with someone you feel is very intelligent and you're on the same page about everything—neither one of you believes in unicorns, for example, or you're talking about politics... You think you've made a connection, and then they'll say something like natural disasters are just God's way of keeping us in line. And you think, whoa—we're really not even the same creature. It is disheartening. Because in one second that sets you apart from the other person, it puts up a wall... It's a horrible end to any kind of dialogue when someone is a fundamentalist (is "fundamentalist" too strong a word used for the example given?). The book I'm working on now [*Henni*] is almost entirely about religious fundamentalism. I'm still drawing it. It's probably going to be a long one.

This is a fictional work?

Someone who's familiar with my work would recognize themes from the first two graphic novels, but at the same time it doesn't even involve humans. It's a very important way to make my point... It features cat-like humans, who look like foolish people running around in fur suits. It's in the format of an epic quest, but a lot of it is about religious fundamentalism.

Why are you still focused on religion? Do you feel like you haven't said everything you wanted to say on the topic?

It's impossible to look at what's going on in the world and not think that one of the biggest conflicts we have is against fundamentalist thinking. It doesn't have to be any particular religion, but fundamentalist thinking... That absolute, unreasonable, irrational type of thinking. It was something I really wanted to do a book about.

The theme of identity often comes up in your work. In "Child Psychology," an early comic in *Escape from "Special,"* Melissa is talking to a child therapist: "I don't want people to know my identity." The therapist asks her: "Well, what is your identity?" and she's frazzled. This story reflects the tension between wanting to be an individual, "special" and unique, but also needing to know where you fit in. Can you tell me more about this issue of identity in your comics?

It's about how you define yourself by what you're struggling against... There are also the labels that are put on you from birth, like being Jewish—someone tells you something like that and you think, *well, what does it mean? I don't feel a particular way.* Being a non-believer from such an early age didn't matter, it didn't remove that Jewish label... And then there was being a special education student. Those are labels that are applied to you, and you have no say in them whatsoever. You end up with an identity that's a composite of what everyone else calls you.

Do you think that happens to you as a woman who creates comics?

Sure. I'm generalizing here, but many people have certain expectations for female cartoonists. They assume that you'll be a bad artist until they see your artwork... When my husband and I are introduced at a party to someone and they're told, *oh, they both do comics*, all the serious questions, any questions about cartooning, go to him, and they assume automatically that he's the professional and that I'm the dabbler and I'm doing a little fanzine and it's scribbly and it's cute and it's going to be about, *oh darn, my favorite shoes, I can't find them*, or something like that. As a female cartoonist, what happens often is that you are almost automatically put into that category of people who can't draw.

There is the preconception that comics are only meant to be read by children. Would you say that *Escape from "Special"* is for young readers?

The touchy thing is parents and what they think is right for their children. When parents come up to me at a convention and they ask: "Is this okay for my eleven-year-old girl?" I put it back in their hands. I say: "Well, is she mature? Is she smart?" And then they say: "Yes, of course..." If they're trying to coddle their kids, then no, it's not the right book for children because they'll just look at specific words, isolated nudity, that kind of thing and make a decision based on that, which is a shame because I think it's more about context than about words or images. But that's what people do—they take things out of context and then get outraged.

What made you decide to turn to writing a fictional work [*Henni*]?

I never did anything autobiographical until I did those two early graphic novels. I did a series called *Aim*, which was kind of based on some of my experiences, but it was a fictional series.[5] And I like to write stories that are fiction. So I think it's more the autobiography that was the deviation from the norm.

How has your working process been different with this book?

I don't think the process changed, although, artistically, I didn't put as much time into the first book because I didn't know if it was going to have a publisher. When I started the first book, it was just for myself, I didn't think there *was* a book. I ended up throwing away a lot of the artwork when I realized I was going to be doing a book. With the second book, I immediately knew that I was creating a book, that it had a publisher and an audience, so I went right into it seriously. I didn't have to throw anything away for the second one, but for the first book I had to throw away a good chunk because it didn't fit what it became.

What about your process in general? Is it true that you draw things to scale because you draw as you're going about your life?

A large chunk of those first two books I drew on the subway. Anytime your hand gets jostled or something, you can fix that in Photoshop and just give it a little nip-tuck. I don't do that anymore. I like to have more control, and more polish. But at the time I was working so many hours and that was the only way I could fit in drawing a book. It was any spare moment. I was working full time. I was pretty busy. Being a cartoonist doesn't pay... Most of us have day jobs.

Do you still draw to scale?

No. I'm doing a standard comic-size page now. Not 100 percent. It's larger, so it will be reduced.

Who influences your work?

In comics, the most influential works have been Katsuhiro Otomo's *Akira* (1982). I read those comics religiously when I was in high school, as they were translated. So my collection stops around issue 40, whenever there was that break in the translations. Also, Jaime Hernandez in particular from Los Bros Hernandez and *Love and Rockets* was a huge influence.

Outside of comics, I'm a huge film buff. I love silent film, I love early film, expressionist film. Alfred Hitchcock, as you know from the books, was a favorite of mine when I was a little girl. Alfred Hitchcock Presents was one of my favorites. I think my storytelling visually—is cinematic.

Where do you get most of your comics?

I go to Bergen Street Comics in Brooklyn or sometimes I go to Jim Hanley's Universe. The House of Twelve Comic Jam is a few doors down.[6] They have a drink and draw about once a month. It's been going on for about a decade. They put out anthology books. House of Twelve books. That's been a chance to do some stuff that's very different from the autobiographical work.

The comic you're working on now is framed as an epic, not as vignettes...

Yeah, it's one sustained narrative. And there are no thought bubbles. That's something that I set out to do for myself. If someone has any kind of internal monologue, it's spoken out loud. That's the extent of it. I still did not include narration because I hate narration. I see narration as giving up, as assuming that the audience can't understand your visual narration so you have to explain what's going on to them.

Outsider themes are weaved into both of your memoirs, notably an image of your persona's face with two Jewish stars, which looked like they'd been tattooed on.

That's what I'm saying about being branded with an identity, whether or not it fits you. It's the visual representation of the branding.

But it doesn't seem like a completely negative thing... At certain points, it's almost like that "special" is helping you think through who you are...

Yeah. I think all my very strong Jewish qualities are not bad qualities. I'm all the things you would stereotypically expect: I'm notoriously cheap. I over-intellectualize everything, as my husband likes to say. I'm hopelessly neurotic or just crazy and very much a Jew. And this is why I still call myself a Jew, even though I've gone out of my way my entire life to do nothing in that direction and to do everything against it. But it's still an inescapable fact that I'm a Jew. It's out of my hands because I just *am* that character. There's no getting around it. Someone might say, you're not a "Jew's Jew." You don't believe, you don't practice, you don't do anything. I often make the joke that I'm a bad Jew, enjoying delicious bread during Passover. Because I don't do any of that... It's much more of a cultural identity than anything else.

We're going up to my family to celebrate Passover. I like the food, I like the family. But it doesn't matter. We could celebrate Kwanza or anything. Everyone gets together, there's food, everyone loves food, there's family. Everyone thinks their cultural identities are so different from everybody else's. It's only in these tiny little details that you see any differences. There's a lot of that in *Henni*. Everywhere she travels, everyone is the same. Everyone has their own creation myth.

Notes

1. Jewesses with Attitude is a blog run by the Jewish Women's Archive. The interview, conducted by Leah Berkenwald and posted on February 14, 2011, was part of a series of interviews of the 18 artists featured in the "Graphic Details" exhibit.

2. The name on the cover page of Lasko-Gross's graphic memoirs is "Miss Lasko-Gross," whereas the name of her persona in the comics is "Melissa."

3. Vanessa Davis is another young and Jewish cartoonist who publishes autobiographical comics, including diary comics. She has published two full length works: the graphic journal, *Spaniel Rage* (2005), and the graphic memoir, *Make Me a Woman* (2010), which includes sketches, long-form narrative comics, and diary comics.

4. This nine-page comic, "The Turd," was published in *A Mess of Everything* and featured in "Graphic Details." It pictures Melissa as a teenager hanging out at a coffee shop with a friend, Terry. After a few minutes of discussing politics with her friend, she goes to the bathroom and, to her horror, the toilet does not flush. The story recounts in detail the anxiety of that incident.

5. *Aim* was Miss Lasko-Gross' very first comic series published by the independent Cryptic Press between 1993 and 2001.

6. House of Twelve Comics is an art collective started by "Cheese" Hasselberger and various friends. The collective publishes digital and print comics, including the House of Twelve anthology, which has often featured work by Miss Lasko-Gross. For more, see their website, http://houseoftwelve.com/.

Bibliography

Antler, Joyce. *Talking Back: Images of Jewish Women in American Popular Culture.* Hanover, NH: Brandeis University Press of New England, 1998.

Biale, David, Michael Galchinsky, and Susannah Heschel, eds. *Insider/Outsider: American Jews and Multiculturalism.* Berkeley: University of California Press, 1998.

Bloom, Lisa E. *Jewish Identities in American Feminist Art: Ghosts of Ethnicity.* New York: Routledge, 2006.

Brodkin, Karen. *How Jews Became White Folks & What That Says About Race in America.* New Brunswick, NJ: Rutgers University Press, 2000.

Gubar, Susan. "Eating the Bread of Affliction: Judaism and Feminist Criticism." *Tulsa Studies* 13.2 (Autumn 1994): 293–316.

Lasko-Gross, Miss. *A Mess of Everything.* Seattle: Fantagraphics, 2009.

_____. *Escape from "Special."* Seattle: Fantagraphics, 2006.

_____. "Graphic Details: Interview with Miss Lasko-Gross." Interview with Leah Berkenwald. *Jewesses with Attitude*, 15 February 2011. http://jwa.org/blog/graphic-details-interview-miss-lasko-gross.

Otomo, Katsuhiro. *Akira* (1982–1990). Serialized by Kodansha. Translated 1989–1995. New York: Marvel.

Prell, Riv-Ellen. *Fighting to Become Americans: Jews, Gender, and the Anxiety of Assimilation.* Boston: Beacon Press, 1999.

Thinking Panoramically

An Interview with Lauren Weinstein

Tahneer Oksman

Lauren Weinstein's *Girl Stories* (2006), originated as a series of short comics on www.gURL.com, a website aimed at teenage girls. *Girl Stories* is a small, brightly colored book, drawn in the bubbly style of a young, creative teenager. The graphic novel follows the life of a girl entering the eighth grade as she experiences the humiliations and exhilarations of her young adulthood. Weinstein has also published less categorizable comics in the form of a short series called "Little Laurie Sprinkles," created for Seattle's independent newspaper, *The Stranger*, and an oversized, beautifully drawn comic book about the adventures of Valkyrie, the great-granddaughter of Thor, entitled *The Goddess of War* [Fig. 52]. Tahneer Oksman interviewed Lauren Weinstein in person on September 20, 2011, at a coffee shop in the small New Jersey town where Weinstein lives. Weinstein discussed how she began writing comics and how her Jewish identity has influenced her project *Girl Stories* (2006), and her current book, its sequel, *Calamity* (in progress).

Each of your books has a different shape and size. What influenced each of your books' unique forms?

Girl Stories was long and looked like a *Garfield* book. It started [as a series] on the web, so that was the easiest size to put all of the work into. As I work on the new book, *Calamity*, which is the same size by default, it makes me think panoramically. With *The Goddess of War*, I was really inspired by old comic strips, like from the 1920s. *Krazy Kat* and all of those old comics. I also love Chris Ware's big books. I wanted to work in the biggest size that I could without making it too much of a publishing issue, but it became a publishing issue. Also, because it's just a pamphlet—it's not even a hardcover—the books get damaged a lot. I don't think I'll ever work in that size again. My originals are really big. It's a daunting thing, to work that big. I do think about a project concept first, and then I design everything around that. The *Girl Stories* books seemed like they should be long and thin and accessible. With *The Goddess of War*, I wanted it to be epic, so I made it big.

How important is packaging for your books and your websites?[1]

The *Girl Stories* website was designed by John Kuramoto. We designed it together. We really wanted it to look like a kid's journal. And then my blog is new—I just started to work

185

Fig. 52. Lauren Weinstein, *The Goddess of War* (New York: Picturebox, 2008) cover.

on it seriously; my intern and I are designing it. She was a student of mine at SVA [the School of Visual Arts].

How do you feel about having an intern?

I was recently talking to a friend who's a painting professor. We were talking about feminism and fine art, and why women don't get ahead more. She was saying that one of the reasons is that there's not a lot of mentorship between older established men and younger women because even if there's nothing going on, it seems weird. It's easier to be a mentor to somebody who's the same sex as you. I think that since I'm at the School of Visual Arts and I'm kind of in a position of power, it's wonderful to have women interns, people that I feel like I can help and connect with other people. I think that's a big deal. It's something that I only recently realized that I could do for people.

Have you ever had a mentor?

I've been really lucky in that I've gotten to meet almost all of my heroes. I've met [Robert] Crumb and Chris Ware—and they've helped me, they've given me advice about different things. I love Gabrielle Bell's work so much, and we go out and draw sometimes. She's a peer—I take her words seriously.

Are you in touch with older women cartoonists?

I've corresponded with some, like Aline Kominsky-Crumb, but not in a serious way. I'm Facebook friends with Carol Tyler. But, in terms of people that have mentored me in comics, not really. Luckily, I met an amazing group of people when I first came to New York ... Danny Hellman was a great mentor. He would do these Max Fish shows, these large cartooning shows, and anybody that was a cartoonist could come and put their work up.[2] So that's how you'd meet everybody. He's really instrumental in my meeting a lot of people.

You have mentioned being in art school and hating it, and only later discovering an interest in cartooning.[3] How did you arrive at that conclusion?

My heart just wasn't in painting. I wanted to tell stories. I saw Lynda Barry's work and Debbie Dreschler's and Chris Ware's and Crumb's, and Dan Clowes's... I got passed the xeroxed "Art School Confidential" comic in my studio in college and I fell down on the floor laughing and I thought, this is exactly my life.[4] I just felt comics was my calling... Not instantly, but after I graduated from college, I thought, this makes the most sense to me. I'm literal-minded, I can't talk the talk of the school gallery world, and I'm not into pastiching. I think that nowadays, people tell stories more in art school, they allow that. But it wasn't cool then. All stories had been told; we were in a world of post-stories. And if you wanted to tell a story, it would be through illustration. The world of cartooning and fine art seemed so separate at that time.

I was a good painter and I was good at handling paint in an emotional way, where it feels like there's somebody behind it. It's not so glossy... I could paint anything but I just wasn't satisfied with any theme because it didn't get to the meat of anything for me. I distinctly remember making this one painting. I didn't know what it was, and then I divided it up into squares, and then I cut up those squares into smaller squares, and then I cut everything up into smaller and smaller squares, and then just threw it all away. I feel that's a sign of someone who's a cartoonist and just hasn't figured it out yet.

Did you start with autobiographical comics?

The first comics that I did were for the school comics magazine that my husband was editing at the time. Now he's [Tim Hodler] the editor of *The Comics Journal*. I made a comic about going to Red Lobster[5] and how I was depressed and the fish were saying: "Well, at least you're not breaded, cheer up." Making that comic came naturally to me. That was the first time I ever did a comic, and it was autobiographical. I was doing all sorts of weird comics when I first started. They were all sort of half art and half comics. I went out for a summer with my friend who was an artist in Connecticut. I was a waitress and I would do landscape paintings on my breaks. At the end of the summer, I put together all of the drawings and I thought, how do I make a comic out of all of this? I decided to turn it into: "Places Where You Could Get Killed in The Litchfield Hills, Conn." [Fig. 53]. And I just put arrows next to each one of the drawings. My first comics were just little moments. After that, I got a job for the website, www.gURL.com.[6] Their idea was for me to write semi-autobiographical stuff about high school, and I thought: I can do that.

How did you find the job?

This was when the internet was just taking off, around 1997/1998. My roommate's girl-friend's friend was the editor of www.gUrl.com, and they needed comics. When I started, I said I would make just one. I didn't realize you were supposed to work bigger. I didn't know any of the rules. I just did it. At the same time, I got a job for *The Stranger* in Seattle, doing these weird little gag comics. To me, I still feel like that was some of the strongest work I've ever done. They're totally bizarre; there's a certain sensibility in them that's hard to wrap your head around and it's not something that women [at the time] were doing necessarily. The Lynda Barry/Debbie Dreschler confessional women's comics thing always kind of bugged me. I didn't want to be pigeonholed like that. That's why I really tried to do other things... But I also feel there's nothing wrong with telling a good story about your life.

Does that mean you find it easier to write memoir?

I do and I don't. Research-wise, it's easier. It's what happened to you, so you can remember or at least piece together what it must have felt like for something to happen. The story is already there, so you just have to craft it into something good.

Can you talk about your new book, *Calamity*?

A lot of the book revolves around my relationship with my mom and this one incident that happened. It never really dawned on me how important my mom's relationship with her parents was, in shaping her and the decisions she made. But, having just had a child myself, there's nothing that puts you more on a continuum. Suddenly you are a mother and a daughter—and so many things come up about your own childhood. I think about the choices that my mom made and it gives me a different perspective. Thinking in this way involves more work, and also more pain. I've been delving into things that have affected the people in my family for years. It's this big, amazing puzzle.

***Girl Stories* is considered separate from your other work, less sophisticated because it's about issues of adolescence.[7]**

I've always felt really conflicted about *Girl Stories*, though less so now because I know that I was just shooting from the hip. There's a lot going on in those comics. For example, I didn't feel like I wanted to include "Am I Fat?" when I first was trying to put together the book, as I thought it was such a frivolous comic.[8] It's not a story, it's not art... And then I thought, how could I not put that comic in? It's exactly what I felt like for so many years. The book is uneven because it's stuff that's collected from my early twenties. I agonized over every story but everything that I chose to go into it was consciously done.

Fig. 53. Lauren Weinstein, "Places Where You Could Get Killed in The Litchfield Hills, Conn.,"
Inside Vineyland (Cupertino, CA: Alternative Comics, 2003) (n.p.).

I'm always taken aback at how differently people respond to memoir when women are creating it versus men. Women's work often seems to be described as "cathartic."

I did not consider the making of *Girl Stories* to be cathartic. It was more like stabbing a wound over and over again. As soon as I decide to do memoir, the story changes. It's crafted.

You draw a lot of places and maps. The "Litchfield Hills" comic is one example, and the poster-sized map you drew for *The Ganzfeld*.[9]

I like diagramming things, and I love looking at maps. I have a horrible sense of direction. I think drawing out maps helps me visualize an entire space or an entire world; it's a good way of fleshing out a world. When I was a kid, I'd draw tons of weird maps... In third grade, I drew this fancy ballroom—a flat view of a ballroom and all the different rooms and kids having a slumber party in a side room. I just love doing stuff like that. I'm really obsessed with Botticelli's work, all those cartooning things that he did where you have four different views of the person on the same path... I'm doing that a lot in my new books. I like the idea that there are no breaks—you're just traveling along this line... That's what I love about cartooning. There's this time and space, and you have complete control over it and a couple of things can be happening at the same time. I find that true in reality, too. Again, having just had a kid, things are arbitrarily moving forward, but there's a lot that's happening in the background, a lot that happened in the past, that's affecting right now.

Can you talk about the theme of alienation that threads through your work?

When I was younger, I felt genuinely lost. I don't feel that so much anymore. I do feel more grounded now—the comics I'm doing [on my blog] these days are about having a child. Those early comics had that feeling of total alienation. And *Girl Stories* was a book about the worst period in my entire life. So there's no better time to show alienation... Like getting into a tub in front of a whole class—I don't know how that happened, but it did.[10]

How does your Jewish identity figure in your works?

It's one of those things that you can't shake. I think maybe I'm an atheist, but a lot of Jews are. There's this really interesting thing with cultural versus religious Judaism—there's a lot of overlap. But I feel like there are certain things, even just the history of cartooning and Judaism, there's something to it. And I don't really know what it is. Maybe it's the idea of making something funny and sad—that funny and sad are basically the same thing, it's just putting a different twist on it. Maybe because Jews like to *kvetch* a lot, there's a *kvetching* aspect to the work. But I don't think you can shake it. *Girl Stories* definitely seems Jewishy to me, even though there's not a lot that's obviously Jewish. There's Latke Boy, for example.[11]

The name of your persona's nemesis in *Girl Stories* is Glenn Schwartz, a very "Jewish" name. Other cartoonists talk about feeling a discomfort around Jewish boys when they are young—they are surrounded by them, yet they feel alienated from them because nice Jewish girls are *supposed* to eventually marry Jewish boys.

That's funny—Glenn Schwartz is not a real person. He's an amalgam of people and maybe some of those people were Jewish and some were not. I go back and forth with the question of Jewish identity in my own work. When I was first drawing, I definitely just wanted to be this person that didn't necessarily have a gender or a religion. And now, I like owning up to it all. I feel like you can't shake Judaism and it's so rich, so why not be a member? I'm on a continuum with all of these people that have complained about things. There is also this idea of martyrdom and self-sacrifice, which is completely selfish at the same time.

These are all themes I'm working on now. There are a couple of scenes in my newest book that deal with being Jewish... My mom got into a car accident, that's the big thing that happened, and we had a *Seder*/Passover in the hospital. And my mother's workaholism I think also has a lot to do with being Jewish—that she carries the weight of the impoverished on her shoulders—that seems very Jewish to me.

Do you mind being labeled a Jewish cartoonist?

I always hate things that pigeonhole people in that way. But then, I also think it's interesting that there is this strain... It's an easy way to box something in—people are going to think of this person's identity first and foremost, rather than, simply, this is a good story.

In *Girl Stories* you compare your persona's looks with that of another young woman, Diana.

Less Jewish looking ... I was obsessed with Barbies, too. That idea of Jewish beauty— her nose is not as *schnozzy* as mine. That was definitely a real feeling I had.

When you draw female characters, do you think a lot about how you want to portray them, or do you portray them how you think you remember them?

I think it changes from panel to panel. That's what I love about comics. There are a couple of moments in *Girl Stories*... When Lauren and Genine write this letter to play a prank on Glenn, and then she [Lauren] doesn't send it, and it's in order to become friends with the other cooler girls. I very intentionally drew myself looking a lot prettier in that panel because I was morphing into those girls. I think that is something you can do. If you feel really pretty for real, you can look pretty. If you feel spazzy, you can look spazzy. I think the best advice anybody ever gave me about drawing was in fourth grade, after school. A guy that was working at the after-school program said: "Draw a portrait of yourself where you feel like you're drawing the inside of your face." I really take that to heart. I want my drawings to feel like you're looking at the inside of your face. Not the musculature or anything like that, but what's going on in your mind. Even if it's really exaggerated, like the eye-balls are bugging out ... I think morphing the way somebody looks—as long as you keep those big iconic markers—means you can make them look like anything [Fig. 54].

Would you agree that autobiographical comics are a constant battle—you're drawing how other people see you, but you're also drawing how you see yourself?

Chris Ware said it best when he said: "Comics is the art of memory." That seems pretty obvious for memoir comics, but comics are the best at constructing a fictional memory. They're so controlled through the filter of somebody else that you're invited into this world that's completely synesthetic, that somebody else is creating. I think that's why dream comics are so popular and why they work better here than in hardly any other medium—you can take a person down a road with you in a very specific way. As a cartoonist, you think about how you're showing every aspect of a situation: what parts of the backgrounds do you put in, and what parts of the person's body are you going to show, and what kind of style are you going to use. It's really layered.

So it's similar to film?

It is like film, but then it's not because you can play around with how the viewer perceives time—your eyes can linger for longer, the format can completely change... You can't do a rant very well in film, but you can do it very well in comics. You could do a comic of somebody walking down the street, ranting about something, and that would be completely compelling

DIANA IS SUCH A SMART, GIVING PERSON THAT I PREDICT THAT IN SIX YEARS SHE WILL BE IN AFRICA SAVING CHILDREN FROM STARVATION AND MALARIA! AND JOHN WILL BE RIGHT BY HER SIDE BEING THE LAMEASS THAT HE IS.

Fig. 54. Lauren Weinstein, "Diana," *Girl Stories* (New York: Henry Holt, 2006) 174.

if the composition and drawing was interesting. In a film it would be boring. I think it's a specific filter and I take [the notion] that comics are the art of memory as a practice. It's not exactly a true memory, but you're creating something so specific that you want the viewer to key into it and be in that space. That's what that whole map piece was about that I did for *The Ganzfeld*. It was just creating all these four different people's lives, a memory of their entire lives, in the course of one day at the park. It's so cool the way you can do that with comics. That's why it's such a humbling task. At every level, there's another thing that you can do, and there's so much that's already been done that you can look at.

Whose work do you look at?

Full disclosure—my husband is the editor of *The Comics Journal*, so every day we get a free box of comics delivered to our house. I've been reading French comics artist Jacques Tardi recently. He does a lot of film noir-ish and weird surrealist stuff. I've been reading him, and his style is just so appealing. I love Lynda Barry. I love Gabrielle [Bell]'s work. I love Vanessa [Davis]'s work... I love *Popeye*, I love slapstick, just do-anything-you-can-do-to-get-that-story-to-move-ahead, funny, rapid-fire stuff. And I love old *Mad Magazines*...

You've mentioned before that you want to write a book about being pregnant...

I took tons of notes when I was pregnant, and I've been interviewing a lot of people. It seems like everyone I know just got pregnant in the last year or so. To me, pregnancy seemed like a second adolescence. And in working on the sequel to *Girl Stories*, a lot of pregnancy things came up even as I was doing something about high school—the way your whole mind changes, trying to wrap itself around something new. Once you're a new parent, it is a bit like being in high school again. You're meeting all of these new moms, and are they going to be the same kind of cool as you? You just want to make sure that your kids like each other and that you like each other. I've started to just put pregnancy stuff online [Weinstein's blog]. I think that will generate an audience and it's going to help sell and help me do the work for it. It's something that seems to write itself... For the first time in a lot of adults' lives, in my life, you're handing your body over to somebody else. There are all these things that happen over the course of a pregnancy, such as genetic testing and all sorts of things that I don't think anyone is really equipped to deal with. It's medical, but it's also about how your whole life changes in kind of an amazing and wonderful way, but nobody writes about it.

There doesn't seem to be a lot written about how pregnancy and becoming a mother affects women's work...

I actually made a comic about this recently. Once I stopped breastfeeding, my drive to work came back. The oxytocin comic.[12] There's this amazing calm that I carried with me when I was pregnant that I loved. I just felt really excited, I couldn't wait to meet Ramona. And I feel like that's an important thing to talk about. I think in my work in general, I strive to get a lot of different angles of a situation. I try to just be honest, even if it's just telling the "emotional truth." For me, the big question is how to organize the book. Like *Girl Stories*, they are visual essays that are anecdotal, but they touch on big themes that people can relate to... And, also, I'd like to include other people's birth stories because I love hearing how the deal went down for people. It's really fascinating. That's what I'm thinking about right now. I've been getting a lot of feedback about the pregnancy stuff recently. I just went to the Small Press Expo and a lot of people came up to me and have been telling me that they've been reading my blog. I have a binder and I keep throwing stuff in for this pregnancy book. I think that, for right now, the Internet is the best way of laying claim to it, of putting it out there.

NOTES

1. Weinstein currently has a web address, www.girlstoriescomics.com, which links both to her blog and to a website centered specifically on *Girl Stories*.

2. Max Fish is a bar and art gallery located on the lower east side of Manhattan. Danny Hellman curated an annual comics show at Max Fish from 1990 to 2000.

3. In her interview with Jesse Sposato, published on SadieMagazine.com (2011), Weinstein talks about her time in art school: "I hated it ... I hated not knowing what I was doing. I really wanted to tell a story and I liked drawing, and you couldn't really do that with painting. And I didn't really know comics yet, although I kind of did— I just didn't realize I liked them so much... I didn't realize that women even made comics; I hadn't seen any comics by women yet. But I graduated and I kept making paintings and never felt like they were doing what I wanted them to do..." Weinstein also talks about her experiences in art school in a recorded interview with Robin McConnell posted July 8, 2009, on www.inkstuds.org. Finally, in an interview with Emily Bobrow printed in *The Believer* (2007), Weinstein also discusses her move to comics.

4. "Art School Confidential" is a short story published by Daniel Clowes as part of his *Eightball* series. It was also adapted into a film directed by Terry Zwigoff in 2006.

5. Red Lobster Seafood Restaurants are an American restaurant chain.

6. gUrl.com was founded in 1996. According to the site, it is a "leading online community and content site for teenage girls."

7. In his introduction to an *Inkstuds* interview, for example, Robin McConnell describes *Girl Stories* as a collection which "I was carefully informed does not represent your work."

8. "Am I Fat?" is a comic, which can be found at the end of *Girl Stories* (191–200), in which Weinstein's teenage persona explores her nagging anxiety about her weight, as well as her general relationship with food and with how women are depicted by the media. The subsequent comic: "Fat Feedback" (201–9), explores the many responses Weinstein received from young women upon the original online publication of the comic.

9. According to its website, *The Ganzfeld* is "an annual book of pictures and prose." It was originally founded in 2000 by three art graduates of Washington University in St. Louis, Dan Nadel, Patrick Smith, and Tim Hodler. In 2008, its final issue (#7) included a full-size, two-sided poster by Weinstein. One side of the poster features a colored drawing of a park with many of the same characters drawn serially on the page, engaging in various activities and taking up different spaces on the page.

10. In "The Tub," another comic published in *Girl Stories* (34–45), Weinstein's persona volunteers in science class to help her teacher demonstrate how Archimedes discovered how to measure volume. The comic depicts her stepping into a trash can lined with a garbage bag at the boys' locker room in the basement of school, in front of her

entire class. In the last panel of the comic, as she walks away, barefoot and shivering in her bathing suit, one of her classmate's speech bubble reads "freak" (45).

11. Latke Boy is featured in "The Chanukah Blues" (64–74). As he describes himself: "I help Jewish boys and girls everywhere get over the Chanukah Blues," 71.

12. This unnamed comic can be found on www.laurenweinstein.com. The comic begins with the opening narrative, "The day I weaned Ramona ..." and continues "... was the same day I got an intern and started to update my website a lot."

BIBLIOGRAPHY

Weinstein, Lauren. *Girl Stories*. New York: Henry Holt, 2006.
_____. *The Goddess of War*. New York: Picturebox, 2008.
_____. *Inside Vineyland*. Gainesville, Florida: Alternative Comics, 2003

"I thought hand wringing about my peculiar form of British-Jewish assimilation was a little niche I had"

Corinne Pearlman Lays Down Her Jewish Cards

PAUL GRAVETT and SARAH LIGHTMAN

Corinne Pearlman has been making comics and cartoons since the early 1970s and was a regular contributor with her series of comic strips "Playing the Jewish Card" in the *Jewish Quarterly* until 2011. She is a director of the Brighton-based publisher Myriad Editions and commissioning editor for their list of graphic novels. For many years she has been art director and a partner in Comic Company, a London based publisher working with comics artists to produce health information. She also is a coordinator of Cartoon County, a cartoonists," group that has been meeting in Brighton since 1993. She lives in London and Brighton. This conversation is based on interviews with Paul Gravett in London in April 2012, and with Sarah Lightman in March 2013.

"Playing the Jewish Card" was a series that ran in the *Jewish Quarterly*, a Jewish cultural journal, yet it could be argued much of it is about your uncomfortable feelings about being Jewish and the Jewish community. Can you talk about this?

Discomfort is at the heart of the original strip I drew for the *Jewish Quarterly*, "The Non-Jewish Jewish Female Cartoonist and Other Confusions," when I was originally asked to contribute to a special women's issue back in 1992 [Fig. 39]. I was asked not because the guest editor, Sonja Lyndon, knew my work, but because of my name. Sonja approached Carol Bennett, who ran a network of women cartoonists called "Fanny," to see if she could recommend a Jewish artist. Carol, of course, knew me as a cartoonist, but not as a Jew, and I felt a little awkward to get the job simply on the strength that I was called Pearlman! So this became the subject of the strip: whether or not, as an assimilated Jew, I was qualified to author the strip. And, if I was, to what extent was I exploiting—as opposed to exploring—my identity in the interests of getting published as a cartoonist? I riffed on this theme in greater detail when Carol asked me for an extended version of the strip in *Dissenting Women* (1992) later that year.

In 2004, the then editor of the *Jewish Quarterly*, Matthew Reisz, asked me to contribute a regular strip. A friend, the late journalist Ian Walker, was very fond of arguing over the dinner table, and preferably about class. He always accused me—usually with a guffaw of

195

triumph—of "playing the Jewish card" when—in his opinion—I was sidestepping my middle-class identity by doing this (as being Jewish was not an obvious part of my life). I included a snippet of such a scene in the original 1992 strip, and I adopted the phrase "Playing the Jewish Card" as the title of the series as it seemed like an apt description of what I would be doing.

Certainly, exploring the roots of assimilation is a legitimate subject for a strip, and it's fair to say that assimilation breeds a heady brew of discomfort, guilt, alienation and all those wonderful negative emotions that comics can visualize so well. However, I've always been aware that dredging up Jewishness in order to maintain a quarterly gig could be seen as a cynical act; sometimes there's a bit too much self-conscious wittering on about that.

You made "Show & Tell" [Figs. 1–2] after reading Michael Kaminer's article and it mentions many artists in "Graphic Details." You talk about not being aware that so many Jewish women were making autobiographical comics...

Kaminer's article alerted me to a *new* generation of Jewish women cartoonists. "Show & Tell" was made in response to that discovery. But back in the early 1970s, when I became a great fan of the underground artists and their autobiographical work, I discovered the fabulous work of Aline Kominsky-Crumb, who drew on her own Jewish background with such humor. So naturally, in the original 1992 strip, I immediately show myself as hugely unqualified to pen an overtly "Jewish" strip compared to Aline, or indeed, her contemporary, Art Spiegelman.

Of course there were other autobiographical cartoonists whom I admired, and who may or may not have been Jewish, but I wasn't exactly seeking them out as a like-minded community. Being slightly embarrassed about what I was doing (exploring or exploiting my identity), I tended to keep my head down about the strip—not just in my cartoonist world, but also among family and friends and work colleagues. I thought hand wringing about my peculiar form of British-Jewish assimilation was a little niche I had, and although it was great if someone happened upon a strip that resonated, it was very much a minority taste and I wasn't going to advertise it to the world at large.

So in "Show & Tell," I show myself not only becoming reacquainted with artists from the past who just happen to be Jewish, but also meeting a new generation of cartoonists who are actively exploring their Jewish identity. You can see my character admiring the pride and politics of this latest crew of creators, but also slightly resenting it!

"Show & Tell" is a fantastic example of your complex language of text, image, humor and object. You beautifully visualize metaphors for feelings, for example: the opening image in your Jewish Playing Card is opening yourself up, looking at your insides, navel gazing. Later on that page you are shown rummaging around "the freezer of your mind." How did you choose these objects, images and metaphors? Does your own work make you laugh?

I'm not conscious of making any of those choices; it's almost as if those layers are already there: life exists in layers, you just have to know how to show them (or switch them off). It's like anything you do, however small, you're both in the moment and outside of it. There's what you look like on the outside, how you perceive yourself, what you think others see, and then there's all this "stuff" inside, which needs an outlet, but it needs to be channeled. A comic provides a framework where you can focus on the clutter; it's a great way of carrying all that information—metaphorical, literary, visual, factual, and humorous. And those juxtapositions are in themselves humorous. I wouldn't say I make myself laugh, but I do enjoy bringing out the humor in a situation. In a way it helps to make sense of something that may not be particularly funny, or it puts something into perspective.

A favorite comic of mine is "Whatever Happened to Great Grandma" (2004)—part of me still feels shocked even after I read it again and again. Can you talk about its creation?

"Whatever Happened to Great Grandma" was the first of the "Playing the Jewish Card" strips. My parents had recently told me a shocking story about my paternal great-grandmother being farmed out to live with my grandfather's non–Jewish business partner during World War II. As the strip reports, she was hugely fat and spoke only Yiddish, and was clearly an embarrassment to them in the smart hotel where they were staying (their flat had been commandeered by the British army). I couldn't believe that I hadn't heard this story before and it gets tragically worse, but it was one of those distressing and shameful episodes that a family hopes will be forgotten. My mother rather bluntly weighed in with the tale—not *her* family after all; my father was obviously pained to have to talk about it.

As well as retelling a good story, I also wanted to focus on what they were going through as they told me, and on my own emotions and thoughts as I heard it. Having worked at Age Concern in the past, I was, and remain, fascinated by how families deal with their aging relatives. I was also horrified but interested by how badly my grandfather betrayed his mother; having myself been accused of betrayal, I sometimes play to the gallery. So, in a weird way, I felt almost liberated to find out about my grandfather. Mind you, the goalposts around people's notions of "loyalty" seem to move.

How British Jews behaved during World War II also interests me. For instance, my mother's family took in a young German refugee (though they soon shunted her off to another relative), while my father's family didn't help anyone (my father's explanation: "well, they were German!"). In the strip, it was quite fun to play on the notion of how I might treat my own parents...

What inspired you to do cartooning?

As a child I always seemed to be in bed with some illness or other, and the great thing about that was my parents bought me loads of comics to read: *Girl, Bunty, Judy, The Topper, The Beezer,* and when I exhausted those there was always my sister's collection of *School Friend Picture Library* (1962–1988), which I read and reread. I also loved delving into my mother's and aunts' collection of school annuals, a heady mixture of cartoon strips and stirring stories for girls, and in particular reading the biographical story strips in the *Girl Annual* for my age group. So these gave me a love of the form. As I became a teenager I graduated with some relish to the story strips and photo stories in *Valentine* and *Romeo* (1957–1974)—but these weren't as inspirational as the earlier works.

I remember once being rather piqued when a friend of mine at school said disparagingly about a drawing of mine: "Oh, that's just a cartoon"—it immediately made me think: so what's wrong with cartoons? I enjoyed art, but the thing I took most pleasure in was filling in my "rough" books with loads of drawings and doodles. In the 1960s these were mostly illustrational and based on my obsession with fashion: often Art Nouveau patterns intertwined with skinny girls and lots of shoes. I was very flattered when a girl in the year below collected my drawings.

You studied English Literature at Oxford University. Did any literary works inspire you or your work?

My time at university was more about the people I met and what I did in the holidays than the works of literature I encountered—with some notable exceptions. I do remember getting very excited about Mark Twain and American literature in general, including the novels of William Carlos Williams. I went through a Samuel Beckett and James Joyce phase—but I suspect the former was influenced primarily by a very trendy lecturer who gave the impression he was Beckett's best mate, and we were all duly smitten (by Beckett and by the lecturer). I recall doing a cartoon of a friend and fellow student, in her purple velvet hot pants being ravished by him in his rooms at St. Peter's College. I don't *think* that happened ... but I'd love to see the cartoon again.

My James Joyce devotion was also inspired by a fellow fan of the lecturer (I think the lecturer was also perhaps a little in love with him), a very good-looking almost-boy-friend who once put a little torn-out piece of card in my "pigeon hole" with the word ZAP on it in a spiky shout cartoon, and a copy of *Finnegans Wake*, inscribed: "Read it with feeling."

In fact, by the time I got to university, most of the inspiring stuff had inspired me... Let's face it, I was a teenager living in London in the 1960s, so I'd had a pretty good time. "Bliss it was in that dawn to be alive; but to be young was very heaven"—a quote from Wordsworth's *The Prelude*, learned at school. I don't think I learned any quotes while at university. So, my influences remain more from school than university—partly because I had a wonderful English teacher at school who made everything come alive, and partly because there was so much exciting stuff going on and happening culturally in London that I felt the world was my oyster. Oxford was a bit of a shock.

Were you cartooning at university?

Not comics, as such, at that time. The best stuff was the informal cartooning, those moments you capture shortly after what you've just seen, and what you think about it, come together: a sketch of a friend with his long hair down to his waist, and tiny little legs. I wish I still had those drawings. My cartoon ephemera, then and now, is what I most value.

I did have a short-lived spell doing "fashion" illustration for the university newspaper *Cherwell,* but I had a minor fashion conversion at the end of my first year, which had mostly been spent walking up and down the King's Road in London, shopping at Mr Freedom, Granny Takes a Trip, and Ossie Clark sales. Perhaps it was the cost, but, suddenly, it didn't seem quite so much fun. So, there marked the end of my days drawing high fashion.

When you left university, you lived in a squat. How did that come about?

I wanted to live affordably with people I liked. One of my Oxford friends, Jamie Gough, was a post-graduate student at the Bartlett School of Architecture, and we had always talked about sharing a place together when we got to London. And so a group of us moved into an empty house in Tolmers Square, near Euston station. It was an area scheduled for demolition by property developers, with the intention of creating more office space. When tenants moved out, they weren't replaced and the houses were boarded up. A campaign had started among students from the nearby School of Architecture to oppose the process, and part of that plan was to move into the empty homes. So it seemed like a "good cause." To install ourselves so centrally, and so cheaply, in Tolmers Square, was also enlightened self-interest. It was our home for six years; we were squatters, yes, but we never called it "a squat."

What did you do for a living?

Unlike many of my friends in the Square, I was no longer a student, or making ends meet on the dole, or infiltrating unions on behalf of the International Marxist Group by becoming a ward clerk at University College Hospital, but had a full-time job as an assistant to the public relations officer at Age Concern. I'd seen a TV programme about the plight of the elderly, and wrote to Age Concern asking if they had a job, saying I wanted to "make comics for old people." I got a job, and I did some cartoons for the organization, but never any comics.

Then a group of friends in the Square decided to put together a comic. I saw it as a great opportunity to do a strip about poor old Gertie who worried about her electricity bill, and eventually died of hypothermia. I wanted to redeem my lack of cartooning at Age Concern, but *Cold Oldies* (1976) made me cringe then, never mind now.

Was that your first comic strip?

I think it was. By then—1973—I'd become a fan of Robert Crumb, which sadly shows in my abominable aping of his artwork. It was really the obscenity trials of the time, such as that brought against *Oz* in 1971 that brought the work of the American underground cartoonists to light in the UK. I was planning a trip to San Francisco and a lawyer friend asked me to pick up some Crumb comics for him. I was knocked out by what I saw—I just loved the honesty, irreverence, wit, rants, sexual fantasies, and cute little Bearzy-Wearzies, all contained by superb artwork in that safe place: the page. I never considered Crumb a misogynist or racist, although certainly he wasn't afraid of playing with stereotypes, to devastating and comical effect, and always at the expense of his characters.

So from 1973 to 1976 I did some cartoon work, but not very much, until I left Age Concern. I decided not to continue in public relations, or to be a journalist, though as a freelancer, I did a bit of both. But at that point I started to concentrate on cartooning.

How did you get work doing cartooning?

I don't think I've ever got work without knowing someone who knows someone.... A friend of mine was working as an editor for educational publishers Mary Glasgow Magazines, and I began doing illustrations and comics for European school children learning English as a foreign language. That gave me a fairly regular income. At the same time, I'd been supplying free cartoons to *The Leveller,* a political magazine set up by left-wing journalists, and I began earning money by producing quite a few political cartoons, mostly for charity publications with whom I'd become involved while working at Age Concern, and then being passed on from one client group to the next. For instance, the Newham Monitoring Project, documenting police bullying of the Asian and black population in Newham, East London. I have to say that political cartooning is not my forte: I was quite heavy-handed and most of my output was wince-worthy. I felt most comfortable when I was reporting rather than commenting: for instance, illustrating "Stephen Lawrence: The story of a racial killing" by Brian Cathcart.[1]

How did you get involved in producing comics for education?

Working for organizations that had a social message, both as an employee, and also as a cartoonist, gave me a background in disseminating information visually and accessibly, and led to other jobs. I'd done a poster illustrating the history of broadcasting for a friend of mine, Peter M. Lewis, and contributed cartoons and cover designs for a community radio magazine *Relay.* This led to a proposal for us to create a full-length book on broadcasting, which was eventually published by Camden Press as *Media and Power: A Graphic Guide* (1986)—my first documentary comic book. I really enjoyed working with the editor, Philip Boys, and got to know the other artists working with him. Together we got the idea to create an anthology about *The Comic Book of First Love*, which was published by Virago Press Limited in 1988. As joint editors, Philip and I set up Comic Company, and brought together a group of artists—then, as now, aided by lots of generous help and advice from one Mr Paul Gravett. *The Comic Book of First Love* was reissued by Fantail, an imprint of Penguin Books, who also published a companion volume *The Comic Book of the Facts of Life* in 1991.

Philip and I believed that these comic book stories by some of the UK's best—and funniest—artists had the potential to become a really useful resource in sex and relationships education. So we showed the books to the Family Planning Association, one of the major UK charities advising on sexual health and contraception, and suggested that they created publications for young people using comic book artists. They commissioned us to create a leaflet about periods for young girls, which I designed and illustrated, and that led to a series of booklets for young people on puberty, contraception, relationships, pregnancy and abortion. Generations of young people have been brought up on *4Boys, 4Girls, 4You* and the other titles; millions of copies have been distributed and they all are still in print.

How did Comic Company get started as a publisher?

Comic Company was also commissioned to create comics for specific health education research projects; a series of workshops on HIV infection, facilitated by comics artists and actors working with groups of young people at risk, produced two comics that got evaluated—and then went nowhere, as there was no mechanism to publish them. When a similar situation arose with a whole raft of comics and print ephemera produced for a "healthy eating education project," funded by Europe Against Cancer Group, Philip's partner Maggie—far more practical than either of us—insisted that we had to publish the resources ourselves.

Nevertheless, although Comic Company did produce some comics over the years, the graphic narrative has been the exception rather than the rule. Our client base has mostly been health promotion agencies that opt for short, colorful messages in a variety of formats, and while the comics' artists who create the materials have been key to their success, sequential art has been seen as an expensive luxury for this audience. That's why it's so gratifying to see the creator-led development of health information in graphic novel format, published in the trade press as comics literature, gaining popularity and reaching a target audience, despite the restrictions of the health promotion industry.

How far do you think comics can be useful social and political tools—and have an impact on the world around them?

Well, where on earth does one start? Comics have an enormous impact in spreading awareness and changing people's perspectives about all kinds of issues. Do we need to mention more than Art Spiegelman's *Maus* which was first published as a three-page strip in 1972? How about Will Eisner's *The Plot: The Secret Story of the Protocols of the Elders of Zion* (2005)? Or Joe Sacco's graphic journalism on Palestine and the war in Bosnia? In the UK, Darryl Cunningham's *Psychiatric Tales* (2010) has provided amazing graphic insight into mental health issues, and his *Science Tales* (2012) has skewered the media's collusion with controversial data. In Europe, comics artists are becoming the new historians of the 21st century, documenting little known wars, or individual experiences of very well known wars, or unsung experiences of the labor movement. Nicola Streeten's work on child bereavement in *Billy, Me & You* (2011) has seen her work highly commended by the British Medical Association—these and so many other graphic works become amazing tools for the advancement of understanding and education. This may not always be the intention of the artist: I defy anyone to find a better illustration of adolescent body changes than in Marjane Satrapi's *Persepolis,* which began publication in installments by L'Association in 2000, but I'm sure she didn't set out to provide that; it was incidental to her autobiography. I'd also say it's true for David Lloyd, the artist who co-created *V for Vendetta* (which first started appearing in 1982) with Alan Moore—it wasn't his intention for his character's masked face to be adopted by the global Occupy movement, but that image has become synonymous with protests worldwide.

Nowadays there isn't a disease or social issue that doesn't have a graphic artist beavering away at bringing it to light, so sometimes it comes as a welcome relief to seize on a work of pure graphic fiction without any message, incidental or otherwise.

You have enabled many new graphic novels to be published through your role at Myriad. Can you talk about your incentives ... and the changes you can see in the comics world in the UK?

I was working freelance as a designer at Brighton-based Myriad Editions, on a series of illustrated, topical atlases—among them was one on climate change, which I had great difficulty visualizing. I remember going to a presentation by Kate Evans about her comic *Funny Weather* (2000)—and thinking: "Never mind the atlas; we must publish the comic!" which we did, as a full-length book, in 2006. Shortly before this, Myriad had decided to branch out into trade publishing with a mixed media anthology, *The Brighton Book* (2005), that reflected the backgrounds and interests of those working for Myriad: my own being comics and cartoons. A short graphic story by Woodrow Phoenix led to Myriad publishing his first full-length graphic novel *Rumble Strip* (2009). Since then, and with Arts Council funding, we have been able to expand both our fiction and graphics publishing, with a commitment to publish three graphic books a year, as well as running a biennial First Graphic Novel Competition.

It's so exciting to be a part of this. I was originally caught up in the comics boom of the late 1980s, where a lot of money was invested by trade publishers, and a lot got burnt by the experience. But now graphic novels have really taken hold and they are here to stay; cartoonists are part of the literary circuit, invited to festivals, exhibited in galleries, and featured in newspapers and winners of top literary awards. The top comics festivals sell out within minutes of going online—the demise of the local bookshop means that selling in person becomes more valuable. And comics artists are an amazing critical mass in social media. That also means that all of one's time can be spent promoting and proselytizing about comics, but that's true of any art form, surely?

Is it difficult to balance working with other comic artists while focusing on your own cartoons? Has editing other comics helped your own work?

I now describe myself as a "resting" cartoonist. I do feel that I've lost the balance over the past couple of years. My *Jewish Quarterly* cartoon was a way of hanging in there. But I recognize that I'd passed my sell-by date, and I needed to move on to something else. Sadly that hasn't happened.

It's not a reflection on the rigors of the editorial job that I'm not doing that right now. It's great to have the opportunity to be able to publish graphic novels; certainly promoting the medium as well as creating it is important for any practitioner. There are several comics artists who also work as editors, particularly in France, but also here—for instance, Woodrow Phoenix, who as well as being author of *Rumble Strip,* is co-editor of the award-winning anthology *Nelson* (2011).

Editing other people's work provides an insight into one's own work (although it also makes the stakes much higher—no surprise my output has been minimal to non-existent recently!). We treat every work as if it's still in progress, even if it's been presented as a finished article. I find structural editing very exciting—when you print out all the pages, and physically shove the book around on the floor, discarding stuff, making a note to add, fixing on an amazing drawing that needs to be made much more of, working out what's missing, identifying what doesn't make sense. And content-wise, too—it's always thrilling when you see a way to make a book more satisfying, identifying what will make a better read, a more fulfilling experience. You may not always be able to persuade the author, and, of course, not every book needs that, but when they do, and it works, it's so great to see it taking shape.

I'm not much of a policewoman: I have no idea how I think a comic should behave. I love trying to find the artist's language and then helping her or him say it better.

Your drawing style is linear and hand drawn, with a wash of color, and there's a lightness … I presume it's a lot of work creating pictures that look this free and natural. How do you plan your panels?

In terms of the landscape (one page) cartoons I do (for invitations or cards or to celebrate or record an event), I adopt quite a rigid format, which conforms to a more or less consistent pattern. But I don't plan anything; it's a kind of organic shaping that springs from a central idea, or topic, or celebration of a personality or event. So, in my head I almost start with some central image, a character, a person, an event, an almond-shaped *mandorla*, which then gets surrounded by cartouches or vignettes illustrating events or characteristics about that person—there may not be a particular narrative development, although there might be an overall text that follows roughly from image to image and culminates in the bottom left-hand corner, and, usually, with a title on the top. In other words, what I'm describing is a complete piece of artwork; at most a double-page spread [DPS] (in landscape) to view, with no page turns. Most of this work is not designed for publication but an example is the illustration I did of the "Graphic Details" symposium [Figs. 8–9].

My strips for the *Jewish Quarterly* were intended to be seen as a double-page spread, and the ones that work best have a central illustration that anchors the two pages (although this was always a problem for them because of the gutter). For instance, I love "Losing the Plot" (2005), which displays the horror of London's Jewish burial grounds in all their glory across the two pages, so to me this is visually more interesting and more successful.

I haven't done more than two pages for a long time, but it's exciting just to approach a longer narrative from a formal point of view: looking at how the page turns and the visual surprise for each spread; it's all a matter of pacing and keeping the eye engaged. As a reader I'm more than happy with a formal panel grid but, looking back, I think my best work is when I treat the DPS as a coherent piece of artwork. One of the earliest strips I did, which shows this, is "Gregory's Passion" in *The Comic Book of First Love* (1988).

As for my art style, here's the process: I make some sketches and notes on anything I have to hand, the back of an envelope, a notebook: preferably not an ancient half-filled-in sketchbook that reminds me of all the things I haven't done for a long time. I'll research on the internet, I may use or take photographs, then if it's a narrative, I might start a script, and roughly work out the panels and possible content. Next comes the landscape watercolor paper, so I'll sketch everything out in pencil. I don't want to lose the informality of my original sketches, so I'll most likely scan them in and blow them up to the appropriate size for my artwork, print it out and trace it onto my watercolor paper using my lightbox. Then I ink in, using a brush pen and normal sable brushes from thin to thick, and then rub out some of it before doing several layers of wash (in grays or color depending on output). Then I scan it all in—crushing my bit of paper to fit it onto the scanner so it looks a right old mess— and try piecing it together on the computer. If it's a one-off drawing I'd probably hand draw the text. However, if it's a text-heavy narrative I'm more likely to add the words in my design document, using a font of my handwriting. Then comes a load of heavy tweaking in Photoshop. I might add a second color at this stage, but it's still best if I've got the tone in the original artwork and then manipulate it later, rather than adding it at the end—otherwise I lose the sweep of the big fat brushwork.

Do you see your comics as visual essays?

I do think of the *Jewish Quarterly* series as visual essays—they usually have a topic that's both explored and then taken further, to a level of fantasy or "what if?" but it's always brought back to some kind of conclusion at the end. The best ones work with that scenario—for instance: "An Assimilated Jew's Guide to the Jewish Calendar" (2005/2006) addresses my ignorance of the Jewish holidays, and then imagines how the nation might benefit if the nation's favorite radio soap opera, *The Archers*, which occasionally slips in public information, were to include Jewish characters who could educate us about the high days and holy days.

The essays aren't all funny. When my father passed away, I wanted to record some of the things that happened or were said at the time—which I did about a year later, in "That Was Alright While It Lasted" (2010). I didn't need to make a point, I just wanted to remember. In "The Jews Who Wouldn't Go Away" (2010), I wanted to record my visit to Lithuania—where I had experiences that I didn't know how to digest, or make sense of (and still don't), but struck me very strongly at the time. For instance: two very elderly ladies greeting each other from opposite sides at a remote, forested section of the Lithuanian–Belarusian border. I think the strips work best when I'm not trying to make a point.

You've also illustrated children's books, which have been among your most successful works.

I've only illustrated two children's books, but I really enjoyed working with the author on developing the stories, and finding a style for the artwork (a very wobbly dip pen and lots of ink wash). The books featured a real cat, Ottoline, who shared a house with me and the author, Sally Craddock, in London's Great Russell Street, and liked to roam next door to the British Museum, in *Ottoline at the British Museum* (1987). Sally and I later took her on another adventure (purely fictional) to the Natural History Museum in *Ottoline at the Natural History Museum* (1990). What great locations to set the stories: I loved finding complicated architectural angles to draw. Although both books are now out of print, Ottoline still features, along with some mummified cats, on a popular postcard sold at the British Museum, and she also graces a whole range of kitchen gloves, egg cups, tea cozies and placemats. And hey, I even get royalties!

What do you consider your best work?

I am very fond of one or two of the comics strips I did for the series called "Playing the Jewish Card"—such as "In Valhalla" (a story about opera and Wagner), or "The Gap Year" [Figs. 87—88] or "Losing the Plot"; the drawings for *4Girls* ... and a couple of the drawings for *Ottoline*. But my ephemera mean the most to me—the cartoons I've done for family and friends, recording moments in our lives; not so much a visual diary but a visual commemoration of special occasions. I don't have many of these, just bits and pieces, really, but they are certainly the most valuable to me.

NOTE

1. Brian Cathcart, *Mindfield*, ed. Susan Greenfield (London: Camden Press, 1998).

BIBLIOGRAPHY

Benn, Melissa, ed. *The Brighton Book*. Brighton: Myriad Editions, 2005.
Boys, Philip, and Corinne Pearlman, eds. *The Comic Book of First Love*. London: Virago Press, 1988.
Cathcart, Brian. *Mindfield*. Ed. Susan Greenfield. London: Camden Press, 1998.
Craddock, Sally, and Corinne Pearlman. *Ottoline at the British Museum*. London: Macdonald & Co., 1987.
_____. *Ottoline at the Natural History Museum*. New York: Simon & Schuster Young Books, 1990.
Cunningham, Darryl. *Psychiatric Tales*. Brighton: Myriad Editions, 2010.
_____. *Science Tales*. Brighton: Myriad Editions, 2012.
Davis, Rob, and Woodrow Phoenix. *Nelson*. London: Blank Slate, 2012.
Eisner, Will. *The Plot: The Secret Story of the Protocols of the Elders of Zion*. London: W.W. Norton, 2006.
Evans, Kate. *Funny Weather*. Brighton: Myriad Editions, 2006.
Lewis, Peter M., and Corinne Pearlman. *Media and Power: A Graphic Guide*. London: Camden Press, 1986.
Lloyd, David, and Alan Moore. *V for Vendetta*. New York: Vertigo/DC Comics, 1982.
Pearlman, Corinne. "Gregory's Passion." In *The Comic Book of First Love*. London: Virago Press, 1988.
_____. *Cold Oldies*. London: The Optimist, 1976.
_____. "The Non-Jewish Jewish Female Cartoonist and Other Confusions." *Jewish Quarterly* 39, no. 3 (Autumn 1992): 57.
_____. *Periods, 4Boys, 4Girls, Is Everybody Doing It?, Abortion, Pregnancy, 4You*, and *Love, Sex, Relationships*. London: Family Planning Association, 1990.
_____. "Playing the Jewish Card: Armchair War Diary." *Jewish Quarterly* 203 (Autumn 2006): 4–5.
_____. "Playing the Jewish Card: An Assimilated Jew's Guide to the Jewish Calendar." *Jewish Quarterly* 200 (Winter 2005-06): 4–5.
_____. "Playing the Jewish Card: The Gap Year." *Jewish Quarterly* 194 (Summer 2004): 4–5.
_____. "Playing the Jewish Card: In Valhalla." *Jewish Quarterly* 195 (Autumn 2004): 4–5.
_____. "Playing the Jewish Card: The Jews Who Wouldn't Go Away." *Jewish Quarterly* 216 (Winter 2010): 26–27.
_____. "Playing the Jewish Card: Losing the Plot." *Jewish Quarterly* 198 (Summer 2005): 4–5.
_____. "Playing the Jewish Card: Show & Tell." *Jewish Quarterly* 214 (Winter 2009): 16–17.
_____. "Playing the Jewish Card: That Was Alright While It Lasted." *Jewish Quarterly* 215 (Summer 2010): 14–15.
_____. "Playing the Jewish Card: Whatever Happened to Great Grandma?" *Jewish Quarterly* 193 (Spring 2004): 4–5.
Phoenix, Woodrow. *Rumble Strip*. Brighton: Myriad Editions, 2008.
Sacco, Joe. *Palestine*. Seattle: Fantagraphics, 2002.
_____. *Safe Area Gorazde: The War In Eastern Bosnia 1992–1995*. Seattle: Fantagraphics, 2002.
Satrapi, Marjane. *Persepolis*. Paris: L'Association, 2000.
School Friend Picture Library. London: Amalgamated Press, 1962–88.
Spiegelman, Art. *Maus*. London: Penguin, 2003.
Streeten, Nicola. *Billy, Me & You*. Brighton: Myriad Editions, 2011.

From the Other Side of the World to North America

An Interview with Racheli Rottner

NOA LEA COHN

As a young cartoonist of 26, Racheli Rottner created her first graphic novel, *The Other Side of the World* (2008). Since its publication, her book has been seen as a groundbreaking achievement in the newly emerging genre of the graphic novel in Israel, where comics have not yet achieved high status.[1] Rottner's work is remarkable in its combination of motifs that allow the work to function both as a normal comic book and as stand-alone art. *The Other Side of the World* is an autobiography describing the maturing of the artist's consciousness. It does this without disengaging from her inner spirit, which lends the book a wistful, naïve voice. Rottner lives in Tel Aviv and is walla.co.il site editor. This interview was conducted by phone between Noa Lea Cohn in Toronto and Racheli Rottner in Tel Aviv on May 17, 2011.

Do you define yourself as a painter or a writer?

A creator, not only a painter and not just a writer. For example, this graphic novel came to me visually and I felt the need to tell the story and to express it using some sort of medium. In this case, I felt it had to be a comic; I spoke this [visual] language. For years I have written literature detached from visual art as a journalist in Israeli magazines like *Rating*[2] or the online [culture and news] website walla.co.il so words come naturally to me. On the other hand I produce art without words. Everything depends on the situation.

When did you discover comics?

I was exposed to comics in a similar scenario to that of many other teenagers when they get bored with reading books, and look for alternatives. Since my childhood I have combined drawing and writing, so it was natural for me to have an affiliation with comics. But in reality I had no specific interest in comics, I did not collect them or try to copy them.

You have to understand that in the past comics were not developed in Israel and it was very difficult to find high quality comics, especially if like me you did not have family abroad that could bring you quality comic books. So I abandoned the field entirely. Even today there are only two or three stores nationwide that sell my comics, even when I studied art in the Hamidrasha.[3] I did not think about comics as an art form.

205

When did things change for you?

When I went away to school a new world opened to me, the world of art, which I did not know as an innocent Orthodox Jewish girl from Netanya. Even when I studied art as a child at school, and in my childhood society, I was always on the periphery. No one ever showed me the artistic drive for new sensations that is at the heart of the artistic conflict. While I was studying at the college, a teacher invited me to a festival of alternative comics, where I met Dudu Geva, an Israeli comics pioneer, and I learned that I could make art that was comics. I learned all about individual comic artists and that I could present a comic page at an exhibition. Though it was not part of the official curriculum of the college, they did emphasize that the medium of artistic expression can be varied.

Who is Dudu Geva and what was the comic group that you joined?

Dudu Geva was an artist who dedicated his life to comics. He was a satirist and humorist and edited a cartoon section in the local newspaper named *The Duck* in the newspaper *Ha-Ir*.[4] After years of comics journalism Dudu Geva decided to prepare alternative and subversive comics, and he founded a group called A4 to prepare an institutional framework to help create and distribute individual comics on A4-size pages, selling them for one shekel each. I had idolized him since childhood and was an avid reader of his comics journalism work; when I met him it opened my eyes to a new world. I was shocked by the fact that I was hanging out with people my father's age, with everyone respecting one another for their professionalism regardless of religion, age or sex. I even started to create a comic book with Dudu Geva, which was interrupted and never completed.

As part of the group I did not have any religious conflicts, even though I could not attend some of the events due to them being held on Friday afternoon close to *Shabbat* [the Jewish Sabbath]. They would bring kosher food and everyone knew my comics contained no obscenities. There was harmony between us and I was exposed to high-quality comics I did not know existed before. I participated in the group's last joint project and we published a joint graphic novel. I was impressed and I hadn't ever imagined such a world. Dudu was an amazing person who took aspiring young artists under his wing; they studied and collaborated with him, and he gave them the gift of a cartoon. He wanted his house to be a venue where artists could come and go. Unfortunately, our contact with this aspirational world was prematurely severed with his sudden death on February 15, 2005.

***The Other Side of the World* seems very autobiographical. Where did the idea to write and publish a book come from?**

During my years studying art, my paintings focused on this theme, so I decided to dedicate the end of the year exhibition to this internal world. An intensive focus gave birth to independent images of myself that draw from a significant period in my life during high school and later, when I left on a two-month excursion to Australia, after finishing National Volunteer Service.[5]

So actually the first sketches were born as part of my thesis while studying art at school. The choice to view comics as a thesis work was very unusual within the student scene and I had a lot of uncertainty about the work I was doing. To my surprise, the teachers' response was enthusiastic and supportive; they saw the works' maturity and sensitivity, and the language of comics was an appropriate medium for my message.

Roee Rosen, my teacher, came up to me at the end of the year and encouraged me to do a graphic novel. His reasoning was that he felt that for all these years my paintings were trying to tell him something but he couldn't put his finger on why they were so quiet. "Give them their own words and don't insist on the muteness of the painting," he said. It was a turning point for me because for years you're taught to analyze art within an academic course and I had some fear that words within the art would lead to a simplistic result. Verbal graphic novels and comics can lead to a simplistic message which loses the strength of the story.

Who were the main influences in the stylistic ideas for your book?

Although art critics typically viewed my comics as based on the artist Miró, my paintings come more from the school of Rafi Lavie and Yair Garbuz, teachers at the Hamidrasha who influenced me greatly. Lavie's *bad painting* style of art was a rebellion aimed at Israeli painting; he advocated the principle of bringing his own world into art and ignoring the classical historical movements. Yair Garbuz's works spoke about the combination of words and painting.

Another artist that influenced me from Hamidrasha is Roee Rosen who drives change by using images in a new fashion, including an obsessive use of hair, something that I used in my book, as well as dealing with the fictitious boundary between reality and imagination, and making use of black as a color in an abstract context that simplifies the painting. Although Rosen's content can be provocative, especially his exhibition *Live and Die as Eva Braun*,[6] I looked at the work within the appropriate context, and took what felt right to me.

Which comic book has influenced you the most?

The comic book that influenced me the most was *Persepolis* by Marjane Satrapi,[7] an Iranian artist. It inspired me to produce a committed autobiography. She understands herself, thereby making art. Her painting style is close to mine—using simplistic graphic language that conveys the most powerful emotions, although I do not relate to the political aspect of the books.

Did you know any other autobiographical comic artists when you created your book? Were you familiar with the artists in "Graphic Details: Confessional Comics by Jewish Women"?

Not at all. Even while I was in the group with Dudu Geva, I knew of no other significant Jewish comics apart from [Art Spiegelman's] *Maus*; we just talked about comics artists in general. Perhaps in the United States the Jewish issue is more prominent within the comic, whereas in Israel most comics artists are Jewish. In terms of the confessional nature of my book, it was born out of deep contemplation and desire, looking at my high school years when I kept to myself and was less sociable. The book is an inner journey; from the time and emotional space of one's present to the eternal adolescence of the soul. It's the kind of book that whispers to you the things you're repressing and fighting, that even when you read it a second time, it still has an impact. So I think my book is quite universal in its message. It's a very personal story, but it does not directly describe situations only affecting an Israeli experience, because it's describing an imaginary internal world that has no geography.

As a journalist, you must always be thinking about the target audience. Who is your audience?

I also do commercial comics, humorous comics that are directed at an audience that expects entertainment. There is almost nothing similar between my commercial comics and this emotionally intense graphic novel. The book's target audience is people like me. That is, confused young people who have not yet found a place in the world, girls probably, because I get amazing reactions from girls. Boys seem less connected to the story. The story describes the experience of feeling alienated and it's a search for meaning, which one needs to relate to to connect to the story. One critic described the story as "A description of the experience of depression without the overtones of sentimentality."[8] It's important for me to note that I drew and wrote this book myself, so it looks more like a personal journal and less like a classic comic book. For many years I did not discuss my feelings or thoughts with anyone. I only started to share those aspects of myself when I studied art, and, gradually, I began to understand that there is a therapeutic value to this type of sharing. I found that art gave me a certain distance and allowed me to look at things askance, offering me a more inspired insight.

I didn't plan to publish it. This story was burning inside me, and I just started drawing it. I thought at most that when I finished the story I could Xerox it and sell copies at comics fairs for 20 shekels. What was most important for me was to describe what I experienced in the most accurate and true possible way.

Your book starts with a visual artistic display—the five little girls in puffy dresses and dominant black hair, with each composition showing a different relationship among them. The first story is called "Dream" with you as an adult, followed by a story called "Gate" that describes your wait at the departure gateway before your trip to Australia when you're twenty years old. And the comic ends with "Home" when you are five years old. Why did you change the chronological order?

I was working on different parts over the course of the year and it was important for me to get the correct order. The visual opening of the book exposes the reader to the motifs and narrative language that are needed to understand the meaning within the textual lines of the book. The chapter "Dream" describes a mature relationship, "Gate" is about a conflict where at the end I come back with nothing but the tools to start over, in my case, art tools, and "Home" describes regression. I felt the order was the right thing to do; the happy ending was not accurate, it was too simple. I'm not a fairy princess solving problems and moving on—I had to create this cycle that never really ends.

Who is Sisal Hedge in "Gate"?

Sisal Hedge is a fictitious TV character [in an Australian programme from the 1990s], a negative figure. Essential to the story is that it takes place in a twilight zone between the real world and the world of television delusions.[9] The meaning of the name is "a thorn," through which the character is trying to remove the heroine from the world and disconnect her from reality. He tries to surround her like the thorn bush around Sleeping Beauty in the fairy tale.

Throughout the stories a cockroach appears, an insect typically found in Israel. Why did you choose this insect? [Figs. 55, 90.]

First of all, I chose to use this visual metaphor as a tool that contains several structured concepts. To begin with I wanted a black spot, without details, without humanity, representing a basic level of life. Hairy little legs were added to the book to allow the feeling of movement. At that moment I thought about the significance of the cockroach as menacing and the fact that there is something very despicable about the cockroach, a threatening foreign presence, that runs and hides, and struggles with man, so the cockroach sometimes becomes the metaphor for the heroine herself and sometimes it represents the world she's trying to approach.

My book does not deal with my experience as an Israeli or even as someone Jewish; there is some expectation that religious artists should represent religion, like an expectation

Fig. 55. Racheli Rottner, *The Other Side of the World* (Tel Aviv: Babel, 2008) 9.

that women should deal with femininity. But for me all these concepts are the outside, both
are my costumes. Inside I'm just a girl. A confused girl looking for her way—and this is the
girl represented in the graphic novel. She is religious—yes—it shows in that she always wears
a skirt. But that's it. She is Israeli, indeed—a fact that appears here and there and even when
she is eating a meal at a Chabad House in Australia. But these are just tools to the narrative,
they are not the essence. When a banner appears saying "Prepare for the Coming of the
Messiah" in a Chabad painting, this is actually a metaphor suggesting that the main character
is waiting for something she was not sure was coming, but that faith in his arrival is the only
thing that defines her at the moment.

**Currently you're a partner with a group called *Armadillo*.[10] What is unique about this
group?**

Armadillo is a unique group of young religious, Jewish artists that provides a platform
aimed at expanding the Israeli art world. The group wants to take an active part in the culture
and create a place for artistic expression. Armadillo members are Orthodox and find this
place a space to express feelings of the heart, doubts and love and dialogue between God
and man. We meet once every two months to share opinions and decide on a common theme
and get together twice a year in Jerusalem. The agenda is not necessarily religious themes,
but all the writers come from the same world view and therefore we are driven toward works
in this direction. An Orthodox world view today surrounds me and I attempt to express it
in my art, but in this faith there are always doubts, especially when you are feeling down.
My book deals with this loss and shattered dreams and works for me on a personal level, too.
This exists as a kind of existential confusion, one that has all kinds of forms of expression
in my Orthodox world view and my life as someone who finds it difficult to grow up.

**Israeli comics have traditionally been mostly male; women have only recently joined
the ranks of comics creators. Do you see your comic as a groundbreaking feminist
expression?**

In general every woman who works independently is a feminist by definition. I feel
that the world of comics in Israel is engaged in more important issues (establishment and
society, religion and secularism, etc.) and I feel that I don't need to emphasize the female
aspect. As comics artists are a minority group already we all work together and focus less on
our differences.

**You have displayed in an exhibition at Tova Oasman's studio in Tel Aviv, published a
graphic novel, participated in a unique Israeli–Polish comic project, are running a private blog called *Shufonim*[11] and are writing and publishing comics. What is your next
step?**

I really don't know, I'm not the type of person that plans ahead and stays in one place,
I create according to the place I'm in and what doors open for me.

NOTES

1. The first comic store in Israel only opened in a suburb of Tel Aviv in 2007.
2. A weekly Israeli entertainment magazine that recently folded.
3. Hamidrasha Art School at Beit Berl College, in Tel Aviv.
4. A comic section that began in a local Tel Aviv newspaper and later was published throughout Israel in the
Haaretz newspaper as *The Silence of the Duck*. The duck character was an anti-hero, the loser. The story was suffused
with black humor and the duck was a cynical survivor who became a symbol of Dudu Geva. See Talma Admon's
"The Loser Protest: On *The Duck* of Dudu Geva," *Maariv*, August 26, 2010 (Hebrew).

5. National Volunteer Service is an alternative to mandatory military service for religious girls in Israel.

6. Roee Rosen, *Live and Die as Eva Braun* (Jerusalem: Israel Museum, 1997).

7. Marjane Satrapi, *Persepolis: The Story of a Childhood* (London: Pantheon, 2004).

8. Liat Elkayim, "*The Bad Channel,*" *Haaretz*, November 11, 2008.

9. Rottner is part of Israel's first generation to grow up with color television (in the 1980s) and to witness the emergence of TV stars becoming an integral part of Israel's culture.

10. www.armadil.net.

11. *Shufonim.* http://israblog.nana10.co.il/blogread.asp?blog=14049.

BIBLIOGRAPHY

Admon, Talma. "The Loser Protests: On *The Duck* of Dudu Geva." *Maariv*, August 26, 2010.

Rosen, Roee. *Live and Die as Eva Braun*. Jerusalem: Israel Museum, 1997.

Rottner, Racheli. *The Other Side of the World*. Tel Aviv: Babel, 2008.

Satrapi, Marjane. *Persepolis: The Story of a Childhood*. London: Pantheon, 2004.

Part IV: "Graphic Details"
Artists, Artworks and Confessions

Vanessa Davis

Figs. 7, 56–58

Born: 1978 West Palm Beach, Florida.
Lives: Santa Rosa, California.
Education: University of Florida (BA).
Publications:
    Make Me a Woman. Montreal: Drawn & Quarterly, 2010.
    Spaniel Rage. Oakland, California: Buenaventura Press, 2005.
Awards:
    2009 Maisie Kukoc Award for Comics Inspiration.
Website: www.spanielrage.com

TAHNEER OKSMAN

I was first introduced to Vanessa Davis's work when, on a whim, I bought *Spaniel Rage*, her collected diary comics and sketchbook illustrations. Reading *Spaniel Rage* was like going back in time to encounter myself in my early twenties, except this self had artistic talent, a sharp wit, and was a lot less, shall we say, reserved. "We were making out... And he stuck his finger up my ass." Davis here records an "incident" that her friend has told her about in the diary comic "Deposit." This event, like most in the book, is reported not just verbally, but also with detailed and compelling sketches. She draws faces and body parts, the insides of restaurants and subway cars. Through these sketchbook fragments, a life emerges, complicated and irresistible for all its seemingly inconsequential revelations. In an unnamed diary comic, dated August 13, 2003, Davis pictures herself splayed across a couch in a bra and polka dot panties, and holding a remote control. Below the image, she writes: "This was me on Saturday, watching *The Breakfast Club*, *Sixteen Candles*, *The Goonies*, *Road House*, and *Boys and Girls*." The pages of Davis's diary are filled with such prosaic moments, which often evoke unexpected familiarities. In another comic, from July 2, 2003, she writes: "I am obsessed with eating *pad kee mao* in front of my air conditioner." Flipping through *Spaniel Rage*, we are brought back to our own forgotten evenings spent eating take-out in a hot, lonely apartment. We feel the hard pavement colliding with our palms from that embarrassing time we tripped on the street after getting out of a cab. We recall the otherwise forgotten green pair of underwear covered with etchings of batik palm trees.

Davis's more recently published *Make Me a Woman* is a continuation of *Spaniel Rage*, this time with full color comics interspersed between her shorter, black and white sketches. *Make Me a Woman* has garnered Davis lots of attention and rightly so. In it, she demonstrates

Fig. 56. Vanessa Davis, "Wild Ride," 2009, ink on paper.

Fig. 57. Vanessa Davis, "Wild Ride," 2009, ink on paper.

Fig. 58. Vanessa Davis, "Wild Ride," 2009, ink on paper.

her ability to thoughtfully—and always charmingly—reflect on everything from her family, to her *goyish* boyfriend, to her assessment of Philip Roth's *Portnoy's Complaint*. The book is worth flipping through for her full page colored portraits alone. Drawn in rich, vibrant tones, Davis draws women costumed in diverse and powerful fashions. A slumped posture, a sidelong gaze: using minor details, she depicts a whole life captured in a single moment.

Bernice Eisenstein

Figs. 10, 43–44, 59–60

Born: 1949 Toronto, Canada.
Lives: Toronto, Canada.
Education: 1972 York University, BA (Hons).
Publications:
  I Was a Child of Holocaust Survivors. Toronto: McClelland and
    Stewart, 2006.
Exhibitions:
  2010 "Charlotte Salomon: Through the Eyes of Jonathan Safran Foer,
    Bernice Eisenstein and Ernst van Alphen." Jewish Historical
    Museum, Amsterdam.
  2008 "Superman and Golem." Frankfurt Jewish Museum.
  2008 "Superheroes and Schlemiels." Jewish Museum of Australia.
  2007 "From Superman to the Rabbi's Cat." Museum of Jewish Art and
    History, Paris.
  2007 "Superheroes and Schlemiels." Jewish Historical Museum,
    Amsterdam.
Awards:
  2008 Adei-Wizo Prize, Italy, Second Prize for Young Readers.
  2007 Canadian Jewish Book Award for *I Was a Child of Holocaust
    Survivors.*

MALCOLM LESTER

In her memoir *I Was a Child of Holocaust Survivors*, Bernice Eisenstein quotes Primo Levi, who said in an interview that writing his book about his survival in Auschwitz worked for him as a sort of prosthesis—an external memory set up like a barrier between his life today and his life then. When I read this, I wondered if we could view Bernice's graphic art this way, that is, as a prosthesis to her text—after all she is a wonderful storyteller; a prosthesis by which she enhances her narrative of growing up in a family haunted by memories of the Holocaust. Though "prosthesis" also suggests something artificial, Bernice's drawings are not that, but are, I feel, a necessary expression of her artistic language.

Yes, you could read Bernice's compelling and ingenious memoir separate from the drawings, but your reading would be woefully incomplete. The edgy sharpness of her drawings extends the text and brings to it a melancholy vitality (nobody smiles much in the drawings). And the vitality often comes from the frequent (and funny) juxtapositions of pop culture

Fig. 59. Excerpted from *I Was a Child of Holocaust Survivors* by Bernice Eisenstein, 52. Copyright © 2006 Bernice Eisenstein. Reprinted by permission of McClelland & Stewart.

references with the historical record. One of my favorites is Bernice's father as a Gary Cooper–like sheriff entering the gates of Auschwitz to bring justice (or is it Judgment?) to the Nazi killers. But what you notice most of all in Bernice's drawings is the alert gaze on the faces of the survivors—whose eyes have seen horrors beyond imagination, and whose lips are invariably closed, as if the unimaginable should not be spoken. So words, yes, and images too—both are indivisible in Bernice's art—and then we can begin to approach the truth.

Fig. 60. Excerpted from *I Was a Child of Holocaust Survivors* by Bernice Eisenstein, 72. Copyright © 2006 Bernice Eisenstein. Reprinted by permission of McClelland & Stewart.

Sarah Glidden

Figs. 45–47, 61–64

Born: 1980 Boston, Massachusetts.
Lives: Chicago, Illinois.
Education: Boston University (BFA).
Publications:
  Comment Comprendre Israël en 60 Jours (ou Moins). Paris: Steinkis, 2011.
  Una judía americana perdida en Israel. Barcelona: Norma Editorial, 2011.
  Israël in 60 dagen. Amsterdam: Oog & Blik, 2011.
  Capire Israele in 60 giorni (e anche meno). Milan: Rizzoli Lizard, 2011.
  Israel Verstehen: In 60 Tagen oder Weniger. Berlin: Panini, 2011.
  How to Understand Israel in 60 Days or Less. New York: Vertigo, 2010.
Contributions (Selected):
  "How to Understand Israel in 60 Days or Less" in *Best American Comics*. New York: Houghton Mifflin Harcourt, 2012.
  "The Waiting Room," *Cartoon Movement*, 2011.
    http://www.cartoonmovement.com/comic/10.
  "State of Palestine," *Cartoon Movement*, 2011.
    http://www.cartoonmovement.com/comic/15.
  "Tents of New York," *Haaretz*, 2011.
  "Occupy Miami," *Cartoon Movement*, 2011.
    http://www.cartoonmovement.com/comic/22.
  "Proximity Talks," *Jewish Quarterly*, 2011.
    http://jewishquarterly.org/2011/09/proximity-talks/
  "Drawing a Line," *Jewish Quarterly*, 2012.
    http://jewishquarterly.org/2012/09/drawing-line/
  "A Walk in Once," *Jewish Quarterly*, 2012.
    http://jewishquarterly.org/2012/11/walk/
  "The Sound of Jade" in *Syncopated: An Anthology of Nonfiction Picto-Essays*. New York: Villard, 2009.
Exhibitions (Selected):
  2012 "Nuvole di Confine: *Graphic Journalism L'arte del reportage a fumetti.*" Musei Internazionale dell'Umorismo dell'Arte, Tolentino.
  2010 "Docu-comix, KinoKino Arts Center." Sandes, Norway.
  2010 "Neointegrity." The Museum of Comic and Cartoon Art, New York, New York.
  2008 "Everything Must Go." Flux Factory, Queens, New York.
  2006 "Works on Paper." Flux Factory, Queens, New York.
  2006 "Secret Clubhouse." Lower Manhattan Cultural Council, New York, New York.

Fig. 61. Sarah Glidden, "Falafel," *How to Understand Israel in 60 Days or Less,* **mini-comic, 2008, ink paper, 3.**

Fig. 62. Sarah Glidden, "Falafel" *How to Understand Israel in 60 Days or Less*, mini-comic, 2008, ink on paper, 4.

Fig. 63. Sarah Glidden, "Falafel," *How to Understand Israel in 60 Days or Less*, mini-comic, 2008, ink on paper, 5.

Fig. 64. Sarah Glidden, "Falafel," *How to Understand Israel in 60 Days or Less*, mini-comic, 2008, ink on paper, 6.

Awards:
2008 Ignatz Award for Promising New Talent.
2008 Masie Kukoc Award for Comics Inspiration.
Website: www.sarahglidden.com

JULIA WERTZ

When Sarah Glidden and I first started exchanging mini comics in 2004, I thought she was a total weirdo. But the more I got to know her, I realized that she was a delightful weirdo. Over the next few years, I watched her work develop from easy, lighthearted autobiographical gag comics into substantial, ardent journalistic comics that offer a sympathetic face to conflicts most Americans tend to ignore or view with bias. Sarah's dedication to her work makes me feel shameful about every fart joke I've ever written. But I can tell you that almost every email she's written has had a subject line that is a guttural noise of disgust or surprise. One would think that "gah!" and "oof" would eventually be made redundant, but they've been going strong for eight years.

She would hate that I said this, but Glidden is a pioneer in the world of journalism comics and she's only getting started.

Miriam Katin

Figs. 19–20, 65–68

Born: 1942 Budapest, Hungary.
Lives: New York, New York.
Publications:
   Letting It Go. Montreal: Drawn & Quarterly, 2013.
   När mamma brände Gud. Stockholm: Epix Bokforlag, 2011.
   Allein Unter Allen. Hamburg: Carlsen Comics, 2007.
   Por Nuestra Cuenta. Tarragona: Ponent Mon, 2007.
   We Are on Our Own. Montreal: Drawn & Quarterly, 2006.
   Seules Contre Tous. Paris: Seuil, 2006.
Contributions (Selected):
   "Live Broadcast." *Beaux Arts éditions La Bande Dessinée,* 2009.
   "Curried Away." First City, New Delhi, 2007.
   "Eucalyptus Nights." Guilt and Pleasure, 2006.
   "Oh to Celebrate!" *Drawn & Quarterly* (2001).
Exhibitions:
   2010 "Helden, Freaks und Superrabbis: Die Jüdische Farbe des
Comics." Jüdisches Museum, Berlin.
   2008 "Superhelden En Sjlemielen." Joods Historisch Museum,
      Amsterdam.
   2008 "Superman Und Golem." Jüdisches Museum, Frankfurt.
   2009 "Superheroes & Schlemiels." Jewish Museum of Australia.
   2008 "Miriam Katin." Expocomic Xi Salón Internacional Del Tebeo
      de Madrid.
   2007 "De Superman au Chat du Rabbin." Musée d'Art et d'Histoire
      du Judaïsme, Paris.
   2007 Holocaust Memorial Exhibition. The Bible Museum, Tel Aviv.
   2006 "The Jewish Graphic Novels." Hebrew Union College
      Museum.
Awards:
   2001 Eisner Award 2001 (Nominee).
   2007 Grand Prix de la Critique.
   2007 l'Association des Critiques et Journalistes de Bande Dessinée.
   2007 Inkpot Award, Comic-Con International San Diego.
Website: www.miriamkatin.com

Fig. 65. Miriam Katin, "Eucalyptus Nights," 2006, pencil on paper.

Fig. 66. Miriam Katin, "Eucalyptus Nights," 2006, pencil on paper.

Fig. 67. Miriam Katin, "Eucalyptus Nights," 2006, pencil on paper.

Fig. 68. Miriam Katin, "Eucalyptus Nights," 2006, pencil on paper.

RANEN OMER-SHERMAN

I have been working in the classroom with Miriam Katin's extraordinary Holocaust memoir *We Are on Our Own* (2006) for the past few years with great success; my Holocaust literature students often praise it as one of the works that most touch them and no matter how often I revisit it, I am astonished by its narrative power and by Katin's visual and textual gifts for poetic understatement. Emboldened by her critical and commercial success with this work, Katin soon began to explore other phases of her tumultuous life, most notably in "Eucalyptus Nights," a visually expressionistic work about her service in the Israel Defense Forces in the early 1960s.

Somehow my acquaintance with her earlier work left me utterly unprepared for the stylistic ferocity and visceral shock of this highly charged and gripping compact work, which is in some respects an equally unsparing work of psychological turmoil and memory. Katin's taut narrative addresses the lust of impatient young soldiers eager to be distracted from the tedium of army life as well as seething ethnic tensions, an uneasy undercurrent in Israeli society especially in its early decades.

Its frenzied, turbulent, and aggressive imagery deftly captures the raw intensity of those days, especially her startling encounter with the seething tensions between Israel's Ashkenazi Jewish establishment and Jews from the Arab world. Yet it also expresses a degree of unabashed nostalgia for the romanticism of that time and in February 2010 she told me: "In the silence of the night you would listen to the whispering leaves, the music they created when the wind changed. There was a smell of dust and dry leaves and gun oil. So much quiet conversation, [so many] hours of contemplation." Even today, she says that these things send her into "dizzy reveries." As a former Israeli soldier, I instantly recognized the truth of that sentiment.

Even though it is clearly set in the early 1960s, this is a timeless, nearly universal statement about Israel, which has always absorbed its waves of immigrants, most recently from Russia and Ethiopia, with a marked degree of ambivalence if not outright hostility and latent racism. The aching conclusion of "Eucalyptus Nights" is about an elusive connection. With its poignant "might have been" flourish, there is a clear-eyed and unsentimental portrayal of a lost moment, the toll intolerance and timidity enact on a promising relationship.

Aline Kominsky-Crumb

Figs. 69–72

Born: 1948 Long Beach, New York.
Lives: France.
Education: University of Arizona BFA (1971).
Publications:
  Need More Love. London: MQ Publications, 2007.
  Love That Bunch. Seattle: Fantagraphics Books, 1990.
Contributions and Joint Projects (Selected):
  Parle-Moi d'Amour. (in collaboration with Robert Crumb). Paris:
    Editions Denoël, 2011.
  Drawn Together (in collaboration with Robert Crumb). New York:
    W.W. Norton, 2011.
  New Yorker stories (in collaboration with Robert Crumb). 1995–2005.
  Self-Loathing Comix 2. Seattle: Fantagraphics, 1995.
  Self-Loathing Comix 1. Seattle: Fantagraphics, 1992.
  Weirdo. San Francisco: Last Gasp, 1986–1993 (contributor, editor)
  Twisted Sisters. San Francisco: Last Gasp, 1995, 1994, 1976.
  Dirty Laundry. San Francisco: Last Gasp, 1974–1977, 1993.
  Wimmen's Comix #1, #2, #4. San Francisco: Last Gasp, 1972–1974.
Exhibitions (Selected):
  2008 "Superman Und Golem." Jüdisches Museum, Frankfurt.
  2009 "Superheroes and Schlemiels." Jewish Museum of Australia.
  2007 "De Superman au Chat du Rabbin." Musée d'art et d'histoire du
    Judaisme, Paris.
  2007 "Superhelden En Sjelmielen." Joods Historisch Museum,
    Amsterdam.

F.K. Clementi

When I was a child my mother tried sharing with me her passion for superheroes and darkly sexy detectives with large fedoras, but these hyper masculine heroes never captured my imagination as deeply and intensely as they had hers. I liked only the comics that made me laugh (*Peanuts*, *B.C.*, *Asterix*); I loathed the unironic infallibles. Today, in retrospect, I realize that none of the dozens of comic books circulating in my house were written or drawn by women. Could a child have sensed that there was no room "for her" in Superman's or Dick Tracy's universe? Theirs are planets where none of my IDs were accepted for entrance. The choice was between the super-funny and the super-heroic: one made *me* the butt of the

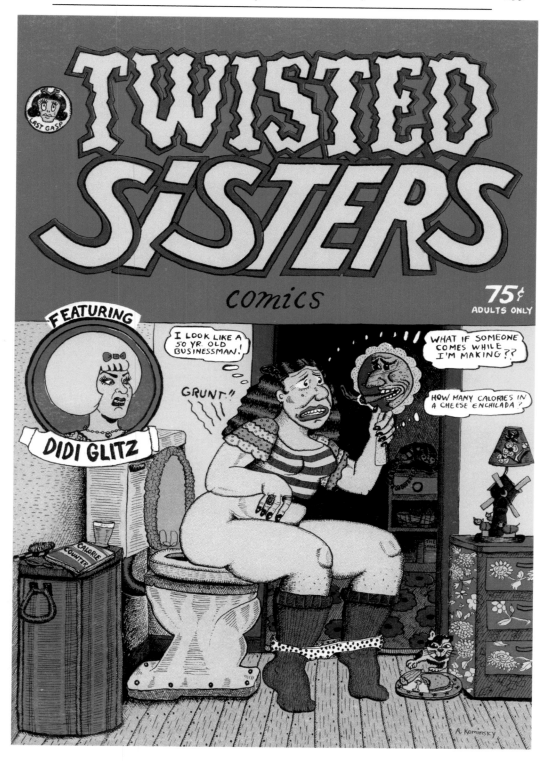

Fig. 69. Aline Kominsky-Crumb, *Twisted Sisters* (cover), 1976.

Fig. 70. Aline Kominsky-Crumb, "Nose Job," *Need More Love* (London: MQ, 2007) 86.

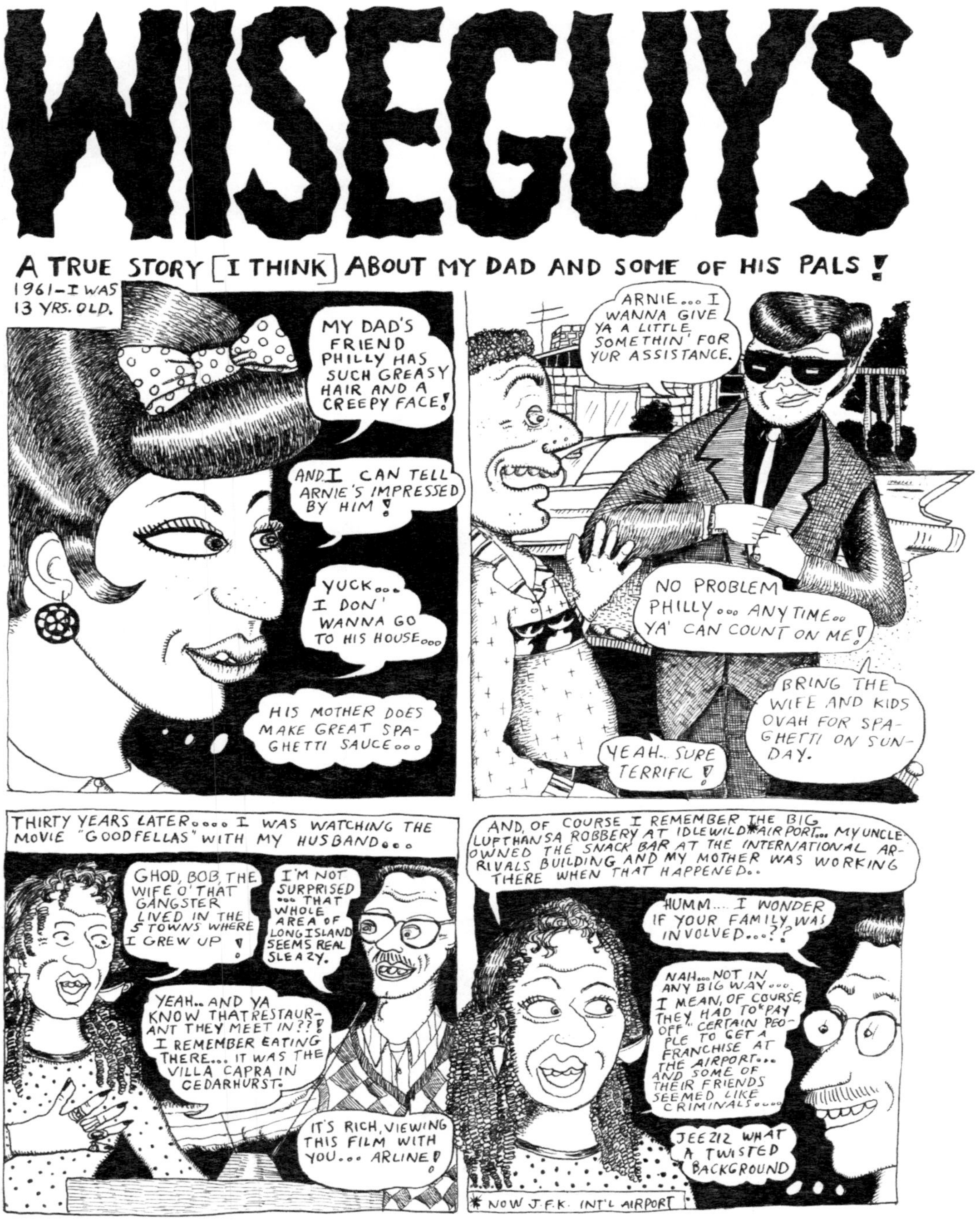

Fig. 71. Aline Kominsky-Crumb, "Wiseguys," 1995, ink on paper, page 1 of 10.

Fig. 72. Aline Kominsky-Crumb, "Wiseguys," 1995, ink on paper, page 2 of 10.

joke; the other left *me* out altogether. Where was the planet for mercurial Jewish girls with unspectacular torsos, slightly downturned noses, and hair that flew *agitato molto* [very agitated] most days?

Enter Aline Kominsky-Crumb with her graphic confession *Need More Love*. God knows I needed *that* book when I was a teenager. Despite the age gap between the author and myself, The Bunch [Aline's drawn character] and I walked on similar paths: I know the planet she hails from awfully well; she is my sister in ways that Lois Lane could never be... I know The Bunch, I have seen The Bunch stare back at me from bathroom mirrors, I am The Bunch, too. The traditional hero is independent and self-reliant (he saves the world because it's his job); The Bunch needs love, has strong emotions, loves friends and beautiful places, changes her mind (whatever!) and evolves spurred by curiosity and deep feelings about everything—*this* sounds healthy to me. No other-planetary breasts, breath-limiting wasp-waist, highway-long legs and hyperluminous hair here: yet The Bunch has the power to turn *me*, the reader, into a superhero who angers at those who make independent-looking and independent-thinking girls feel inadequate, who empathically shares The Bunch's insecurities, bleeds at the cuts of her self-deprecating humor and learns to be proud of her own unusual choices in life. Surviving, as The Bunch did, in this world of hypocritical family ideals, ideological parochialism, patriarchal mythologies, brutal consumerism, chauvinism, bigotry, compulsive homogeneity—where even dissent is commodifiable—she *is* the stuff of superheroes and superheroines. Aline Kominsky-Crumb's acerbic humor is her majestic weapon: the truths it reveals are like kryptonite to our planet, which is still largely controlled by *superior*-men. While comics often mask the human to make them superhuman, Kominsky-Crumb's autobiographical comics use humor to undress the characters of their performative costumes and show their humanity—often a struggling, sad, beaten, certainly always complex humanity.

Miss Lasko-Gross

Figs. 3, 37–38, 50–51, 73–75

Born: 1977 Boston, Massachusetts.
Lives: Lower East Side, New York, New York.
Education: Communication Design, Pratt Institute (BFA).
Books:
  A Mess of Everything. Seattle: Fantagraphics, 2009.
  Escape From "Special." Seattle: Fantagraphics, 2006.
Contributions (Selected):
  Womanthology: Heroic. San Diego, CA: IDW, 2012.
  "Indie Spinner Rack." *Awesome 2: Awesomer.* Portland: Top Shelf,
    2009.
  "Next Door Neighbor." SMITH Magazine, 2009.
Exhibitions:
  2012 "Kirby Enthusiasm." Maxwell's.
  2005 "Comiclysm." Sputnik, Brooklyn.
  2001 "Legal Action Comics Show." CBGB's 313 Gallery.
  1996 "Alt.Youth.Media Show." New Museum of Contemporary Art.
Awards:
  2009 Booklist Top 10 Graphic Novels.
  2008 Young Adult Library Services Association Great Graphic Novels
    (Nominee).
Website: www.misslaskogross.com

ROB CLOUGH

Miss Lasko-Gross's self-caricature of Melissa in her semi-autobiographical comics is an amalgam of a typical teen with low self-esteem and that of an indignant outsider determined to make her increasingly confident voice heard—and loudly. From a young age, Melissa understands that she doesn't fit in and is in fact constantly bombarded by that message. As a reader, I quickly identified with that sense of being outside of consensus ideas of behavior, looks and style and admired the bold volume of Melissa's voice. In a group of vignettes that cohere into a narrative through sheer accretion, Melissa's stubborn individuality and sense of generalized outrage is directed toward anything resembling authority, especially when she begins to understand that maneuvering through authority structures is simply a matter of understanding that it's all a game. Lasko-Gross has a particular thematic bent to her comics, but the use of vignettes to break up the narrative helps remove some of the temptation to make more sense out of one's own life story than is really there. Indeed, she goes out of

Fig. 73. Miss Lasko-Gross, "The Gruswerk's Sabbath," *Escape from "Special,"* 2002, ink on paper.

Fig. 74. Miss Lasko-Gross, "The Gruswerk's Sabbath," *Escape from "Special,"* 2002, ink on paper.

Fig. 75. Miss Lasko-Gross, "The Gruswerk's Sabbath," *Escape from "Special,"* 2002, ink on paper.

her way to be not just self-effacing, but to point out that she's a sort of "type" (the rebel), with a whole host of expected behaviors—an idea that seemed equally clear to me in my own high school experiences. Lasko-Gross's greatest strengths as a cartoonist are her character design and use of body language and gesture. It's the way she stages her characters that makes looking at each page interesting. She uses a muted palette on pages that are filled with gray, and jams every panel with decorative details. Lettering also serves as a way to depict exaggeration, and the organic quality of her lettering often reveals emotional states in a more direct way than the actual words themselves. What elevates these books above simple teen rage is Melissa's burgeoning sense of self-awareness and how her actions and anger affect those around her. Her outrage is not just directed at societal structures in general, but rather her sense that qualities such as honesty, empathy and compassion are not only discouraged by the culture-at-large but openly derided. What's most appealing about Lasko-Gross's work is her warts'n'all portrayal of Melissa, and that forsaking of idealization made it all the easier to identify with her. The slightly grotesque and expressionistic art is a perfect match for the way Melissa looks at the world and herself, as faces and bodies are distorted to reflect emotional tumult. She's not an easy person for the reader to like; she's cranky, argumentative and prone to outbursts of rage. Her eccentricities are not affected, however; and how she manages to deal with authority while embracing the qualities that make her different is inspiring.

Sarah Lazarovic

Figs. 48–49 , 76–77

Born: 1979 Montreal, Quebec, Canada.
Lives: Toronto, Ontario, Canada.
Education: Florida State University (BA)
  Concordia University, Montreal (BFA)
  The New School, New York (MA)
Publications (Selected):
  "A Bunch of Pretty Things I Did Not Buy." thehairpin.com, 2012.
  "How T.O." *National Post* 2010–2012 (weekly comic).
  Mireille Silcoff, *National Post* 2010–2012 (weekly illustration).
  "Another Week" *Ottawa Citizen* 2006–2010 (weekly cartoon).
  Benjamin Errett, *Jew and Improved*. Toronto: HarperCollins,
    2010 (illustrations and cover design).
Exhibitions (Selected):
  2012 "Summer Special." Honest Ed's with Koffler Centre of
    the Arts, Toronto.
  2009 "Keyframes." Harbourfront, Toronto.
  2009 "Older." Luminato Box, BCE Place, Toronto.
  2007 "One Inch Punch." Lennox Contemporary, Toronto.
  2006 "Midnight Snack." *Nuit Blanche*, Toronto (Curator).
  2005 "What's Your Pleasure?" Steam Whistle Gallery, Toronto.
Awards (Selected):
  2011 Writer's Guild of Canada Jim Burt Screenwriting Award
    (Nominee).
  2010 HarperCollins Canadian Short Story Contest (Runner Up).
  2010 Green Innovation Award, City of Toronto.
  2008 Chalmers Fellowship, Ontario Arts Council.
  2007 Annual Illustration Award, *Applied Arts Magazine*.
  2005 Toronto Jewish Arts Council Visual Arts Grant.
  2005 Framework Foundation's Artist Commission (Shortlisted).
  2006 Filmmaker Assistance Program Grant, National Film Board of
    Canada.
  2004–6 Grants from Toronto Arts Council, Ontario Arts Council.
Website: www.SarahL.com

Fig. 76. Sarah Lazarovic, "Abstained," 2007, print on paper.

Fig. 77. Sarah Lazarovic, "Shop til you Stop," 2008, print on paper.

ALISON BROVERMAN

In Sarah Lazarovic's illustrated world, everyone's a bit wittier, a bit prettier, and a bit better dressed. She draws and writes with a distinctly feminine sensibility, undercut by a sharp intelligence and curiosity and a wry sense of humor that isn't above a well-placed pun or two. Whether she's relating a moment from her own life, or examining a civic issue, her wit shines through in both her words and images. She draws with casual assurance and frequently pulls off a rare blend of elegance and goofiness. Her light touch and springy colors are equally effective whether she's eviscerating a local politician or fondly recounting an anecdote about her daughter.

As the only female member of a graphic novel bookclub (although to be fair, my male counterparts are some of the most enlightened and sensitive fellas you could hope to meet), I'm sometimes overwhelmed by the maleness of many of the comics that our group chooses to read. As a reader, I love stories about how contemporary women interpret and live in the world, and Sarah's work often explores just such stories.

I'm fortunate enough to count Sarah as a friend and colleague, and we have long shared a more than passing interest in baked goods. Much to my sweet-toothed delight, it's a theme that appears often in her work—and the lady draws a mean croissant.

Miriam Libicki

Figs. 5, 78–79

Born: 1981 Columbus, Ohio.
Lives: Coquitlam, British Columbia, Canada.
Education: Emily Carr University of Art and Design, Vancouver, Canada (BFA).
Publications (Selected):
"Turning Right on Cassady." *22 Journeys*. Vancouver: Cloudscape Comics, 2011.
"Jewish Memoir Goes Pow! Zap! Oy!" *The Jewish Graphic Novel: Critical Approaches*, eds. Samantha Baskind and Ranen Omer-Sherman. New Brunswick, NJ: Rutgers University Press, 2008 (essay and cover).
"*jobnik!*" *Jews and American Comics*. Ed. Paul Buhle. New York: The New Press 2008 (excerpt).
jobnik! An American Girl's Adventures in the Israeli Army. Coquitlam, British Columbia: Real Gone Girl Studios, 2008.
Exhibitions:
2008 Israel Arts Week, HUB Gallery, Seattle.
2008 Jewish Arts Month. University of Washington Hillel, Seattle.
2008 "Inkstuds". Jem Gallery, Vancouver.
2007 "Salty: Three Tales of Sorrow." El Camino College Art Gallery, Torrance, CA.
2006 Jewish Arts Month. University of Washington Hillel, Seattle.
2006 Graduate Show. Concourse Gallery, Vancouver.
2005 "View to an End." Concourse Gallery, Vancouver.
2004 "Kweer Show." Concourse Gallery, Vancouver.
Awards:
2009 Gene Day Award for Canadian Self-Publishing (Finalist).
2009 Hadassah-Brandeis Institute Research Grant.
2008–09 International Fellowship in Jewish Studies, Memorial Foundation for Jewish Culture.
Website: www.realgonegirl.com

RANEN OMER-SHERMAN

What first struck me about Miriam Libicki's marvelous graphic memoir *jobnik!* was her bravery in exploring painful aspects about her vulnerable search for love and belonging even while witnessing the foibles of Israeli society, especially the hallowed institution of the Israel Defense Forces [IDF]. *jobnik!* encompasses a series of provocative vignettes portraying Miriam's struggles as an American immigrant soldier in Israel that illuminate a range of

249

Fig. 78. Miriam Libicki, *jobnik!* (Coquitlam, British Columbia: Real Gone Girl Studios, 2008) 72, pencil on paper.

Fig. 79. Miriam Libicki, *jobnik!* **(Coquitlam, British Columbia: Real Gone Girl Studios, 2008) 73, pencil on paper.**

critical issues concerning Jewish identity, gender politics, sexuality, and politics. Like many other critics and readers, I was stirred by her capacity for portraying uncomfortable experiences with raw urgency, conviction, and immediacy. Initially I saw in this young artist's story a reflection of my own experiences as a young immigrant from California serving in the IDF decades earlier. My own ardent, pathetic desire to prove myself, to gain a sense of belonging, my desperate, witless hope to instantly embody the "new Jew" of martial coolness and virility, made her story seem very familiar at first. But the more I read, the more I came to appreciate Miriam's brilliantly drawn portraits of everyday Israeli society as well as army life, her ironic, witty, and profoundly humane perspectives on the myriad absurdities and tragedies she witnessed. Very soon my nods of recognition turned into little gasps of gratitude for her graceful and subtle renderings of Israel's physical and psychological landscapes. More than a personal memoir, *jobnik!* synthesizes innovative research and clear exposition with a bold, engaging style. Again and again, Miriam proves herself a tender and incisive observer of all she experienced during her tumultuous time in Israel.

Sarah Lightman

Figs. 12–14, 80–82

Born: 1975 London.

Lives: London.

Education: Central/St Martins Art School (Art Foundation).
  Slade School of Art, UCL (BA Hons).
  Slade School of Art, UCL (MFA).
  University of Glasgow, PhD (ongoing).

Exhibitions (Selected):
  2013 "The Book of Sarah." Occupy My Time Gallery, London.
  2013 "Family Line-ups: Trans-generational Encounters in Family
    Photography." University of Bucharest.
  2012 "Publicly Private." New Media Gallery, Oranim College, Israel.
  2011 Ruth Borchard: Self-Portrait Competition. King's Place Gallery,
    London.
  2010 "The Moment of Privacy Has Passed." The Collection, Lincoln.
  2009 "In Memoriam." New Hall College Art Collection, Cambridge.
  2008 "Diary Drawing." Northampton University, and The Centre for
    Recent Drawing (curator).
  2007 "Bomberg's Relevance." Ben Uri Gallery, London Jewish Museum
    of Art (curator).
  2005 "Sarah Lightman, Drawings and Film." Berwin Leighton Paisner,
    London.

Awards:
  2013 European Association for Jewish Culture.
  2012, 2011, 2010 Research Grants, University of Glasgow.
  2006 Camden Small Grants for the Arts.
  2001 Young Jewish Artist Award.
  2001 Post Graduate Award AHRB British Academy Award.
  2001 Travel and Expeditions Award, UCL.
  1999, 1998, 1996 The Slade School of Art Awards.

Website: www.sarahlightman.com

Roger Sabin

"It is a curious sensation... When your heart is broken, your boats are burned: Nothing matters any more. It is the end of happiness and the beginning of peace."—George Bernard Shaw
  Sarah Lightman's triptych "Dumped Before Valentine's" is about a moment of shock. Her relationship ends, on the bank of the Thames, the news being conveyed via her cell

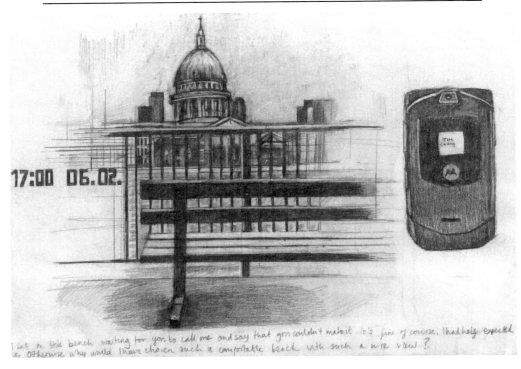

I sat on this bench waiting for you to call me and say that you couldn't make it. It's fine of course. I had half expected it. Otherwise why would I have chosen such a comfortable bench with such a nice view?

I watched the water, I knew you meant more in your no show than you cared to admit

Top—Fig. 80; *bottom*—fig. 81. Sarah Lightman, "Dumped Before Valentine's," 2007, pencil on paper.

And it wasn't just this afternoon I was going to spend on my own.

Fig. 82. Sarah Lightman, "Dumped Before Valentine's," 2007, pencil on paper.

phone in the oblique but unmistakable form of a cancelled liaison. Her heart is broken, and nothing matters anymore. We move from a scene of a bench and a "nice view," with the phone depicted adjacent; then a close-up of the cityscape across the river; and finally, the bench again, this time isolated in white space, and the phone, lingering, displaying a "call ended" message.

There's a wonderful sense of time standing still. The close-up at the center of the three images reveals construction cranes dotted along the London skyline. The city is being rebuilt, just as Sarah will have to rebuild her life. Words, impossible to form at the moment of the call's impact, appear handwritten as a commentary beneath each drawing—a retrospective reckoning with a moment of "curious sensation." It turns out that Sarah half-knew what was going to happen—"it's fine, of course," she writes, capturing perfectly the feeling of wounded stoicism we all recognize.

Is it a "sacred moment," also? The religious references are there if you look for them—and they're mostly Christian. The view is dominated by St Paul's Cathedral; the idea of a triptych is associated with altarpieces; and "Valentine" is named after Saint Valentine (Even the idea of a "confessional" is a little bit Catholic.). It's never emphasized, but maybe—there and then—Sarah is a Jew in a Christian world, another situation over which she has no control.

Is this the "end of happiness" and the "beginning of peace" for Sarah, as Shaw predicted? Luckily, we can find out, because "Dumped..." is just one episode in a vast and compelling narrative that she has been constructing over a period of 15 years. *The Book of Sarah* (yes, another religious reference) is more a visual diary than a comic strip, and takes in many further autobiographical tales of love and loss. The fascination, as ever, is in the (graphic) details.

Diane Noomin

Figs. 21–22, 83–86

Born: 1947 Brooklyn, New York.
Lives: Connecticut.
Education: Pratt Institute, New York (BA).
Publications:
    Dangerous Drawings. New York: Juno Books, 1997.
    The New Comics Anthology. New York: Maxwell MacMillan, 1991.
    Twisted Sisters. San Francisco: Last Gasp 1976 and 1994 (editor).
    Weirdo. San Francisco: Last Gasp 1981–1993.
    Contributions to *Wimmen's Comix.* San Francisco: Last Gasp
      1972–1992.
    Young Lust San Francisco: Last Gasp (and others) 1970–1990.
    Lemme Outa Here. San Francisco: The Print Mint, 1978.
    Arcade: The Comics Revue. San Francisco: The Print Mint 1975–1976.
Exhibitions:
    1996 "Twisted Sisters Show." White Columns Gallery (curator).
    1995 The Museum of Cartoon Art of San Francisco.
    1994 Solo Exhibition. Little Frankenstein Gallery in San Francisco.
    1991 La Luz de Jesus Gallery in Los Angeles.
Awards:
    1995 Harvey Award (nominated).
    1995 Eisner Award (nominated).
    1994 Ink Pen Award.
Website: www.dianenoomin.com

SARAH LIGHTMAN

Tragi-Comic—the term seems made for Diane Noomin's "Baby Talk: A Tale of 3 4 Miscarriages"—is the graphic art of personal tragedy that remains resolutely funny. It might explain also why I'm always desperate to talk about Noomin's fertility history. I bask in her visual intelligence and when I see the awkwardness in my audience's faces (they'd only asked how my PhD was going to make conversation), I also feel the sharp cracks of ice that are societal norms—and I am reminded of her bravery. People just don't talk about miscarriages. But that doesn't stop them happening. And when I talk about Noomin's comic, I watch my audience transform—they start a conversation, previously unimaginable, about their own gynecological experiences, in the cold hands of callous doctors.

Noomin draws the unfairness of life. I am moved by the drawn Diane, who is dragged

Fig. 83. Diane Noomin, "Baby Talk: A Tale of ~~3~~ 4 Miscarriages," 1993, ink on paper, page 1 of 12.

Fig. 84. Diane Noomin, "Baby Talk: A Tale of 3 4 Miscarriages," 1993, ink on paper, page 2 of 12.

Fig. 85. Diane Noomin, "Baby Talk: A Tale of ~~3~~ 4 Miscarriages," 1993, ink on paper, page 3 of 12.

Fig. 86. Diane Noomin, "Baby Talk: A Tale of ~~3~~ 4 Miscarriages," 1993, ink on paper, page 4 of 12.

unwillingly to star in her own comic, breaking her own autobiographical pact. She hadn't dressed for the occasion. Frazzled and ungroomed, but now immortalized, Noomin's comic reminds me of what I look like most days. And in a comic about her own miscarriages, Noomin reminds the reader how others are so careless with her own heart's desire. DiDi Glitz is Noomin's drinking, demanding and glamorous alter ego. DiDi often neglects and forgets her daughter, Crystal. And to add salt to the drawn wound, is it just me or does ice-cream loving Crystal look like a little Diane? With no small touch of irony, Noomin reminds the reader that, in a story about childlessness, art is an act of creation, capable of reflecting the complexities of parenting: DiDi's self-centered demands overshadow Diane's own existential crisis and personal agony: "What happens to **me** if **you** crack up!!" [Fig. 86].

"Baby Talk" oozes the alchemy of great art—when form harmonizes with content to unsettle the viewer. Deconstructing this comic's skillful edifice of narrative, watching each miscarriage take place, is to helplessly observe as a beautiful and fragile heart gets broken, again and again. Diane Noomin described to me how she cried when she made "Baby Talk." With a sharp ink line that marks like scratchboard, a comic has never cut so deep.

Corinne Pearlman

Figs. 1–2, 8–9, 87–88

Born: 1949 Amersham, UK.
Lives: Brighton and London.
Education: Hilda's College, Oxford (BA).
Publications:
　Hate Thy Neighbour: Dividing Lines of Race and Colour (Mindfield).
　　London: Camden Press, 1998.
　Ottoline at the British Museum. London: Macdonald, 1987;
　　London: British Museum Press, 1993.
　The Comic Book of the Facts of Life. Philip Boys and Corinne Pearlman.
　　London: Fantail/Penguin, 1991.
　The Comic Book of First Love. Philip Boys and Corinne Pearlman,
　　London: Virago Press 1987; London: Fantail/Penguin, 1991.
　Ottoline at the Natural History Museum. London: Simon & Schuster,
　　1990.
　Media & Power: A Graphic Guide. Peter M. Lewis and Corinne
　　Pearlman. London: Camden Press, 1986.
Contributions (Selected):
　"Playing the Jewish Card." *The Jewish Quarterly*, 2009–2011.
Exhibitions (Selected):
　1997 "The Cartoonists' Progress." Gardner Arts Centre, University of
　　Sussex, and National Theatre, London.
　1996 "The 100." Gardner Arts Centre, University of Sussex.
　1995 "The Cartoon Stripped." Gardner Arts Centre, University of
　　Sussex.
　1993 Cartoon County inaugural exhibition. Gardner Arts Centre,
　　University of Sussex.
Awards:
　1988 Mother Goose Award, "The Most Exciting Newcomer to
　　Children's Book Illustration" Books for Children (shortlist).
Website: www.comicopera.co.uk

Arthur Oppenheimer

Jewish humor is not vicious; the man slipping on a banana skin has no place in Jewish humor. For many years *bar mitzvah* boys used to receive as a gift "The Treasury of Jewish Humor"—735 pages of comical hindsights into a Jewish milieu that existed in the Pale of Settlement, the Diaspora and in the murky world of god, heaven and devils. Anti-Semitism

Fig. 87. Corinne Pearlman, "Playing the Jewish Card: The Gap Year," 2004, ink on paper.

Fig. 88. Corinne Pearlman, "Playing the Jewish Card: The Gap Year," 2004, ink on paper.

and pessimism played a part in this history. It's good being a cynical pessimist—you are prepared and anticipate the worst that can happen and so are pleasantly surprised when enjoyable events spring out of the undergrowth.

It is this interplay between the Jewish culture and the surrounding world that makes Corinne Pearlman's work graphically distilled, relevant and sensitive. Corinne takes the situation of Anglo-Jewry and frames it with intelligent analysis, understanding and irony. Her comic strips contain a sympathetic hidden language, which shows how Jews carry with them cultural and religious memories of the past in an increasingly multicultural world. She continues in the tradition of Jewish humor but creates a synthesis of Jewish memory and contemporary life. Jewish life and humor covers major life events—birth, marriage, death (or in the language of *The Jewish Chronicle* "hatch, match and dispatch"). Corinne's characters project themselves into these three dimensions—whether reminiscing on student life on a kibbutz, memories of chicken soup at some long closed restaurant, the position of their father's grave or the trials and tribulations of being an assimilated Jew. Her comic strips are simultaneously poignant, amusing and revealing.

Corinne's graphics are wonderful—you can see the nerve endings dangling in the chopped liver (not necessarily kosher). There is amusing compassion for all the feuding, loving, meandering relationships that define life and in each episode there is a penetrating X-ray on Anglo-Jewish lifestyle.

Perhaps it is because I come from a similar background that Corinne's storyline resonates so strongly with my own experience: when being a North London Jew meant Banning the Bomb, realizing that one's ancestry was both religious and political, and trusting that psychiatry would replace electric shock treatment. In those days, our emotional geography was bounded by the northern stretches of London's tube network—Hampstead, Belsize Park and Golders Green were a supportive enclave, and although we knew that there were places called Tooting Bec and Morden at the other end these were more alien than Jerusalem or New York. Her work is placed within a framework of contemporary and tender scenes, which wryly, but without rancor, recapture a time when we thought the world was going to get better and better and better ... until suddenly, it didn't.

Trina Robbins

Fig. 89

Born: New York. Laydeez do not have to give their ages!
Lives: San Francisco, California.
Education: Expelled from two of New York's best schools: Cooper Union and Queens College.
Publications (Selected):
> *The Chicagoland Detective Agency* #1–4. Minneapolis: Graphic Universe 2009–2012 (author).
> *Marvel's Girl Comics.* New York: Marvel Worldwide, 2012.
> *Lily Renee, Escape Artist.* Minneapolis: Graphic Universe, 2011 (author).
> *Womanthology: Heroic.* San Diego: IDW, 2011.
> *GoGirl!* graphic novels 1–3. Image/Dark Horse, 2000–2006.
> *From Girls to Grrlz.* San Francisco: Chronicle Books, 1994.
> *Wimmen's Comix.* San Francisco: Last Gasp, 1972–1992.
> *Girl Fight #1* and 2. San Francisco: The Print Mint, 1972–1974.
> *It Ain't Me, Babe.* San Francisco: Last Gasp, 1970.

Awards:
> 2011 Moonbeam Children's Book Awards, Gold Medal.
> 2011 Sydney Taylor Jewish Library Association Silver Medal.
> 2011 Little Nemo Award.
> 2010 Norton Award.
> 2010 Junior Literary Guild Selection.
> 2002 Haxtur, Gijon, Spain.
> 2000 Firecracker Alternative Book Award.
> 2000 Friends of Lulu Female Cartoonist Hall of Fame.
> 2000 Lulu of the Year.
> 1997 Friends of Lulu.
> 1994 Parents' Choice Award.
> 1990, 1991 NOW Outstanding Feminist Award.
> 1989 Special Achievement award, San Diego Comicon.
> 1989 Media Alliance Meritorious Achievement Award.
> 1977 Inkpot Award for Achievement in Comic Arts.

Website: www.trinarobbins.com

RACHEL POLLACK

Trina Robbins and I share a birthday, a fact I find comforting in moments of weakness and doubt. Other people who share our day include Davy Crockett, Mae West, and Marcus

Fig. 89. Trina Robbins, "Big Sister Little Sister," 1989, print on paper.

Garvey. In my vainer moments I like to pretend these three define who I am, but I always know they're really all about Trina.

Like Davy Crockett, Trina is a pioneer and a fighter. Her work on the early women cartoonists, and other aspects of women in comics, has greatly enlarged our knowledge of this very American form of the popular arts. Trina's own comics may be light and fun, but they always carry meaning. Trina will fight for what she believes, and her beliefs are passionate but also clear-headed. To be honest, I'm not sure just how clear Mr. Crockett's head was, but we can count on Trina's research and the depths of her thought. And unlike Davy, who (Mr. Disney assures us) "kilt himself a b'ar when he was only three," Trina is a passionate respecter of all life. Really, Disney should do a TV series about Trina. Well, maybe HBO.

Like Mae West, Trina is brash, funny, uppity, smart, irreverent, and sexy. Doesn't that sound a bit like the Girl Scout oath? I can hear Trina exclaiming how wonderful the Girl Scouts are, for their inclusive policies, and well, because they're girls. A few years ago Trina gave me the honor of writing the foreword to her book *Eternally Bad: Goddesses with Attitude.* I had known most of the stories in this book for years, but only in academic accounts or well-intended uplifting publications for young readers. Trina brought these heroines alive as no one had ever done—daring, hilarious, and fighters for women. I think it was about then that Trina began to describe herself as "the oldest grrl in San Francisco." It's because I want to be like Trina when I grow up (I will turn 67 on our next joint birthday) that I sometimes sign email postings as Artemisgrrl.

Sadly, Marcus Garvey is the least known of our famous birth mates. An early Black liberationist, he founded the Back to Africa movement. Like Garvey, Trina is politically committed, tireless, and devoted to her cause: feminism in the service of all humanity. She is, however, much funnier than Garvey. Also prettier. Trina reminds us, in her person and her comics, that feminism can dress up, look wonderful, and have fun. Trina Robbins is a national treasure.

Racheli Rottner

Figs. 55, 90

Born: 1982 Netanya, Israel.
Lives: Tel Aviv, Israel.
Education: Hamidrasha School of Art, Beit Berl College, Tel Aviv.
Publication: *The Other Side of the World.* Tel Aviv: Babel, 2008.

ARIEL KAHN

I first came across Racheli Rottner's work *The Other Side of the World* in a Steimatsky's in a Tel Aviv mall. In a pizzeria nearby, my nephew and niece were wreaking havoc, and I had sought refuge in the relative peace of the bookstore, which faced the pizzeria so I could still see them. The title leapt out at me. *The Other Side of the World* was precisely where I wished to be at that moment. What I found was not safety or escape, but something more elusive, and more precious.

Racheli's work made me genuinely afraid, as the best fairy tales had when I was a child. My encounter with Sisal Hedge, a spiky insect/man like an imaginary friend gone bad, allowed me to be more forgiving of the food fight I could observe in silence through the glass. Hedge was like a little corner of my own unconscious come to life, his blots and jagged edges a Rorschach of my own fears of isolation and abandonment. He reminded me, too, of that term for "The Other Side" from my childhood—the *Sitra Achra*: the dark, demonic side of existence, which was used in school to threaten us into obedience like a Jewish bogeyman. Here was an artist bravely exploring her own *sitra achra*.

As I read on, I saw there was also tenderness, humor—that Sisal Hedge was a little like Edward Scissorhands, and that the novel was playing a kind of literary "What if?"—What if Kafka's Gregor Samsa had taken a lover, one who was not repulsed by his insect body, one who could meet him in dreams, and drink coffee? Through Rottner's work, I felt I was traveling somewhere new, which was, at the same time, a place I had known since my childhood. Sisal gave me a sense of rediscovery and awakening to those moments of fear in my adolescence, that I might never find someone who would really see me. It was a rare experience of shared dreaming, of feeling that some of my own imaginings had torn loose and taken on independent life.

In *The Other Side of the World* I found a companionship all the more powerful for being fictive. The strength of Racheli's protagonist as she dealt with her demons stayed with me long after I left the bookstore, and my experience of that other space her comic had taken me to made me a little more empathetic, for that afternoon at least. In my braver moments, I try to return there.

Fig. 90. Racheli Rottner, *The Other Side of the World* (Tel Aviv: Babel, 2008) 7.

Sharon Rudahl

Figs. 91–94

Born: 1947 Arlington, Virginia.
Lives: Los Angeles, California.
Education: Cooper Union (BFA), 1969.
Boston University (PG) 1971–1972.
Publications (Selected):

It Started in Wisconsin. By Paul and Mari Jo Buhle. London: Verso, 2011.

Robin Hood, People's Outlaw. By Paul Buhle, illustrations by Chris Hutchinson, Gary Dumm and Sharon Rudahl. Oakland: PM Press, 2011.

Yiddishkeit. Ed. Harvey Pekar and Paul Buhle. New York: Abrams Comicarts, 2011.

Art in Time. By Dan Nadel—reprint of 32-page "Crystal Night." New York: Abrams, 2010.

Comics in Wisconsin. By Paul Buhle. Madison, WI: Borderland Books, 2009.

Studs Terkel's Working. Adapted by Harvey Pekar, ed. Paul Buhle. New York: The New Press, 2009.

Jews and American Comics. Ed. Paul Buhle. New York: The New Press, 2008.

Wobblies, a Graphic History. Eds. Paul Buhle and Nicole Shulman. London: Verso, 2005.

Story Time. Eds. Anne Chang-Blaeske and Phil Yeh. San Francisco: Friends of Lulu, 2000.

A Dangerous Woman: The Graphic Biography of Emma Goldman. New York: The New Press, 2007.

All American Hippie Comix. Northampton, MA: Kitchen Sink Press, 1994.

The Best Contemporary Women's Humor. Ed. Roz Warren. Berkeley: Crossing Press, 1994.

A Century of Women Cartoonists. Ed. Trina Robbins. San Francisco: Chronicle Books, 1993.

Underground Classics. San Francisco: Rip Off Press, 1992.

Gates of Eden. Ed. Mitch Cohen. New York: Fantaco Publishers, 1982.

Aftershock. Ed. Rebecca Wilson. San Francisco: Last Gasp, 1981.

Adventures of Crystal Night. Northampton, MA: Kitchen Sink Press, 1980.

Wimmen's Comix #1–8. San Francisco: Last Gasp, 1972–1977.

Titters. Ed. Deanne Stillman and Anne Beatts. New York: Macmillan, 1976.

Comix Book #2–3. New York: Marvel Comics, 1973–1974.

Fig. 91. Sharon Rudahl, "The Star Sapphire," 1975, ink on paper.

Fig. 92. Sharon Rudahl, "The Star Sapphire," 1975, ink on paper.

Fig. 93. Sharon Rudahl, "The Star Sapphire," 1975, ink on paper.

Fig. 94. Sharon Rudahl, "The Star Sapphire," 1975, ink on paper.

Awards:
2012 Eisner Award (shortlisted).
2007 Young Adult Award.
1989 National Chess Journalists' Cartoonist/Illustrator Award.
1969 National Merit Scholarship; Ford Foundation Fellowship.

PAUL BUHLE

As publisher of the one-shot *Radical America Komiks* (1969) and steady reader/collector/sometime interviewer of the U.G. comics and their artists, I admired Sharon Rudahl hugely for several decades before we got in touch. It was a great thing for me to get her several pages on Emma Goldman for *Wobblies!*—and then to secure a contract for her graphic biography of Emma. Since then, we seem to have worked together pretty steadily. We are only a half-dozen years apart in age, and I feel that Sharon and I have been spending lifetimes together, separated by geography but connected by social movements. I am very, very lucky to be collaborating with a brilliant artist, serious thinker and perpetual activist. I continue to be amazed by the detail of her work and her ability to blend social history—most particularly, but not only, of women—with great care for historical detail and narrative strength. Every Rudahl story is of intrinsic interest, as well as being lovely and highly skilled work. This detail will keep readers of new generations reading her for many decades to come.

Laurie Sandell

Figs. 95–99

Born: 1971 Long Island, New York.
Lives: Santa Monica, California.
Education: University of Wisconsin–Madison, 1993 (BA).
Publications:
  Truth and Consequences: Life Inside the Madoff Family. New York: Little, Brown, 2011.
  The Impostor's Daughter. New York: Little, Brown, 2009.
Award: Eisner Award (nominee).
Website: www.lauriesandell.com

MICHAEL KAMINER

The first thing that struck me about Laurie Sandell's work was its modesty: simple lines, clean shapes, straightforward composition. Then I read and reread *The Impostor's Daughter*, the graphic novel that, astonishingly, represented her debut as a cartoonist. Every panel yielded some detail that sparked a smile, raised an eyebrow, pierced the heart. And I realized that Laurie's almost naïve style doesn't just represent stylistic choices; it's a sly, skillful way of disarming readers. By the time you're immersed in her book, you—like her—are too deeply engaged in her father's deceptions, and too emotionally invested in Laurie's own story, to stop reading. As a masterful writer, she could have chosen to relate *The Impostor's Daughter* as a straightforward narrative. Lucky for us, she chose comics—with their multiple layers of storytelling, fluidity of form, and freedom to riff—as her vehicle. Her almost unbelievable story is all the more powerful for it.

Fig. 95. From *The Impostor's Daughter* by Laurie Sandell, 37. Copyright © 2009 by Laurie Sandell. By permission of Little, Brown and Company. All rights reserved.

Fig. 96. From *The Impostor's Daughter* by Laurie Sandell, 198. Copyright © 2009 by Laurie Sandell. By permission of Little, Brown and Company. All rights reserved.

Fig. 97. From *The Impostor's Daughter* by Laurie Sandell, 199. Copyright © 2009 by Laurie Sandell. By permission of Little, Brown and Company. All rights reserved.

Fig. 98. From *The Impostor's Daughter* by Laurie Sandell, 200. Copyright © 2009 by Laurie Sandell. By permission of Little, Brown and Company. All rights reserved.

Fig. 99. From *The Impostor's Daughter* by Laurie Sandell, 201. Copyright © 2009 by Laurie Sandell. By permission of Little, Brown and Company. All rights reserved.

Ariel Schrag

Figs. 6, 32–36, 42, 100–102

Born: 1979 Berkeley, California.
Lives: Brooklyn, New York.
Education Columbia University (BA).
Publications:
  Awkward and Definition. New York: Simon & Schuster, 2008.
  Likewise. New York: Simon & Schuster, 2008.
  Potential. New York: Simon & Schuster, 2008.
  Stuck in the Middle: 17 Comics from an Unpleasant Age. New York:
    Viking, 2007.
Awards:
  2009 Lambda Literary Award (nominee).
  2000 Eisner Award (nominee).
Website: www.arielschrag.com

NOAH BERLATSKY

If there's a characteristic danger of autobiographical comics, it would be narcissism. Creating art about yourself can cause you to spiral into numbingly mundane depictions of clipping your toenails or cultivating your angst in an endless round of hermetic inconsequence.

Perhaps the thing I love most about Ariel Schrag's work is the way in which her autobiographical comics are so thoroughly un-hermetic. Don't get me wrong; Ariel definitely gives you mundane details and tons (and tons!) of angst. But the mundanity and the trauma are always routed through, and involved with, relationships. The first panel in Ariel's first book, *Awkward*, written when she was a high school sophomore, is emblematic. It shows her on the phone talking to her friend Julia about a crush on a guy in her PE class. The scribbly, mostly unshaded linework and the overstuffed captions rush you into a world of schoolgirl crushes and breathless sharing. The panel borders, violated by starburst infotext and arrows, don't so much isolate as encourage crossing over.

As Schrag's work got more sophisticated, her identity (most notably as a lesbian) became more defined. But that only means that those relationships—especially with her girlfriend Sally—become even more central and more defining. One of the funniest scenes in *Likewise*, Schrag's chronicle of her senior year, is when she and her male friend Zally go to a strip club. Zally gets a lap dance and quickly does that thing that guys do when they get lap dances. Ariel tries to imitate him, but ends up instead thinking about the experience of the stripper

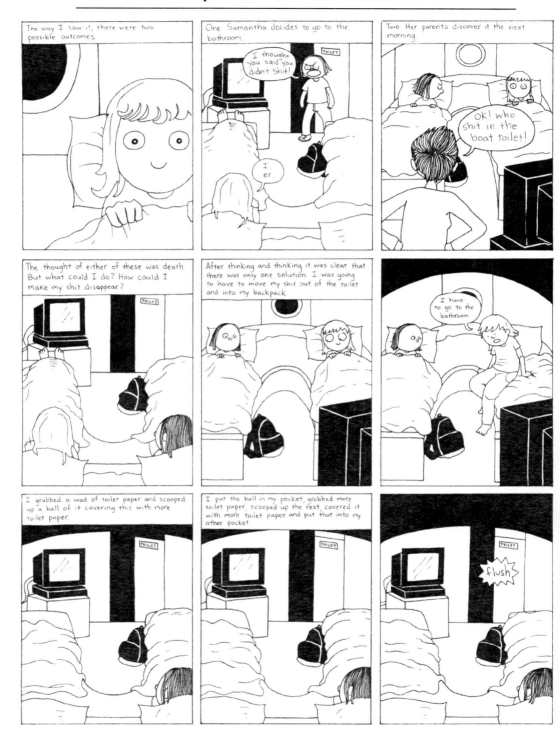

Fig. 100. Ariel Schrag, "Shit," 2003, ink drawing on paper, page 2 of 4.

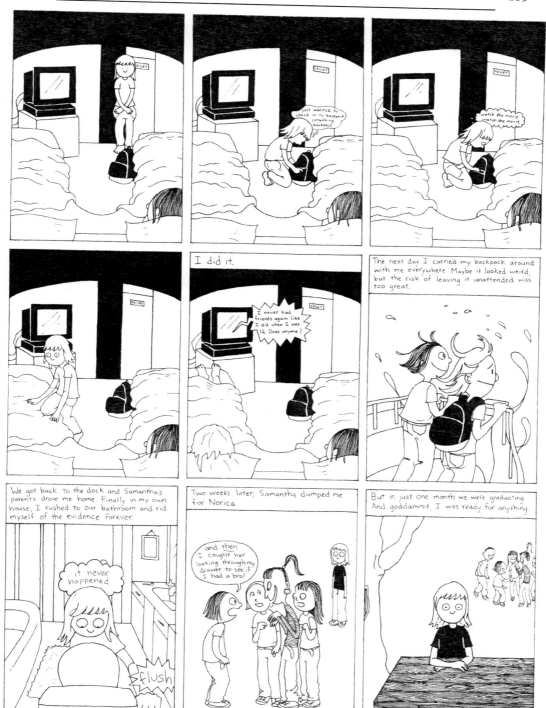

Fig. 101. Ariel Schrag, "Shit," 2003, ink drawing on paper, page 3 of 4.

Fig. 102. Ariel Schrag, "The Chosen," 2008, ink on paper.

who is performing for her. The private expression of her lust ends up being about Zally and about the stripper—in short, about everybody but her.

"The Chosen" presents the same dynamic in a lighter vein, as Ariel, half by accident, half on purpose, plays up her Jewish roots in order to please a Hasidic acquaintance named Joseph. In the penultimate panel, as swirled concentric half circles reminiscent of her *menorah* [Jewish candelabra lit during the festival of Hanukkah] spiral behind her, she worries that her ruse has been discovered, and that Joseph has figured out that she's not really a believer. But in the final panel, the question loses its urgency. The point is not what she truly is or isn't, but rather who she was friends with—not that she's Jewish in herself, but that she was, at least for a little while in someone's eyes, "one of the Chosen." For Schrag, the story of the self is the story of those around you—which is a pretty Jewish way of looking at the world.

Lauren Weinstein

Figs. 40–41, 52–54, 103–104

Born: 1975 Boston, Massachusetts.

Lives: Maplewood, New Jersey.

Education: 1997 Vermont Studio Center Residency.
Washington University in St. Louis, School of Art (BFA).

Publications:
The Goddess of War. Brooklyn, New York: Picturebox, 2008.
Girl Stories. New York: Henry Holt, 2006.
Inside Vineyland. Self-published, 2003.

Contributions:
Best American Comics. Guest edited by Neil Gaiman. Boston:
Houghton Mifflin, 2010.
The Ganzfeld. Issues 1 (2000), 2 (2001), and 7 (2008). New York:
Picturebox.
Best American Comics. Guest edited by Chris Ware. Boston: Houghton
Mifflin 2007.
Stuck in the Middle: 17 Comics from an Unpleasant Age. Edited by Ariel
Schrag. New York: Viking Juvenile, 2007.
An Anthology of Graphic Fiction. Edited by Ivan Brunetti. New Haven:
Yale University Press, 2006.
Kramer's Ergot #4. Oakland, CA: Buenaventura Press, 2003.
Hotwire. Seattle: Fantagraphics, 2006.

Exhibitions:
Ongoing "Lit Graphic," touring show, Norman Rockwell Museum and
Munson-Williams-Proctor Arts Institute, Utica, New York.
2009 Fumetto Festival in Lucerne, Switzerland.
2006 "Telling Tales: Contemporary Women Cartoonists." Adam
Baumgold Gallery, New York.

Awards:
2007 Booklist Top 10 Graphic Novels for Teens.
2005 Ignatz Award.
2004 Xeric Grant for Self Publishing.
1993–1997 Conway Proetz Full Tuition Merit Scholarship.

Website: www.laurenweinstein.com

Fig. 103. Lauren Weinstein, "This Is the Book of Lauren R. Weinstein," 2006, ink drawing on paper, n.p.

Fig. 104. Lauren Weinstein, "This Is the Book of Lauren R. Weinstein," 2006, ink drawing on paper, n.p.

Nicole Rudick

The first comic I saw by Lauren Weinstein was a single-panel poster, from 2008, in which the meanderings of two people through a park are plotted atemporally. We see them meet up, make out, bear a child, raise the child, and grow old—until he dies of a heart attack and she waves goodbye to her grown son as he embarks on his first romantic relationship and leaves the park. It is an exhilarating diagram of movement and an eloquent and pithy panorama of human life. The comic makes sense to me, too, in thinking about the milestones of Weinstein's career: from bright and candid tales of Barbies and middle-school Weltschmerz, to witty, reliably oddball gag cartoons and vignettes, to the sophisticated story of a brash and lovesick goddess of war who sets off on her own, and to remarkable sequences exploring the gnawing self-doubt of drawing comics with a child on her hip. A constant throughout is her humor; as witty as it is silly, it enlivens everything she does. I'm trying to picture myself now in one of her "self-actualization activities," standing on the edge of a restless ocean with a bear named Smokey, and all I can think about is what my thighs would look like in the "Sit-Down Test."

Ilana Zeffren

Figs. 26–31, 105–107

Born: 1972 Rechovot, Israel.
Lives: Tel Aviv, Israel.
Education: West Galilee College, Vizo Haifa Art School (BA).
Publications:
  Achbar Hair, Rishumon. Jerusalem : Shoken, 2006–2013 (weekly
    comic column).
  "Zina," "Moadim" "Lesimcha," "Playlist," "Kipa." *Masmerim Literary
    Journal*, Israel, 2006–2012.
  Hair. Jerusalem: Shoken, 2007–2008 (weekly caricatures).
  "Paragraph no. 19." *The Direction Is East Literary Journal*. Bimat
    Kedem, Israel, 2008.
  "Pussycat." *Alma, Yedioth Ahronoth*, Israel, 2006–2007 (comic strip).
  "Lesbix." *The New Time*, Israel, 2005 (comic strip).
  Pink Story. Tel Aviv: Mapa, 2005.
Exhibitions:
  2012 "The First Friedel Stern Humorous Cartoon Contest." The Israeli
    Cartoon Museum.
  2010 "X+Y." The Israeli Cartoon Museum.
  2006 "Cats." Eretz Israel Museum.
Website: www.ilanazeffren.com

GIL HOVAV

My 15 seconds of fame lie in Ilana Zeffren's graphic novel *Pink Story*, depicting Israel's gay history. On page 127, I am in one tiny frame, looking skinnier than I usually do, wearing a green shirt and a smile. I got the book from my daughter and her mother stating: "From now on, you are officially a minor celebrity!" Well, well. It is not easy to get your daughter to admit that her mom is half-famous. I opened the book, started reading it and fell in love instantly. Not with Ilana Zeffren. With Spageti, her cat.

Ever since I've been an avid fan of *Rishumon*, Ilana's weekly comic column in our local magazine, admiring her partner, her two talking cats (that are more intelligent than all of us), her humor and her talent. In one of her columns, she even included my late cat, Aznavour, who was not as intelligent (or, alas, as feminist) as her own cats, but is now immortalized as a minor-celebrity feline.

I love Ilana Zeffren's wit, I love her style, I admire her talent and super-dry humor. And let's face it: I'm still in love with that cat.

292

Fig. 105. Ilana Zeffren, " Neither shall a man put on a woman's garment," *Pink Story* (Tel Aviv: Mapa, 2005) 82–83.

Rishumon Ilana Zeffren

Under Spageti's tuna lies a dignified past

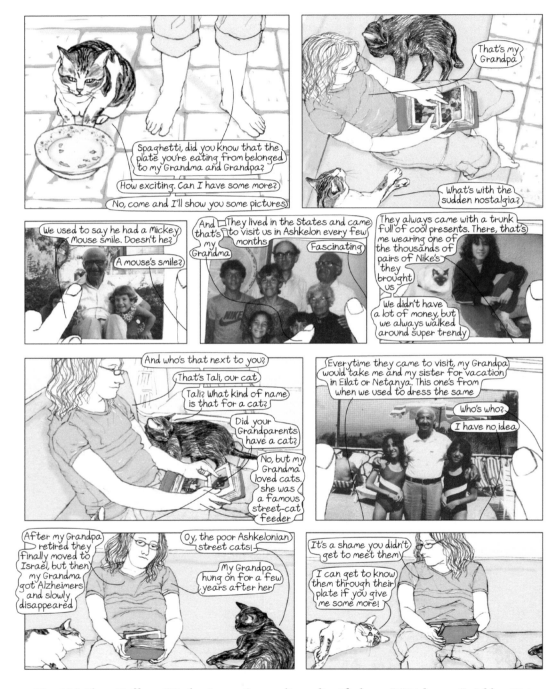

Fig. 106. Ilana Zeffren, "Under Spageti's tuna lies a dignified past," "*Rishumon*," *Achbar Hair*, 2007.

Fig. 107. Ilana Zeffren, "Yes, I too was once straight," "*Rishumon*," *Achbar Hair*, 2007.

About the Contributors

Judy **Batalion** is a Canadian writer, performer and art historian based in New York City. Her personal essays, journalism and criticism have appeared in *The New York Times*, *Salon*, *The Washington Post*, *The Jerusalem Post*, *Contemporary Theatre Review*, *Nerve*, *Babble*, *The Frisky*, *The Jewish Daily Forward* and many other publications. She edited the academic collection *The Laughing Stalk: Live Comedy and Its Audiences* (Parlor Press, 2011) and co-curated the exhibition "Home and Garden" at the Geffrye Museum of Domestic Interiors, London.

Heike **Bauer** is a senior lecturer in English and gender studies at Birkbeck College, University of London. Her publications include a monograph, *English Literary Sexology 1860–1930* (Palgrave Macmillan, 2009), a three-volume anthology on *Women and Cross-Dressing 1800–1930* (Palgrave Macmillan, 2006) and a collection of co-edited essays, *Queer 1950s* (Palgrave Macmillan, 2013). She is writing a book about Jewish sexologist Magnus Hirschfeld and the violent shaping of modern queer culture.

Noah **Berlatsky** edits the comics blog "The Hooded Utilitarian." He writes for *The Atlantic*, *Salon*, *Reason*, and *Splice Today*. His book on the original Wonder Woman comics will be published by Rutgers University Press in early 2015.

David **Brauner** is a reader in English and American literature at the University of Reading. He is the author of three books: *Post-War Jewish Fiction: Ambivalence, Self-Explanation and Transatlantic Connections* (Palgrave Macmillan, 2001), *Philip Roth* (Manchester University Press, 2007) and *Contemporary American Fiction* (Edinburgh University Press, 2010). He is co-editing the *Edinburgh Companion to Modern Jewish Fiction*.

Alison **Broverman** is a Toronto-based writer and broadcaster. Her play *Expiry Dating* won the Toronto Fringe Festival's New Play Contest in 2007. Since then, her work has appeared in newspapers and magazines across Canada. On the radio, her work has been featured on several national CBC programs.

Paul **Buhle** was the founder of the student new left journal *Radical America* in 1967, later of Cultural Correspondence, which followed trends in comic art, and has been editor of eight comic art volumes of nonfiction history since 2005. His latest project is gathering and sharing comic art on working conditions and labor history from across the globe.

F.K. **Clementi** is an assistant professor of Jewish studies at the University of South Carolina. Her work focuses on Jewish women's personal and historical experiences as expressed in their literature and art. She is the author of *Holocaust Mothers and Daughters: Family, History, and Trauma* (Brandeis University Press, 2013), on the bond and conflict between Jewish mothers and daughters during the *Shoah*. She is a feminist and eco-activist.

Rob **Clough** grapples with cancer as a function of his day job, and writes about comics and women's college basketball at night. His work may be found at www.tcj.com, www.high lowcomics.blogspot.com, and *The Comics Journal*.

Noa Lea **Cohn** was born in Netanya, Israel, and is a PhD candidate in Jewish art history at Bar-Ilan University. She graduated from Hebrew University, Jerusalem, with a BA and an MA in art history and Jewish thought. She teaches art in several colleges in Jerusalem and lectures on writing programs for the Ministry of Education. She has also written for several newspapers in Israel including *Makor Rishon*.

Ariela **Freedman** is an associate professor at Liberal Arts College, Concordia University, Montreal. She is the author of *Death, Men and Modernism* (Routledge 2003), and her articles and reviews have appeared in numerous journals, including *Literature Compass, Modernism/Modernity, Journal of Modern Literature* and *Vallum*. She is working on word and image in the work of Charlotte Salomon and on the representation of pain and illness in comics.

Dan **Friedman** is the managing editor of *The Jewish Daily Forward*. Formerly *The Jewish Daily Forward*'s award-winning arts and culture editor, he has also written for *The New York Times, The Financial Times, The Wall Street Journal* and *Da Ali G Show*. He has a PhD in comparative literature from Yale University and an MA in English literature from Cambridge University—where he also earned a blue for association football. He is writing a book about the rock band Tears for Fears.

Paul **Gravett** is a London-based freelance journalist, curator, lecturer, writer and broadcaster. He is the co-author, with Peter Stanbury, of the books *Manga: 60 Years of Japanese Comics* (Laurence King, 2004), *Graphic Novels: Stories to Change Your Life* (Aurum Press, 2005), and *Great British Comics* (Aurum Press, 2006), and he is the editor of *The Mammoth Book of Best Crime Comics* (Robinson, 2008). His newest book is *Comics Art* (Tate, 2013) and he is co-curator of the first major exhibition of British comics at the British Library.

Gil **Hovav** is an Israeli author, publisher and television personality. He has published one novel and two collections of short stories about the Jerusalem of his childhood that no longer exists and more than 15 cookbooks. He lives in Tel Aviv.

Sarah **Jaffe** is an independent journalist based in New York, writing about politics, economic justice, gender, pop culture, music and comics. Her work has been published in *The Nation, Rolling Stone, The Guardian, Bitch, Bust, Truthout, Jacobin*, and many other publications. She was the labor and media editor at *AlterNet.org* and a regular contributor to Newsarama.com, where she covered comics and gender.

Ariel **Kahn** received an MA in African and Indian literature at SOAS, University of London. He is a senior lecturer in creative writing at Roehampton University, where he teaches courses on comics, and was a contributor to *The Jewish Graphic Novel*. He is writing a novel for his doctorate about a young female Kabbalist in contemporary Israel. He is on the faculty of the London School of Jewish Studies teaching prayer, Jewish thought and mysticism.

Michael **Kaminer** is a journalist in New York and co-curator of "Graphic Details: Confessional Comics by Jewish Women." He wrote the 2009 *Jewish Daily Forward* story that inspired "Graphic Details." He is the restaurant critic for the *New York Daily News* and contributes travel and food coverage to *The New York Times, The Washington Post, The Jewish Daily Forward*, and other media. Michael also collects original cartoon art, most of it by women.

Joanne **Leonard** is a distinguished university professor emerita, University of Michigan, and a widely exhibited photographer, photo-collage artist, writer and feminist whose work has contributed to the field of autobiography studies. Her varied publications include her visual memoir *Being in Pictures: An Intimate Photo Memoir* (University of Michigan Press, 2008) and an essay "Being in Pictures: A Commentary on Feminist Visual Narratives in the Digital Age" in *Exposure* (Spring 2012).

Malcolm **Lester** has been active in Canadian publishing since 1964. He is best known as the president of Lester & Orpen Dennys which he co-founded in 1973. *The Literary Review of Canada* named three of L&OD's publications among the 100 most important books ever published in Canada. He is publisher at large at Malcolm Lester & Associates where, among other things, he produces limited editions of books for individuals and organizations.

Zachary Paul **Levine** is a curator at Yeshiva University Museum and he adapted "Graphic Details" into its traveling form. He completed a PhD in the Hebrew and Judaic studies and history departments at New York University where he studied clandestine aid programs to East European Jews during the Cold War. He holds an MA in history from Central European University and BAs in government and politics, and Jewish studies from the University of Maryland.

Sarah **Lightman** is an artist and curator with degrees from the Slade School of Fine Art. She is a PhD student at the University of Glasgow and has contributed to *Trauma, Narratives and Herstory* (Palgrave Macmillan, 2013) and *The Routledge Handbook to Contemporary Jewish Cultures* (Routledge, 2014), among others. She has a forthcoming autobiographical graphic novel, *The Book of Sarah* (Myriad Editions, 2015), and she is chair of the Women in Comics conferences and director of Laydeez do Comics, a unique graphic novel forum. She is co-curator of "Graphic Details: Confessional Comics by Jewish Women."

Tahneer **Oksman** is an assistant professor of academic writing and director of the Writing Program at Marymount Manhattan College. She earned a doctorate in English literature at the Graduate Center at CUNY, with a focus on Jewish women's graphic memoirs. Her articles have been published in *Studies in Comics* and *Studies in American Jewish Literature*. She has taught courses in comics, visual media, and American literature at NYU-Gallatin, Brooklyn College, and Rutgers University.

Ranen **Omer-Sherman** is a professor of English and Jewish studies at the University of Miami. His essays have appeared in many periodicals, including *Journal of Jewish Identities, Journal of Modern Jewish Studies, Journal of Modern Literature, Prooftexts,* and *Shofar*. His books include *Diaspora and Zionism in Jewish American Literature* (Brandeis University Press, 2002) and the co-edited volume *The Jewish Graphic Novel: Critical Approaches* (Rutgers University Press, 2008). His research addresses literary and cinematic narratives of the kibbutz.

Arthur **Oppenheimer** was a computer programmer for many years. He was awarded a special fellowship by the Alumni Society of the University of Sussex in recognition of his work and involvement with the Centre for German-Jewish Studies.

Natalie **Pendergast** is a PhD candidate at the University of Toronto. She specializes in contemporary autobiographical graphic novels and *bande dessinée*. Under the supervision of Professor Julie LeBlanc at the Centre for Comparative Literature, she engages in studies of theory including Peircean semiotics and psychoanalysis, as well as methodologies of analysis like *la critique génétique*.

Rachel **Pollack** is the author of 34 books, including two award-winning novels, and *78 Degrees of Wisdom,* described around the world as "the Bible of Tarot Readers." She is also a poet, a translator and a visual artist. Her books have been published on every continent, in 15 languages, and she has lectured and taught across America and Canada, Europe, Australia, and New Zealand. She is a senior faculty member of Goddard College's MFA program for creative writing.

Pnina **Rosenberg** is an art historian specializing in the art and legacy of the Holocaust, subjects she is teaching in the Technion, Haifa, and the Yezreel Valley College, Israel. She has written a book, *L'art des indésirables: L'art visuel dans les camps français* (L'Harmattan, 2003), as well as scholarly articles, including "Art of the Holocaust" and "Women-Artists in Auschwitz" in *The Last Expression* (1999 and 2002, respectively). She is also the art editor of *Prism: Journal for Holocaust Educators.*

Nicole **Rudick** is the managing editor of *The Paris Review.* Her criticism has appeared in *The New Yorker, Artforum, The Comics Journal, Bookforum, The Los Angeles Review of Books,* and elsewhere. She has written on the work of numerous artists, including Gary Panter, Destroy All Monsters, Diane Noomin, Alison Bechdel, Adrian Tomine, Ben Jones and Lynda Barry.

Roger **Sabin** is a reader in popular culture at Central Saint Martins College of Arts and Design, University of the Arts, London. His books include *Adult Comics: An Introduction* (Routledge, 1993) and *Comics, Comix and Graphic Novels* (Phaidon, 2001). He serves on the editorial boards of many of the key academic journals in the field of comics scholarship and reviews graphic novels for the press and radio.

Evelyn **Tauben** is a producer, curator and writer based in Toronto. With an MA in art history from the Tyler School of Art, she has worked at the Philadelphia Museum of Art, the Smithsonian American Art Museum and the National Museum of American History. She was the first head of programs and exhibitions at the Koffler Centre of the Arts where her work was integral to the Toronto presentation of "Graphic Details."

Julia **Wertz** is the author/illustrator of the unfortunately titled *The Fart Party Volumes* (Atomic Book Company, 2007) and the Eisner-nominated *Drinking at the Movies* (Three Rivers Press, 2010). Her latest book is *The Infinite Wait and Other Stories* (Koyama Press, 2012).

Index

Page numbers in **_bold italics_** indicate pages with illustrations.

A4 (comics group) 205
Achbar Hair (magazine) 98
Achinstein, Sharon: on Jews and excrement 138
Ahmed, Sarah 98, 102
Aim see Lasko-Gross, Miss
Akira (Katsuhiro Otomo) 183
Allen, Patrick 199
Allen, Woody *11*, 19, 25, 144, 145, 150, 153
Altneuland see Herzl, Theodor
"Another Week" (series) 173; "Abstained" 158, *246*; "Shop til you Stop" 158, *247*
anti–Semitism 23; Holocaust: 51–3, 63; self–hatred 137–45, 150, 152–3; *see also* Eisenstein, Bernice; Katin, Miriam; Salomon, Charlotte; *We Are on Our Own*
Arendt, Hannah 38, *39*
Armadillo (Jewish artists' group) 210
Arnovitz, Andi 70–1
Arnowitz, Jo Ann 4
Art of the Holocaust 163
Art School Confidential see Clowes, Daniel
Atkinson, Paul on drawn lines 114
Attie, Shimon 52
Austin, Carolyn 43
Awkward see High School Comic Chronicles of Ariel Schrag
Aylon, Hélène: *The Liberation of G-d* 70, *71*

"Baby Talk: A Tale of 3 4 Miscarriages" 23, 79–97, *82–83*, 150–2, 157, 256–61, *257–60*
Barefoot Gen 42
Barry, Lynda 187, 188; *One Hundred Demons* 87
Baskind, Samantha 145; on Jews and the graphic novel 19

Batalion, Judy 297; on confessional comedy 149–59
Bauer, Heike 297; on Ilana Zeffren 98–109
Bauer, Ute Meta 4
Bechdel, Alison 98–9, 178; method 116, 118
Being in Pictures: An Intimate Photo Memoir see Leonard, Joanne
Bell, Gabrielle 168, 187
Benjamin, Walter 42, 43
Bennett, Carol 195
Bergen Street Comics 183
Berger, John 23
Bergson, Henri 42
Berlatsky, Paul 297; on Ariel Schrag 283, 287
"Big Sister Little Sister" 157, *267*
Boltanski, Christian 94; "Holocaust Effect" 51–2
The Book of Alfred Kantor 163
The Book of Sarah *54*, *56*, *57*; "Families" 55–9, *56*, *57*; postmemory 51, 53; as scroll 53–4
Boys, Philip 199–200
Brauner, David 297; on the comedy of self–hatred 131–159
The Brighton Book (mixed media anthology) 201
Brinkley, Nell 3
Broverman, Alison 297; on Sarah Lazarovic 248
Brown, Chester 115
Bruce, Lenny 153 (Jesus joke)
Buhle, Paul 297; *Jews and American Comics* 19, 145; on Sharon Rudahl 276; 297
Bunch online magazine 174
Busch, Wilhelm 41

Calamity 185, 188, 191
Caricature see Clowes, Daniel
Cartoon Art Museum, San Francisco 1

Cartoon Country (Brighton group) 195
catalogue for "Graphic Details..." exhibition 5–6, 21–3; front cover *22*
Chambers, Ross: on "loiterature" 111
Chase, Alisia Grace 3–4
The Chosen 133, 138, 141, 154, *286*, 287
Chute, Hillary 41, 87, 98, 139
Clementi, F. K. 6; 297–8; on Aline Kominsky-Crumb 234, 239
Clough, Rob 298; on Miss Lasko-Gross 240, 244
Clowes, Daniel: *Art School Confidential* 187; *Caricature* 119; on Vanessa Davis 18
Coat of the Chained Woman see Arnovitz, Andi
Cohn, Noa Lea 298; interview with Racheli Rottner 205–11
The Comic Book of First Love 200, 202
The Comic Book of the Facts of Life 200
Comic Company 200
Comic Company (publisher) 195
The Comics Art Show (1983 exhibition) 5
The Comics Journal 188, 192
Comics, Manga and Graphic Novels: A History of Graphic Narrative 39
The Comics Stripper 99 and 101, *100*
Crumb, Robert 52, 187, 199

Davis, Vanessa 178; biography 214; on Charlotte Salomon 46, 48; *see also Make Me a Woman*; *Spaniel Rage*
DC Comics 20, 167
Deepwell, Katy 4

Definition see *High School Comic Chronicles of Ariel Schrag*
"Diary Drawing" (touring show) 2
Different Combinations of Me and Tim 29, 154, 192–3
Don't Talk to Women see Nicholls, Jacqueline
Doucet, Julie 7
Dreschler, Debbie 187, 188
Dumped Before Valentine's 1, 32–3, 253–5, *254–5*
Dyke March 31, 32
Dykes to Watch Out For see Bechdel, Alison

Eisenstein, Bernice 219–220, *220*, *221*; *I Was a Child of Holocaust Survivors* 38, *39*, 48, 156–7, *164*, *165*; interview 162–166
Eisner, Will 6, 145, 200
Errett, Ben 173, 174
Escape from "Special" 18, 133, 176, 182; "Child Psychology" 181; "The Gruswerk's Sabbath" 133, 136–7, 153, *241–3*; "Kidnapped" 178, *179*; "Of Little Faith II" 179, *180*, 181
Eternally Bad: Goddesses with Attitude see Robbins, Trina
"Eucalyptus Nights" 32, *229–32*, 233
Evans, Kate 201

"The Faces of Race and Memory" (installation) see Haim, Maor
"Fanny" (women's cartoon network) 195
The Female Eunuch 102
Finck, Liana see *The Shul Detective*
Fingeroth, Danny: on Jews and the graphic novel 145
For Better or For Worse see Johnston, Lynn
Frank, Anne 90; in Bernice Eisenstein strip *165*; parents 12
Freedman, Ariela 298; on Charlotte Salomon 38–50
Freeman, Elizabeth 99
Freud, Sigmund: on humor 149, 150
Friedman, Dan 298; on "Graphic Details..." exhibition 21–4
"From Superman to the Rabbi's Cat" (touring show) 3
Fun Home 178
Funny Weather see Evans, Kate

Gammel, Irene: on autobiographical narrative 111
The Ganzfeld 190, 192
Garbuz, Yair 207

Gerard, Shannon 116, 118
Geva, Dudu 206
Girl Fight (first all-women comic) 19
Girl Stories 185, 188, 190, 191, 193; "Chanukah Blues" 19; "Diana" *192*; "Last Dance" 150, *150*, *151*; "This Is the Book of Lauren R. Weinstein" *289–90*
Glidden, Sarah 222–7; interview 167–72; see also *How to Understand Israel in 60 Days or Less*
Gloeckner, Phoebe 141
Glückel of Hameln 26
Goddess of War 185, *186*
"Goldie: A Neurotic Woman" 19
Goldman, Emma (feminist anarchist) 276
Gough, Jamie 198
"Graphic Confessions of Jewish Women: Exposing Themselves Through Pictures and Raw Personal Stories" 2, 7, 18–20, 21, 90, 144–5, 196
"Graphic Details: Confessional Comics by Jewish Women" (touring exhibition) 1–7, *27*, 133, 149, 164, 174, 175; Dan Friedman on 21–4; see also "Talking about Jewish Women and Comics" (one-day symposium)
Graphic Women 41, 98, 139
Gravett, Paul 145; 200, 298; interview with Corinne Pearlman 195–204
Greer, Germaine: *The Female Eunuch* 102
"Gregory's Passion" 202
Grosz, George 41, 44
Growing up Female 89
The Guerrilla Girls 93
gURL.com 185, 188

Haim, Maor 52
Hamidrasha School of Art 205–7
Hartman, Tova 4
Hatfield, Charles: on cartoon self-image 119
Hayden, Malin Hedlin 4
Heer, Jeet 44
Hellman, Danny 187
Henni 176, 181, 182, 183
Hernandez, Jaime 183
Herriman, Chris see *Krazy Kat*
Herzl, Theodor 25
Heyman, Abigail see *Growing Up Female*
High School Comic Chronicles of Ariel Schrag: *Awkward* 120, 283; *Definition* 112–14, *113*, 120; *Potential* 19, 116, 120, *117*, *121*, 122, 126; *Likewise* 19, 118–9, 120–27, *123*, *125*, 283, 287

Hill, Edward: on drawing 114–15
Hirsch, Marianne 51
History of Art: feminist revision 93
Hitchcock, Alfred 183
Hodler, Tim 187–8, 192
Home for the Holidays 154, *155*
The House of Twelve Comic Jam 183
Hovav, Gil 298; on Ilana Zeffren 292
How to Understand Israel in 60 Days or Less 19–20, 32, 62–4, 65–6, 67, 68, 72–3, 144; comedy in 153; "Falafel" *223–6*; "Sleep" *169–71*

I Was a Child of Holocaust Survivors see Eisenstein, Bernice
The Impostor's Daughter see Sandell, Laurie
"In the Name of the Father" see Rosenhouse-Ben Zion, Daniela
Israel, army experience see "Eucalyptus Nights"; Glidden, Sarah; Katin, Miriam; Libicki, Miriam
Israeli women artists see Rottner, Racheli; Zeffren, Ilana

Jaffe, Sarah 298; on women as story tellers 29–34
Jagose, Annamarie 98
Janson, Anthony see *History of Art*
Jew and Improved 174
Jewesses with Attitude, blog 176
The Jewish Daily Forward 2, 5–6, 21–3, 46, 90
The Jewish Institute for Jewish Research (YIVO) 25
Jewish Museum of Florida 4
Jewish Quarterly 141–3, 195–6, 202, 203
Jews and American Comics see Buhle, Paul
Jews and Words (book) 9, 12
Jim Hanley's Universe 183
jobnik! 19, *30*, 32, 33, 62, 65–6, 67–8, 72, 73, 249–52, *250–51*
Johnston, Lynn 110
Journal of a Miscarriage 79, 84–94, *85*; "Now and Then" *88*; "Reproduction" *86*
Journal series (Fabrice Neaud) 119
journalism, graphic 168, 172, 199, 200–1

Kafka, Franz 269; "impossibilities" 45–6
Kahn, Ariel 298; on Racheli Rottner 269
Kahn-Harris, Keith: on self-hatred 139

Kalman, Maira: influence of Charlotte Salomon 46
Kaminer, Michael 299; interview with Bernice Eisenstein 162–6; interview with Sarah Glidden 167–72; interview with Sarah Lazarovic 173–5; on Laurie Sandell 277; *see also* "Graphic Confessions of Jewish Women: Exposing Themselves Through Pictures and Raw Personal Stories"
Kantor, Alfred 163
Katin, Miriam 23, 72, 233; biography 228; *see also* "Eucalyptus Nights"; *We Are On Our Own*
Kestenbaum Ben-Dov, Ruth 52
Kirschenblatt-Gimblett, Barbara 69
Koffler Center of the Arts 1, 4
Kominsky-Crumb, Aline 12, 145, 177, 196, 234–9; *Twisted Sisters* 92–3, 139, *235*; *Wimmin's Commix* 141; *see also* "Goldie: A Neurotic Woman"; *Love That Bunch*; *Need More Love*
Krazy Kat 185
Kunzle, David 41
Kuramoto, John 185

The Ladies Guild Collection 71
Lasko-Gross, Miss 19, 145, 240–44; *Aim* 182; biography 240; cover image for "Graphic Details..." exhibition catalogue 22–3, *22*; interview 176–84; *see also Escape from "Special"*; *Henni*; *A Mess of Everything*
Lavie, Rafi 207
Layne, Linda *see Motherhood Lost*
Lazarovic, Sarah: Ben Errett 173, 174; biography 245, 248; "A Bunch of Pretty Things I Didn't Buy" *174*; interview 173–5; *see also* "Another Week" (series)
Le Guin, Ursula 3
Lejeune, Philip: on diary as antifiction 111
Leonard, Joanne 299; *Being in Pictures: An Intimate Photo Memoir* 87; *Letting Her Go with Difficulty* 90; *My Journal of a Miscarriage* 79, 84–94, *85*, *86*, *88*; *Not Losing Her Memory* 87; *Romanticism is Ultimately Fatal* 93
Leone of Modena, Rabbi 25
lesbianism, representation *see* Schrag, Ariel; Zeffren, Ilana
Lessons of Darkness 51–2
Lester, Malcolm 299; on Bernice Eisenstein 219

The Leveller (political magazine) 199
Levi, Primo 38, *39*, 43, 219
Levine, Zachary Paul 299; on comics within Jewish literature 25–8
Lewis, Peter M. 199
Liberation of G-d see Aylon, Helène
Libicki, Miriam 34, 138–9; biography 249; "Jewish Memoir Goes Pow! Zap! Oy!" 69; "Towards a Hot Jew: The Israeli Solider as Fetish Object" 62; *see also jobnik!*
Life? or Theatre? (Leben? oder Theater?): absence from comics history 38, 41; aunt's suicide 38, *40*, 43–4; deportation 44–5; epigraph 42–3; Gurs 45; insignia 43; legacy 46–8; Nazi Germany 44; *see also* Salomon, Charlotte
Lightman, Sarah 299; biography 253; "Confessions of a Co-Curator, Editor and Artist" 1–12; influence of Charlotte Salomon 46, *47*, 53; influence of Diane Noomin 256, 261; interview of Corinne Pearlman 195–204; Pearlman portrait 144; *see also The Book of Sarah*; *Dumped Before Valentine's*
Likewise see High School Comic Chronicles of Ariel Schrag
Lilith Magazine 12, 64
Literature Compass (journal) 41
Lloyd, David 201
Louis Riel see Brown, Chester
Love and Rockets (Jaime Hernandez) 183
Love That Bunch 139–141, 144
Lowenthal Felstiner, Mary: on Charlotte Salomon 12, 39, 41, 44, 46, *47*
Lyndon, Sonia 195

Make Me a Woman 23, 32, *33*, 214, 218; "Toys in Babeland" 149, 156; "Wild Ride" *215–17*
Margles, Judy 4
Marion, Philippe: on drawn lines 114
"Masters of American Comics" (touring exhibition) 3
masturbation 19, 112, *113*, 122, 123–7, *123*, *125*
Maus see Spiegelman, Art
McCloud, Scott 21, 42, 115
McIntyre, Sandra 22
Megillat Esther see Waldman, T. J.
A Mess of Everything 18–19, 137–8, 176–7; "The Turd" 23,

29, 132–3, *134–135*, 137, 139, 157, 178
Messick, Dale 3
miscarriage *see* "Baby Talk: A Tale of 3̶ 4 Miscarriages"; *Journal of a Miscarriage*
Molotui, Andrei 5
Moore, Alan 201
Motherhood Lost 91
Mulvey, Laura 23
Munson, Kim 5
Myriad Editions 7, 195, 201

Nakazawa 42
National Foundation for Jewish Culture 145
Neaud, Fabrice 119
Need More Love 239; "Nose Job" *236*; "Wiseguys" 152, *237–8*
Nelson see Phoenix, Woodrow
Neustein, Joshua 68
Nicholls, Jacqueline 71–2
Noomin, Diane: biography 256; *Twisted Sisters* 6–7, 92–3, 256; *Wimmin's Commix* 6; *see also* "Baby Talk: A Tale of 3̶ 4 Miscarriages"
"Nose Job" *see Need More Love*
Not Losing Her Memory see Leonard, Joanne
Nussbaum, Felix (surrealist painter) 163

Oasman, Tova 210
Oksman, Tahneer 299; interview with Lauren Weinstein 185–94; interview with Miss Lasko-Gross 176–84; on Vanessa Davis 214–18
Old Mistresses: Women, Art and Ideology (book) 4
O'Malley, Brian Lee 115
Omer-Sherman, Ranen 299; on Jews and the graphic novel 145; on Miriam Libicki 249–52
One Hundred Demons 89
Oppenheimer, Arthur 300; on Corinne Pearlman 262, 265
Oregon Jewish Museum 1, 4
The Other Side of the World 205, 206, 207–8, *209*, 269, *270*
Otomo, Katsuhiro 3
Our Bodies, Ourselves 89
Our Foremothers see Snyder, Joan
Oz, Amoz 9, 12
Oz-Salzburger, Fania 9, 12
"The Painter and the Hassid" *see* Kestenbaum Ben-Dov, Ruth

Parker, Rozsika *see Old Mistresses: Women, Art and Ideology*
Parker Royal, Derek 145
Paying For It see Brown, Chester

Pearlman, Corinne biography 262, 265; "Confessions about Jewish Women and Comics Symposium: Academia or Comics?" 8, *36–7*; early works 199–200, 202, 203; interview 195–204; *see also* "Playing the Jewish Card"
Pekar, Harvey 29, 139–40, 177
Pendergast, Natalie 300; on Ariel Schrag 110–30
Persepolis see Satrapi, Marjane
Peterson, Robert 39
Phair, Liz 32
Phoenix, Woodrow 201
Pink Story 102, 292; "Neither shall a man put on a woman's garment" *293*; "Everything Was Brand New" 102, *103*, 104
"Places Where You Could Get Killed in The Litchfield Hills, Conn." 188, *189*, 190
"Playing the Jewish Card": "An Assimilated Jew's Guide to the Jewish Calendar" 203; "The Gap Year" 157, 203, *263–4*; "In Valhalla" 142, 203; "The Jews Who Wouldn't Go Away" 203; "Losing the Plot" 156, 202, 203; "The Non-Jewish Female Cartoonist" 141–2, *143*, 195; "Show & Tell" *10–11*, 12, 141, 144, 152, 153, 195–7; "That Was Alright While It Lasted" 203; "Whatever Happened to Great Grandma" 142–4, 197; "Your Global Community Needs You" 144
Poletti, Anna 106–7
Pollack, Rachel 300; on Trina Robbins 266, 268
Pollock, Griselda 4, 41, 42, 44, 45
Potential see High School Comic Chronicles of Ariel Schrag
Proust, Marcel 42; compared to Ariel Schrag 112, 119–22, 124, 126–7

Rating (Israeli magazine) 205
RAW magazine 163
Reisz, Matthew 195
Relay (community radio magazine) 199
Rich, Adrienne: on "lesbian continuum" 99
"*Rishumon*" 98, *101*, *104*, *105*, *106*, 292, *294*, *295*
Rivers, Joan 150
Robbins, Trina 5, 19; on "American Masters of Comic Art" 3; "Big Sister Little Sister" 157, *267*; biography 266, 268; *Eternally Bad: Goddesses with Atti-*

tude 268; *Wimmin's Commix* 6–7
"Romanticism is Ultimately Fatal" *see* Leonard, Joanne
Rosen, Roee 206–7, 207
Rosenberg, Harold 61
Rosenberg, Pnina 300; on Sarah Lightman 51–60
Rosenhouse-Ben Zion, Daniela 52–3
Roth, Laurence 145
Roth, Philip *11*, 139, 139n37, 144, 145; *Portnoy's Complaint* 25, 218
Rottner, Racheli 206, 207, 210, 269; interview 205–11; *see also The Other Side of the World*
Rubinstein, Rochelle 72
Rudahl, Sharon biography 271, 276; Emma Goldman 276; *The Star Sapphire* *272–5*
Rudick, Nicole 300; on Lauren Weinstein 291
Rumble Strip see Phoenix, Woodrow

Sabin, Roger 300; on Sarah Lightman 253–5
Salomon, Charlotte 6, 38–50; Albert and Paula Salomon 12; influence on Bernice Eisenstein 38, *39*, 162–3; influence on Diane Noomin 80; influence on Maira Kalman 46; influence on Sarah Lightman 53; influence on Vanessa Davis 46–7; *see also Life? or Theatre?*
Sandell, Laurie biography 277; *The Impostor's Daughter* 33, 157–8, 277, *278–82*
Sanders Peirce, Charles 112, 114
Satrapi, Marjane 102, 201, 207
Schnur, Susan 12
School Friend Picture Library (1962–88) 197
Schrag, Ariel 110–30, 144–5; biography 283, 287; as lesbian 110, 116, 119–22, *121*, 126, 283; masturbation 122, 123–6, *123*, *125*; *see also* "The Chosen"; "Dyke March"; *High School Comic Chronicles of Ariel Schrag;* "Home for the Holidays"; "Shit"
Schroll Guz, Savannah 70
Scott Pilgrim (Brian Lee O'Malley) 115
Seinfeld 25; Swiss-army knife sketch 153–4
sexism 2–7, 12, 23, 61, 69–72, 89, 90, 92–3, 157, *267*
Sfar, Joann *see* "From Superman to the Rabbi's Cat"
Shiff, Melissa: wedding to Louis Kaplan 69–70

"Shit" 29, 131–2, 133, 137, 138, 139, *284–5*
Sh'ma: A Journal of Jewish Ideas 99
"Show & Tell" *see* "Playing the Jewish Card"
Shufonim (blog) 210
The Shul Detective 64–5, *65*, *66*, 68–9, 72, 74
Shulz, Bruno 38, *39*
Silverman, Sarah 153
Skrubbe, Jessica Sjöholm 4
Snyder, Joan 72
Spaniel Rage 18, 19, 20, 214
Spiegelman, Art 145; *Maus* 21, 141, 163, 196, 200
The Star Sapphire see Rudahl, Sharon
Starr, Lori 4
Steinberg, Michael P. 41
Stetz, Margaret D. 4
The Stranger (Seattle newspaper) 185, 188
Der Stürmer (Nazi newspaper) 44
synagogue 73; *see also The Shul Detective*

Tablet magazine 174
"Talking about Jewish Women and Comics" (one-day symposium) 3, 8; Corinne Pearlman strip *36–7*
Tardi, Jacques 192
Tauben, Evelyn 300; on Jewish identity 61–78
Things I Wish I Told You see Gerard, Shannon
To Paint Her Life: Charlotte Salomon in the Nazi Era 12, 44, 46, *47*
The Tongue Mothers (Miss Lasko-Gross, *Self Portrait*) 22–3, *22*
Töpffer, Rodolphe 41
"Toys in Babeland" *see Make Me a Woman*
Traub, Valerie 102
The Treasury of Jewish Humor 262
Twisted Sisters see Kominsky-Crumb, Aline; Noomin, Diane

Understanding Comics: The Invisible Art see McCloud, Scott
Unspent Love see Gerard, Shannon

V for Vendetta 201
Vertigo *see* DC Comics

Waldman, T.J. 145
Walker, Brian 5
Walker, Ian 195–6

walla.co.il (culture and news website) 205
Ware, Chris 185, 187, 191
Washington, D.C., Jewish Community Center 1, 4
We Are On Our Own 66-7, 74, *75*, *76*, 233
Weinstein, Lauren biography 288, 291; blog 185-7, 192; "Different Combinations of Me and Tim" 29, 154, 192-3; "Horse Camp" 19; interview 185-194; "Little Laurie Sprinkles" 185; "Places Where You Could Get Killed in The Litchfield Hills, Conn." 188, *189*,
190; Tim Hodler 187-8, 192; *see also Calamity*; *The Ganzfeld*; *Girl Stories*; *The Goddess of War*
Weinstein, Simcha: on the appeal of graphic novel form 145
Wertz, Julia 300; on Sarah Glidden 227
Whitlock, Gillian 106-7
Wiesel, Elie 38, *39*
"Wild Ride" *see Make Me a Woman*
Wimmin's Commix 6, 141
"Wiseguys" *see Need More Love*
Wisse, Ruth 149, 158
Wonder Woman 32
"Writing on the Wall" (installation) *see* Attie, Shimon

Yeshiva University Museum 1, *27*, 149; *see also* "Talking about Jewish Women and Comics" (one-day symposium)
Youngman, Henny 152, 156

Zawatsky, Carole 4
Zeffren, Ilana biography 292; as lesbian artist 98-109; *see also* "The Comics Stripper"; *Pink Story*; "*Rishumon*"
Zegher, Catherine de 4
Ziv, Avner 149